# Pragmatism
# in Law and Society

D0060808

# New Perspectives on Law, Culture, and Society
*Robert W. Gordon and Margaret Jane Radin,*
*Series Editors*

*Pragmatism in Law and Society,* edited by
Michael Brint and William Weaver

*Feminist Legal Theory: Readings in Law and Gender,* edited by
Katharine T. Bartlett and Rosanne Kennedy

FORTHCOMING

*Wittgenstein and Legal Theory,* edited by
Dennis M. Patterson

*The Philosophy of International Law: A Human Rights Perspective,*
Fernando R. Teson

*In Whose Name? Feminist Legal Theory*
*and the Experience of Women,*
Christine A. Littleton

# Pragmatism in Law and Society

EDITED BY
## Michael Brint
## and William Weaver

## Westview Press
BOULDER • SAN FRANCISCO • OXFORD

*New Perspectives on Law, Culture, and Society*

All rights reserved. No part of this publication may be reproduced or transmitted in any form or by any means, electronic or mechanical, including photocopy, recording, or any information storage and retrieval system, without permission in writing from the publisher.

Copyright © 1991 by Westview Press, Inc.

Chapters 2, 5, 7, 8, 12, 13, and 14 copyright © 1990 by the *Southern California Law Review;* Chapter 6 copyright © 1991 by Lynn A. Baker; Chapter 9 copyright © 1991 by Joan C. Williams; Chapter 16 copyright © 1991 by Daniel R. Ortiz; Chapter 19 copyright © 1991 by Ronald Dworkin

Excerpt from "Democratic Vistas" on page 1 is taken from *Complete Poetry and Collected Prose of Walt Whitman* (New York: Viking Press, 1982).

Excerpt from "On the Road Home" on page 132 is taken from *The Collected Poems of Wallace Stevens* (New York: Knopf, 1954).

Published in 1991 in the United States of America by Westview Press, Inc., 5500 Central Avenue, Boulder, Colorado 80301-2847, and in the United Kingdom by Westview Press, 36 Lonsdale Road, Summertown, Oxford OX2 7EW

Library of Congress Cataloging-in-Publication Data
Pragmatism in law and society / edited by Michael Brint and William
  Weaver.
    p.  cm.
  Includes bibliographical references and index.
  ISBN 0-8133-8309-9. — ISBN 0-8133-8310-2 (pbk.)
    1. Sociological jurisprudence.  2. Judicial process—United
States.  3. United States—Constitutional law—Interpretation and
construction.  4. Pragmatism.  I. Brint, Michael.  II. Weaver,
William, 1956–   .
K376.P73  1991
340′.115—dc20                                                            91-35084
                                                                              CIP

Printed and bound in the United States of America

The paper used in this publication meets the requirements of the American National Standard for Permanence of Paper for Printed Library Materials Z39.48-1984.

10    9    8    7    6    5    4    3    2    1

# Contents

# Acknowledgments

On behalf of the Political and Social Thought program at the University of Virginia, we owe our sincere appreciation to all the authors who participated in this project. In addition, the generosity and efforts of a number of persons throughout the University of Virginia made this work possible. For their financial and intellectual support we are grateful to Paul Gross, chair of the Center for Advanced Studies; R. Edward Freedom, head of the Olsson Foundation at the Colgate Darden School of Business; Robert M. O'Neil, former president of the University of Virginia; Thomas Jackson, dean of the School of Law; Ralph Cohen, director of the Commonwealth Center; and Clifton McCleskey and the members of the Woodrow Wilson Department of Government and Foreign Affairs.

We also owe our thanks to Ken Abraham, Cora Diamond, Walter Benn Michaels, George Rutherglen, and David Thomas, who offered important criticism and help concerning the conference. Nancy Fraser also helped us to clarify some of the philosophical issues regarding pragmatism and the public domain. Joan C. Williams and Martha Minow offered a number of useful suggestions for the organization of this work. Special thanks are owed to Patricia Bennet and David Hennigan for the untold hours they spent in helping to organize this effort and to Mary and Richard Rorty, who opened their home to the participants in the conference on pragmatism in law and politics held at the University of Virginia in November 1990.

The essays by Martha Minow and Elizabeth V. Spelman, Richard A. Posner, Hilary Putnam, Margaret Jane Radin, Richard Rorty, Catharine Wells, and Cornel West were previously published in Volume 63 (September 1990) of the *Southern California Law Review*. To Peter Juzwiak and the staff of the *Southern California Law Review*, we are grateful for their permission to reprint these essays. We are also grateful to Pasquale A. Cipollone for permission to reprint the essay Stanley Fish delivered to the Virginia conference on pragmatism. Stanley Fish's "Almost Pragmatism: Richard Posner's Jurisprudence" was published in Volume 57 (Fall 1990) of the *University of Chicago Law Review*.

Professor Fish revised and expanded his essay for publication in this volume.

Finally, to Anne and Camille, and especially to our children, Shay and Case, with whom the multivalent possibilities of the real future lie, we lovingly dedicate this work.

*Michael Brint*
*William Weaver*
Charlottesville, Virginia

# Introduction

*Michael Brint and William Weaver*

Far, far, indeed, stretch, in distance, our Vistas! How much is still
to be    disentangled, freed!

—Walt Whitman

For John Dewey, the never-ending, open possibilities of novel
events, experiences, and social structures in the United States "facilitated
the birth of a philosophy which regards the world as being in continuous
formation, where there is still place for indeterminism, for the new and
for a real future." Unlike older philosophies, burdened by an inherited
stock of ideas, prejudices, and metaphors, this new philosophy of
pragmatism was dedicated to constructing the multivalent possibilities of
this real future.

Social philosophers in the Deweyan mold have long held optimistic
and constructive outlooks on the possibilities of social progress, but
recent    advocates    have    tended    to    emphasize    pragmatism's
antifoundationalism, the idea that truths are created, not found; situated,
not objective; changing, not timeless; partial, not absolute. Armed with
these antiessentialist claims, pragmatists have been consummately
(notoriously) skilled in dismembering the foundations of historical
determinism, philosophical realism, and moral absolutism.

Yet, once things have been taken apart—when truth becomes what
is good in the way of belief, when law becomes what the judges say it
is, and when no discourse occupies the privileged position of "getting the
world right"—we still have to decide what to do with the pieces. In
good pragmatic fashion, the question becomes: What constructive role,
if any, can antifoundationalism play in dealing with life's practical
struggles? More specifically, can one deduce from pragmatism a given

*1*

political doctrine, set of public programs, or ethical commitments? Does it offer new and better ways of orienting public debate? Or does it provide novel ways of handling interpretive controversies like those revolving around judicial decisionmaking or the meaning of the Constitution?

In an effort to present a broad and diverse range of views on this subject, we asked a number of prominent scholars from law, literature, philosophy, and political science to respond to these questions. Their answers, contained in the essays that follow, form a lively, vital, and often contentious debate on the current status of pragmatism in law and society. Although any strategy used to organize these essays risks severing some of their important interconnections, we have divided this book into two sections. The articles contained in the first section tend to focus on the general question: What difference, if anything, does pragmatism make to law and society? The second part is composed of essays that take up the more specific relation between pragmatism and the practice of judicial decisionmaking and constitutional interpretation.

It will come as no great surprise that one of the most often contested issues in the contemporary debate on pragmatism concerns the very definition of pragmatism itself. In the first two essays, Thomas C. Grey and Richard A. Posner confront this issue directly. In appropriately nonessentialist terms, Judge Posner suggests that

> there is nothing practical to be gained from attaching the pragmatist label to any philosophy that does not have all three [of the following] elements. The first is a distrust of metaphysical entities ("reality," "truth," "nature," etc.) viewed as warrants for certitude whether in epistemology, ethics, or politics. The second is an insistence that propositions be tested by the consequences, by the difference they make—and if they make none, set aside. The third is an insistence on judging our projects, whether scientific, ethical, political, or legal, by their conformity to social or other human needs rather than to "objective," "impersonal" criteria.

Though most would agree with Posner's basic characterization, Thomas Grey offers a further dimension to pragmatism that has aroused more controversy. In his depiction of its intellectual genealogy, Grey reminds us not only of pragmatism's relation to the tradition of empiricism, but of its origin in the intellectual currents of evolutionary biology, historicism, and Romanticism as well. "The Romantics," he tells us, ". . . particularly stressed the interaction between mind or culture and external reality through the transformative power of human imagination." It is the social optimism often anchored to this Romantic feature of pragmatism that has drawn the wrath of Stanley Fish.

In fact, one of Fish's most vigorous claims is that a pragmatic account of law entails neither programmatic consequences nor romantic visions of future possibilities. Accepting the antifoundationalism of pragmatism, Fish rejects its links to social optimism. In his comment on Fish's essay, E. D. Hirsch suggests that there is a tension in his account of pragmatism. According to Hirsch, this "tension arises from Fish's claim of the rhetoricity of pragmatism, coupled with his simultaneous claim of the nonconsequentiality (hence nonrhetoricity) of pragmatism. If pragmatism is rhetorical, then its implicit program is to change peoples' minds and practices for the better. If pragmatism has no such programmatic consequences, then it is at best bad or ineffectual rhetoric."

Richard Rorty admits that there is no logical or philosophical entailment binding antiessentialism to Romanticism. Nevertheless, he endorses both of these elements under the umbrella of pragmatism. In Rorty's view, jurists as diverse as Stanley Fish and Ronald Dworkin accept what is by now the rather banal claim of antifoundationalism in law. But for Rorty, "pragmatism" stands for more than just a set of increasingly less controversial philosophical arguments and judicial practices. It stands for a visionary and egalitarian tradition of social hope that calls into question the basic terms of our social life.

But problematizing this tradition does not guarantee a more promising substitute. In her chapter, Lynn A. Baker discusses the tension between the prophetic and antifoundational aspects of Rorty's thought. In her view, neither pragmatism's antifoundationalism nor its prophesy are of much use in achieving progressive social change. Unlike Baker, Cornel West sees pragmatism as a potential source of such change. Against Rorty, he urges what he calls the "new" pragmatism not to repeat the mistakes of the "first wave of pragmatism [that] foundered on the rocks of cultural conservatism and corporate liberalism." Instead he accents the existential, communal, and political dimensions of pragmatism's "prophesy." The existential dimension concerns our commitment to the humanity of others; the communal dimension is dedicated to cultural criticism and the flourishing of democracy; and the political dimension is guided by freedom as "a perennial quest for self-realization and self-development that resists all forms of oppression." In his portrayal of its prophetic dimensions, West revives the "Romantic" elements of pragmatism as a form of *praxis* and social reform.

Heeding West's warning, Margaret Jane Radin analyzes the relationship between pragmatism and feminism. Among the many themes raised in her essay, she explores the situation of the double bind that women experience under a system of domination. She also employs William James's distinction to dismantle the polarities conventionally used to characterize women as "tender" rather than "tough" minded. Joan Williams also confronts multiple dimensions of the relation between pragmatism and feminism. She suggests that the romantic idealization of the "strong poet" (to which thinkers like Rorty are drawn) carries with it the peculiarly masculine assumption that self-realization involves the solitary autonomy of the quest. In contrast to this "masculinized" romantic portrait, she questions the private/public distinction upon which such solitary quests are predicated.

Jean Bethke Elshtain approaches the private/public distinction from a different perspective. She analyzes the relation between the family, state, and civic identity in the respective writings of G.W.F. Hegel and Jane Addams, an exemplar of Progressive reform who was strongly influenced by the tradition of pragmatism in the United States. Portraying Addams's double bind, Elshtain points to the complex and often paradoxical relations between her social responsibilities and her familial commitments. In Elshtain's words: "It was, for Addams, a 'monstrous absurdity' for society to refuse to recognize the contributions of parents, especially mothers, and to force them into situations that compromise *both* the family and the social claim."

Concentrating on what he might well describe as yet another "monstrous absurdity" in the liberal-democratic state, Milton Fisk criticizes liberal theory's attempt to legitimize punishment on "essentialist" grounds. According to Fisk, there is only an internal justification for punishment in the liberal state. Though coming to the same critical (antiessentialist) conclusions as a pragmatist, Fisk advocates a Marxist approach to punishment and legitimacy. Legitimacy, he contends, can be affirmed only with a reduction in the antagonistic social divisions associated with the structure of the liberal state. Blind to this critical issue, he argues, pragmatism overlooks the possibility of successfully moralizing certain forms of punishment from other than a purely internal perspective.

The first section concludes with Hilary Putnam's pragmatic justification for democracy. He begins by reconsidering the relationship between Dewey's political commitments and his antiessentialism. According to Putnam, Dewey's philosophy was dependent on empirical hypotheses that entailed the advocacy of democratic principles. Rejecting all transcendental forms of logic in his philosophical writings, Dewey employed these empirical arguments to justify his political claims. Seen in this light, Putnam demonstrates the consistency in Dewey's view of pragmatism in law and society.

Martha Minow and Elizabeth V. Spelman open the second part of this work by responding to the common charges that pragmatism leads to unhealthy forms of moral relativism and/or political complacency. In terms of the former they argue that pragmatism endorses contextual judgments, not relativistic theories. Highlighting this element of contextualism, they claim that although pragmatism does not endorse any particular political agenda, it "does signal a commitment to consider and reconsider the meaning of moral and philosophical purposes in light of . . . persistent patterns of power, based on lines of gender, racial, class, and age differences."

In specific relation to judicial decisionmaking, Catharine Wells also stresses the contextual dimension of all deliberation. By recognizing the situated character of abstract reasons and structures, she contends, we can better consider what reasons and structures are pragmatically appropriate to a particular decision. In this way, without completely rejecting formalism, she declares, we can move closer to fulfilling our aspirations for just decisionmaking practices.

Initiating a discussion of constitutional interpretation, Sanford Levinson forces us to reconsider the distinction between interpretations that result from the practice of judicial decisionmaking and amendments that are "officially" added to the text of the Constitution. Continuing this discussion, Daniel R. Ortiz lays out both the positions and the reasons for the deadlock in the debate between originalists, those people who hold that the Constitution must be interpreted according to the framers' or ratifiers' original intent and the noninterpretivists or nonoriginalists, those who believe that constitutional meaning hinges upon changing social value. Although Ortiz clearly associates pragmatism with the latter view, Steven Knapp links (antifoundational) pragmatism to (at least his own particular brand of) originalism. In contrast, David Hoy argues that pragmatism and Knapp's originalism are philosophically incompatible.

Offering a highly charged account of pragmatism in law, Ronald Dworkin takes Rorty's pragmatism to task for successfully defeating a position no one actually holds. In his essay, Dworkin also defends his claim that there are right answers in hard cases. This claim is not metaphysically preposterous, he insists, but "a commonsensical, extremely weak proposition of law that . . . it would be silly ever to announce if it had not been denied by so many legal philosophers." In the course of making these points, Dworkin responds directly to the articles by Grey, Rorty, Fish, and Knapp contained in this volume.

At the end of their chapters, Steven Knapp and Stanley Fish respond to Dworkin's analysis. For many readers it may be surprising to find how little genuine disagreement there is between Knapp and Fish, who notoriously take a position "against theory," and Dworkin, a thinker renowned for his theoretical approach to judicial decisionmaking. For instance, both Knapp and Dworkin emphasize the rational components of interpretation and the constraints of genre. The main area of disagreement appears to be that Knapp insists that these reasons and constraints must be focused solely on the interpretation of an author's intention (as in the case of the framer's intended meaning of the Constitution). In contrast, Dworkin codifies and purifies what he conceives to be the standards of legal reasoning and generic constraints of interpretation that good legal practitioners actually do and should employ in their decisionmaking. In describing legal practice, both Fish and Dworkin acknowledge the fact that the skill of being a good judge requires a theoretical component insofar as reflection is a part of the practice of judging. For his part, however, Fish maintains that theory itself is not a privileged component of this practice, only a necessary component of what it means to be a skilful judge. In contrast, for Dworkin, theory plays the crucial role of articulating the principles that animate and vivify our legal and political institutions. Despite these differences, the gap between Fish and Dworkin seems to have narrowed considerably. As in the specific case of Fish and Dworkin, the chapters contained in this book will certainly not end, but will clarify and sharpen the controversies surrounding the use of pragmatism in law and society.

# What Difference Does Pragmatism Make to Law and Society?

PART ONE

What Difference Does Pragmatism
Make to Law and Society?

# 1

# What Good Is Legal Pragmatism?

*Thomas C. Grey*

My aim here is to give a short and straightforward general statement of what the current pragmatist revival means for legal thought. Such programmatic statements of pragmatist theory are better kept short. Any attempt to state a version of pragmatism in the form of constructive generalizations risks falling into unpragmatic dogmatism by omitting the proper qualifications; but going on and on with those qualifications can only bore everyone to death.

The main job of the pragmatist theorist is critique of more ambitious (nonpragmatist) theories. As Dewey said, philosophy is best thought of as cultural criticism, and it follows that metaphysics (First Philosophy) then consists in drawing "the ground-map of the province of criticism."[1] The best constructive work done in the pragmatist spirit will not seem, to normal theory-buffs, theoretical enough or even theoretical at all. In the face of all these drawbacks, the idea of drawing up an accessible, short, and constructive statement of pragmatist theory may not seem like a promising project. But as a teacher of jurisprudence and legal theory, I myself would find such a summary or manifesto or survey pedagogically useful, and so here is my shot at supplying one.

To keep the sketch from being unrelievedly general, I will lead into it by setting out a practical legal problem and later lead out of it by trying to say how that problem seems to me illumined by what has come in between. The problem is how or whether to regulate discriminatory verbal harassment on the campus. This problem creates a dilemma, bringing into conflict the important principles of equal opportunity and free expression. It is not, I should specify right here, a problem to which, in my opinion, pragmatist theory dictates a unique solution. In general, pragmatism undermines the imperial ambitions of theorists;

pragmatist theory as such dictates almost nothing. Pragmatists presume that good theories will supply only heuristic guides and partial perspectives and will be none the worse for the limitation. Heuristic theories can facilitate good work of a more concrete and immediately practical kind. Theories can also, and often do when their scope and power is exaggerated, strangle good work in the cradle. Pragmatism is freedom from theory-guilt; it frees us from the admonitory voice that paralyzes us by saying "we cannot deal with this problem because we do not yet have a comprehensive theory of _____." You can fill in the space with your own candidate.

As I spell out what I mean by pragmatist theory, I must confront an obvious challenge. This is the claim that, in its ecumenical spirit, pragmatism simply leaves things as they were before, and so is of no earthly practical good—except to those with a vested interest in the status quo. This is a plausible and thoroughly pragmatic criticism, one that requires an answer. Indeed the issue of the practicality hovers over the whole enterprise of pragmatist theorizing. Pragmatism reminds us of the recurrent relevance of the self-reflexive question "what difference does *this* make?" At the same time, the pragmatist theorist, whose creed it is to keep this question in focus, must not prematurely close off the question about what it means for a theory to be practical. Theorizing can make many and different kinds of difference. The less obvious of these derive from theory's sometimes concealed attractions as a form of play, on the one hand, and as something approaching a form of religious devotion on the other. It stretches the usual sense of the term only a little to suggest that it may be *practical* to enjoy yourself or to give meaning to your life.

I

One practical problem of theory arises right at the beginning with the very act of naming—the use of the term "pragmatism" itself. We need a name for a naturalistic, flexible, experimental, and this-worldly philosophy, even apart from its application to legal theory. But in its century or so of life the term "pragmatism" has come to connote both antiintellectualism and unprincipled short-run expediency, connotations that must undercut its appeal not only to legal theorists but to anyone of a critical or reflective cast of mind. George Bush, for example, is often said to be a pragmatist.

So we have to consider whether other advantages offset the costs of these connotations. One philosopher sometimes associated with pragmatism, W.V.O. Quine, thinks not. He has said that the term "draws a pragmatic blank" as a name for a philosophical school or tendency. The word "pragmatism" adds nothing, in his view, that we do not already have from the older, more familiar, and serviceable term "empiricism."[2] As Quine doesn't add, the latter term has the virtue of not immediately summoning associations with the maneuvers of a politician who survives by closely tracking the opinion polls.

The issue of *naming* takes us back a century or so to the origins of pragmatism as an intellectual movement. This historical tour is practical, I would argue; intellectual genealogy is of more than "merely historical" (antiquarian) interest. Living intellectual movements are not constituted wholly out of the present and its anticipations of the future. They also carry with them the marks of their context of origin.

In the case of pragmatism, that origin, to put it somewhat oversimply, has two components. One is the Enlightenment empiricist positivism of the *philosophes* and the Benthamite radicals that came down from the eighteenth century. The other is the mix of nineteenth-century contributions to the synthesis: evolutionary biology, historicism, and Romanticism.

Reminding ourselves of this originating context can help us answer Quine's very plausible challenge. Why not name our movement "empiricism"? It is the vigorous continued influence within the pragmatist movement of its Romantic and historicist origins that marks it off from even the sophisticated contemporary forms of scientific empiricist philosophy—those represented by Quine, among others. Romanticism and historicism lend a scope to pragmatism that no philosophy drawing inspiration entirely from the natural sciences can have.

Still, it is crucial as well to recall that the early pragmatists *were* centrally inspired by the achievements of nineteenth-century science. The influence of Charles Darwin on the founding of pragmatism has been thoroughly mapped by intellectual historians.[3] The theory of evolution located humanity firmly within the animal kingdom and helped lead to a biologically based conception of the human mind as a set of survival-adaptive structures or functions, not in principle different from upright posture and the opposable thumb.

Here is one point of origin for pragmatism's assault on the mind-body distinction, that central assumption of all thinkers of the Enlightenment—the British empiricists as well as René Descartes and his followers. And from Darwinians also comes the pragmatist's sense that the categories of mind themselves, like the biological species, are fluid devices of classification, changing with time, adaptable to different needs and purposes. A belief, said Charles Peirce, is "a habit of mind." He added, following Alexander Bain, that it is something on which a person will act.[4] Finally mind itself, to the pragmatist, is simply an umbrella term for the higher action-guiding capacities of the human organism.

A frequent mistake has been to overstress pragmatism's roots in the Darwinian evolutionary perspective (itself an extension of the great success story of natural science). This mistake comes at the expense of the equally important influence of nineteenth-century Romanticism and historicism. Among the human organism's basic capacities are those that allow it to create and develop languages and cultures. With early roots in the ideas of thinkers such as Vico, Herder, and Burke, and major origins in Hegel and the Romantics, the leading historicists stressed the constitutive force of society and culture on individual personality. They also made central to their approach the importance of cultural evolution and variation as features of human social life.

The Romantics (many of whom were also historicists) particularly stressed the interaction between mind or culture and external reality through the transformative power of human imagination. Human nature should not be conceived as an unchanging set of needs and faculties facing an essentially unchanging external environment. Rather it is, above all, a set of capacities for adaptation and change, typically exercised in a collectivity, a society with its own distinctive language, culture, and history. Of course many Romantics stressed the importance of *individual* creativity as a factor in cultural evolution. (In the American context, it generally works pretty well to translate "the Romantics" as "Emerson," in which case history, custom, and the collectivity become "Fate.")

Out of its mixed Darwinist-historicist-Romantic heritage, pragmatism developed an account of mind and inquiry that was in two senses thoroughly *practical*. As Justice Oliver Wendell Holmes (himself an early pragmatist) put it, all thought is at once "social" and "on its way to action."[5] First, thought always comes embodied in practices—culturally embedded habits and patterns of expectation, behavior, and response. This is the *contextual* side of pragmatism, the side that derives from historicism and theories of cultural evolution.

On the other, Darwinian, side, the pragmatists learned equally to stress mind as an adaptive device for coping with the external environment, practical in the sense that it is *instrumental* to survival. In its most evolved, distinctively human form, mind enables conscious reflection and deliberation aimed to solve the problems that arise in the source of acting on the unreflective and habitual substratum of customary practice. And deliberative inquiry itself modifies culture, feeding back upon the substratum itself. It can change the customary baseline of default options or tacit beliefs that guide action in that great majority of cases in which no conscious inquiry intervenes. This *instrumentalist* element reflects the inheritance of the Enlightenment, whose lasting message, as Kant said, is "Think for yourself!"

Earlier accounts of pragmatism primarily emphasized its instrumental side, but the recent reinterpretation of the movement gives equal stress to its historicist and Romantic roots. Neopragmatism thus brings to the fore the contextualist thesis that thought is always essentially embedded in a context of social practice. It is, to repeat, this equal stress on context that sharply distinguishes pragmatists from the orthodox scientific positivists with whom they have often been conflated in the past. Further, it was mainly contextualism that led to pragmatism's most important philosophical innovation—its Deweyan critique of the quest for certainty, the longstanding Western project of placing solid and impersonal *foundations* under human beliefs.

The Enlightenment philosophers had followed a much older tradition in presuming that knowledge, if it is to be trustworthy at all, must be grounded in a set of indubitable truths. These could be the immediate deliverances of the senses, as the empiricist thought. Or as the rationalist party contended, the foundations of knowledge could be intuitions that survive the effort at universal doubt—"I think therefore I am." In either case, the foundationalist procedure is to strip away habitual and conventional ways of thought and to build a new structure of knowledge based on logically unimpeachable inferences from certifiably indubitable premises.

This is an impossibility, argues the pragmatist. You cannot, as Peirce said, set out to think *either* by "doubting everything," *or* by "observing 'the first impressions of sense.'" You rather "set out" from "the very state of mind in which you actually find yourself," in which inevitably you are "laden with an immense mass of cognition already formed." Of that mass, "you cannot divest yourself if you would," and if you could do so, how could you think at all?[6] The zero-based foundationalist method of inquiry is not an option.

This antifoundationalism, taken by itself, might seem to entail a kind of skeptical intellectual conservativism. And, indeed, this seems to be confirmed when we find William James (in his *Pragmatism* lectures) making Peirce's critique vivid by saying that "in this matter of belief, we are all extreme conservatives," who try to hold on as much as we can to our inherited "stock of old opinions," so that "the most violent revolutions in an individual's beliefs leave most of his old order standing."[7] But as anyone who has read James knows, the conservative rhetoric is misleading; the whole thrust of his work reveals a temper of mind that is open, innovative, experimental, free of imprisoning dogma.

Generally, pragmatists are not skeptical or irrationalist conservatives. That variety of anti-Enlightenment thought (for short, the "Burkean") is alien to pragmatism. We pragmatists do hold that human thought always and necessarily takes place in a situated complex of beliefs, largely of social origin. We do believe that on any given occasion the great mass of these beliefs must be left tacit and used, not made explicit and subject to doubt, if thought and action are to proceed at all. But unlike skeptical conservatives, pragmatists grant no special normative authority to unconscious beliefs, to habits formed from experience, or to slowly evolved social practices. When we pragmatists are romantic, it is about imagination, not about custom. For the pragmatist, custom is not sacred, it is just *there*. As Holmes put it, "continuity with the past is only a necessity, not a duty."[8]

Pragmatists recognize that action according to unquestioned habit constantly runs human beings into problematic situations, from which a combination of imaginative reflection and systematic deliberation can sometimes successfully extract them. Innovative problem solving is as natural and as human (though not as easy) as is customary conduct. This is the central point made on the familiar *instrumentalist* side of pragmatism; it is the future-directed offset to the backward-looking tendencies of the pragmatist stress on the importance of context.

Beliefs cannot be doubted all at once, but this does not privilege any particular belief or set of beliefs against being put in question at any time. Nor does it erect any presumption against pushing a conceptual innovation as far as it can usefully go, even to the point of revolution. That revolutions leave most of the old *conceptual* order standing does *not* make them, for practical human purposes, less revolutionary.

Indeed a recognition of the robust character of context and the tacit substratum in some respects makes the pragmatist *more* open to change than the foundationalist, who is inclined to hold practical change in abeyance until it has gained the kind of complete foundational justification that it can never have. On the other hand, there *is* a kind of foundationalist radicalism based on the delusion of being in possession of a genuinely all-encompassing theory. This secular equivalent of religious fanaticism, when brought to bear on social and political questions, is perhaps the most dangerous temper of mind characteristic of this century.

Instrumentalism says that thought is shaped and tested by its use in the pursuit of human ends. What does pragmatism have to say about the nature of those ends? Since long before the pragmatists came on the scene, it has been common for instrumentalist thinkers to postulate some dominant human drive—toward pleasure, security, survival, power, sex, or whatever—and deduce from it a systematic and all-encompassing theory of society, morals, and politics. Such are the systems of Hobbes, of Bentham, and of the classical economists.

These theories are not pragmatist in spirit. They cultivate the instrumentalist side of pragmatism, but entirely neglect its emphasis on context and culture. Undiluted instrumentalist theories in fact seek to establish dominant and fixed ends as theoretic *foundations* for a science of human nature. Very often, these theories posit *biologically* fixed ends, sometimes supported by appeal to Darwinian considerations, and so draw on the evolutionary origins of pragmatism. But biological reductionism neglects what neopragmatists insist upon: that habit, history and culture, the actions and judgments of others, all shape our goals, wants, and preferences. So do the dreams, visions, and musings of ourselves and our fellows.

Here as elsewhere, one side of the pragmatist concept of *the practical* can check the potential excesses bred by a too-exclusive focus upon the other. We pragmatists keep in the back of our minds the reminder that we are thinking to some end—thinking *instrumentally*. We also keep there a reminder that we are thinking against a background of tacit presupposition of which we can never be fully aware—thinking *contextually*.

## II

What does pragmatism, conceived as a synthesis of contextualism and instrumentalism, contribute to legal theory? In considering pragmatism and legal thought, an initial question arises that is like the one Quine raised at the philosophical level. He asked: "Isn't it really empiricism that you are talking about?" On the legal side, one naturally asks: "Isn't the right term 'instrumentalism'?" A practical and down-to-earth jurisprudence, it seems, is quintessentially instrumentalist—a recognition that law is not a self-contained system but rather a set of human directives aimed at socially desired ends.

This was, in fact, a large part of Justice Holmes's view of law. Yet when Harold Laski and others described Holmes's theory by the then new-fangled term "pragmatism," Holmes objected that "the judging of law by its effects and results did not have to wait for W[illiam] J[ames]."[9] And indeed, the *instrumental* conception of law had been promulgated by Bentham a century earlier, and the utilitarian positivists enthusiastically spread it in the years since. Holmes himself drew many of his jurisprudential ideas from Bentham's disciple John Austin.

But Holmes did add something new to the ideas of Bentham and Austin. Unlike them, he basically accepted the main tenets of what in his time was called the Historical School of Jurisprudence. This was the movement, associated with Friedrich Karl von Savigny in Germany and Sir Henry Maine in England, that saw law essentially as custom, a body of historically evolved and culturally specific norms of conduct, analogous in many ways to a natural language. Something like this had always been the largely uncontested jurisprudence of the English common-law tradition, expounded and celebrated in countless bar dinner speeches, as well as in the pages of Coke, Hale, and Blackstone.

Bentham abhorred this whole tradition; he proposed his instrumentalist Analytical Jurisprudence as an antidote to its imprecision and complacency. Benthamism was meant to bring an end to judges-made law through the triumph of universal codification. The proponents of the Historical School and the defenders of common-law tradition answered Bentham's scorn for them in kind and focused their energies on frustrating the drive for codification.

This is where the American legal pragmatists came in. Holmes, and after him Roscoe Pound, Benjamin Cardozo, Karl Llewellyn, and Lon Fuller, as well as John Dewey in his writings on law, all are distinguished by their refusal to find contradiction in the opposition of legal instrumentalism and historicism. They saw these as usefully complementary perspectives on the complex set of ideals, institutions, and practices that constitute law. In the synthesis they promoted, we can see the two faces of pragmatism. Contextualism emphasizes law's rooting in practice and tacit know-how; instrumentalism requires judging these practices by how well they produce desired results in problematic situations.

How then does the old duality of historical and utilitarian jurisprudence—legal contextualism and instrumentalism—reflect itself in present-day legal thought? The answer should be evident to anyone who knows the current scene. Contemporary legal theory is marked by a strong division of the same kind we find in the nineteenth century. On the one side are a cluster of hermeneutic and contextualist approaches, which stress the centrality to law of history, culture, language, ideology, and interpretation. On the other are instrumentalist theories derived from economics, rational choice theory, and social contract political philosophy.

This spirit parallels a similar division in philosophy, where analytic approaches oriented to science confront phenomenological or hermeneutic humanistic perspectives. And in the study of society we likewise have the schism between positivist social science, on the one hand, and interpretive social theory and cultural study on the other. As legal scholarship has (only recently) become less intellectually parochial, these larger divisions in the intellectual world have impinged on it ever more directly. But, as the struggle over codification in the nineteenth century illustrates, similar schisms have often divided lawyers and legal commentators in the past.

The dominant tendency in present-day legal thought is to see the rational choice approach and the hermeneutic approach to law as opponents. Pragmatism speaks against this tendency. The pragmatist urges: "Don't try to resolve this conflict at the level of theory. Whatever side you find yourself inclining toward, hear the other side." Just as William James proposed a pragmatic mediation between tough-minded positivists and tender-minded idealists in his time, so today the legal pragmatist proposes to the contending instrumentalist and contextualist schools: "Good health to both your houses."

Let me now construct and confront two imagined representative criticisms of legal pragmatism; each will offer an unfriendly interpretation of the ecumenical pragmatist proposal as I have just enunciated it. The first critic focuses on politics and finds pragmatist theory reasonable—all *too* reasonable. It reminds him of Polonius's smooth assent to the manic Prince Hamlet's various cloud-theories. The cloud (which is to say law) *does* indeed look like a camel, but (if the young Prince pleases) it is also like a weasel. And a whale? "Very like a whale." So, is law economic analysis? "Very like." Literary criticism? ᵒ"Very like that, too." Hermeneutic phenomenology? "Eh? Oh, of course . . . whatever you say."

Polonius, one may say, is a kind of pragmatist, the George Bush kind. He represents a certain sort of law-firm senior partner or old-time doctrinal law professor. He (definitely *he*) humors the antic young legal theorist, secure in the conviction that none of this theory business will ever matter in practical terms.  His strategy is to let the theory-minded play in their intellectual sandbox: At least it keeps them out of trouble, away from the real (concrete) issues of law and politics.  Pragmatism viewed in this light is useless as a guide to legal action, though perhaps ideologically useful for cynical protectors of the status quo.

A second kind of critic sees the pragmatist tendency to embrace and mediate between apparent theoretic alternatives as founded in irrationalism.  On this view, legal pragmatists wave off theoretical dilemmas not because they think theory is irrelevant.  Rather they have a theory—one that privileges some mystical capacity for making particular decisions ("intuition" or "judgment") over the requirements of intellectual consistency.  P and not-P can cohabit promiscuously in the house of pragmatism because it is action driven by gut reaction that counts; the discursive formulations that purport to justify action are mere epiphenomena.

Notice that this intellectual critique can converge with the political challenge raised by the first critic.  Interpreted as a mystical or irrationalist doctrine, pragmatism may occasionally sponsor a kind of spasmodic legal radicalism, freed from the confining checks of articulate criticism based on canons of consistency.  But given the recruitment and reward structure of legal institutions, the more likely pervasive effect of legal-theoretic irrationalism is conservative after the Burkean manner—the self-satisfied relaxation back into the familiar habits and prejudices that guide unreflective practice, just as Polonius planned it.

Let me start with the first, explicitly political, critic.  A beginning point for response is that the pragmatist *has* no absolute conception of what counts as theory.  Absolute theorists take the *foundations* of a subject as their object of inquiry; pragmatists do not believe that such foundations exist.  For the pragmatist, "theory" is not marked off sharply from the practical; there exists only a continuum of increasingly broad generalizations made by lawyers and commentators and aimed at legal subject matter.  As Holmes put the point, "the process [of legal thought] is one, from a lawyer's statement of a case . . . up to the abstract universals of jurisprudence"; jurisprudence is "simply law in its most generalized part."[10]

When legal generalizations strike the average practitioner (or legal scholar) as too abstract to be practical, they are naturally described as theoretical—a term that in this context is pejorative.  Theory, then, is *by definition* whatever is commonly thought impractically general or abstract by practitioners or commentators.

The pragmatist defense of theory is then simply a denial of final or absolute authority to the average practitioner's (or average doctrinal commentator's) intuitions about which generalizations are useful. Experienced common sense is certainly worthy of consideration, but questions like this have to be decided at retail. A wholesale endorsement of practical common sense could only rest on the supposition that habitual ongoing practice is always all right as it is. But this is just the fallacy of Burkean conservatism. Sometimes established ways of doing things require correction; sometimes correction can be had through the application of unfamiliar material imported from outside an institutionally going practice. And sometimes those with some distance from the fray (the theorists) can see this more clearly than do the busy practitioners.

Further, to suppose that practical legal doctrine can ever be complete in the sense of stating all its own operative premises is a mistake—a mistake that ignores the teachings of pragmatist contextualism. Behind the articulated propositions alleged to guide practice at any point, there is always a body of presupposed tacit beliefs. Some of these may be inconsistent with others; others may simply clash with the facts. The critical task of theory is to make tacit presuppositions explicit *when they are causing trouble*. (The task—to repeat—is *not* the impossible foundationalist project of making all working premises explicit or entirely eliminating tacit presuppositions.)

What then counts as "trouble"? Pragmatists do not guarantee in advance any comprehensive theoretic answer to this question—which itself is a practical one. Nor is any group of people, or any institution, finally in charge of deciding what "trouble" or "a problem" is. Polonius is not, but neither is Hamlet; the law-firm senior partners are not, but neither are the members of the free-floating intelligentsia. This latter point gives one formulation of the democratic theme within pragmatist thought—a constant theme of Dewey's, upon which Richard Rorty has also spoken to good effect.[11]

But the question of criteria for what "works" or what counts as "trouble" leads naturally to the second set of criticisms that are naturally aimed at pragmatists—criticism more intellectual than political. Anyone who aspires to establishing strongly determinate theoretical foundations for legal judgment will naturally see pragmatist formulations as circular. How can we talk about what "works" or what "causes trouble" without a well developed Theory of the Right and the Good? Secondly, these critics will find pragmatist theory to be formulated in deliberately sloppy and imprecise terms. Indeed, they will often convict the ecumenical pragmatist of full-fledged irrationality—tolerance of actual contradiction.

To take the last point first, the pragmatist firmly denies the charge of contradiction—and does so in a way that also answers the charge of inappropriate imprecision. Useful theoretical generalizations, at least in areas such as law that are concerned with the complexities of human and social relations, are likely to be heuristic in intent and probabilistic in content rather than axiomatic and universal. Clashing presumptions and clashing probabilistic generalizations do *not* contradict each other—when they are stated with the proper qualifications.

A case may belong to one class, for which a presumption prescribes one treatment, subject to the proviso "unless overriding factors dictate otherwise." At the same time, the same case belongs to another class, for which an equally good presumption dictates different treatment, subject to a similar proviso. For example: Do not regulate the content of speech, unless necessary to achieve a compelling interest; do not create an institutional environment discriminatorily hostile to traditionally stigmatized groups, unless necessary to achieve a compelling interest. Both directives validly apply to the case of campus verbal harassment. (The qualified imperatives can be recast as probabilistic generalizations: "It is usually a bad idea to. . . .") There is no contradiction here, once the provisos are put in. Nor is there any guarantee that some other well-established generalization will be available to decide the conflict—theory often turns out to be incomplete when it is used as a resource for solving practical problems.

The pragmatist is not surprised to come upon the situation in which the best available applicable generalizations simply conflict, though without logically contradicting each other. Such a situation is just the lawyer's familiar "hard case"—the case that established generalizations do not decide. This is not to say the generalizations are useless in such a case. They provide the decisionmaker with a finite range of alternative ways to frame the problem. They direct attention to relevant values to be "balanced"—to invoke the over-optimistic metaphor lawyers use for the process of decision in such cases. (Because there are no agreed-upon scales and no agreed metric of weight, "mediated" or "accommodated" are less misleading terms.)

Perhaps upon reflection the case will itself suggest a tentative generalization that justifies striking the balance one way rather than another. Perhaps with more testing and experience that generalization may ripen into a "theory." Perhaps not. In any event, the generalization will remain more or less tentative, as even the best-established heuristic principles are.

By contrast to the pragmatist, the theoretical absolutist is likely to frame this situation as one involving a contradiction. This can easily be done by sharpening the conflicting heuristic generalizations into exceptionless axioms, and thus forcing choice between them. But from a pragmatic perspective, this is no benefit if the practicalities of the situation do not justify the increased precision.

An insistence on precision often stands in the way of either accuracy or helpfulness. Consider the question "How tall was the robber?" "Pretty tall" may be a more accurate (though less precise) answer than "six feet two" and a more helpful one than "I can't say—I couldn't measure him." Similarly with "When should I lie?" "Usually not" is more accurate than "never" (and maybe than any precise theory) and more helpful than "it depends." This is the pragmatist's central defense against the charge of sloppiness—to remind of the offsetting inconvenience of excessive precision. At the same time, the pragmatist pleads by confession and avoidance to the charge of circularity; the absence of a single foundational theory makes inescapable the process of justifying practical judgments in a wide benign circle—what Rawls calls the search for reflective equilibrium.

The pragmatist notes, and without disparaging, the motives that make theorists love to create precise and elegantly noncircular theories. When exceptionless theories do hold true, they are enormously useful—the great triumphs of classical physics over the range where its laws hold prove the point well enough. But there are also other worthy motives for this kind of theorizing beyond the immediately practical ones.

Making theory is a form of intellectual activity, of play. It can be serious and absorbing *deep* play, comparable to art in intrinsic satisfaction. Nor should we sharply distinguish this intrinsic motive for theorizing from more utilitarian aims. Just as the play of young animals is practice for "real life," so the play of theoreticians often spins off benefits that are practical in the instrumental sense, but would never have been attained without the play motive. And even when no such benefits turn up, theorizing is itself a practice, a satisfying and meaningful pastime, even a lifetime's project—as writing poetry or composing music is. What is the instrumentally practical an instrument *for*, if not to clear the way for poetry, music, and theory-lovers (and just plain lovers) to do what they love to do?

Finally, there are what might be called the religious motivations for theorizing. Theorists make seek sharp and broad theories to give definition to life situations that otherwise seem formless and meaningless. This is surely no contemptible motive. We have a right to believe, as

James said, and many of us try to give our workaday worlds meaning beyond the quotidian.  But when meaning giving takes the form of the a priori preference for sharp and definitive theories, it should not be considered tough-mindedly practical—as it is, all too often, in today's intellectual climate.

Rather this form of theory pursuit is itself a *tender-minded* indulgence in that same Jamesian right to believe—a flight from the baffling complexity of the world, driven by the kind of fear that underlies the absolutist quest for certainty.  Many of the theoretically minded are particularly moved by such considerations.  Again, these are not unworthy or illegitimate considerations *if* they are acknowledged and brought out in the open.  But such airing is too rare among those whose religious yearnings are dominated by what Holmes called "that longing for certainty and for repose that is in every human mind."[12]

## III

I now want to come back to my example to illustrate the workings of the pragmatist conception of legal theory.  Recall that this is the problem of how to deal with campus verbal harassment of women and racial minorities.  The problem, as I said earlier, creates a dilemma.  It seems to require regulation of speech on the basis of content in order to achieve official nondiscrimination—thus bringing two very basic values into conflict.

On one side is the legal principle that an employer who tolerates abuse and harassment of women or racial minority employees provides those employees with a differentially hostile work environment and so is guilty of sex or race discrimination with respect to terms and conditions of employment.  To avoid this kind of discrimination, the employer must take reasonable steps to prevent employees from harassing each other, verbally as well as physically.  Such steps may well include some content-based regulation of employee speech—"Don't call other employees x, y, and z" (listing some familiar hate epithets).

When the government uses antidiscrimination law to induce an employer to regulate in this way, it is, in effect, engaging in official censorship itself.  That seems to violate well-established First Amendment principles, though few civil libertarians have worried much about this as long as it was confined to the employment context.  But once the concept of hostile environment discrimination moved from the workplace to the university, the conflict it generated between antidiscrimination and free speech immediately began to attract the attention of legal commentators.

I should say that I have been involved with this problem in a practical way myself, as a drafter of Stanford University's student harassment ordinance—that is what leads me to select it as my example of legal pragmatism in action. But I must disclaim from the start any suggestion that pragmatist theory by itself can supply the pragmatist solution to the harassment problem. My pragmatism tells me that there is no uniquely correct solution nor is any particular solution dictated by pragmatist precepts or methods. But I do think that a pragmatist approach usefully illuminates this problem and facilitates dealing with it intelligently—partly, indeed, by undercutting the expectation that practical problems such as the harassment issue should normally find ready solution through the straightforward application of broad theories or principles.

This problem involves theory at a rather low level, if we take the perspective of the average philosopher or legal theorist. Most of them would deny that it is theoretical at all as I have formulated it. On the other hand, most practitioners and many doctrinal writers would find my analysis of the problem theoretical in the pejorative sense—more abstract and general than is useful. The conflicting responses are another illustration of the *relativity* of the concept of "theory."

I interpret the harassment dilemma as an instance of a broader conflict, one that pits against each other what I call civil-rights and civil-liberties mentalities. (I use terms like "mentalities" or "approaches," rather than those like "models," to emphasize the imprecision of the ideational clusters involved.) What are the characteristics of these competing approaches?

First, the civil-liberties approach holds to a strong public-private distinction or state-action requirement, and, second, it downplays the significance of psychic disturbance as a ground for government action—offense is no ground for coercive intervention. (For example, offended patriotic sensibilities are not enough to justify banning flag burning.) The approach is closely associated with an individualistic view of law and politics and with the general set of assumptions about human beings and their social life that underlie rational-choice theory. It is social contractarian, classically liberal, prescribing a night watchman state in the arena of culture. It does not call for hermeneutic inquiry—examination of the *meaning* of social practices—indeed, it is very suspicious of any such thing, holding that government officials are peculiarly ill-suited for the task.

The civil-rights approach, by contrast, is suspicious of the state-action requirement; it holds that inequalities are enforced as effectively and perniciously through the private social and economic structures of civil society as through the laws and practices of states and their officers. Accordingly, it tends to prohibit invidious discrimination by powerful but formally private actors as well as by government—hence the application of civil-rights acts to private landlords, employers, innkeepers, and the like.

Further, the civil-rights mentality treats harm to "hearts and minds" (or "stigma" from insulting stereotypes) as one of its paradigmatic forms of wrong. In identifying stigma, it requires lawyers and judges to engage in enthnographic interpretation; they must read the message sent by social practices. Civil-rights analysis treats social groups as meaningful units; it is thus methodologically collectivist, drawing on the language and approach of sociology and anthropology, as civil-liberties analysis draws on social contract political philosophy, or on economics ("the marketplace of ideas"). The two approaches clash at almost every point.

In the face of this contrast of mentalities or approaches, the standard untheoretical lawyer might ask: Who needs all this baggage of mentalities, classical liberalism, hermeneutics, and so on? We have a tough legal issue; let's analyze the cases, principles, and rules and try to resolve the conflict. In response, I would argue that the actual narrow conflict is indeed illuminated and its solution facilitated by placing it in the broader theoretical context of conflict between the two approaches I have outlined. I cannot make out the case as fully as I would like in the space available here, but perhaps you can see how the argument would go.[13]

The rigorous theorist would have a response very different from that of my postulated practical lawyer. Theoretically, the two approaches I have sketched are readily translated into normative theories that flatly contradict each other—perhaps a rigorously formulated version of social contract liberalism and communitarianism. The theorist's tendency would be to broaden the scope of the theories, and (more to the point) to *sharpen* them from vague approaches into precise models so as to enhance their capacity to clash with each other. Using this approach, the practical conflicts would be seen as simply instances of the broader theoretical contradiction, to be solved as one or the other of the opposed lemmas is selected as the logically dominant one.

Sometimes this sharpening approach is indeed useful in solving problems; it is an important component in the collection of strategies of inquiry called "scientific method." In my view, the preference for precise and testable theses is *not* useful on the issue of harassment. I reach this conclusion not on a priori grounds, but only after I have thought about the problem as carefully as I can, and after (through practice) I have made myself fairly adept at looking at the problem through the alternative lenses they supply. This convinces me that to exclude either approach in the name of the other would be a mistake.

Though neither approach *dictates* a solution when both thus remain in the case, both do inform my own particular practical resolution of the harassment problem. This is to prohibit only harassing speech that both discriminates invidiously and falls within certain established narrow exceptions to the First Amendment—fighting words, and words calculated to inflict severe emotional distress.

In its civil-rights-based restriction to *discriminatory* harassment, this solution conflicts with the civil-liberties principle of content neutrality. On the other hand, it falls far short of what a pure civil-rights approach would demand—requiring university authorities to take all potentially effective steps that might tend toward abolishing a discriminatorily hostile environment on campus. Civil-liberties considerations counsel strongly against so sweeping a requirement.[14]

I do not mean to defend the details of this particular solution here. Its relevant characteristic for my theoretical purposes is that it *mediates* between the civil-liberties and civil-rights approaches to the problem. What is more, it does so in a way that I cannot justify on the basis of any overarching theory or principle. The highest-level theories that I find useful in working out the problem are the civil-liberties and civil-rights approaches that I have roughly sketched here. These approaches speak in different terms to the problem and so are *incommensurable* as applied to it. Still, my practical resolution borrows fragments from each and would not have the shape it does without both of them.

In summarizing the practical lessons of pragmatist theory from this case, I should repeat a caveat. Pragmatism in law is primarily a theory about how to use theory; it is not a recipe for solving practical problems. In particular, it does not invariably dictate, though it may tend to favor, mediated or compromised solutions to concrete practical problems like the question of what campus harassment code to adopt. Sometimes a clear-cut, simple, and "principled" solution—one that follows straightforwardly from a single theoretical formulation—will indeed be the most practical one.

But the pragmatist knows that this will very often not be so. In many situations, solutions that mediate between overlapping and incommensurable theories will be best. Further, there is no overall foundational theory to tell us when mediation is better, and when principled choice—though, again, there are partial (and sometimes conflicting) heuristic guidelines to help with this choice too.

If you are a pragmatist in legal theory, you will not find this either a surprising or a deplorable state of affairs. Pragmatist theory did not dictate my solution to the campus harassment problem. It *dictates* solutions to almost no practical problems. What it does is to free us, when faced with an immediate practical problem, to explore more space than other conceptions of theory open up.

Pragmatism reminds us of the territory below the level of articulate justification. This is the substratum of ordinary unreflective experience: of habit and of the feelings that sometimes spontaneously rebel against what habit dictates. It is this level of experience that determines most of our actions, and also influences (by supplying the context for) all of our self-conscious reflection. As pragmatists, we have learned to respect both the power and the (sometime) wisdom of experiential know-how of this kind.

Less obviously, perhaps, pragmatism opens up to our practical reflections and deliberations the space of theory—the space above the most familiar level of articulate abstraction, the level of doctrine familiar to the practitioner. It is here that pragmatist theorists mostly work. It is here that we seek to ensure the continued freedom of the inquirer to pursue the imagination's possibilities past where they would otherwise be closed off by another product of the same imagination—the restraining glass ceiling of imagined theoretical impossibility.

### Notes

This is a version of a talk delivered at the University of Virginia pragmatism symposium, November 7, 1990. Some passages in it are taken from my article "Holmes and Legal Pragmatism," *Stanford Law Review* 41 (April 1989): 787—870. My thanks to Barbara Babcock, Dan Farber, Stanley Fish, Toni Massaro, and Robin West for their helpful suggestions.

1. John Dewey, *Experience and Nature*, 2nd ed. (New York: Dover, 1958), 412—413.

2. W.V.O. Quine, "The Pragmatists' Place in Empiricism," in *Pragmatism: Its Sources and Prospects*, ed. Robert Mulvaney and Philip Zeltner (Columbia: University of South Carolina Press, 1981), 23.

3. See especially Philip Wiener, *Evolution and the Founders of Pragmatism* (Cambridge, Mass.: Harvard University Press, 1949).

4. Charles S. Peirce, "The Fixation of Belief," in *Collected Papers of Charles Sanders Peirce* 5:358. See 5:912 for Peirce's reference back to Bain's aphorism. Full citation in bibliography.

5. Oliver Wendell Holmes, Jr., "John Marshall," in Holmes, *Collected Legal Papers* (New York: Peter Smith, 1920), 270.

6. Peirce, "What Pragmatism Is," *Collected Papers*, 5:411, 416.

7. William James, "Pragmatism," in *The Writings of William James*, ed. John J. McDermott (Chicago: University of Chicago Press, 1977), 382—383.

8. Holmes, "Law in Science, Science in Law," in *Collected Legal Papers*, 211.

9. *The Holmes-Laski Letters*, ed. Mark Howe (Cambridge: Cambridge University Press, 1953) 1:20.

10. Holmes, "The Path of Law," *Collected Legal Papers*, 211.

11. See Richard Rorty, "The Priority of Democracy to Philosophy," cited in bibliography.

12. Holmes, "The Path of the Law," in *Collected Legal Papers*, 181. The point that reductive accounts of human behavior are, however hard-headed they may sound, tender-minded in terms of James's famous distinction is lucidly made in Margaret Jane Radin, "The Pragmatist and the Feminist," *Southern California Law Review* 63 (September 1990): 1712—1719. Reprinted as Chapter 8 in this book.

13. See, for my proposal, with a much fuller discussion of the doctrinal difficulties and the competing approaches than I can give here, Thomas Grey, "Civil Rights vs. Civil Liberties: The Case of Discriminatory Harassment," *Social Philosophy and Policy* (forthcoming, 1991).

14. The University of Michigan harassment rule struck down on the first amendment grounds in *Doe v. University of Michigan*, 721 F. Supp. 852 (E. D. Mich. 1989) went the whole way with the civil-rights approach; its language tracked the regulations of the Equal Employment Opportunity Commission defining discriminatory harassment in the workplace.

# 2

# What Has Pragmatism to Offer Law?

*Richard A. Posner*

*[T]he great weakness of Pragmatism is that it ends by being of no use to anybody.*

—T. S. Eliot[1]

## I

The pragmatic movement gave legal realism such intellectual shape and content as it had. Then pragmatism died (or merged into other philosophical movements and lost its separate identity), and legal realism died (or was similarly absorbed and transcended). Lately pragmatism has revived, and the question I address in this chapter is whether this revival has produced or is likely to produce a new jurisprudence that will bear the same relation to the new pragmatism as legal realism bore to the old. My answer is no on both counts. The new pragmatism, like the old, is not a distinct philosophical movement but an umbrella term for diverse tendencies in philosophical thought. What is more, it is a term for the same tendencies; the new pragmatism is not new. Some of the tendencies that go to make up the pragmatic tradition were fruitfully absorbed into legal realism, particularly in the forms articulated by Oliver Wendell Holmes and Benjamin Cardozo; others led, and still lead, nowhere. The tendencies that many years ago were fruitfully absorbed into legal realism can indeed help in the formulation of a new jurisprudence, but it will be new largely in jettisoning the naive politics and other immaturities and excesses of legal realism.[2] This refurbished, modernized realism will owe little or nothing, however, to the new pragmatism—if indeed there is such a thing, as I doubt.

Histories of pragmatism[3] usually begin with Charles Sanders Peirce, although he himself gave credit for the idea to a lawyer friend, Nicholas St. John Green, and anticipations can be found much earlier—in Epicurus, for example.[4]   From Peirce the baton is (in conventional accounts) handed to William James, then to John Dewey, George Mead, and (in England) F.S.C. Schiller.   Parallel to and influenced by the pragmatists, legal realism comes on the scene, inspired by the work of Holmes, John Chipman Grey, and Cardozo and realized in the work of the self-described realists, such as Jerome Frank, William Douglas, Karl Llewellyn, Felix Cohen, and Max Radin.  Pragmatism and legal realism join in Dewey's essays on law.[5]  But by the end of World War II both philosophical pragmatism and legal realism have expired, the first superseded by logical positivism and other "hard" analytic philosophy, the other absorbed into the legal mainstream and particularly into the "legal process" school that reaches its apogee in 1958 with Hart and Sacks's *The Legal Process*.   Then, beginning in the 1960s with the waning of logical positivism, pragmatism comes charging back in the person of Richard Rorty, followed in the 1970s by critical legal studies—the radical son of legal realism—and in the 1980s by a school of legal neopragmatists that includes Martha Minow, Thomas Grey, Daniel Farber, Philip Frickey, and others.  The others include myself, and perhaps also, as suggested by Professor Rorty in his essay, Ronald Dworkin—despite Dworkin's overt hostility to pragmatism[6]—and even Roberto Unger.  The ideological diversity of this group is noteworthy.

In the account I am offering (not endorsing), pragmatism, whether of the paleo or neo varieties, stands for a progressively more emphatic rejection of Enlightenment dualisms such as subject and object, mind and body, perception and reality, form and substance; these dualisms being regarded as the props of a conservative social, political, and legal order.

This picture is too simple.   The triumphs of science, particularly Newtonian physics, in the seventeenth and eighteenth centuries persuaded most thinking people that the physical universe had a uniform structure accessible to human reason.   It began to seem that human nature and human social systems might have a similarly mechanical structure.  This emerging world view cast humankind in an observing mold.  Through perception, measurement, and mathematics, the human mind would uncover the secrets of nature (including those of the mind itself, a part of nature) and the laws (natural, not positive) of social interaction—including laws decreeing balanced government, economic behavior in accordance with the principles of supply and demand, and moral and legal principles based on immutable principles of psychology and human behavior. The mind was a camera, recording activities both natural and social and alike determined by natural laws, and an adding machine.

This view, broadly scientific but flavored with a Platonic sense of a world of order behind the chaos of sense impressions, was challenged by the Romantic poets (such as Blake and Wordsworth) and Romantic philosophers. They emphasized the plasticity of the world and especially the esemplastic power of the human imagination. Institutional constraints they despised along with all other limits on human aspiration, as merely contingent; science they found dreary; they celebrated potency and the sense of community—the sense of unlimited potential and of oneness with humankind and with nature—that an infant feels. They were Prometheans. The principal American representative of this school was Ralph Waldo Emerson, and he left traces of his thought on Peirce and Holmes alike. Emerson's European counterpart (and admirer) was Friedrich Nietzsche. It is not that Peirce or Holmes or Nietzsche was a "Romantic" in a precise sense, if there is such a sense. It is that they wished to shift attention from a passive, contemplative relation between an observing subject and an objective reality, whether natural or social, to an active, creative relation between striving human beings and the problems that beset them and that they seek to overcome. For these thinkers, thought was an exertion of will instrumental to some human desire (and we see here the link between pragmatism and utilitarianism). Social institutions—whether science, law, or religion—were the product of shifting human desires rather than of a reality external to those desires. Human beings had not only eyes but hands as well.

Without going any further, we can see that "truth" is going to be a problematic concept for the pragmatist. The essential meaning of the word is observer independence, which is just what the pragmatist is inclined to deny. It is no surprise, therefore, that the pragmatists' stabs at defining truth—truth is what is fated to be believed in the long run (Peirce), truth is what is good to believe (James), or truth is what survives in the competition among ideas (Holmes)—are riven by paradox. The pragmatist's real interest is not in truth at all, but in belief justified by social need.

This change in direction does not necessarily make the pragmatist unfriendly to science (there is a deep division within pragmatism over what attitude to take toward science).[7] But it shifts the emphasis in philosophy of science from the discovery of nature's laws by observation to the formulation of theories about nature that are motivated by the desire of human beings to predict and control their environment. The implication, later made explicit by Thomas Kuhn, is that scientific theories are a function of human need and desire rather than of the way things are in nature, so that the succession of theories on a given topic need not bring us closer to "ultimate reality" (which is not to deny that scientific *knowledge* may be growing steadily). But this is to get ahead of the story, because I want to pause in 1921 and examine the formulation of legal pragmatism that Benjamin Cardozo offered in his book published that year, *The Nature of the Judicial Process*.[8] Most of what Cardozo has to say in this book (and elsewhere) is latent in Holmes's voluminous but scattered and often cryptic academic, judicial, and occasional writings. But the book is worthwhile and important as a clear, concise, and sensible manifesto of legal pragmatism and harbinger of the realist movement.

"The final cause of law," writes Cardozo, "is the welfare of society."[9] So much for the formalist idea, whose scientistic provenance and pretensions are evident, of law as a body of immutable principles. Cardozo does not mean, however, that judges "are free to substitute their own ideas of reason and justice for those of the men and women whom they serve. Their standard must be an objective one"—but objective in a pragmatic sense, which is not the sense of correspondence with an external reality. "In such matters, the thing that counts is not what I believe to be right. It is what I may reasonably believe that some other man of normal intellect and conscience might reasonably look upon as right."[10]

The thing that counts the most is that legal rules be understood in instrumental terms, implying contestability, revisability, and mutability.

> Few rules in our time are so well established that they may not be called upon any day to justify their existence as means adapted to an end. If they do not function, they are diseased. If they are diseased, they need not propagate their kind. Sometimes they are cut out and extirpated altogether. Sometimes they are left with the shadow of continued life, but sterilized, truncated, impotent for harm.[11]

A related point is that law is forward-looking. This point is implicit in an instrumental concept of law—which is the pragmatic concept of law, law as the servant of human needs, and is in sharp contrast to Aristotle's influential theory of corrective justice. That theory is quintessentially backward-looking. The function of law as corrective justice is to restore a preexisting equilibrium of rights, while in Cardozo's account "[n]ot the origin, but the goal, is the main thing. There can be no wisdom in the choice of a path unless we know where it will lead. . . . The rule that functions well produces a title deed to recognition. . . . [T]he final principle of selection for judges . . . is one of fitness to an end."[12] The "title deed" sentence is particularly noteworthy; it is a rebuke to formalist theories that require that for a law to be valid it must be "pedigreed" by being shown to derive from some authoritative source.

Where does the judge turn for the knowledge that is needed to weigh the social interests that shape the law? "I can only answer that he must get his knowledge . . . from experience and study and reflection; in brief, from life itself."[13] The judge is not a finder, but a maker, of law. John Marshall "gave to the constitution of the United States the impress of his own mind; and the form of our constitutional law is what it is, because he moulded it while it was still plastic and malleable in the fire of his own intense convictions."[14]

The focus of *The Nature of the Judicial Process* is on the common law, but in the last quoted passage we can see that Cardozo did not think the creative powers of the judicial imagination bound to wither when confronted by the challenge of textual interpretation. Although the self-described legal realists (from whom Cardozo, conscious of their excesses, carefully distanced himself)[15] added little to what had been said by Cardozo and before him by Holmes, a notable essay by Max Radin[16] clarifies and in so doing emphasizes the parity of statutes and the common law. Judges, it is true, are not to revise a statute, as they are free to do with a common law doctrine. But interpretation is a creative rather than contemplative task—indeed judges have as much freedom in deciding difficult statutory (and of course constitutional) cases as they have in deciding difficult common law cases.

Yet, despite Radin's notable essay and the realists' salutary effort to refocus legal scholarship from the common law to the emergent world of statute-dominated law, legislation proved a challenge to which the realist tradition, from Holmes to the petering out of legal realism in the 1940s and its replacement by the legal process school in the 1950s, was unable to rise. The trouble started with Holmes's well-known description of the judge as an interstitial legislator, a description that Cardozo echoes in *The Nature of the Judicial Process*. The implication is that judges and legislators are officials of the same stripe—guided and controlled by the same goals, values, incentives, and constraints. If this were true, the judicial role would be greatly simplified; it would be primarily a matter of helping the legislature forge sound policy. It is not true. The legislative process is buffeted by interest-group pressures to an extent rare in the judicial process. The result is a body of laws far

less informed by sound policy judgments than the realists in the heyday
and aftermath of the New Deal believed. It is no longer possible to
imagine the good pragmatist judge as one who acts merely as the faithful
agent of the legislature. Indeed, the faithful-agent conception has
become a hallmark of modern formalism—judges as faithful agents
*despite* the perversity of so many of the statutes that they are
interpreting.

A closely related failing of legal realism was its naive enthusiasm for
government, an enthusiasm that marked legal realism as a "liberal"
movement (in the modern, not nineteenth-century, sense) and is part of
the legacy of legal realism to today's neopragmatism. As strikingly
shown by the other chapters in this book, today's legal pragmatism is so
dominated by persons of liberal or radical persuasion as to make the
movement itself seem (not least in their eyes) a school of left-wing
thought. Yet not only has pragmatism no inherent political valence, but
those pragmatists who attack the pieties of the Right while exhibiting a
wholly uncritical devotion to the pieties of the Left (such as racial and
sexual equality, the desirability of a more equal distribution of income
and wealth, and the pervasiveness of oppression and injustice in modern
Western society) are not genuine pragmatists; they are dogmatists in
pragmatists' clothing.

Another great weakness of legal realism was the lack of method.
The realists knew what to do—think things not words, trace the actual
consequences of legal doctrines, balance competing policies—but they
didn't have a clue as to how to do any of these things. It was not their
fault. The tools of economics, statistics, and other pertinent sciences
were insufficiently developed to enable a social-engineering approach to
be taken to law.

I want to go back and pick up the thread of philosophical
pragmatism. When *The Nature of the Judicial Process* appeared, John
Dewey was the leading philosopher of pragmatism, and it is his version
of pragmatism that is most in evidence in Cardozo's book and other
extrajudicial writings.[17] Dewey continued to be productive for many
years, but until the 1960s there was little that was new in pragmatism.
Yet much that was happening in philosophy during this interval
supported the pragmatic outlook. Logical positivism itself, with its
emphasis on verifiability and its consequent hostility to metaphysics, is
pragmatic in demanding that theory make a difference in the world of
fact, the empirical world. Karl Popper's falsificationist philosophy of
science is close to Peirce's philosophy of science; in both, doubt is the
engine of progress and truth an ever-receding goal, rather than an

attainment. The anti-foundationalism, anti-metaphysicality, and rejection of certitude that are leitmotifs of the later Ludwig Wittgenstein and of W.V.O. Quine can be thought of as extensions of the ideas of James and Dewey. By the 1970s and 1980s, the streams have merged and we have a mature pragmatism represented by such figures as Donald Davidson, Hilary Putnam, and Rorty in analytical philosophy, Jurgen Habermas in political philosophy, Clifford Geertz in anthropology, Stanley Fish in literary criticism, and the academic lawyers whom I mentioned at the outset.[18]

There is little to be gained, however, from calling this recrudescence of pragmatism the "new" pragmatism. That would imply that there were (at least) two schools of pragmatism, each of which could be described and then compared. Neither the old nor the new pragmatism is a school. The differences between a Peirce and a James, or between a James and a Dewey, are profound. The differences among current advocates of pragmatism are even more profound, making it possible to find greater affinities across than within the "schools"—Peirce has more in common with Putnam than Putnam with Rorty, and I have more in common (I think) with Peirce, James, and Dewey than I have with Cornel West or Stanley Fish. What is more useful than to attempt to descry and compare old and new schools of pragmatism is to observe simply that the strengths of pragmatism are better appreciated today than they were thirty years ago and that this is due in part to the apparent failure of alternative philosophies such as logical positivism, but more to a growing recognition that the strengths of such alternatives lie in features shared with pragmatism, such as hostility to metaphysics and sympathy with the *methods* of science as distinct from faith in the power of science to deliver final truths.

If both the old and the new pragmatisms are as heterogeneous as I have suggested, the question arises whether pragmatism has any common core, and, if not, what use the term is. To speak in nonpragmatic terms, pragmatism has three "essential" elements. (To speak in pragmatic, nonessentialist terms, there is nothing practical to be gained from attaching the pragmatist label to any philosophy that does not have all three elements.) The first is a distrust of metaphysical entities ("reality," "truth," "nature," etc.) viewed as warrants for certitude whether in epistemology, ethics, or politics. The second is an insistence that propositions be tested by their consequences, by the difference they make—and if they make none, set aside. The third is an insistence on judging our projects, whether scientific, ethical, political, or legal, by their conformity to social or other human needs rather than to "objective," "impersonal" criteria. These elements in turn imply an outlook that is progressive (in the sense of forward-looking), secular, and experimental, and that is commonsensical without making a fetish of common sense—for common sense is a repository of prejudice and ignorance as well as a fount of wisdom. R. W. Sleeper has helpfully summarized the pragmatic outlook in describing Dewey's philosophy as "a philosophy rooted in common sense and dedicated to the transformation of culture, to the resolution of the conflicts that divide us."[19] Also apt is Cornel West's description of the "common denominator" of pragmatism as "a future-oriented instrumentalism that tries to deploy thought as a weapon to enable more effective action."[20]

## II

It should be apparent that what I am calling the core of pragmatism or the pragmatic temper or outlook is vague enough to embrace a multitude of philosophies that are profoundly inconsistent at the operating level (anyone who still doubts this after the examples I gave earlier would do well to recall that Sidney Hook and Jurgen Habermas are both distinguished figures in pragmatic philosophy), including a multitude of inconsistent jurisprudences. Indeed there is a serious question—the question raised by the quotation from T. S. Eliot that is the epigraph of this chapter—whether pragmatism is specific enough to have any use, specifically in law. To that question I devote the balance of the essay. I shall be brief and summary; the reader is referred to my forthcoming book[21] for elucidation of the points that follow and for necessary references.

1. There is at least one specific legal question to which pragmatism is directly applicable and that is the question of the basis and extent of the legal protection of free speech. If pragmatists are right and objective truth is just not in the cards, this may seem to weaken the case for providing special legal protections for free inquiry, viewed as the only dependable path to truth. Actually the case is strengthened. If truth is unattainable, the censor cannot appeal to a higher truth as the ground for foreclosing further inquiry on a subject; but the libertarian, in resisting censorship, can appeal to the demonstrated efficacy of free inquiry in enlarging knowledge. One can doubt that we shall ever attain "truth," but not that our knowledge is growing steadily. Even if every scientific truth that we accept today is destined someday to be overthrown, our ability to cure tuberculosis and generate electrical power and build

airplanes that fly will be unimpaired. The succession of scientific theories not only coexists with, but in fact contributes greatly to, the growth of scientific knowledge.

The pragmatist is apt also to be sympathetic to the argument that art and other nondiscursive modes of communication, and the "hot" rhetoric of the demagogue, and even of the flag or draft-card burner, ought to be protected. The pragmatist doubts that there are ascertainable, "objective" standards for establishing the proprieties of expression and therefore prefers to allow the market to be the arbiter. It is a plausible extension of Holmes's marketplace-of-ideas approach—an approach that rests on a pragmatist rejection of the proposition that there are objective criteria of truth.

2. The pragmatic outlook can help us maintain a properly critical stance toward mysterious entities that seem to play a large role in many areas of law, particularly tort and criminal law. Such entities as mind, intent, free will, and causation are constantly invoked in debates over civil and criminal liability. Tested by the pragmatic criterion of practical consequence, these entities are remarkably elusive. Even if they exist, law has no practical means of locating them and in fact ignores them on any but the most superficial verbal level. Judges and juries do not, as a precondition to finding that a killing was intentional, peer into the defendant's mind in quest of the required intent. They look at the evidence of what the defendant did and try to infer from it whether the deed involved advance planning or other indicia of high probability of success, whether there was concealment of evidence or other indicia of likely escape, and whether the circumstances of the crime argue a likelihood of repetition—all considerations that go to dangerousness rather than to intent or free will. The legal factfinder follows this approach because the social concern behind criminal punishment is a concern with dangerousness rather than with mental states (evil or otherwise), and because the methods of litigation do not enable the factfinder to probe beneath dangerousness into mental or spiritual strata so elusive they may not even exist.

Similarly, while interested in consequences and therefore implicitly in causality, the law does not make a fetish of "causation." It does not commit itself to any side of the age-old philosophical controversy over causation, but instead elides the issue by basing judgments of liability on social, rather than philosophical considerations. People who have caused no harm at all because their plans were interrupted are regularly punished for attempt and conspiracy; persons may be held liable in tort law when their acts were neither a necessary nor a sufficient condition of the harm that ensued (as where two defendants, acting independently, simultaneously inflict the harm, and only one is sued); and persons whose acts "caused" injury in an uncontroversial sense may be excused from liability because the harm was an unforeseeable consequence of the act. The principle of legal liability can be redescribed without reference to metaphysical entities such as mind and causation. This redescription is an important part of the project of a pragmatic jurisprudence, although it will not please those for whom law's semantic level is its most interesting and important.

There is nothing new about endeavoring to puncture the law's metaphysical balloons. It was a favorite pursuit of the legal realists. But they did it with a left-wing slant. They were derisive of the proposition that a corporation had natural rights, since a corporation is just the name of a set of contracts. But they were not derisive of the idea of corporate taxation, though, since the corporation is not a person, it cannot bear the burden of taxation. The ultimate payors of the corporate income tax are flesh-and-blood persons, by no means all wealthy, for among them are employees as well as shareholders.

3. Pragmatism remains a powerful antidote to formalism, which is enjoying a resurgence in the Supreme Court. Legal formalism is the idea that legal questions can be answered by inquiry into the relation between concepts and hence without need for more than a superficial examination of their relation to the world of fact. It is, therefore, anti-pragmatic as well as anti-empirical. It asks not, What works? but instead, What rules and outcomes have a proper pedigree in the form of a chain of logical links to an indisputably authoritative source of law, such as the text of the United States Constitution? Those rules and outcomes are correct and the rest incorrect. Formalism is the domain of the logician, the casuist, the Thomist, the Talmudist.

The desire to sever knowledge from observation is persistent and, to some extent, fruitful. Armed with the rules of arithmetic, one can drop a succession of balls into an urn and, if one has counted carefully, one will *know* how many balls there are in the urn without looking into it. Similarly, if the rule of the common law that there are no nonpossessory rights in wild animals can be thought somehow to generalize automatically to the rule that there are no such rights in *any* fugitive natural resource, then we can obtain the "correct" rule for property rights in oil and gas without having to delve into the economics of developing these resources. The pragmatic approach reverses the sequence. It asks, What is the right rule—the sensible, the socially apt, the efficient, the fair rule—for oil and gas? In the course of investigating this question, the pragmatist will consult the wild animal law for what (little) light it may throw on the question, but the emphasis will be empirical from the start. There will be no inclination to allow existing rules to expand to their semantic limits, engrossing ever greater areas of experience by a process of analogy or of verbal similitude. The tendency of formalism is to force the practices of business and lay persons into the mold of existing legal concepts, viewed as immutable, such as "contract." The pragmatist thinks that concepts should be subservient to human need and therefore wants law to adjust its categories to fit the practices of the nonlegal community.

4. The current bulwark of legal formalism, however, is not the common law, but statutory and constitutional interpretation. It is here that we find the most influential modern attempts to derive legal outcomes by methods superficially akin to deduction. The attempts are unlikely to succeed. The interpretation of texts is not a logical exercise and the bounds of "interpretation" are so expansive (when we consider that among the verbal and other objects that are interpreted are dreams, texts in foreign languages, and musical compositions) as to cast the utility of the concept into doubt. Pragmatists will emphasize the role of consequences in "interpretation," viewed humbly as the use of a text in aid of an outcome. They will point out, for example, that one reason we interpret the sentence "I'll eat my hat" as facetious is that the consequences of attempting to eat one's hat are so untoward.

In approaching an issue that has been posed as one of statutory "interpretation," pragmatists will ask which of the possible resolutions has the best consequences, all things (that lawyers are or should be interested in) considered, including the importance of preserving language as a medium of effective communication and of preserving the separation of powers. Except as may be implied by the last clause, pragmatists are not interested in the authenticity of a suggested interpretation as an expression of the intent of legislators or of the framers of constitutions. They are interested in using the legislative or constitutional text as a resource in the fashioning of a pragmatically attractive result. They agree with Cardozo that what works carries with it the best of title deeds; they prefer the sturdy mongrel to the sickly pedigreed purebred.

Take the old jurisprudential chestnut, discussed briefly in *The Nature of the Judicial Process*,[22] whether a "murdering heir" shall be allowed to inherit. The wills statute allows testators who comply with certain formalities to leave their property to whomever they please. There is no exception for the eventuality in which the beneficiary named in the will murders the testator. Should such an exception be interpolated by the courts? The answer, to the pragmatist, depends on the consequences. On the one hand, it can be objected that by interpolating an exception the courts will relax the pressure on legislators to draft statutes carefully and will violate the principle that legislatures rather than courts prescribe the penalties for criminal behavior. On the other hand, there is a natural concern that allowing the murderer to inherit will encourage murder; a reluctance to pile more work on already overburdened legislatures; and recognition that disinheriting the murderer is apt to fulfill, rather than to defeat, the testator's intentions, which is the ultimate purpose of the wills statute. A testator who foresaw the murder would not have made the murderer a beneficiary under the will; so if no exception to the wills statute is recognized, farseeing testators may decide to insert express provisions in their wills disinheriting murdering beneficiaries. The courts can save them the trouble by interpolating such a provision by interpretation. All these consequences have somehow to be analyzed and compared if the courts are to interpret the wills statute pragmatically.

Further complicating the interpretive picture in general is our current understanding of the legislative process, a more critical understanding than reigned when Cardozo, the legal realists, and the realists' successors in the legal process school wrote. We no longer think of statutes as typically, let alone invariably, the product of well-meaning efforts to maximize the public interest by legislators who are devoted to the public interest and who are the faithful representatives of constituents who share the same devotion. The wills statute can probably be viewed in faithful-agent terms, but many other statutes cannot be. The theory of social choice has instructed us about the difficulties of aggregating preferences by the method of voting, while the interest-group theory of politics in the version revived by economists has taught us that the legislative process often caters to the redistributive desires of narrow coalitions and, in so doing, disserves the public interest, plausibly construed. Under pressure of the insights of both theories it becomes unclear where to locate statutory meaning, problematic to speak of judges discerning legislative intent, and uncertain why judges should seek to perfect through interpretation the decrees of the special-interest state. The main choices in "interpretive" theory that the new learning allows are either some version of strict construction or a pragmatic approach in which, recognizing the difficult and problematic nature of statutory interpretation, judges use consequences to guide their decisions, always bearing in mind that the relevant consequences include systemic ones such as debasing the currency of statutory language by straying too far from it.

Mention of systemic concerns should help demolish the canard that legal pragmatism implies the suppression of such concerns in favor of doing shortsighted substantive justice between the parties to the particular case.[23] The relevant consequences to the pragmatist are long run as well as short run, systemic as well as individual, the importance of stability and predictability as well as the importance of justice to the individual parties, and the importance of maintaining language as a reliable method of communication as well as the importance of interpreting statutes and constitutional provisions freely in order to make them speak intelligently to circumstances not envisaged by their drafters.

5. Pragmatism has implications, some already sketched under the rubrics of formalism and interpretation, for the theory of adjudication—of what judges do and should do. Although professional discourse has always been predominantly formalist, most American judges have been practicing pragmatists, in part because the materials for decision in American law have always been so various and conflicting that formalism was an unworkable ideal.[24] But after a bout of conspicuous judicial activism that lasted several decades, there is renewed interest in approaches that favor continuity with the past over social engineering of the future—approaches embraced by many quondam judicial activists eager to conserve the work of the past decades against inroads by conservative judges, and by many conservatives who believe that the judiciary remains committed to liberal policies. There is renewed talk of tradition, of embodied but inarticulate wisdom (embodied in precedent, in professional training, in law's customary language), of the limitedness of individual reason and the danger of precipitate social change. The cautionary stance implicit in these approaches is congenial to the pragmatist, for whom the historical record of reform efforts is full of sobering lessons. But pragmatists are not content with a vague neotraditionalism. They know it will not do to tell judges to resolve all doubts against change and freeze law as it is, let alone to return to some past epoch in legal revolution (1950? 1850?). As society changes, judges, within the broad limits set by the legislators and by the makers of the Constitution, must adapt the law to its altered environment. No version of traditionalism will tell them how to do this. For this they need ends and an awareness of how social change affects the appropriate means—how, for example, the coming of the telegraph and the telephone altered the conditions for regulating contracts. They need, in short, the instrumental sense that is basic to pragmatism.

6.    This brings me to the question of the relation between pragmatism and our most highly developed instrumental concept of law, the economic.  Among the recurrent criticisms of efforts to defend the economic approach as a worthwhile guide for legal reform is that the defenders have failed to ground the approach securely in one of the great traditions of ethical insight, such as the Kantian or the utilitarian.  The criticism is sound as observation, but not as criticism.  The economic approach to law that I defend—the idea that law should strive to support competitive markets and to simulate their results in situations in which market-transaction costs are prohibitive—has affinities with both Kantian and utilitarian ethics: with the former, because the approach protects the autonomy of people who are productive or at least potentially so (granted, this isn't everyone); with the latter, because of the empirical relation between free markets and human welfare.  Although it is easily shown that the economic approach is neither deducible from nor completely consistent with either system of ethics, this is not a decisive objection from a pragmatic standpoint.  Pragmatists are unperturbed by a lack of foundations.  We ask not whether the economic approach to law is adequately grounded in the ethics of Kant or Rawls or Bentham or Mill or Hayek or Nozick—and not whether any of those ethics is adequately grounded—but whether it is the best approach for the contemporary American legal system to follow, given what we know about markets (and we are learning more about them every day from the economic and political changes in Communist and Third World countries), about American legislatures, about American judges, and about the values of the American people.

The economic approach cannot be the whole content of legal pragmatism.  Because it works well only where there is at least moderate agreement on ends, it cannot answer the question whether abortion should be restricted, although it can tell us something, maybe much, about the efficacy and consequences of the restrictions.  One value of pragmatism is its recognition that there are areas of discourse where lack of common ends precludes rational resolution; and here the pragmatic counsel (or one pragmatic counsel) to the legal system is to muddle through, preserve avenues of change, do not roil needlessly the political waters.  On a pragmatic view, the error of *Roe v. Wade*[25] is not that it read the Constitution wrong—for there are plenty of well-regarded decisions that reflect an equally freewheeling approach to constitutional interpretation—but that it prematurely nationalized an issue best left to simmer longer at the state and local level until a consensus based on experience with a variety of approaches to abortion emerged.

7. To those who equate economics with scientism and who consider pragmatism the rejection of the scientistic approach to philosophy,[26] my attempt to relate the economic approach to pragmatism will seem perverse. But scientistic philosophy—the attempt to construct a metaphysics, a theory of action, an ethical theory, a political theory or what have you that has the rigor and generality that we associate with the natural sciences—is not at all the same thing as social science, which is the application of scientific method to social behavior. Most pragmatists have not disbelieved in the utility of scientific method. Quite the contrary, pragmatism in the style of Peirce and Dewey can be viewed as a generalization of the ethic of scientific inquiry—open-minded, forward-looking, respectful of fact, willing to experiment, disrespectful of sacred cows, anti-metaphysical. And this is an ethic of which law needs more. I am not saying that the economic approach to law is rooted in or inspired by pragmatism, for in truth it is rooted in and inspired by a belief in the intellectual power and pertinence of economics. But economic analysis and pragmatism are thoroughly, and I think fruitfully, compatible.

8. There is renewed interest in the rhetoric of law.[27] This may appear to have nothing to do with pragmatism, but the appearance is misleading. By making the concept of "objective truth" problematic, the pragmatic distrust of foundations expands the range in which metaphor and other forms of emotive argument may legitimately upset belief. In Holmes's pragmatic metaphor of the marketplace of ideas, competing theorists, ideologues, and reformers hawk their intellectual wares. Knowing how important persuasion is in the market for goods and services, we should not be surprised to find it playing a big role in the market in ideas as well. We should expect change in law to be related not only to politics and economics and not only to the correction of error, but also to new slogans, metaphors, imagery, and other means of bringing about changes in perspective.

### III

With muddling through offered as one method of pragmatic jurisprudence (see point 6), one may wonder whether that jurisprudence has progressed an inch beyond *The Nature of the Judicial Process.* Certainly the essence of that jurisprudence is in Cardozo's book and indeed can be found much earlier, though in a more elliptical form, in Holmes's writings, especially "The Path of the Law."[28] But there has been some progress since 1921. Reviewing my eight items, we can see that Cardozo had a solid pragmatic grasp of the weakness of formalism (point 3) and a good pragmatic theory of adjudication (point 6), but free speech was not an issue about which he was much concerned (point 1); the critique of intention and causation (point 2) was less developed than it is today and certainly less salient in Cardozo's thinking; he was uninterested in interpretation and unrealistic about the legislative process (point 3); and he was innocent of the economic approach to law as a self-conscious methodology (point 6)—it did not exist in 1921, or indeed until half a century later—but like most good common law judges he had intuitions of it.[29]   A closely related point is that the application of scientific method to law lay in the future (point 7). Cardozo in his judicial opinions was very much the rhetorician (point 8), but his essay on judicial rhetoric[30] is a disappointment—cute, civilized, but unanalytic.

Although pragmatic jurisprudence embraces a richer set of ideas than can be found in *The Nature of the Judicial Process* or "The Path of the Law," one can hardly say that there has been much progress, and perhaps in the nature of pragmatism there cannot be.   All that a pragmatic jurisprudence really connotes—and it connoted it in 1897 or 1921 as much as it does today—is a rejection of a concept of law as grounded in permanent principles and realized in logical manipulations of those principles, and a determination to use law as an instrument for social ends.   It signals an attitude, an orientation, at times a change in direction.   It clears the underbrush; it does not plant the forest.

## Notes

This is the revised text of a paper presented at the Symposium on the Renaissance of Pragmatism in American Legal Thought, held at the University of Southern California Law Center on February 23 and 24, 1990.   I thank Cass Sunstein for helpful comments on a previous draft.

1. T. S. Eliot, "Francis Herbert Bradley," in *Selected Prose of T. S. Eliot*, ed. Frank Kermode (London: Faber and Faber, 1975), 204 (essay first published in 1927).

2. I present my full argument for this new jurisprudence in my book *The Problems of Jurisprudence* (Cambridge, Mass.: Harvard University Press, 1990).

3. See entries under Hollinger, Smith, and Thayer in bibliography.

4. See Martha Nussbaum, "Therapeutic Arguments: Epicurus and Aristotle," in *The Norms of Nature*, ed. Malcom Schofield and Gisela Striker (Cambridge: Cambridge University Press, 1986), 31, 41, 71—72.

5. Notably John Dewey's essay "Logical Method and Law," *Cornell Law Quarterly* 17 (December 1924): 17—27.

6. See note 23 below. Also see Richard Rorty, "The Banality of Pragmatism and the Poetry of Justice," Chapter 5, and Ronald Dworkin, "Pragmatism, Right Answers, and True Banality," Chapter 19.

7. See, for example, Isaac Levi, "Escape From Boredom—Education According to Rorty," *Canadian Journal of Philosophy* 11 (December 1981): 589—601.

8. Benjamin Cardozo, *The Nature of the Judicial Process* (New Haven: Yale University Press, 1921).

9. Ibid., 66.

10. Ibid., 88—89.

11. Ibid., 98—99.

12. Ibid., 102—103.

13. Ibid., 113.

14. Ibid., 169—170.

15. See Benjamin Cardozo, "Jurisprudence," in *Selected Writings of Benjamin Nathan Cardozo: The Choice of Tycho Brahe*, ed. M. Hall (New York: Bender, 1947).

16. See Max Radin, "Statutory Interpretation," *Harvard Law Review* 43 (April 1930): 863—885, esp. 884.

17. I discuss the matter of Cardozo's pragmatism at greater length in my Cooley Lectures, *Cardozo: A Study in Reputation* (Chicago: University of Chicago Press, forthcoming).

18. For good recent discussions of pragmatism from a variety of perspectives see entries in bibliography under Simpson, Margolis, Rorty, West, Levi, Mulvaney and Zeltner, and Putnam and Putnam. For the work of the new legal pragmatists, see entries under Farber, Grey, and Minow.

19. R. W. Sleeper, *The Necessity of Pragmatism: John Dewey's Conception of Philosophy* (New Haven: Yale University Press, 1986).

20. Cornel West, *The American Evasion of Philosophy: A Genealogy of Pragmatism*, 5.

21. See Note 2 above.

22. The case is *Riggs v. Palmer*, 115 N.Y. 506, 22 N.E. 188 (1889), and the discussion is in Benjamin Cardozo, *The Nature of the Judicial Process*, 41—43.

23. An implication readers might draw from Dworkin's statement in *Law's Empire* that "the pragmatist thinks judges should always do the best they can for the future, in the circumstances, unchecked by any need to respect or secure consistency in principle with what other officials have done or will do." Ronald Dworkin, *Law's Empire* (Cambridge, Mass.: Harvard University Press, 1986), 161. This is an impoverished conception of pragmatism, one that merges pragmatism with act utilitarianism.

24. Against the suggestion that "pragmatism provides the best explanations of how judges actually decide cases," Dworkin argues that it "leaves unexplained one prominent feature of judicial practice—the attitude judges take toward statutes and precedents in hard cases—except on the awkward hypothesis that this practice is designed to deceive the public, in which case the public has not consented to it." Ronald Dworkin, *Law's Empire*, 161. Dworkin is inferring judges' attitude from the rhetoric of judicial opinions, and this is perilous, because judges are not always candid and also because they often are not self-aware. Even if judges are consistently and deliberately deceptive, this would not impair the soundness of the pragmatic *explanation* of judicial behavior. Similarly, a lack of public consent would have nothing to do with the explanatory power of the pragmatic explanation. The issue of consent is in any event artificial, since judicial opinions are with rare exceptions written to be read by lawyers, not by lay people, and have in fact virtually no lay readership. Since Dworkin knows all these things as well as I do, I infer that his discussion of judicial behavior and legitimacy, like so much discussion in law, is itself highly rhetorical.

25. 410 U.S. 113 (1973).

26. For a clear statement of this rejection, see Richard Rorty, "Philosophy as Science, as Metaphor and as Politics," in *The Institution of Philosophy: A Discipline In Crisis?* ed. Avner Cohen and Marcelo Dascal (La Salle, Ill.: Open Court, 1989), 13—33.

27. See Richard Posner, *Law and Literature: A Misunderstood Relation* (Cambridge, Mass.: Harvard University Press, 1985), 269—316 and references therein.

28. Oliver Wendell Holmes, "The Path of the Law," *Harvard Law Review*, 10 (March 1897): 457—478.

29. Professor Landes and I discuss an example—Cardozo's decision in *Adams v. Bullock*, 227 N.Y. 208, 125 N.E. 93 (1919)—in William Landes and Richard Posner, *The Economic Structure of Tort Law* (Cambridge, Mass.: Harvard University Press, 1987), 97—98.

30. Benjamin Cardozo, "Law and Literature," in *Selected Writings of Benjamin Nathan Cardozo: The Choice of Tycho Brahe*, 339.

# 3

## Almost Pragmatism:
## The Jurisprudence of Richard Posner, Richard Rorty, and Ronald Dworkin

*Stanley Fish*

### I

In *The Problems of Jurisprudence*,[1] Richard Posner announces that he is a pragmatist, by which he means that he rejects many if not most of the goals of legal theory, and especially the chief goal of offering an account of the law that is at once comprehensively abstract, strongly normative, and predictive of outcomes, that is, of decisions and holdings. He begins by declaring that he will "argue against 'artificial reason,' against Dworkin's 'right answer' thesis, against formalism, against overarching conceptions of justice such as 'corrective justice,' 'natural law,' and 'wealth maximization' . . . against 'strong legal positivism'" (26), and he ends by proclaiming that the search for "an overarching principle for resolving legal disputes" (302) has failed and that "no keys were found" (455). The process of finding no keys gives the book its structure. In other treatises on jurisprudence the argument is built up step by step into what promises to be a magnificent edifice (or empire), but here "there is no edifice" (69), only the repeated attempt to lay still another foundation that is almost immediately found to be as "rotten" as the last one (392).

Something of the feel of this negative project emerges early on in the discussion of objectivity. Objectivity, Posner tells us, comes in three flavors. First, and most ambitiously, there is "objectivity as correspondence to an external reality" (7); second, the scientific sense of objectivity as a procedure that is replicable independently of the differences between agents who execute it: "A finding is replicable in this sense if different investigators, not sharing the same ideological or other preconceptions . . . would be bound to agree with it" (7); and, third, there is objectivity in the sense of "merely reasonable—that is, as not willful, not personal, not (narrowly) political, not utterly indeterminate though not determinate in the ontological or scientific sense, but as amenable to and accompanied by persuasive though not necessarily convincing explanation" (7).

The first kind of objectivity—the conforming of our procedures to an independent and external truth—"is out of the question in most legal cases" (31). The second, scientific or replicable and convergent objectivity, "is sometimes attainable, but given the attitudes of and the constraints on the legal profession, and the character of the problems it deals with, often not"; and the third form of objectivity, named by Posner "conversational objectivity," the objectivity that seems achieved in moments (however temporary) of successful persuasion, "is attainable—but that isn't saying much" (31). It isn't saying much because its attainability is not a matter of method or planful design (conversational objectivity cannot be generated by a mechanical procedure; if it could it would be replicable and scientific objectivity) and therefore it is in some sense fortuitous; in any situation it may or may not occur, depending on the degree of homogeneity in the relevant community, the relation of available argumentative resources to skillful advocates, the pressures for generating a conclusion in one direction or another, the routes by which that decision might be reached, and innumerable other *contingencies* that may or may not meet together in a happy conjunction.

In a word, conversational objectivity is a *political* achievement, and therefore an achievement that is the antithesis of objectivity as many understand it, a state of certitude that attends the identification and embrace of bedrock and abiding fact and/or principle. To those for whom objectivity can only come in this (hard) form, the temporary outcomes of an indeterminate and messy institutional "conversation" hardly meet the test. Neither is the test met by scientific or replicable objectivity as Posner describes it, because it is distinguishable from the softer, conversational, kind only in degree. "The only way to make [the law] more objective"—the only way to kick legal objectivity up a notch from the conversational to the replicable—"is to make the courts and the legislatures more homogeneous, culturally and politically" (32).

In short, the only difference between scientific and conversational objectivity is a difference between a community in which assumptions are widely shared and firmly in place, and a community in which assumptions differ and agreement must be repeatedly negotiated. And since the stability of the first community is itself a contingent matter, a stage in the history of a discipline or a society, it is a stability that can always be upset by an unforeseen circumstance.[2] Scientific or replicable objectivity is therefore no less political than conversational objectivity; it is just a matter of how much homogeneity the powers that be have managed to achieve. "Legal thought cannot be made objective by being placed in correspondence with the 'real' world. It owes whatever objectivity it has to cultural uniformity rather than to metaphysical reality or methodological rigor" (30).

If methodological rigor goes south in the pragmatist wind, can formalism be far behind? Formalism is the hope that legal outcomes can be generated by a procedure that is not hostage to any a priori specification of value: "the only prerequisite to being a formalist is having supreme confidence in one's premises and in one's methods of deriving conclusions from them" (40). However, adds Posner, the formalist's confidence is unfounded since the premises are always contestable and therefore incapable of providing a firm foundation for the reasoning that flows from them. So long as one does not notice the contestability, "decisions will appear to be strongly objective because logically deducible" (48); but once the curtain is lifted the observer will "see that the decisions are no more objective in an ultimate sense than those made under [a] more frankly ad hoc regime" (48). One may intone with "great resonance" the "idea of treating like things alike," but the "idea is empty without specification of the criteria for 'likeness'; and . . . those criteria are political" (42). So much for what H.L.A. Hart calls the idea of justice in its simplest form ". . . the notion that what is to be applied to a multiplicity of different persons is the same general rule, undeflected by prejudice, interest, or caprice."[3]

What is true of large abstractions like the "idea of justice" is no less true of rules; they too are political in their operation, says Posner, because although they may be invoked as formal and universal, they are almost always employed in the service of "ad hoc exceptions and adjustments" (46). Rules of a truly formal kind may perhaps be found in games where the player is not free to decide, for example, that his rook will simply not "be captured by his opponent's queen" (50), but in the law judges can do just that and say that "they are doing so in order to comply with a higher level rule" (50). In games the rules apply to carefully circumscribed and static worlds, but the world in which legal rules function is protean and ever changing: the richness of its phenomena is richly in excess of any attempt to formally contain it.

Since "[r]ules make dichotomous cuts in continuous phenomena" (46), a rule "suppresses potentially relevant circumstances of the dispute" (44) and a judge is free to decide what will or will not be suppressed.

Thus, rather than constraining judges, rules offer judges the opportunity to engage in temperamentally preferred activities by allowing them either to confine or expand the judicial gaze. Judges who are tolerant of "untidiness, even disorder" will be "highly sensitive to the particulars of each case," while judges who are invested in tradition and continuity will defer to already in place authorities, "legislators, the founding fathers, higher or earlier judges" (49). Although judges of both kinds will employ rules, the rules will function not as checks on personal preferences (the standard account of rules and their value), but as their vehicle: "judges are not *bound* by the rules to do anything" (47). Here is the formalist fear writ large, a legal system that is no system at all, but a ramshackle non-structure made up of bits of everything and held together (when it is held together) by transitory political purposes: "The common law is a vast collection of judge-made rules, loosely tethered to debatable interpretations of ambiguous enactments" (47).

Loose tethering, however, turns out to be all the tethering one needs in the Posnerian vision, for while "exact inquiry" (71) and "pure" reason are unrealizable ideals, practical reason takes up the slack. Practical reason "is a grab bag that includes anecdote, introspection, imagination, common sense, empathy, imputation of motives, speaker's authority, metaphor, analogy, precedent, custom, memory, 'experience'" (73). In one sense, as Posner points out, the list is too long, because its components are not all of a kind and are sometimes not discrete; but it is also too short because some of the entries can be divided and subdivided. It is that untidiness that makes practical reason what it is, not a self-enclosed mode of algorithmic or mechanical calculation, but an ever changing collection of rules of thumb, doctrines, proverbs, precedents, folk-tales, prejudices, aspirations, goals, fears, and, above all, beliefs.

In the realm of formal objective reasoning (if there were such a thing) belief (personal preference) is precisely what is kept at bay so that the impersonal logic of the deductive machine can run smoothly, without interference. But in the (real) world of practical reasoning, beliefs—the intuitions "that lie so deep that we don't know how to question them" (73)—serve as the premises of all reasoning, and rather than being controlled or trumped by evidence (as they are in the popular picture of "good" reasoning) beliefs pass on the usefulness and relevance of different kinds of evidence and put the kinds together in ways that sort with an already-in-place structure. "Pure" reasoning generates a basis for the taking up of purposes; but practical reasoning begins with purposes, with inclinations toward the inhabiting and building of this or that world, and it is those inclinations that influence and direct the way evidence is marshalled and even seen.

Posner illustrates the point with the doctrine of precedent. The doctrine is that precedent controls, but, says Posner, what really controls is how one "chooses to read the precedent"; "the key to the decision is precisely that choice, a choice not dictated by precedent—a choice as to what the precedent *shall* be" (95). That choice will not have been logically driven, but driven by the direction in which the judge wanted to go. This does not mean that the judge can decide in any direction he or she pleases; the routes of choice, indeed the alternative forms in which choice can even appear, are constrained by the present shape of practical reasoning, by what arguments will work, what categories are firmly in place, what distinctions can be confidently invoked.

Posner asks if a precedent could be distinguished on the basis that in the earlier case "the plaintiff had been left-handed and in the present one the plaintiff is right-handed," and answers, "it could not—but only because there is no consideration of policy or ethics that would justify so narrow an interpretation" (96). That is, the distinction between left- and right-handedness cannot be grabbed hold of by a judge who wants to arrive at a certain conclusion; the state of the culture, of what it will hear as reasonable (not the force of reason itself) bars him, at least now; but there might come a day (perhaps in the context of a new and persuasive account of criminal behavior) when the left-handed/right-handed distinction carries a legal weight, means something in terms related to the concerns of the legal community. Practical reasoning is not a fixed category and its content will not always be the same, but whatever it contains, its mode of calculation will be rhetorical rather than logical, a matter first of determining or sensing where the lines of authority lie—what previous holdings will strike one as settling a question, what rules can be invoked without challenge or qualification, what maxims ("no one should be permitted to profit from his own wrong") will close down discussion, what analogies have stood the test of time, "what politically accredited source" (82) has issued what citable pronouncements, what goals now go virtually unquestioned in the realm of "rational" deliberation—and then of "working" these "authoritative" materials in the direction of one's purposes, one's inclinations, one's intuitions, one's beliefs.

In this vision authority itself is rhetoricized and politicized; that is, authorities do not come ready made in the form of a pure calculus or a scriptural revelation; rather they are made, fashioned in the course of debate and conflict, established by acts that are finally grounded in nothing firmer than persuasion (another name for practical reasoning) and so finally fashioned and maintained by force: "To be blunt, the *ultima ratio* of law is . . . force—precisely what is excluded even by the most latitudinarian definitions of rationality" (83). Posner here endorses and expands on the view of Holmes which he had earlier quoted: "I believe that force, mitigated so far as may be by good manners, is the *ultima ratio*, and between two groups that want to make inconsistent kinds of world I see no remedy except force" (19 n. 29). The conclusion is of course a shocking one, but it follows inevitably from every other part of Posner's argument and it does so for a reason Holmes's sentence nicely highlights: disputes between "groups who want to make inconsistent kinds of world" could be resolved by rational rather than forceful means only if the content and method of rationality could be stipulated apart from the agenda of any particular group; but it is just that kind of specification Posner rules out as a possibility when he declares unavailable to the law (and to much else) objectivity in the ontological sense and grants to the law only scientific or replicable objectivity ("sometimes attainable") and conversational objectivity (contingently attainable).

As I have already observed the second and third senses of objectivity are actually one and the same, since they are distinguished not by an epistemological, but by a social/political condition. In a discipline that can be said to display scientific objectivity—for example science or at least some corners of it—potentially disputable premises are simply not in dispute for reasons of history, disciplinary politics, societal expectations, etc. In a discipline characterized by conversational objectivity, disputes are everywhere and basic premises are often seen to be "up for grabs" (although as Posner correctly points out, not all of them will be so seen at the same time). In either disciplinary situation—the one of potential but quiescent dispute or the one of pervasive and continuing dispute—the settling of dispute, should it break out, can only be accomplished by political means, by the invoking of some sacrosanct (but itself contestable if anyone dared, or even thought, to contest it) first principle of the enterprise ("if we are to remain a government of laws, not men . . ."), or by the pronouncement of someone in a position to make his or her pronouncements stick or by the taking of a vote as the result of which the dispute has been officially or administratively settled (but is sure to erupt on another day) or by the intervention of an armed force.

In this list (certainly not exhaustive) of possibly "authoritative" actions, only the last is usually given the name "force," but in the absence of any neutral calculus or principle to which disputants might have recourse, the other actions are but softened versions of the last, instances of what Holmes refers to as the mitigation of "good manners." To be sure this is a mitigation not to be lightly dismissed; without good manners—a weak phrase for the willingness to refrain from bashing one's opponent's head in—civilization itself would fail, not because, as some have been telling us recently and others had been telling us even before Juvenal's third satire, we have lost hold of first principles and basic truths, but because, given the unavailability of such principles and truths to limited mortals (the phrase is redundant), we would fall instantly to fratricide (and to matricide, and patricide and genocide and every other cide) did we not invest our energies in procedures and habits designed (as it has become fashionable to say) to keep the conversation going. Force, in short, comes in hard and soft versions, and all things being equal, soft is better than hard (a reversal of the usual masculinist metaphor underlying much of academic discourse). But not always, because all things are not equal. That is, at any moment one is always committed to goals and premises in such a way that certain challenges to them will be perceived as socially, not personally, disastrous; and when those challenges arise, it will seem that a soft response—turning the other cheek, writing another page—is a betrayal of one's values and of one's responsibility to the world.

At that point there will be invoked the distinction between legitimate and illegitimate force, a distinction that, as H.L.A. Hart saw, is basic to the law's claim to be law rather than force in law's clothing, but a distinction that will then be invoked in another form—the line differently but just as sincerely drawn—by those whose depredations you feel compelled to resist. At bottom—and the situation of having to confront "at bottom" is what most of life is devoted to avoiding—what is unreasonable is what the other fellow believes, and illegitimate force is the action he is taking in defense of his beliefs. As Learned Hand put it in a statement Posner also cites: "'Values are incommensurable. You can get a solution also by a compromise, or *call it what you will*. It must be one that people won't complain of too much; but you cannot expect any more objective measure'" (129 n.10).[4]

You cannot expect any more because of the condition whose strong acknowledgement is the basis of all pragmatist thinking, the condition as

Posner names it, of heterogeneity or difference as I would name it. (The fact that pragmatism too has its foundational premise is not a contradiction of its antifoundationalism because this particular premise—the irreducibility of difference—*is* antifoundationalism.) In a heterogeneous world, a world in which persons are situated—occupying particular places with particular purposes pursued in relation to particular goals, visions, and hopes as they follow from holding (or being held by) particular beliefs—no one will be in a situation that is universal or general (that is, no situation at all), and therefore no one's perspective (a word that gives the game away) can lay claim to privilege. In that kind of world, a world of difference, in our world according to Posner and according to me, the stipulation both of what is (of the facts) and of what ought to be will always be a politically angled one, and in the (certain) event of a clash of stipulations, the mechanisms of adjudication, whether in the personal or institutional realms, will be equally political.

How then does the business of law get done? "If two social visions clash, which prevails? . . . How does a judge choose between competing social visions?" (148). Posner's answer to these questions will be troubling to those who seek a jurisprudence in which policy considerations have been either eliminated or subordinated (à la Dworkin), but it is an inevitable answer given everything that precedes the question: "Often the choice will be made on the basis of deeply held personal values, and often these values will be impervious to argument" (148—149). This last is particularly devastating, since argument, in the sense of the marshalling of evidence that will be compelling to any actor no matter what his or her "personal values," is supposedly the very life of the law. This is not to say, Posner hastens to add, that because a judge's personal values are impervious to argument, they are impervious to change. Change can and does occur, not however by a process of "reasoned exposition" (149), but through conversions, defined nicely as "a sudden deeply emotional switch from one non-rational cluster of beliefs to another that is no more (often less) rational" (150).

And what brings that switch about? Almost anything and nothing in particular. That is, there is no sure route—no sequence of formalizable or even probabilizable steps—to conversion, nor are there means or stimuli that are "by nature" too weak to produce it. Conversion can follow upon anything—reading at random a verse from the Bible, falling off one's horse on the road to Damascus, suddenly seeing the first gray hair—for anything, given the right history, psychology, pressuring circumstances, etc., can "jar people out of their accustomed ways of thinking" (150).

Posner's example is the women's movement, which he says, has become influential because "[m]any women and some men" have been brought to see the role of women "in a different light," not however "by being shown  evidence that this is the way things 'really' are, but by being offered a fresh perspective that, once glimpsed, strikes many with a shock of recognition" (150). But not all.  The metaphors, analogies, revisionist histories, slogans ("the personal is the political") that have struck some as a revelation ("once I saw through a glass darkly") have struck others as absurd or irrelevant.  If the minds of people, including judges, are changed by conversion rather than by the operation of reason and logic, then change is a *contingent* matter and predictability—both prized and claimed by the law—is a chimera.  Of course, contingency can sometimes take hold, not however as the result of a plan or campaign, but as the result of notions or vocabularies that somehow get to be "in the air" and effect a "change of outlook" which when it is noticed (by a historian or social commentator) will be seen to have been caused by no one in particular and certainly not by any rational process. It is just that something that was once "virtually unthinkable" (151) now goes without saying.  "My point," concludes Posner, "is that the great turning points in twentieth-century law (and in law, period) [were] not the product of deep reflection on the meaning of the Constitution . . . but instead reflect changing outlooks" (152).

II

With statements like this, Posner puts the cap on his anti-essentialist, anti-foundational, anti-rational (in the strong sense), anti-metaphysical and deeply pragmatist view of the law, and it is perhaps superfluous for me to say that I agree with him on almost every point.  Indeed, as I look back on the preceding pages, I see little effort to separate my account of Posner's argument from my own elaborations of it.  Of course I have some quibbles, but that's why they are, even though I shall now be so ungenerous as to rehearse them.

When Posner says that "[a] judicial holding normally will trump even a better-reasoned academic analysis because of the value that the law places on stability" (95), he seems to accord both a privilege and an independence to "reason" that he elsewhere withholds.  Would it not be truer to his larger argument to replace "better-reasoned" with "differently-reasoned" and so recognize that the desire for stability is itself a reason, and one no better or worse than the academic reasons that are put forward in the context of institutional norms? And when Posner criticizes the "plain-meaning approach" of excluding consideration of "the communicative intent and broader purposes" of statutes, he seems to think that such an exclusion is possible, that one could, in fact, read in a way that bracketed purposes and intentions not already "in" the writing; but (as I have argued elsewhere and at length) language is only construable within the assumption of some or other human purpose. No act of reading can stop at the plain-meaning of a document, because that meaning itself will have emerged in the light of some stipulation of intentional circumstances, of purposes held by agents situated in real world situations. The difference between ways of reading will not be between a reading that takes communicative intent into account and a reading that doesn't, but between readings that proceed in the light of differently assumed communicative intents. Formalist or literalist or "four corners" interpretation is not inadvisable (as Posner seems to suggest); it is impossible.

And finally in this short list of occasional but not fatal lapses or slips, it really will not do, in the context of the book's informing spirit, to contrast "persuasion by rhetoric" to "the coolest forms of reasoned exposition" (149). Reasoned exposition (which will have different shapes at different times in different disciplines) is itself just one form of rhetoric, cooler perhaps if the measure of heat is a decibel count, but impelled by a vision as partisan and contestable as that informing any rhetoric that dares to accept that name.

As I have already said (twice), these disagreements with Posner do not amount to much, but that should not be taken to indicate that I have no real quarrels with this book, for there is a strain in it, muted at first but heard more often in its second half, that I believe to be at deep odds with Posner's strongest insights. Let me try to focus my criticism by returning to the moment when Posner declares that of the three kinds of objectivity, the third—conversational objectivity—is attainable in the law, but, he adds, "that isn't saying much" (31). It seems to me, however, that in the following pages he sometimes thinks that too much follows from having said "that." Indeed, in my view *anything* that would be said to follow from the fact of "conversational objectivity" would be too much, for it would be to confuse a pragmatist account of the law with a pragmatist program.

A pragmatist *account* of the law speaks to the question of how the law works and gives what I think to be the right answer: the law works not by identifying and then hewing to some overarching set of principles, or logical calculus, or authoritative revelation, but by deploying a set of ramshackle and heterogeneous resources in an effort to reach political resolutions of disputes that must be framed (this is the law's requirements and the public's desire) in apolitical and abstract terms (fairness, equality, what justice requires). By the standards applied to determinate and principled procedures, the law fails miserably (this is the charge made by Critical Legal Studies); but by the pragmatist standard—unsatisfactory as a standard to formalists and objectivists, as well as to deconstructors—the law gets passing and even high marks because it *works*. A pragmatist *program* asks the question "what follows from the pragmatist account?" and then gives an answer, but by giving an answer pragmatism is unfaithful to its own first principle (which is to have none) and turns unwittingly into the foundationalism and essentialism it rejects.

Posner's answer—his program—takes the form of a pro-scientific, no nonsense empiricism that is obviously related to the tradition of legal realism. Signs of this "realist" stance surface early, when in the course of setting out the book's plan, he questions the utility of interpretation as an explanatory concept and declares, "We might do better to discard the term" (31). Discarding terms and much else is a favorite move in legal realist polemic and no one performed it with more flair than Felix Cohen.[5] Cohen begins by heaping scorn on the notion of a corporation as a legal abstraction, as a fictional entity. "Where is a corporation?" he asks, and replies that it is "not a question that can be answered by empirical observation" (810). "Nor is it a question," he goes on, "that demands for its solution any analysis of political considerations or social ideals. It is, in fact, a question identical in metaphysical status with the question which scholastic theologians are supposed to have argued at great length, 'How many angels can stand on the point of a needle?'"[6] In short, a question directed at a speculative, mythical non-object which, because it was produced by superstition rather than observation, gets in the way of seeing things as they really are. Unfortunately, the law is not (yet) a science and is therefore susceptible to the appeal of "myths [that] impress the imagination . . . where more exact discourse would leave minds cold."[7] The result, Cohen laments, is a world of circular legal reasoning (815) in which jargon-of-the-trade terms interact with one another "without ever coming to rest on the floor of verifiable fact."[8]

The remedy for this sorry state is implicit in the indictment: sweep away the magical but substanceless words that make up the vocabulary of jurisprudence so that we will have an unobstructed view of the situation and problems to which we could then address ourselves. If notions of "'property' and 'due process' were defined in non-legal terms"

(820)—defined that is in a descriptive vocabulary truly in touch with "empirical social facts" (821)—we might be able "to substitute a realistic, rational scientific account of legal happenings for the classical theological jurisprudence of concepts."⁹ If we wean ourselves from "supernatural entities which do not have a verifiable existence except for the eyes of faith" we may at last come into contact with "actual experience."¹⁰ Once this happens, once "statistical methods" have brought us close to the "actual facts of judicial behavior,"¹¹ the "realistic advocate" or judge will be able to "rise above" all distorting lenses including both the lens of "his own moral bias" and the lens of "the moral bias of the legal author whose treatise he consults."¹² No longer will he be "fooled by his own words"¹³ or by anyone else's.

In these quotations (which could have easily been supplemented from the pages of Jerome Frank and other early realists) we see that the basic realist gesture is a double, and perhaps contradictory, one: first dismiss the myth of objectivity as it is embodied in high sounding but empty legal concepts (the rule of law, the neutrality of due process) and then replace it with the myth of the "actual facts" or "exact discourse" or "actual experience" or a "rational scientific account," that is, go from one essentialism, identified with natural law or conceptual logic, to another, identified with the strong empiricism of the social sciences.

The problem with this sequence was long ago pointed out by Roscoe Pound who, while acknowledging the force of many of the realists' observations, declares himself "skeptical as to the faith in ability to find the one unchallengeable basis free from illusion which alone the new realist takes over from the illusion-ridden jurists of the past."¹⁴ Given the realist insistence on the unavoidability of bias and on the value laden nature of all human activities, the recourse to a brute fact level of uninterpretive data seems, to say the least, questionable, as does the assumption that if we could only divest ourselves of the special vocabulary of the legal culture (no longer be fooled by our own words) we could see things as they really (independently of any discursive system whatsoever) are. Cohen and Frank are full of scorn for theological thinking and for the operation of faith, but as Pound sees, they are no less the captives of a faith, and of the illusion—if that is the word—that attends it.

That is, however, *not* the word, for "illusion" implies the availability of a point of view uncontaminated by metaphysical entities or by an a priori assumption of values, and as the realists (and Posner after them) argue in their better moments, there is no such point of view, no realm of unalloyed non-mediated experience and no neutral observation language that describes it. The advocate or jurist who moves from the conceptual apparatus codified in law to the apparatus of statistical methods and behaviorist psychology has not exchanged the perspective-specific facts of an artificial discursive system for the real, unvarnished facts; rather he or she has exchanged the facts emergent in one discursive system—one contestable articulation of the world—for the facts emergent in another. It is not that there is no category of the real; it is just what fills it will always be a function of the in-place force of some disciplinary or community vocabulary; eliminate the special jargon of the law, as the realists urge, and you will find yourself not in the cleared ground of an epistemological reform ("now I see face to face") but in the already occupied ground of some other line of work no less special, no less hostage to commitments it can neither name nor recognize.

Much of what Posner writes in *The Problems of Jurisprudence* suggests that he should be in substantial agreement with the previous paragraph. Steeped as he is in the writings of Peirce, Wittgenstein, Kuhn, Rorty, and Gadamer (not to mention Fish), he should be immune to the lure of empiricist essentialism, but he is not. At the end of the chapter on practical reasoning he complains that the law still carries too much conceptual baggage and avers that "the situation would be improved if law committed itself to a simple functionalism or consequentialism," that is, to a program of adjusting the operations of law to precisely specified social goals in relation to which the law would be self-consciously subordinate and secondary:

> Suppose the sole goal of every legal doctrine and institution was a practical one. The goal of a new bankruptcy statute, for example, might be to reduce the number of bankruptcies . . . and if the statute failed to fulfill [that goal] . . . it would be repealed. Law really would be a method of social engineering, and its structures and designs would be susceptible of objective evaluation, much like the project of civil engineers. This would be a triumph of pragmatism. (122)

This is a complicated statement that looks forward to several arguments Posner will later elaborate, including the argument (more modest than one might have expected) for law and economics. In his chapter on that approach Posner rehearses the familiar thesis that even though the law may not self-describe its operations in economic terms, its history indicates that those terms or something approximating them are impelling legal actors whether they are aware of it or not. It is as if somewhere deep down, in the realm of tacit rather than explicit knowledge, "judges *wanted* to adopt the rules, procedures and case outcomes that would maximize society's wealth" (356). "We should be no more surprised that judges talk in different terms while doing economics than that businessmen equate marginal cost to marginal revenue without using the terms and often without knowing what they mean" (372—373).

Here is the meeting point of Posner's declared pragmatism and his previous self-identification with the law and economics movement. When Posner says that the goal of every legal doctrine should be a practical one, he means (in good realist fashion) that legal doctrine should be reconceptualized so as to accord with the nitty-gritty facts of social life, and that means reconceptualized in the language of law and economics, since in his view the language of law and economics is the language of real motives and actual goals. If "the object of pragmatic analysis is to lead discussion away from issues semantic and metaphysical and toward issues factual and empirical" (387), then by Posner's lights pragmatic analysis and the pragmatic program will succeed when legal concepts and terms have been replaced by economic ones or when "the positive economic theory of law will be subsumed under a broader theory—perhaps, although not necessarily, an economic theory—of the social behavior we call law" (374).

This could possibly happen, but if it ever does, we will not have escaped semantics (merely verbal entities) and metaphysics (faith-based declarations of what is) but merely attached ourselves to new versions of them. As many commentators have observed, "wealth-maximization," efficiency, pareto superiority, the Kaldor Hicks test, and the other components of the law and economics position are all hostage to metaphysical assumptions, to controversial visions of the way the world is or should be. A transformation such as Posner seems to desire would not lead to methods "susceptible of objective evaluation" but to methods no more firmly grounded than the wholly contestable premises that "authorize" them. Moreover, and this is the more important point, should that transformation occur, the result would not be a more empirically rooted law, but no law at all. The law, as a separate and distinct area of inquiry and action, would be no more; an enterprise of a certain kind would have disappeared from the world (itself not fixed, but mutable and revisable) of enterprises.

At issue here is the nature of the desire to which law is a response. In Posner's view (although he doesn't put it this way), the law is answerable to a desire that can be pragmatically defined (the desire to prevent bankruptcy or protect the integrity of the family); given this view, it makes sense that its forms and vocabulary should match up with that desire, and that they should be criticized when they do not. But I would describe the desire that gives rise to law differently and more philosophically, in a loose sense of that word. Law emerges because people desire predictability, stability, equal protection, the reign of justice, etc., and because they want to believe that it is possible to secure these things by instituting a set of impartial procedures. This incomplete list of the desires behind the emergence of law is more or less identical with the list of things Posner debunks in the course of his book, beginning with objectivity, and continuing with determinate rules, value free adjudication, impersonal constraints, the right of privacy, freedom of the will, precedent, intention, mind, judicial restraint, etc. Repeatedly he speaks of himself as "demistifying" (184) these concepts in the service of "the struggle against metaphysical entities in law" (185), and he writes deprecatingly of the delusions, pretensions, and false understandings with which actors in the legal culture deceive themselves.

But the result of success in this struggle, should he or anyone else achieve it, would not be a cleaned-up conceptual universe, but a universe deprived of the props that must be in place if the law is to be possessed of a persuasive rationale. In short, the law will only work—not in the realist or economic sense but in the sense answerable to the desires that impel its establishment—if the metaphysical entities Posner would remove are retained; and if the history of our life with law tells us anything, it is that they *will* be retained, no matter what analysis of either an economic or deconstructive kind is able to show.

The curious fact is that Posner knows this with at least part of his mind. Anticipating the objection that the adoption of a behaviorist vocabulary (which would have the advantage, he says, of eliminating "fictitious" entities like minds, intentions, the conscience, and guilt) will "strip the moral as well as the distinctively human content from the . . . law" (178), he replies:

> There are no . . . grounds for fearing that speculations in the philosophy of mind are likely to affect respect for, let alone observance of, law. . . . Philosophers who believe in determinism behave in their personal lives just like other people. If freedom is an illusion, it is one of those illusions . . . that we cannot shake off no matter what our beliefs or opinions are. (178)

This is exactly right, not (as Posner implies) because human beings obstinately cling to their "illusions," but because the set of purposes that will lead one to do philosophy of mind and the set of purposes that lead one to administer or make law are quite different and there is no reason to assume that a conclusion reached in one area will have an effect on the central tenets of the other. (More of this later.) Law is centrally *about* such things as conscience, guilt, personal responsibility, fairness, impartiality, and no analysis imported from some other disciplinary context "proving" that these things do not exist will remove them from the legal culture, unless of course society decides that a legal culture is a luxury it can afford to do without.

What Posner calls the "illusions" with which public actors sustain their roles are in fact the assumptions (no more or less vulnerable than any others) that constitute those roles; take them away (not, as he acknowledges, an easy task) and you take away the role and all of the advantages it brings to the individual and the community. As Posner correctly observes, "most judges believe, without evidence (indeed in the face of the evidence . . .) that the judiciary's effectiveness depends on a belief by the public that judges are finders rather than makers of law" (190). The implication is that the belief would be better founded if independent evidence of it could be cited; but this particular belief is itself founding, and constitutes a kind of contract between the legal institution and the public, each believing in the other's belief about itself and thus creating a world in which expectations and a sense of mutual responsibility confirm one another without any external support. Similarly when judges persuade "themselves and others that their decisions are dictated by law" (193), the act of persuasion is not a conscious strategic self-deception, but something that comes with the territory, with the experience of law school, of practice, of a life in the courts, etc. The result is not, as Posner would have it, a "false sense of constraint" (193), but a sense inseparable from membership in a community from whose (deep) assumptions one takes one's very identity. But as I have said, Posner knows all and he even knows that the fictions he debunks are necessary, that "the belief that judges are constrained by law . . . is a deeply ingrained feature of the legal culture" (194), and that this "situation is unlikely to change without profound *and not necessarily desirable* changes in the political system" (193).

## III

Perhaps he knows something even deeper, which is that the call for a pragmatist program, for a demistifying of the legal culture, for a clearing away of the debris of faith-based conceptual systems, is at odds with the insight of heterogeneity, with the recognition that difference is a condition that cannot be overcome by attaching ourselves to a bedrock level of social/empirical fact because that level, along with the facts seen as its components, is itself an interpretive construction, an imaginative hazarding of the world's particulars that is finally grounded in nothing stronger that its own persuasiveness (with persuasiveness a function of the number of desires this particular story about the world manages to satisfy).

I said earlier that once pragmatism becomes a program it turns into the essentialism it challenges; as an account of contingency and of agreements that are conversationally not ontologically based, it cannot without contradiction offer itself as a new and better basis for doing business. Indeed, if the pragmatist account of things is right, then everyone has always been a pragmatist anyway; someone may pronounce in the grand language of foundational theory, but since that theory will always be a rhetoric—an edifice supported by premises that might be contested at any moment—such pronouncing is no less provisional and vulnerable that "those made under [a] frankly ad hoc regime" (48). Nor will their advent of a frankly ad hoc regime—one in which contingency and the heterogeneity of value are publicly announced—make any operational difference; awareness of contingency allows one neither to master it (as if knowledge of an inescapable condition enabled you to escape it) nor to be better at it (a quite incoherent notion). Once a pragmatist account of the law (or anything else) has shown that practice is not after all undergirded by an overarching set of immutable principles, or by an infallible and impersonal method, or by a neutral observation language, there isn't anything more to say ("to say that one is a pragmatist is to say little" [28]), anywhere *necessarily* to go; and you certainly can't go from a pragmatist account, with its emphasis on the ceaseless process of human construction and the endless and unpredictable achieving and reachieving of conversational objectivity, to a brave new world from which the constructions have been happily removed. Indeed, if you take the antifoundationalism of pragmatism seriously (as Posner in his empiricism finally cannot) you will see that there is absolutely nothing you can do with it.

The point is one that puts me in a minority position in the pragmatist camp, for most advocates of pragmatism (I have never been one myself) assume that something must follow from the pragmatist argument, that there are, in the words of Richard Rorty's title, consequences of pragmatism.[15] Rorty himself thinks that, although at times it seems that the consequences he identifies are so loosely related to pragmatism that the claim doesn't amount to much. Nevertheless he does repeatedly attach at least a hope to the possible triumph of pragmatism, not Posner's hope for "a method of social engineering . . . susceptible of objective evaluation" (122), but the hope that if we give up the search for just such a method, write it off as an investment that didn't pan out, we will turn from the (vain) search for "metaphysical comfort"[16] to the comfort we can provide each other as human beings in the same afoundational boat: "In the end, the pragmatists tell us, what matters is our loyalty to other human beings clinging together against the dark, not our hope of getting things right."[17]

The idea is that if people would only stop trying to come up with a standard of absolute right which could then be used to denigrate the beliefs and efforts of *other* people, they might spend more time sympathetically engaging with those beliefs and learning to appreciate those efforts. Those who do this will be improving what Rorty believes to be a specifically pragmatist skill, the "skill at imaginative identification," the "ability to envisage, and desire to prevent, the actual and possible humiliation of others."[18] Moreover, although this ability is in some sense an anti-method in that it involves the proliferation of perspectives rather than the narrowing of them to the single perspective that is right and true, one acquires it, according to Rorty, by a technique that is itself methodical if not methodological: one practices "rediscription," not rediscription in the direction of what is really true, but rediscription as a temperamental willingness to try out vocabularies other than our own in an effort "to expand our sense of 'us' as far as we can."[19] "We should stay on the look out for marginalized people—people we still instinctively think of as 'them' rather than 'us'. We should try to notice our similarities to them."[20] In that way, we may "create a more expansive sense of solidarity than we presently have."[21] In the process, Rorty hopes, philosophy will lose its orientation toward truth and become "one of the techniques for reweaving our vocabulary of moral deliberation in order to accommodate new beliefs (for example that women and blacks are capable of more than we white males had thought, that property is not sacred, that sexual matters are of merely private concern)."[22]

My problem with Rorty's formulations can be surfaced by focusing on this last sentence which suggests, as other sentences do, that there is a general non-specific skill or ability which, if we hone it, will make us the kind of people likely to see that women and blacks are capable of more than we white men had thought, that property is not sacred, that sexual matters are of merely private concern. But in my view the direction is the other way around: first an issue is raised, by real life pressures as felt by men and women who must make decisions or perform in public and private contexts, and then, in the course of discussion or by virtue of the introduction of a new and arresting vocabulary, or by the pronouncements of a particularly revered figure, or by a thousand other contingent interventions, some of us might come to see the situation and its components in new and different ways. Moreover, this "conversion" experience, if it occurs, will not be attributable to a special skill or ability that has been acquired through the regular practice of rediscription—through empathy exercises—but rather to the (contingent) fact that for this or that person a particular argument or piece of testimony or preferred analogy or stream of light coming through a window at the right moment just happened to "take."

My point is that moments like that, which could be described (although inaccurately I think) as expansions of sympathy, cannot be planned, and cannot be planned *for* by developing a special empathetic muscle. This leads me to proclaim Fish's first law of tolerance-dynamics (tolerance is Rorty's pragmatist virtue where Posner's is contextual clarity): *Toleration is exercised in an inverse proportion to there being anything at stake.* If I go to hear a series of papers on John Milton, I listen to them with an attention whose content includes my own previously published work, the place of that work in Milton studies, projects presently in process, etc., and therefore as I listen (not after I listen) I perform *involuntary* acts of approval ("that's right"), disapproval ("Oh, not that tired line again"), anger ("he's got me all wrong") and others too embarrassing to mention. But if I go to hear a series of papers on George Eliot, whose novels I have read but not written about or even formulated a position on, I listen in quite a different mode, one that allows me to take a relatively cool pleasure at a display of contrasting interpretive skills. Indeed I might even be successively convinced by five speakers and never feel obliged to render a judgment of the kind they are directing at one another. Now obviously I will be exercising more tolerance, engaging more empathetically, in the second scenario as opposed to the first, but that will be because I have no investment in George Eliot whereas my investment in Milton has been

growing for more than twenty-five years and is at this point inseparable
from my sense of my career and therefore from my sense of myself.

What the example shows, I think, is that tolerance (or, if you prefer,
sympathy) is not a separate ability, a virtue with its own
context-independent shape, but is rather a way of relating or attending
whose shape depends on the commitments one already feels. The
Rortian injunction "be ye tolerant" or "learn to live with plurality"[23] or
"notice suffering when it occurs" (93) or "expand our sense of 'us' "[24]
is like the biblical injunction, "be ye perfect" or the parental injunction
"be good"; one wants to respond, yes, but in relation to what? One
cannot *just* be tolerant; one is tolerant (or not) in the measure a given
situation, complete with various pressures and with the histories of its
participants, allows. "Avoid cruelty" is a directive that cries out for
contextualization and when put in a more qualified way—avoid cruelty
when you can, or avoid cruelty, all other things being equal, or avoid
cruelty except when the alternative seems worse—it is even clearer that
its force depends on how everything is filled in, on what is already felt
to be at stake in the situation. It is this sense of there being something
at stake, something not just locally but universally, crucially, urgent, that
Rorty would like to see lessened if not eliminated; although, as he
reports ruefully, William James himself seemed unable to let go of the
feeling that life is "a real fight in which something is eternally gained for
the universe by success."[25] It is Rorty's hope—ungrounded, as it must
be given his (anti)principles—that if "pragmatism were taken
seriously"[26]—if we conceived of ourselves as creatures clinging together
in a foundationless world rather than as philosophers in search of a
foundation—we might cease experiencing life as a fight and we would
be less likely to confront one another across firmly drawn lines of battle.

As Rorty presents it, the vision is certainly an attractive one, but his
utopian consequence no more follows from pragmatism than does
Posner's empiricist consequence. Both theorists begin by asserting the
irreducibility of difference and the concomitant unavailability of
overarching principles, but then go unaccountably to the proclamation of
an overarching principle, in one case to the principle of undistorted
empirical inquiry and in the other to the principle of ever more tolerant
inquirers. The two programs differ markedly, but they are similarly
illegitimate in having as their source an account from which no particular
course of action necessarily or even probably follows. In short, to repeat
myself, they confuse a pragmatist account with a pragmatist program and
thereby fail to distinguish between pragmatism as a truth we are all living
*out* and pragmatism as a truth we might be able to live *by*. We are all

living *out* pragmatism because we live in a world bereft of transcendent truths and leak proof logics (although some may exist in a realm veiled from us) and therefore must make do with the ragtag bag of metaphors, analogies, rules of thumb, inspirational phrases, incantations, and jerry-built "reasons" that keep the conversation going and bring it to temporary, and always revisable, conclusions; but we could only live by pragmatism if we could grasp the pragmatist insight—that there are no universals or self-executing methods or self-declaring texts in sight—and make it into something positive, use an awareness of contingency as a way either of mastering it or perfecting it (in which case it would no longer be contingency), turn ourselves (by design rather than as the creatures of history) into something new. But while contingency may be the answer to the question "what finally underwrites the law?", it cannot be the answer to the question, "how does one go about practicing law?" The answer to *that* question is "by deploying all of the resources (doctrines, precedents, rules, magic metaphors, standard concepts) the legal culture offers." As an analyst or observer of the law you may know that those resources cannot finally be justified outside the culture's confines; but as a practitioner justification from the outside is not your business (you are not a philosopher or an anthropologist); as a practitioner, you take your justifications where you can get them.

IV

One place you are unlikely to get them is in the practice of describing the practice for which you are seeking a justification. The mistake both Rorty and Posner make (albeit in different ways) is the mistake of thinking that a description of a practice has cash value in a game other than the game of description. You may find (as Posner, Rorty, and I all do) that it is with pragmatist categories that one can best describe the law; but that doesn't mean that it is with pragmatist categories that one can best practice the law or that with a pragmatist description in place you have a new source of justification; or there is no reason to think that the results of an effort at description can be turned into a recipe either for performance or the act of justifying. Description is *itself* a practice performed, with its own conventions, requirements, and *internal* justifications, all of which are *necessarily* distinct from the terms of the practice that is its object.

The point speaks directly to the other large disagreement I have with Posner's book, his position on the question of legal autonomy. Posner believes that the ragtag eclectic content of legal doctrine means that it cannot be a distinctive thing. The reasoning is simple: since the law manifestly makes use of and invokes as authoritative, materials, doctrines and norms from any number of other disciplines and even non-disciplines (there seems no limit to its indiscriminate borrowings) it must itself be multi-disciplinary and therefore not autonomous. "Interdisciplinary legal thinking is inescapable" (439), he says, if only because "there is no such thing as legal reasoning" (459), only a "grab bag of informal methods" (455), which includes rules, but rules that are "vague, open-ended, tenuously grounded, highly contestable, and not openly alterable but frequently altered" (455). But the fact that an area of inquiry and practice incorporates material, concepts, and methods from other areas in a mix that is volatile and variable does not mean that there is nothing—no distinctive purpose or perspective—guiding and controlling the mix. The reasoning that if law is not pure, then law is not law, a discipline with its own integrity, holds only if disciplinary integrity is understood in what Posner calls the "strong" sense, "a field that rather than battening on other fields [is] adequately—and indeed optimally—cultivated by the use of skills, knowledge and experience that owed nothing to other fields" (431).

Posner quite correctly observes that the law cannot meet this strong requirement, but then neither can anything else. No field is self-sufficient in these absolute terms; every field depends both for its legitimacy and operations on assumptions and materials it does not contain but on which it draws, often in the spirit of "it goes without saying" or "if you can't assume this, what can you assume?". What makes a field a field—makes it a thing and not something else (a poor thing but mine own)—is not an impossible purity, but a steadfastness of purpose, a core sense of the enterprise, of what the field or discipline is *for*, of why society is willing (if not always eager) to see its particular job done. The core sense of disciplinary purpose is not destroyed by the presence in the field of bits and pieces and sometimes whole cloths from other fields because when those bits and pieces enter, they do so in a form demanded by the definitions, distinctions, convention, problematics, and urgencies already in place.

This does not mean that a field remains unaltered at its core by the entrance into it of "alien stuff"; a purpose that expands itself by ingesting material previously external to it does not stay the same, but even in its new form, it will still be the instantiation in the world of the enterprise's project, a project whose shape may vary so long as it retains its diacritical identity as the shape now being taken by a particular job of work (ensuring justice, understanding poetry, explaining finance, recovering the past). There is no natural reason that any of these projects should continue forever; the world may one day find itself without economics or literary criticism or history as identifiable disciplinary tasks; but before that happens, the natural conservatism of disciplines—the survival instinct that make them institutional illustrations of Fish's first law (tolerance is exercised in an inverse proportion to there being anything at stake) will work to prevent borrowed material from overwhelming the borrower. Despite the recent millenarian calls to interdisciplinarity, disciplines will prove remarkably resilient and difficult to kill.

I will have more to say about the lure of interdisciplinarity in a moment, but for now I want to underline the point I have been making; legal autonomy should not be understood as a state of impossibly hermetic self-sufficiency, but as a state continually achieved and re-achieved as the law takes unto itself and makes its own (and in so doing alters the "own" it is making) the materials that history and chance put in its way. Disciplinary identity is asserted and maintained not in an absolute opposition to difference but in a perpetual recognition and overcoming of it by various acts of assimilation and incorporation.

That is why it is beside the point to complain, as Posner does, that when the law takes up foreign concepts and materials it often does so in crude and sloppy ways, failing to avail itself of the latest up-to-date techniques and formulations. Early on, he observes that although the law is obviously dependent on "ethical insights," it declines "to look for the ethical and political materials of judgment . . . in scholarly materials [and] statistical compendia," relying instead on its own "previous decisions" (94); and later he makes a similar point with respect to the philosophy of language:

> If philosophers mount cogent attacks on simple minded ideas of textual determinacy—ideas that as it happens are the unexamined assumptions of many lawyers and judges engaged in interpreting statutory and constitutional texts—can the legal profession brush aside the attacks with the assertion that what lawyers and judges do when they interpret legal texts is its own sort of thing?" (440).

And by the same reasoning, shouldn't the "pieties of jurisprudence . . . be discarded" so that "at long last" judges would "abandon the rhetoric and the reality of formalist adjudication"? (462).

The answer to these questions was given long ago by Dean Pound in response to the realist program of "beginning with an objective scientific gathering of facts."[27]  Facts, declares Pound, "have to be selected and what is significant will be determined by some picture or ideal of the science and of the subject it treats."[28]  In other words (my words), the particular form in which materials from other disciplines enter the law will be determined by the law's sense of its own purpose and of the usefulness to that purpose of "foreign" information.  Pound notes that there have always been calls for jurisprudence to "stand still" until metaphysicians or ethicists or psychologists concluded their debates and determined an authoritative scientific viewpoint, and yet, as he puts it, "certain general ideas . . . served well enough for the legal science of the last century."[29]  Jurisprudence "can't wait for psychologists to agree (if they are likely to) and there is no need of waiting" since we "can reach a sufficient psychological basis for juristic purposes from any of the important current psychologies."[30]

"*For juristic purposes.*"  It is those purposes and not the purposes at the core of the quarried discipline that rule.  The fact that a notion of the self or of the text or of intention is regarded by psychology or philosophy or literary theory as the best notion going does not mean that it is the notion that best serves juristic purposes.  To this Posner might object that it is irresponsible for jurists or anyone else to go about their business in the company of discarded or discredited accounts of important matters; but again one must point out that accounts are specific to enterprises, to projects informed by their own sense of what needs to be done and for what (usually metaphysical) reasons; and it makes no sense to require that projects impelled by a *different* sense of what needs to be done in relation to different (usually metaphysical) reasons be faithful to, or even mindful of, the state of the art in the areas they invade.  Law will take what it needs, and "what it needs" will be determined by *its* informing rationale and not the rationale of philosophy, or literary criticism, or psychology, or economics.  (That is why psychoanalysis in its classic form, discarded by mainstream psychology today, is alive and well and productively so in English departments.)

Posner doesn't see this because he has a different view of what enterprises are or should be: he thinks that the point of an enterprise is to get at the empirical truth about something; and that enterprises are different only in the sense that they have been assigned (or assigned themselves) different empirical somethings—the mind, the past, the economy, the stars, the planets—to get at the truth of.  The trouble with law is that it has not accepted such an assignment in the true empirical spirit: "Law is not ready to commit itself to concrete, practical goals across the board," but instead keeps prating on about "intangibles such as the promotion of human dignity, the securing of justice and fairness, and the importance of complying with the ideals or intentions of the framers of the Constitution" (123). In short, the law is a rogue discipline that refuses to join the general effort to get things right and that is why the list of legal concepts ("metaphysical entities") that must be discarded is so long as to amount to the discarding of the entire legal culture.

This is not a conclusion the Posner himself reaches (in more than one place he seems to affirm the distinctiveness he elsewhere denies), but it is nevertheless a conclusion that follows inevitably from his strong empiricism. If the "intangibles" he finds "too nebulous for progress" (123)—justice, fairness, the promotion of dignity—are removed in favor of "concrete facts," the disciplinary map will have one less country, and where there was law there will now be social science. Were we to heed Posner's advice to get "rid of" the "carapace of falsity and pretense" that has the effect of "obscuring the enterprise" (469), we would end up getting rid of the enterprise. In doing so we would suffer a loss, not because justice, fairness, and human dignity will have been lost—I believe them to be rhetorical constructions just as Posner does—but because we will have deprived ourselves of the argumentative resources those abstractions now stand for; we would no longer be able to say "what justice requires" or "what fairness dictates" and then fill in those phrases with the courses of action we prefer to take. That, after all, is the law's job—to give us ways of re-describing limited partisan programs so that they can be presented as the natural outcomes of abstract impersonal imperatives. Other disciplines have other jobs—to rationalize aesthetic tastes or make intelligible pasts—and they too have vocabularies that do not so much hook up with the world as declare one.

Disciplines should not be thought of as joint partners co-operating in a single job of work (one world and the ways we describe it); they are what make certain jobs (and worlds) possible and even conceivable (lawyering, literary criticism, economics, etc., are not natural kinds, but the names of historical practices); and if we want this or that job to keep on being done—if we want to use notions of fairness and justice in order to move things in certain directions—we must retain disciplinary vocabularies, not despite the fact that they are incapable of independent justification, but *because* they are incapable of justification, except from the inside.

Posner sees the matter differently because he does think that there is a single job of work to do—the job of getting the empirical facts right—and he thinks of disciplines as either participating in the task or going off into self-indulgent "theological" flights. He is, in other words, at least part of the time, an essentialist (the dismissal of categories as merely "verbal" [468] is a dead giveaway), someone for whom the present state of disciplinary affairs with its turf battles and special claims will in time be "subsumed under a broader theory" (374), that is, under a general unified science.   Despite the many acknowledgments of heterogeneity in the book, he is finally committed to a brave empirical future in which heterogeneity will have been, if not eliminated, at least grounded and firmly tethered to something more real.

That is why he is an advocate of interdisciplinary work which has the effect, he says, of "blurring the boundaries between disciplines" (432). Presumably at some future date the "blurring" will amount to a wholesale effacing and the disciplines will number only one. (Thou shalt have no other disciplines before me.) This is the basic premise and declared hope of interdisciplinarity (more a religion than a project) as it has recently been described by Julie Thompson Klein.[31]   Klein identifies the interdisciplinary impulse with the desire for "a unified science, general knowledge, synthesis, and the integration of knowledge."[32] Disciplinary boundaries, she tells us, divide fraternal paths of inquiry and also force individuals to develop specialized parts of themselves and ignore the "whole person,"[33] and the result is a society that is itself fragmented and must therefore be "restored to wholeness."[34]   Klein deplores the combative vocabulary characteristic of both intra- and inter-disciplinary discussions, which, she says, leads to "imperialistic claims"[35] and a sense of disciplines as "warring fortresses,"[36] and she laments the fact that our very "vocabulary—indeed our whole logic of classification—pre-disposes us to think in terms of disciplinarity."[37]

The suggestion is that if we could only change our vocabulary, no longer speak in a way that created hierarchies and divisions, we would not experience ourselves as locally situated, but as members of a vast interconnected community.   The suggestion, in short, is that through interdisciplinarity, we can eliminate difference (ye shall see the interdisciplinary truth and it shall make you free). Difference, however, is not a remediable state; it is the bottom line fact of the human condition, the condition of being a finite creature, and therefore a creature whose perspective is not general (that would be a contradiction in terms), but partial (although that partiality can never be experienced as such and those who think it can be unwittingly re-instate the objective viewpoint they begin by repudiating). The "predisposition," as Klein puts it, to think in terms of selves and others, better and worse, mine and yours, right and wrong, to think, that is, in terms rooted in local experiences, is not one that could be altered unless we ourselves could be altered, could be turned from situated beings—viewing and constituting the world from an angle—into beings who were at once nowhere and everywhere. That is the implicit and sometimes explicit goal of the interdisciplinary program, and it is also the goal whether acknowledged or not, of a program that would tie all disciplinary work to a single universal task. The promise of interdisciplinarity, like the promise of a pragmatism that offers either expanded sympathy (Rorty) or bed-rock reality (Posner) is the promise that we shall become as gods. Eve believed it. I don't.

## V

In what is presumably an effort to do his part in bringing about a world marked by expanded sympathy and tolerance, Rorty invites everyone he knows to come in under the pragmatist umbrella. The invitation is declined by Ronald Dworkin who, for a moment, sounds almost like me when he declares that "there is nothing in [pragmatism] to accept";[38] but it would seem that the skepticism we both display toward pragmatism as a program is differently inflected. Dworkin means that there isn't enough of a program in pragmatism, whereas I have been saying that pragmatism, at least in the forms put forward by Rorty and Posner, is too much of a program. It is this difference between us, perhaps, that leads Dworkin to pick up the threads of our earlier quarrels.

Dworkin continues to be exercised by my effort to devalue theory in favor of what I call an "enriched notion of practice." It is his view that my account of practice renders it "flat and passive, robbed of the reflective, introspective, argumentative tone . . . essential to its character," and he asserts that I everywhere underestimate "the complexity of the internal structure of practices that people can quite naturally fall into."[39] Needless to say, I disagree, and indeed I would contend that it is Dworkin who underestimates the complexity of the internal structure of practice, and that it is this underestimation that leads him into a futile and unnecessary search for constraints that practice, properly understood, already contains. This is not to say (as Dworkin does) that practice, in at least some forms, is inseparable from theory, but that (1) competent practitioners operate within a strong understanding of what the practice they are engaged in is *for*, an understanding that generates without the addition of further reflection a sense of what is and is not appropriate, useful, or effective in particular situations; and that (2) such a sense is not theoretical in any interestingly meaningful way.

Let me clarify the point by focusing on a single sentence from Dworkin's important and influential essay, "Hard Cases": "If a judge accepts the settled practices of his legal system—if he accepts, that is, the autonomy provided by its distinct constitutive and regulative rules—then he must, according to the doctrine of political responsibility, accept some general political theory that justifies these practices."[40]

The first question to ask is, what would it mean for a judge *not* to accept the settled practices of the legal system? Would it mean that he or she would not recognize the authority of the Supreme Court or would refuse, as an appeals judge, to note or take into account the ruling of a lower court, or would decide a case without reference to any other case that had ever been decided, or would decide a case by opening, at random, to a page in the Bible or in *Hamlet* and taking direction from the first phrase that leapt to the eyes or would simply refuse to decide? The question is rhetorical in the technical sense that it enumerates kinds of action that would be *unthinkable* for anyone self-identified as a judge. I emphasize the word "unthinkable" to indicate that the issue is not one of considering options—to accept or not to accept, that is not the question—but of comporting oneself in ways inseparable from one's position in a field of institutional activity. If one asks, "what does a judge do?", among the answers are, "a judge thinks about cases by inserting them into a history of previous cases that turn on similar problems," or "a judge operates with a sense of his or her place in a hierarchical structure that is itself responsible to other hierarchical structures (a legislature, a Justice Department)," or "a judge is someone who, in the performance of his or her duty, consults certain specified materials which (at least in our tradition) do *not* include (except as occasional embellishments) the Scriptures or the plays of Shakespeare" or even more simply, "a judge is someone who decides."

It must be emphasized that these are not things a judge does in addition to, or in the way of a constraint on, his mere membership in a profession. They are the *content* of that membership; there is no special effort required to recall them, and no danger that a practitioner, short of amnesia, will forget them. Nor was there a moment when they were offered as practices for approval or disapproval. No one ever said to a law student or a young lawyer, "Now these are the ways we usually deal with contracts; do you think you can go along with them?" Rather, one learned about contracts—about consideration, and breach, and remedies for breach—and as one learned these "facts" one learned too (not also) the appropriate, and indeed obligatory, routes by which outcomes might be produced. The normative aspect of the law is not placed on top of its nuts and bolts (like icing on a cake); it comes along with them and someone who is able to rehearse the points of doctrine in a branch of law knows not only what a practitioner does but what he or she is obliged to do by virtue of his or her professional competence.

In short, there is nothing volitional in the relationship between a professional and the practices in which he is settled and therefore no sense can be given to the notion of accepting or rejecting them. Nevertheless, could it not be said that in the course of internalizing the routines of practice, a prospective judge at the same time internalizes a justification of those routines, internalizes a theory? It depends, I think, on what one means by justification. If you ask a contract lawyer to "justify" his or her recourse to categories like "offer and acceptance," "mistake," "impossibility," "breach," etc., you are likely to be met with a blank look equivalent to the look you would receive from an accountant asked to justify a reliance on statistics or a carpenter asked to justify a reliance on hammers and nails. Simply to *be* a contract lawyer or an accountant or a carpenter is to rely, unreflectingly, on those tools. But if you asked a contract lawyer for a "deeper" justification of his routine deployment of certain vocabularies, you might in some cases, but not all, be told the standard story of "classical" contract doctrine, in which two autonomous agents bargain for an exchange of goods or services whose value they are free to specify in any way they like. Such an answer would be equivalent to a theory, and therefore those who were able to give it could fairly be said to have a theory of their practice.

This, however, does not mean that the theory would be necessary to, or generative of, that practice. A theoretical account produced on demand might be little more than the rote rehearsal of something learned years ago at law school and have no relationship at all to skills acquired in the interim. Self-identified theoreticians would then be practicing in ways that could not be accounted for by their theory and yet their practice would not be impaired by this lack of fit. Moreover, other lawyers and jurists who were either incapable of or uninterested in responding to the demand for theoretical justification might nevertheless be among the most skilled practitioners of a trade. A strong proponent of theory might reply (à la Chomsky) that those who are good at their job but cannot produce a theory of it are nevertheless operating on the basis of theoretical principles; they are just not skilled at articulating them, and if they were to become skilled, if they were able to discourse volubly about the pre-suppositions of their professional performances, they would be even better performers, approaching perhaps the ideal represented by Dworkin's Hercules. But this would be like saying that a cyclist who would be able to explain the physics of balance would be, by virtue of that ability, a better cyclist, or that a motorist who could calculate the relationship between automobile weight, velocity and road conditions with respect to braking distances would be a safer or more skillful driver. It is not that the skills of explaining and calculating in these examples are not genuine or admirable; just that they are skills different from the skills necessary to the performances of which they might, on occasion, provide a "theoretical" account.

To be sure, in some practices, as Dworkin points out, the relationship between explanatory and performance skills is closer than in others. Judging is one such practice, for, as I put it in an earlier essay, "judging . . . includes as a part of its repertoire self-conscious reflection on itself."[41] This means that in the course of unfolding an opinion, a judge might well think it pertinent to invoke some legal "principle" such as "a court cannot police the bargains of competent private individuals" or, more abstractly, "the law must be color-blind with respect to the safeguarding of rights"; but at the moment of their invocation, such "principles" would be doing rhetorical, not theoretical, work, contributing to an argument rather than presiding over it. Such principles (and there are loads of them) form part of the arsenal available to a lawyer or judge—they are on some shelf in the storehouse of available arguments (the concept is, of course, Aristotelian)—and the skill of deploying them is the skill of knowing (it is knowledge on the wing) just when to pull them off the shelf and insert them in your discourse. Once inserted, they are just like the other items in the storehouse, pieces of verbal artillery whose effectiveness will be a function of the discursive moment; they do *not* stand in a relation of logical or philosophical priority to more humble weapons, although their force will depend to some extent on the reputation they have for being prior. Aristotle advised his students to lard their orations with maxims because they give a show of wisdom to a speech. Augustine told preachers to quote the Scriptures as often as possible, and his seventeenth-century pupil, the poet George Herbert, recommended expressions of piety because they "show holiness." Similarly, a legal master rhetorician might urge the regular invocation of principle as a way of convincing the appropriate audience of one's high seriousness. I should add that there is no question of insincerity here. The orator or preacher who cites a maxim or a precept will almost certainly believe in it; it is just that the maxim or precept will be only a part of the case he is building and as a part no more or less foundational than the other parts (statistics, precedents, empirical examples) that go to make up a coherent story.

In short, while theory or theory talk will often be a *component* in the performance of a practice, it will not in most cases be the driving force of the performance; rather it will appear in response to the demands of a moment seen strategically, a moment when the practitioner asks himself or herself, "What might I insert here that would give my argument more weight?" Of course many practices are devoid of such moments because the giving of reasons is not a feature of their performance. As Dworkin notes, referring to an earlier essay of mine, "Denny Martinez never filed an opinion,"[42] meaning, I take it, that Martinez's resistance to theory (as evidenced in a conversation with a sportswriter) can be explained by the fact that the activity he is engaged in is not a reflective one, as opposed say, to the activity of lawyering. The distinction is a real one and important, but it is a distinction not between practices informed by theory and practices innocent of theory, but between practices in relation to which the introduction of "theory-talk" will be useful and practices in relation to which the introduction of theory-talk would be regarded as odd and beside the point ("that kid thinks too much to be a good shooter").

In Dworkin's view this distinction marks a hierarchy in which the reflective practitioner is superior, even morally superior, to the practitioner who just goes about his business. Indeed, so committed is Dworkin to this valorization of the reflective temperament (his version of philosophy's age-old claim to be the master art underlying all the other arts) that he finds it even in places where he has just declared it absent: "Even in baseball . . . theory has more to do with practice than Fish acknowledges. The last player who hit .400, fifty years ago, was the greatest hitter of modern times, and he built a theory before every pitch."[43] Now I yield to no one in my admiration for Ted Williams who has been my idol since boyhood (perhaps Dworkin's too, since we are both natives of Providence, R.I., a Red-Sox happy town); for years I carried a picture of the Splendid Splinter in my wallet until it was so worn that it fell into pieces. But the fact that Williams was a student of hitting and wrote a much admired book on the subject does not mean either that his exploits are the product of his analyses or that players (like Babe Ruth or Mickey Mantle) less inclined to technical ruminations on their art were lesser performers. Williams himself testifies (indirectly) to the absence of a relationship between theory and practice when he reports the view of another "thinking man's" hitter, Ty Cobb. "Ty Cobb

. . . used to say the direction of the stride depended on where the pitch was—inside pitch, you bail out a little; outside you'd move in toward the plate."[44]   Of Cobb's analysis Williams says flatly, "This is wrong because it is impossible," and then goes on to explain that, given the distance between pitcher and batter, and the speed of the ball, "you the batter have already made your stride before you know where the ball will be or what it will be."[45]  What this means is that Cobb, possessor of the highest lifetime batting average in baseball history (.367), did not understand—theoretically, that is—what he was nevertheless doing and doing better than anyone else who ever played the game, including Ted Williams (lifetime average, .344).  Later in the book Williams calls Cobb the "smartest hitter of all,"[46] and we must assume that his intelligence, as exemplified in his day-to-day performance, had nothing to do with his theoretical skills, which were, as Williams has demonstrated, deficient.

What then was the content of the intelligence Williams so much admires if it was not theory?  Perhaps we can infer an answer from Williams's account of his own "theoretical" practice.  Early on he identifies the chief constituents of intelligent hitting as "thinking it out, learning the situations, knowing your opponent, and most important, knowing yourself."[47]  To academic ears this last may have a Socratic ring and seem to gesture in the direction of a deep introspection; but Williams here means no more (or less) than knowing your own physical abilities, where your power lies, the quickness of your bat, the strength (or lack thereof) of your arms and legs.  You must know yourself in the same sense that you must know the situations and your opponent; that is, you must be *alert* to the components of your task and avoid inattention and lack of concentration.  The point becomes clear when Williams declares that "guessing or anticipating goes hand in hand with proper thinking."[48]  A hitter who observes that "a pitcher is throwing fast balls and curves and only the fast balls are in the strike zone . . . would be silly to look for a curve."[49]  The smart hitter, in short, *pays attention* and engages in the kind of thinking Williams images in this hypothetical scenario:

> First time up, out on a fast ball.  Looking for the fast ball on the next time up.  But you go out on a curve.  Third time up, seventh inning, you say to yourself, "Well, he knows I'm a good fast ball hitter, and he got me out on a curve.  I'm going to look for the curve, even though he got me out on a fast ball first time up."[50]

It's all there; knowing the situation (it's the seventh inning, and the end of the game is approaching), knowing your opponent (he's smart enough to be thinking this), knowing yourself (I'm a good fast ball hitter), and the skill is to pay attention to all these things at once. "Paying attention," however, is not a skill separable from an experienced player's "feel" for the game, nor is it a skill that is in any meaningful way theoretical (unless it is a matter of theory to attend watchfully to all of the variables in play when you are crossing at a busy intersection; for if it is, then theory is just a name for making your way through life and there's nothing much to say about it or claim for it); it is just the skill that attends being good at what you do.

Now it may be that when Dworkin speaks of the theoretical component of practice he is referring to nothing more exalted than the habits of being alert and paying attention, and if this is so then the difference between us is merely terminological and doesn't amount to very much at all. (This is what he claims in the conclusion to the essay written for this volume.) But somehow I don't think so, for in every formulation that seems to bring us closer together there is something that reopens a gap, as when he declares that a good judge "will naturally see that he must be, in Fish's terms, a theoretician as well as, and in virtue of, occupying his role as a participant."[51] What troubles me here is the slight equivocation (papered over by a strategically placed "and") between "as well as" and "in virtue of." The first suggests that being a theoretician is something in excess of the role of participant, while the second folds the theory *into* the role. But if the theory is folded into the role, as Williams's alertness to the pitcher and to previous moments in the games is folded into his performance as a batter, there seems to be little reason to call it theory, since it is simply the quality of not falling asleep on the job; and, on the other hand, if theory is used in a more exalted sense and refers to something that must be added to ("as well as") the role of participant, we are back in the realm of meta-commentary and high abstraction despite Dworkin's insistence that he really doesn't live there. A similar equivocation attends the assertion the "theory itself is second nature"[52]; if it is truly second nature, and just comes along with each and every territory, then it simply confuses matters to separate it out and give it an honorific name; and if it is second nature in the sense that it must perfect a first nature that is "flat and passive" without it, then theory is a special project undertaken only by heroic souls like Dworkin's Hercules. That finally is what is at stake in the debates between us, whether or not Dworkin has a project. The question of project also marks my disagreements (much less sharp) with Posner and Rorty, both of whom believe, despite their declared pragmatism, in some benefit to be derived for practice from the pursuit of theory or anti-theory. Whatever differences separate Posner, Rorty, and Dworkin, they are alike in thinking that they have something to recommend, something that will make the game better. (Rorty's version of this, as we have seen, is the most tentative and least robust.) All I have to recommend is the game, which, since it doesn't need my recommendations, will proceed on its way undeterred and unimproved by anything I have to say.

# Notes

1. Richard A. Posner, *The Problems of Jurisprudence* (Cambridge, Mass.: Harvard University Press, 1990). All page numbers in the text refer to this book.

2. This is the great lesson of Thomas Kuhn's *The Structure of Scientific Revolutions* (cited in bibliography).

3. H.L.A. Hart, *The Concept of Law* (Oxford: Oxford University Press, 1961), 202.

4. Quoting Learned Hand, "A Personal Confession," in *The Spirit of Liberty: Papers and Addresses of Learned Hand*, 3rd ed. (New York: Knopf, 1960), 307 (emphasis added).

5. Felix S. Cohen, "Transcendental Nonsense and the Functional Approach," *Columbia Law Review* 35 (June 1935): 809—848.

6. Ibid., 809—810.

7. Ibid., 812.

8. Ibid., 814.

9. Ibid., 820—821.

10. Ibid., 822.

11. Ibid., 833.

12. Ibid., 841.

13. Ibid.

14. Roscoe Pound, "A Call for a Realist Jurisprudence," *Harvard Law Review* 44 (March 1931): 699.

15. Richard Rorty, *Consequences of Pragmatism* (cited in bibliography).

16. Ibid., 166.

17. Ibid.

18. Richard Rorty, *Contingency, Irony, and Solidarity*, 93 (cited in bibliography).

19. Ibid., 196.

20. Ibid.

21. Ibid.

22. Ibid.

23. Ibid., 67.

24. Ibid., 196.

25. Rorty, *Consequences of Pragmatism*, 174.

26. Ibid.

27. Pound, "A Call for a Realist Jurisprudence," 700.

28. Ibid.

29. Ibid., 706.

30. Ibid.

31. Julie Thompson Klein, *Interdisciplinarity: History, Theory, and Practice* (Detroit, Mich.: Wayne State University Press, 1989).

32. Ibid., 19.

33. Ibid., 23.

34. Ibid., 41.

35. Ibid., 79.

36. Ibid., 78.

37. Ibid., 77.

38. Ronald Dworkin, "Pragmatism, Right Answers, and True Banality," 369 (Chapter 19 in this volume).

39. Ibid., 382.

40. Ronald Dworkin, *Taking Rights Seriously*, 105.

41. Stanley Fish, *Doing What Comes Naturally*, 378—379.

42. Dworkin, "Pragmatism, Right Answers, and True Banality," 382.

43. Ibid.

44. Ted Williams and John Underwood, *The Science of Hitting* (New York: Simon & Schuster 1986) 47.

45. Ibid.

46. Ibid., 84.

47. Ibid., 14.

48. Ibid., 29.

49. Ibid.

50. Ibid., 32.

51. Dworkin, "Pragmatism, Right Answers, and True Banality," 381.

52. Ibid., 382.

# 4

## Comment on Paper by Stanley Fish

### E. D. Hirsch, Jr.

Even before I received Stanley Fish's essay, I looked forward with some pleasure to commenting on it. I anticipated that whatever his subject, the paper would be clear, lively, and well written, and I was not disappointed. But I was surprised to find the customary tone of the *enfant terrible* so moderated, the views so richly qualified, the observations so judicious, the tone so wise. Thus superannuation doth make moderates of us all, and thus the native hue of feistiness is sicklied o'er with the pale cast of middle-aged geniality. I'm going to be fairly genial, too.

Many, many years ago, I read with admiration a piece by Fish called "What is stylistics and why are they saying such terrible things about it?" It made the much-needed observation that no formal method of stylistic analysis can lead to a right interpretation or, indeed, to any independent interpretation, because stylistic analysis is predicated on the very meanings it thought it was discovering through its analysis. This early attack on empty formalism and mindless reliance on methodology was shrewd and timely. Some of the best parts of Fish's subsequent work, both in Chapter 3 and in his other writings continue to press an attack on method-mongering, and thus continue the fundamental insight that the supposed method is actually discovering what its constructions had put there in the first place.

In turning this insight upon the law and legal theory, Fish has entered a rich and vast field for deflating methodological pretensions. In this effort, he is not, of course, alone. He joins a lot of lawyers early and late who have been highly skeptical of the law's pretensions to reliable, objective methodology. Already in the nineteenth century, Georg Simmel remarked that in human affairs a show of pure disinterested objectivity is usually a mask for a boundless subjectivism.

That debunking insight is an old story in the law. John Q. Public is well aware of it. Public discussions of the hidden predispositions of Supreme Court nominees show that the insight is hardly news.

Hence, it is fair to assume that anything Fish or I or anyone else might say on the law's nonobjectivity will be a variation on a widely accepted theme. The way to make news would be to say the opposite, to issue a man-bites-dog story claiming to show that, despite public prejudices to the contrary, a high degree of disinterested objectivity really dominates the law. One big question that Fish faces in his review of Richard Posner's book is whether the rhetoric of legal theory could possibly make the law more objective in some desirable sense.

Fish's answer to that practical question is complex and full of internal tensions. He expresses the view in Chapter 3 that theoretical rhetoric will not make the law more truly objective because, for starters, there is no such thing as absolutely objective law. At best, your theoretical rhetoric will help the cause of your group's interested and partial view of what desirable practice should be. Legal theory can't make that pretheoretical determination.

Before I describe the internal tensions that seeth under this view, let me illustrate what I think is behind those tensions by adverting to the simple empirical observation Fish makes regarding tolerance. He enunciates Fish's first law of tolerance dynamics as follows: "Toleration is exercised in an inverse proportion to there being anything at stake." As illustration of the point, he says he can tolerate other peoples' views about George Eliot because he has little personal investment in Eliot. But he will always perform "involuntary" acts of approval, disapproval, and even anger when the subject is John Milton, in whom he has a substantial investment, perhaps 20 percent of his intellectual portfolio.

I am drawn to this example because it seems to bear upon the sphere where theory about the law *could* programmatically influence practice. Fish's first law is, as I'm sure he recognizes, an extremely old law. A judge who has an interest in the outcome of a case regularly recuses herself on that ground. Book reviewers who have an existential interest in the argument of a book, sometimes decline to review, or alternatively, they sometimes state their interest, so the reader of the review can factor in Fish's first law. Whence arises a secondary law: that persons who have an interest in a case sometimes, for that very reason, lean in the opposite direction. The phenomenon is called leaning over backwards. That this effect does occasionally operate could be offered as the second law of tolerance dynamics.

Fish and others would no doubt argue that a person attempting impartiality in such a case might do so only because there is a greater existential reward for that person in leaning over backwards than in following her other existential interests. Sure. But then wouldn't it be good public policy to encourage just that sort of existential interest, to reward or praise people for leaning over backwards, or better still for staying upright in trying to make fair judgments? Fish's own self-knowledge in the case of Milton, his alertness to his own existential interest, so far from debunking the enterprise of fairness and toleration, is potentially the best instrument for coming closer to achieving it. His theoretical account of the law's nonobjectivity takes place at far too high and uniform a level of generality regarding a phenomenon that is so variable. Judges and book reviewers differ noticeably from person to person in their ability to factor out their existential interests. I take it that such an ability is what is meant by the phrase "judicial temperament," which some judges are rightly thought to have in a greater degree than others.

The question of whether different degrees of judicial temperament are a reality or a fiction seems to me an empirical rather than a theoretical one. Whether judicial temperament can be taught or successfully encouraged in law schools is a question about which pragmatism does, as I shall explain, have something programmatic to say, as it does also on two other questions: Should judicial temperament be debunked as a fiction? Should legal theory try to foster the ideal of impartiality?

Fish's views on these matters are, as I said, complex. At times he unambiguously and wisely says that we must vigorously pursue such fictions as impartiality:

> Law emerges because people desire predictability, stability, equal protection, the reign of justice, etc., and because they want to believe that it is possible to secure these things by instituting a set of impartial procedures. . . . [These] props must be in place if the law is to be possessed of persuasive rationale. In short, the law will only work . . . if the metaphysical entities Posner would remove are retained; and if the history of our life with law tells us anything, it is that they will be retained. (p. 61)

At other places, Fish denies that pragmatism implicitly fosters any program at all. In fact, one of his most vigorous claims is that logic compels us to distinguish a pragmatic account of the law, which is a consistent enterprise, from a pragmatic program in law, which is rather like deriving an ethical program from nuclear physics. Pragmatism, he says, has no programmatic consequences because it is just an account of the way things are. It is wrong, he says, to think that a pragmatic account of the law has consequences or that anything necessarily follows from pragmatism, except perhaps the activity of writing reviews of books by Posner, or giving papers at conferences.

The tension in Fish's view arises not just from the embarrassing result that if pragmatism has no programmatic consequences it runs the risk of complete triviality. The greater tension arises from Fish's claim of the rhetoricity of pragmatism, coupled with his simultaneous claim of the nonconsequentiality (hence nonrhetoricity) of pragmatism. If pragmatism is rhetorical, then its implicit program is to change peoples' minds and practices for the better. If pragmatism has no such programmatic consequences, then it is at best bad or ineffectual rhetoric.

This tension in Fish's account between pragmatism as rhetoric and pragmatism as description is hard to resolve. I am not persuaded by his claim that nothing in rhetoric can be shown to be an agency that changes peoples' minds. Minds, he says, just change unpredictably. But the history of rhetoric, and certainly of demogoguery, shows that rhetoric can help change peoples' minds. To remove this tension in his ideas, Fish needs to abandon the empirically false claim that the rhetoric of pragmatism has no implicit program. Perhaps he is really saying that the programmatic consequences of pragmatism are unstable and historically contingent, that they depend upon pragmatism's own historical development. If Fish accepted that refinement of his claim he could thereby remove the serious tension with another element of his thought in which he finds it undesirable and impossible to give up the law's ideals of predictability, stability, equal protection, impartiality, and so on.

If Fish did make that adjustment, I could then see him taking a further step. He could decide to become as skeptical of antimetaphysics as he is of metaphysics. Legal pragmatism as now enunciated by Fish seems unnecessarily dogmatic regarding the absence of metaphysical foundations. To state dogmatically that there are no metaphysical foundations is to speak as metaphysically and pseudoapodictically as to say that there are such foundations. A self-consistent skepticism about metaphysics needs to stay skeptical all the way down. When Fish and other appropriators of pragmatism say that at last we know there are no foundations, they proceed as if they had at last found the right foundation. A self-consistent pragmatism would say nothing of that kind at all. It would leave everything of that sort up for grabs, and get on with the job of fostering the most desirable consequences—as, in our contingent world, they are currently conceived to be.

# 5

## The Banality of Pragmatism and the Poetry of Justice

### *Richard Rorty*

Thomas Grey, in his *Holmes and Legal Pragmatism*, says: "From a certain philosophical perspective, Holmes' pragmatist theory of law is . . . essentially banal. At its most abstract level it concludes in truisms: Law is more a matter of experience than of logic, and experience is tradition interpreted with one eye on coherence and another on policy."[1]

I think it is true that by now pragmatism is banal in its application to law. I also suspect that Grey is right when he claims that "pragmatism is the implicit working theory of most good lawyers."[2] To that extent, at least, everybody seems to now be a legal realist. Nobody wants to talk about a "science of law" any longer. Nobody doubts that what Morton White called "the revolt against formalism"[3] was a real advance, both in legal theory and in American intellectual life generally.

It is true that Ronald Dworkin still bad-mouths pragmatism and insists that there is "one right answer" to hard legal questions. On the other hand, Dworkin says that he does not want to talk about "objectivity" any more. Further, Dworkin's description of "law as integrity" in *Law's Empire*[4] seems to differ only in degree of elaboration from Cardozo's account of "the judge as legislator" in *The Nature of the Judicial Process*.[5] So I find it hard to see what the force of the phrase "one right answer" is supposed to be. Dworkin's polemics against legal realism appear as no more than an attempt to sound a note of Kantian moral rigorism as he continues to do exactly the sort of thing the legal realists wanted done.[6] I think Margaret Radin is right when she says that Dworkin's criticism of pragmatism amounts to little more than "gerrymandering the word 'pragmatism' to mean crass instrumentalism."[7]

Since neither Dworkin nor Richard Posner nor Roberto Unger has any use for what Posner calls "formalism"—namely "the idea that legal questions can be answered by inquiry into the relation between concepts"[8]—it seems plausible to claim that the battles that the legal realists found in alliance with Dewey have essentially been won.[9] The interesting issues now seem to cluster around formalism in a wider sense, one that Unger defines as "a commitment to . . . a method of legal justification that contrasts with open-ended disputes about the basic terms of social life, disputes that people call ideological, philosophical, or visionary."[10]

Even under this broader definition of formalism, however, it is not so easy to find a good example of a formalist among legal theorists. Dworkin sometimes suggests that judges are prevented by their office from being open-ended in this way, although theorists are not. Dworkin proposes that helping the law work itself pure by means of an ever more radical egalitarianism is a matter not for "the princes of law's empire"—the judges—but rather for philosophers, the "seers and prophets of that empire."[11] But Dworkin is ambiguous on the question of whether Hercules, in his official capacity, can take heed of open-ended disputes of the sort Unger has in mind. On the one hand, Dworkin says that the work of Critical Legal Studies theorists is "useful to Hercules," but on the other, he warns that Critical Legal Studies may be merely "an anachronistic attempt" to make legal realism—"that dated movement"—reflower.[12] Yet surely Critical Legal Studies adherents like Allan Hutchinson and Peter Gabel are not interested in formulating a general theory of the sort exemplified by legal realism. Instead, they are, if you like, interested in being useful to Hercules. They want to open up the discourse of the legal profession to issues that Hercules will eventually find raised in half of the briefs he must read.

For myself, I find it hard to discern any interesting *philosophical* differences between Unger, Dworkin, and Posner; their differences strike me as entirely political, as differences about how much change and what sort of change American institutions need. All three have visionary notions, but their visions are different. I do not think that one has to broaden the sense of "pragmatist" very far to include all three men under this accommodating rubric.

The very ease by which these three men are accommodated under this rubric illustrates the banality of pragmatism. Pragmatism was reasonably shocking seventy years ago, but in the ensuing decades it has gradually been absorbed into American common sense. Nowadays, Allan Bloom and Michael Moore seem to be the only people who still think pragmatism is dangerous to the moral health of our society.[13] Posner, therefore, raises a good question when he asks whether the so-called "new" pragmatists have anything to contribute—anything that we have not already internalized as a result of being taught by people who were raised on Dewey.[14]

My own answer to this question is that the new pragmatism differs from the old in just two respects, only one of which is of much interest to people who are not philosophy professors. The first is that we new pragmatists talk about language instead of experience or mind or consciousness, as the old pragmatists did. The second respect is that we have all read Thomas Kuhn, N. R. Hanson, Stephen Toulmin, and Paul Feyerabend, and have thereby become suspicious of the term "scientific method."[15]   New pragmatists wish that Dewey, Sidney Hook, and Ernest Nagel had not insisted on using this term as a catchphrase, since we are unable to provide anything distinctive for it to denote.[16]

As far as I can determine, it is only these doubts about scientific method, and thus about method in general, that might matter for legal theory.   The first respect in which the new pragmatism is new—its switch from experience to language—has offered philosophy professors some fruitful new ways to pose old issues of atomism-vs.-holism and representationalism-vs.-anti-representationalism (as in the controversies between Hilary Putnam and David Lewis, Donald Davidson and Michael Dummett, Daniel Dennett and Jerry Fodor). But these issues are pretty remote from the concerns of non-philosophers.[17] By contrast, as Judge Posner's article shows,[18] *method* can still seem important.

Posner says that "lack of method" was "a great weakness" of legal realism.[19] He distinguishes between "scientistic philosophy" and "social science . . . the application of scientific method to social behavior" and says that his own economic approach to law is "rooted in and inspired by a belief in the intellectual power and pertinence of economics."[20] My own Kuhnian-Feyerabendian doubts about scientific method make me wish that Posner had been content with this last remark and not added the sentences about method. Social scientists, like novelists, poets, and politicians, occasionally come up with good ideas that judges can use. For all I know, the brand of economics that centers on considerations of efficiency may provide Hercules with some very useful ideas. But I am fairly certain that it would be hard for Posner to explain what was especially scientific about either the genesis or the application of these ideas.[21]   My assurance on this point is the result of watching many philosophers try and fail to find an epistemic or methodological, as opposed to a sociological or moral, distinction between science and non-science.[22]

I agree with Grey that one advantage of pragmatism is freedom from theory-guilt.[23] Another advantage is freedom from anxiety about one's scientificity. So I think it is in the spirit of Dewey to say that the test of the power and pertinence of a given social science is how it works when you try to apply it. The test of law and economics is whether judges agree in finding Posner's ideas useful when, as Grey puts it, "interpreting tradition with one eye on coherence and the other on policy."[24]

On the other hand, I agree with Posner that judges will probably not find pragmatist philosophers—either old or new—useful. Posner is right in saying that pragmatism clears the underbrush and leaves it to others to plant the forest.[25] I would add that the underbrush in question is mostly specifically philosophical underbrush. The "new" pragmatism should, I think, be viewed merely as an effort to clear away some alder and sumac, which sprang up during a thirty-year spell of wet philosophical weather—the period that we now look back on as "positivistic analytic philosophy." This clearance will restore the appearance of the terrain that Dewey landscaped, but it will not do more than that.

To accomplish more, and in particular to avoid the complacency that Radin rightly sees as the danger of coherence theories of knowledge,[26] we have to turn to Dewey the prophet rather than Dewey the pragmatist philosopher. We have to read the Emersonian visionary rather than the contributor to *The Journal of Philosophy* who spent forty years haggling over definitions of "true" with E. B. McGilvary, Arthur O. Lovejoy, Bertrand Russell, C. I. Lewis, Ernest Nagel, and the rest. This is the Dewey whom Cornel West describes as calling for "an Emersonian culture of radical democracy,"[27] the Dewey who is grist for Critical Legal Studies mills. Like the "prophetic pragmatism" for which West calls, this Dewey is "a child of Protestant Christianity wedded to left romanticism."[28]

No argument leads from a coherence view of truth, an anti-representationalist view of knowledge, and an anti-formalist view of law and morals, to Dewey's left-looking social prophecies. The Heidegger of *Being and Time* shared all those views, but Heidegger looked rightward and dreamed different dreams.[29] These were anti-egalitarian, nostalgic dreams, which resembled those of T. S. Eliot and Allen Tate rather than the one that Dewey embodied in a quote from Keats:[30]

> [M]an should not dispute or assert, but whisper results to his
> neighbor, and thus, by every germ of spirit sucking the sap from
> mold ethereal, every human being might become great, and Humanity
> instead of being a wide heath of Furze and briars with here and there
> a remote Pine or Oak, would become a grand democracy of Forest
> Trees![31]

This romantic side of Dewey is not banal. When one comes across such passages as this, one wakes out of the slumber induced by what Grey calls "the good gray liberal expounds the mild virtues of the theoretic middle way."[32] But this side of Dewey is not distinctively *pragmatist* either. These passages do not let one know, as Grey rightly says Wallace Stevens does, what it *feels like* to be a pragmatist—what it feels like to have overcome the dualisms of fiction and reality, imagination and reason. The pragmatists provided good philosophical arguments against some of the philosophical presuppositions of formalism that Morton White describes, the revolt whose success lets us find much of Dewey platitudinous, owed as much to visionary carrots as to argumentative sticks.

Dewey's Keatsian vision was shared by many social democrats in many countries at the turn of the century.[33] As Putnam rightly says, it is not a vision that can be successfully backed up by a Habermas-Apel style argument about the presuppositions of rational discourse.[34] But visions do not really need backup. To put forth a vision is always one of Fitzjames Stephen's "leaps in the dark."[35] Thus, insofar as we late-comers can get more platitudes from Dewey, it will be because we are able to read our own specific egalitarian hopes into his generic ones, not because we can still use his anti-formalist arguments as weapons.

As examples of attempts to actualize specific hopes, consider such debatable decisions as *Brown v. Board of Education*,[36] *Roe v. Wade*,[37] Judge Sand's recent decision that begging is a first amendment right,[38] various state supreme court decisions holding that all school districts within the state must have the same per-pupil expenditure, and some future Supreme Court decision that will strike down anti-sodomy laws. These are cases in which the courts have done, or might do, what Posner claims "the pragmatic counsel . . . to the legal system" would warn them against.[39] They have "roil[ed] needlessly the political waters."[40] They have "prematurely nationalized an issue [that many thought] best left to simmer longer at the state and local level until a consensus based on experience with a variety of approaches . . . emerged."[41]

Undoubtably, an ideally unromantic and bland pragmatist would offer such advice, but Dewey the visionary would not. Dewey the romantic would have been delighted that the courts sometimes tell the politicians and the voters to start noticing that there are people who have been told to wait forever until a consensus emerges—a consensus within a political community from which these people are effectively excluded.[42] Dewey the pragmatist would not, I think have accepted Dworkin's quasi-Kantian claim that in these cases the courts were simply "taking rights seriously" rather than being visionary—for he would have thought "rights" a good example of what Posner calls "the law's metaphysical balloons."[43] Unlike Dworkin, Dewey would not have attempted to formulate a general legal theory that justified the practice of making leaps in the constitutional dark.[44]  Rather I imagine Dewey would say that to suddenly notice previously existing but hitherto invisible constitutional rights is just the quaint way in which our courts are required to express a conviction that the political waters badly need roiling.

In terms Radin uses, this conviction can be restated as the claim that a paradigm shift is needed in order to break up "bad coherence."[45] Such a shift can be initiated when visionary judges conspire to prevent their brother Hercules, the "complacent pragmatist judge" whom Radin describes, from perpetuating such coherence.  The cheer we egalitarians raise at such breakthroughs into romance—at such examples of the poetry of justice—is, I think, what justified Posner's statement that although it was "not . . . a good judicial opinion," Holmes's *Lochner* dissent was "the greatest judicial opinion of the last hundred years."[46] I read that dissent as saying, in part, "Like it or not, gentlemen, trade unions are part of our country too." I think of *Brown* as saying that, like it or not, black children are children too.  I think of *Roe* as saying that, like it or not, women get to make hard decisions too, and of some hypothetical future reversal of *Bowers v. Hardwick*[47] as saying that, like it or not, gays are grown-ups too.

I can share Ronald Dworkin's and John Ely's concerns over the "unprincipled" character of such decisions—their concern at the possibility that equally romantic and visionary, yet morally appalling, decisions may be made by pragmatist judges whose dreams are Eliotic or Heideggerian rather than Emersonian or Keatsian.  But as a pragmatist, I do not believe that legal theory offers us a defense against such judges—that it can do much to prevent another *Dred Scott* decision. In particular, I do not see that such judges will have more or less "integrity" than those who decided *Brown* or *Roe*.  I agree with Grey when he says: "Pragmatism rejects the maxim that you can only beat a theory with a better theory. . . . No rational God guarantees in advance that important areas of practical activity will be governed by elegant theories."[48]

Further, I think that pragmatism's *philosophical* force is pretty well exhausted once this point about theories has been absorbed. But, in American intellectual life, "pragmatism" has stood for more than just a set of controversial philosophical arguments about truth, knowledge, and theory. It has also stood for a visionary tradition to which, as it happened, a few philosophy professors once made particularly important contributions—a tradition to which some judges, lawyers, and law professors still make important contributions. These are the ones who, in their opinions, or briefs, or articles, enter into what Unger calls "open-ended disputes about the basic terms of social life."[49]

# Notes

1. Thomas Grey, "Holmes and Legal Pragmatism," *Stanford Law Review* 41 (April 1989): 814.

2. Thomas Grey, "Hear the Other Side: Wallace Stevens and Pragmatist Legal Theory," *Southern California Law Review* 63 (September 1990): 1590.

3. Morton White, *Social Thought in America: The Revolt Against Formalism* (New York: Viking, 1949).

4. Ronald Dworkin, *Law's Empire* (Cambridge, Mass.: Harvard University Press, 1986), 176—275.

5. Benjamin Cardozo, *The Nature of the Judicial Process* (New Haven: Yale University Press, 1921).

6. See A. D. Woozley, "No Right Answer," in *Ronald Dworkin and Contemporary Jurisprudence*, ed. Marshall Cohen (London: Duckworth, 1983), 173—182. In a reply to Woozley, Dworkin echoes Dewey by saying that "a concept of truth that somehow escapes the fact that all our concepts, including our philosophical concepts, take the only meaning they have from the function they play in our reasoning, argument, and conviction" is a "mirage." Ronald Dworkin, "A Reply by Ronald Dworkin," in *Ronald Dworkin and Contemporary Jurisprudence*, 277. Dworkin's reply ends by saying that he is content with the statement that "in hard cases at law one answer might be the most reasonable of all, even though competent lawyers will disagree about which answer is the most reasonable" (278). This gloss neutralizes whatever anti-pragmatist and anti-legal realist force there might have been in the "one right answer" slogan.

In Dworkin's view (with which pragmatists heartily agree) that "objectivity" (in a sense interestingly different from "inter-subjectivity") is an unnecessary notion for an accurate description of the decisionmaking process. See Dworkin, "A Reply by Ronald Dworkin," 267.

7. Margaret Radin, "The Pragmatist and the Feminist," *Southern California Law Review* 63 (September 1990): 1722. Reprinted as Chapter 8 in this book.

8. Richard Posner, "What Has Pragmatism to Offer Law?" *Southern California Law Review* 63 (September 1990): 1663. Reprinted as Chapter 2 in this book.

9. The battles have been won among theorists, if not among the more recently appointed members of the Supreme Court. The latter have not garnered much supporting theory for their views;  E. D. Hirsch, Jr., the leading representative of intentionalism in the theory of interpretation, was quick to disassociate himself from their use of the concept of "the Framers' intention." See E. D. Hirsch, Jr., "Counterfactuals in Interpretation," in *Interpreting Law and Literature*, ed. Steven Levinson and Sanford Mailloux (Evanston, Ill.: Northwestern University Press, 1988), 55—68.

10. Roberto Unger, *The Critical Legal Studies Movement* (Cambridge, Mass.: Harvard University Press, 1986), 1.

11. See Dworkin, *Law's Empire*, 407.

12. Ibid., 272—273.

13. Allan Bloom, *The Closing of the American Mind* (New York: Simon and Shuster, 1986); Michael Moore, "A Natural Law Theory of Interpretation," *Southern California Law Review* 58 (1985): 279—398.

14. Posner, "What Has Pragmatism to Offer Law?" 1658—1659.

15. The two respects in which the new pragmatism differs from the old are connected in that without the so-called "linguistic turn," the topic of "theory-neutral observation language" could not have been posed. Without Rudolph Carnap's and Carl Hempel's attempts to develop logics of confirmation and explanation by treating theories as (potentially axiomatizable) sets of propositions whose deductive consequences could be phrased in such an observation language, this topic would not have seemed urgent. Also, without W.V.O. Quine's attack on the analytic-synthetic distinction (an attack that is less easily mounted against the pre-linguistic-turn necessary-vs.-contingent distinction), and Wilfrid Sellars's attack on the notion of "pure sense-datum report," Kuhn's reception would have been colder than it was.

16. For reasons why Dewey's use of that phrase was misleading and unhelpful, see Richard Rorty, "Introduction," in *John Dewey: The Later Works*, ed. Jo Ann Boydston (Carbondale, Ill.: Southern Illinois University Press, 1986), 8.ix—xviii, and Richard Rorty, "Pragmatism Without Method," in *Sidney Hook: Philosopher of Democracy and Humanism*, ed. Paul Kurtz (Buffalo, N.Y.: Prometheus, 1983), 259—275.

17. Insofar as concern with language as such has entered into legal theory, it has done so in the form of the "deconstructionist" wind of the Critical Legal Studies movement. For some powerfully argued criticisms of the claim that deconstructionism has something to contribute to legal theory, see Joan Williams, "Critical Legal Studies: The Death of Transcendence and the Rise of the New Langdells," *New York University Law Review* 62 (1987): 429—497. Whereas Radin suggests that with Dewey you do not need Derrida, see Radin, "The Pragmatist and the Feminist" (1719), Willams's point is that if you have Wittgenstein, you do not need Derrida. I think the latter claim is slightly more accurate, since the later Wittgenstein updates Dewey by working out a non-representational approach to *language*, as opposed to a non-representationalist approach to inquiry. Wittgenstein thus lets one meet the deconstructionists on their own turf.

18. Posner, "What Has Pragmatism to Offer Law?"

19. Ibid., 1659.

20. Ibid., 1668—1669.

21. For some skepticism about the scientificity of economics, see Donald McCloskey, *The Rhetoric of Economics* (Madison: University of Wisconsin Press, 1985).

22. See Richard Rorty, "Is Natural Science a Natural Kind?" in *Construction and Constraint: The Shaping of Scientific Rationality*, ed. Ernan McMullin (Notre Dame, Ind.: Notre Dame University Press, 1988), 49—75.

23. Grey, "Hear the Other Side: Wallace Stevens and Pragmatist Legal Theory," 1569.

24. Grey, "Holmes and Legal Pragmatism," 814.

25. Posner, "What Has Pragmatism to Offer Law?" 1670.

26. Radin, "The Pragmatist and the Feminist," 1710.

27. Cornel West, *The American Evasion of Philosophy: A Genealogy of Pragmatism* (Madison: Wisconsin University Press, 1989), 104.

28. Ibid., 277.

29. See Martin Heidegger, *Auf der Erfahrung des Denkens* (Pfullingen: G. Neske, 1954).

30. On the overlap between Dewey and Heidegger, see Mark Okrent, *Heidegger's Pragmatism* (Ithaca, N.Y.: Cornell University Press, 1988), 3—10, 280—281.

31. John Dewey, *Art as Experience* (London: George Allen and Unwin, 1934), 347.

32. Grey, "Hear the Other Side: Wallace Stevens and Pragmatist Legal Theory," 1592.

33. See James T. Kloppenberg, *Uncertain Victory: Social Democracy and Progressivism in European and American Thought 1870-1920* (New York: Oxford University Press, 1986), 26—27.

34. Hilary Putnam, "A Reconsideration of Deweyan Democracy," *Southern California Law Review* 63 (September 1990): 1687—1688. Reprinted as Chapter 12 in this book.

35. Ibid., 1693—1694.

36. 347 U.S. 483 (1954).

37. 410 U.S. 113 (1973).

38. *Young v. New York City Transit Authority*, 729 F. Supp. 341 (S.D.N.Y. 1990), *rev'd in part, vacated in part*, 903 F.2d 146 (2d Cir. 1990).

39. Posner, "What Has Pragmatism to Offer Law?" 1668.

40. Ibid.

41. Ibid.

42. It might be objected that this phrase is inapplicable to *Roe v. Wade*, since women are included in the relevant community. I am not sure they are, both on Ely-like grounds of under-representation and on the vaguer but more powerful ground that (as banners at a pro-choice demonstration recently put it) "if men got pregnant, they would have made abortion a sacrament."

43. See Posner, "What Has Pragmatism to Offer Law?" 1663.

44. See Daniel Farber, "Legal Pragmatism and the Constitution," *Minnesota Law Review* 72 (June 1988): 1331—1378. I agree with Farber that we do not need "a unified principle that would provide the basis for judicial decisions" (1334), and with Farber's criticism of Dworkin's attacks on pragmatism (1343—1349). But I think that Farber concedes too much to the opposition when he contests John Hart Ely's claim that "when a majority has chosen to invade an arguably fundamental right, courts have no principled way of determining whether the right should be considered fundamental" (1355). Farber is right, of course, if what he means by "principled" in these contexts is simply susceptible to being supported by a reasonable argument—but this is not what Dworkin and Ely mean. Dworkin and Ely want a distinction between principle and policy, which pragmatists must refuse them.

45. Radin, "The Pragmatist and the Feminist," 1710.

46. Richard Posner, *Law and Literature: A Misunderstood Relation* (Cambridge, Mass.: Harvard University Press, 1985), 285. I am grateful to my colleague George Rutherglen for helping me see that Harlan's dissent in *Lochner* was, romance apart, a far better example of what one expects judicial opinions to look like. I am also grateful to him for looking over a draft of this article and saving me from some howlers.

47. 478 U.S. 186 (1986).

48. Grey, "Holmes and Legal Pragmatism," 814—815.

49. Unger, *The Critical Legal Studies Movement*, 1.

# 6

## "Just Do It": Pragmatism and Progressive Social Change

### *Lynn A. Baker*

What use is pragmatism for achieving progressive social change? This question has been central to the recent renaissance of interest in pragmatism within the legal academy. The scholars who have written on this issue not surprisingly have shared a core concern: the persistent marginalization and disempowerment of certain groups in our society.[1] More striking, however, is these scholars' substantial agreement that pragmatism is useful for alleviating such oppression in modern America.[2]

In this chapter I suggest, despite the popularity of claims to the contrary, that pragmatism is of scant use in achieving progressive social change. My analysis focuses on the writings of Richard Rorty for two reasons. First, he is the acknowledged philosophical leader of the recent revival of interest in pragmatism. Second, an examination of Rorty's work uncovers important, and previously undiscussed, inconsistencies in his own assessment of pragmatism's usefulness for progressive social change.

I begin with an analytical summary of two distinct, but previously unseparated, strands in Rorty's discussion of progressive social change, which I term the "prophetic" and the "processual." In Section II I examine two popular responses legal academics have made to Rorty's views: their criticism of his seeming defense of the status quo and their praise of his concern for marginalized people. I argue that in both instances the response may be problematic if it fails to distinguish between the different strands in Rorty's view of progressive social change.

In Sections III and IV I evaluate, by Rorty's own pragmatist terms, his claims for a pragmatist ("postmetaphysical") culture. Section III examines whether the postmetaphysical culture that Rorty advocates would have any advantages over our current foundationalist one for achieving progressive social change, as Rorty defines it. Section IV considers whether, regardless of the background culture, the prophets who are necessary for progressive social change under Rorty's view would be better served by subscribing to pragmatism or to foundationalism.

## I. Rorty on Progressive Social Change

Legal scholars have discussed Richard Rorty's views on progressive social change as if they were of a single genus. Close analysis, however, reveals two importantly distinct strands in Rorty's discussion: the "prophetic" and the "processual." Identifying and separating these threads is necessary for understanding both Rorty's claims and legal scholars' (mis)conceptions of them.

The prophetic strand in Rorty's discussion consists of two major parts. One is his definition of "progressive social change," which necessarily embodies his vision of a better world. The other is his suggestion of the means for getting from the present to that better world. The processual strand consists of Rorty's description of the process or mechanism by which his suggested means moves us closer to his vision of a better world. Thus, one might agree with Rorty about the likely efficacy of a suggested means for realizing his utopian vision (prophetic strand), but disagree about the process by which that means will effect social change (processual strand).

The central element of Rorty's prophetic strand is his definition of progressive social change. Although he frequently eschews the notion of "progress," Rorty is willing to employ it in the context of moral and social change. Progressive change, according to Rorty, is that which moves a society closer to realizing his three interrelated hopes: that suffering and cruelty will be diminished;[3] that freedom will be maximized;[4] and that "chances for fulfillment of idiosyncratic fantasies will be equalized."[5] Rorty derives these hopes from his premise that "the aim of a just and free society [is] letting its citizens be as privatistic, 'irrationalist,' and aestheticist as they please so long as they do it on their own time—causing no harm to others and using no resources needed by those less advantaged."[6]

Rorty does not attempt a theoretical or metaphysical defense of this premise or the hopes it embodies, "hav[ing] abandoned the idea that those central beliefs and desires refer back to something beyond the reach of time and chance."[7] They are simply "ungroundable desires" for which there is "no noncircular theoretical backup."[8]

What means does Rorty suggest we employ to reach his utopian end, to move from our present world to the better world he envisions? Rorty repeatedly asserts: "There is no method or procedure to be followed except courageous and imaginative experimentation."[9] Nonetheless, he suggests two major means by which social progress has occurred in the past and might do so in the future: narratives and separatist groups. Rorty does not mean to imply, however, that these are the only two means by which social change has occurred or could someday occur. They are simply the two means that he has thus far chosen to examine at greatest length.

Rorty's account of the processes or mechanisms by which narratives and separatist groups might yield progressive social change constitutes the "conceptual" strand of Rorty's views on progressive social change. By narratives Rorty means novels, docudramas, ethnographies, and journalists' reports, for example, that provide "detailed descriptions of particular varieties of pain and humiliation."[10] According to Rorty, the narrative can be authored by one of the oppressed or by someone else, and is an attempt to interpret the situation of the oppressed group to the rest of their society. Such narratives increase human solidarity by expanding the sympathies of persons who are not members of the oppressed group so that they come to see the oppressed "as 'one of us' rather than as 'them'."[11] Increased human solidarity, however, is not synonymous with an "us" admitting a "them" to membership through an act of noblesse oblige. Rather, according to Rorty, the narrative process of interpretive description encompasses the nonoppressed as well as the oppressed; it "is a matter of detailed description of what unfamiliar people are like *and of redescription of what we ourselves are like.*"[12]

Through narratives we may each come to know better not only persons whom we do not (yet) think of as one of us, but also "the tendencies to cruelty inherent in searches for autonomy" that we ourselves possess,[13] the "sorts of cruelty we ourselves are capable of."[14] In this way, we may each become more generally aware of, more sensitive to, the suffering around us and our role in it.[15] "Such increased sensitivity," according to Rorty, "makes it more difficult to marginalize people different from ourselves by thinking, 'They do not feel it as *we* would,' or 'There must always be suffering, so why not let *them* suffer?'"[16] Solidarity, then, is "the ability to see more and more traditional differences . . . as unimportant when compared with similarities with respect to pain and humiliation."[17]

Among existing narratives, Rorty classifies the work of Dickens, Olive Schreiner, and Richard Wright as giving us "the details about kinds of suffering being endured by people to whom we had previously not attended."[18] The work of Choderlos de Laclos, Henry James, and Vladimir Nabokov, in contrast, "gives us the details about what sorts of cruelty we ourselves are capable of, and thereby lets us redescribe ourselves."[19]

Separatist groups, according to Rorty, are a second means by which society might progress toward his utopian vision. The creation of a separatist group depends on at least one member of the oppressed group having "the imagination it takes to hear oneself as the spokesperson of a merely possible community, rather than as a lonely, and perhaps crazed, outcast from an actual one."[20] That courageous individual will begin to work out a new story about who she is, which will require, in order to achieve semantic authority over even herself, that she hear her own statements as part of a shared practice.[21] Thus, according to Rorty, she may persuade other members of the oppressed group to band together with her in an exclusive club in order to "try out new ways of speaking, and to gather the moral strength to go out and change the world."[22]

Changing the world is a risky business, however. The separatist group may be ruthlessly suppressed (its members thus doubly oppressed). Or, preferably, over generations, "those in control [may] gradually find their conceptions of the possibilities open to human beings changing" and "[t]he new language spoken by the separatist group may gradually get woven into the language taught in the schools."[23] That is, the formerly oppressed group gradually achieves "'full personhood' in the eyes of everybody, having first achieved it only in the eyes of fellow-members of their own club."[24] The test of whether this larger full personhood has been achieved, according to Rorty, is whether powerful people in the society (still) thank God that they do not belong to the (formerly) oppressed group.[25]

The contemporary feminist movement, Plato's Academy, the early Christians who met in the catacombs, "the invisible Copernican colleges of the seventeenth century,"[26] and the working people who gathered to discuss Tom Paine's pamphlets are all examples that Rorty cites of "clubs which were formed to try out new ways of speaking, and to gather the moral strength to go out and change the world."[27]

In sum, separatist groups, according to Rorty, move society towards his utopian vision through the creation of new linguistic practices, while narratives do so through an expansion of individual empathy. This distinction is not intended to obscure the obvious interrelatedness of the two mechanisms, however: The creation of new linguistic practices can occur simultaneously with, cause, or result from, an expansion of individual empathy. Thus, Rorty also describes narratives as "aimed at working out a new *public* final vocabulary . . . , a vocabulary deployed to answer the question 'What sorts of things about what sorts of people do I need to notice?'"[28] And he portrays separatist groups also as "trying to get people to feel indifference or satisfaction where they once recoiled, and revulsion and rage where they once felt indifference or resignation."[29]

At the center of both the narrative and separatist group processes of progressive social change, as Rorty describes them, is a prophet—an interpreter or a leader with a vision of a better world. The author(s) of a narrative must have both a vision and a sense of how to translate the experiences of either the oppressed or the cruel group into a language that others might not only understand but be transformed by in the direction of that vision. Similarly, the leader of a separatist group must not only be able to suggest particular ways in which a society's language and institutions might be changed. She must ultimately have a *transformative* vision which includes "some sort of blueprint for the results of transformation (in the way in which Jefferson and Adams, or Lenin and Trotsky, did, and Abbie Hoffman did not)."[30] Above all else, then, both the narrator and the leader of a separatist group must have imagination—and sometimes a special kind of courage.

Given these prophetic and processual strands, what in Rorty's views on progressive social change is uniquely the product of his pragmatism? This issue can be examined without confronting the vastly larger and less tractable question of what pragmatism in general is, by focusing on pragmatism's antifoundationalist core: metaphysical entities such as "reality," "truth," and "nature" are not considered "warrants for certitude."[31] In the context of social change, this antifoundationalism more specifically entails: (1) a recognition of the pervasiveness of contingency; (2) the absence of metaphysical notions when guiding, evaluating, or conceptualizing processes of social change; and (3) the absence of metaphysical notions when providing or evaluating justifications or arguments for social change.[32]

Applying these criteria to the prophetic strand in Rorty's views on progressive social change, there would not appear to be anything distinctly antifoundationalist about the *substance* of Rorty's premise or the three hopes it embodies. Indeed, the only antifoundationalist aspect of that strand is the way in which Rorty "justifies" his central hopes. Rorty's claim that his premise simply embodies "ungroundable desires" for which there is "no noncircular theoretical backup"[33] is an example of pragmatism's antifoundationalist distrust of metaphysical entities as warrants for certitude. Another example of this distrust is Rorty's suggestion that "[w]e should learn to brush aside questions like 'How do you *know* that freedom is the chief goal of social organization?'" and instead "should see allegiance to social institutions as no more matters for justification by reference to familiar, commonly accepted premises—but also as no more arbitrary—than choices of friends or heroes."[34]

At bottom is pragmatism's antifoundationalist acknowledgment of contingency: Choices of prophecies, of social institutions, "cannot be preceded by presuppositionless critical reflection, conducted in no particular language and outside of any particular historical context."[35] Thus, Rorty seems to suggest, borrowing from Rawls, that the justification for the substance of his prophecy "is not its being true to an order antecedent and given to us, but its congruence with our deeper understanding of ourselves and our aspirations, and our realization that, given our history and the traditions embedded in our public life, it is the most reasonable doctrine for us."[36] In the end, Rorty justifies the premise and the hopes that constitute his prophecy with an antifoundationalist, historically contingent congruence—not a metaphysical correspondence to Truth.

Applying the above pragmatist criteria to the processual strand in Rorty's views on progressive social change reveals it to be antifoundationalist, through and through. In his account of the processes by which progressive social change takes place, Rorty does not portray either separatist groups or narratives as reaching toward a metaphysical "truth" or "objective reality." They strive toward "increasingly useful metaphors rather than . . . increasing understanding of how things really are."[37]

Rorty conceives of separatist groups as trying to create new linguistic practices through which they will simultaneously forge a new and more useful identity for persons like themselves within the larger society. And he conceptualizes the authors of narratives as, *inter alia*, helping us see the effects on others of our social practices and institutions and of our private idiosyncrasies. In this way, Rorty suggests, narratives enable us usefully to redescribe both others and ourselves. The world is changed not as separatist groups and narratives discover and communicate truths, but as they provide useful redescriptions of the world and its inhabitants. For Rorty, "a talent for speaking differently, rather than for arguing well, is the chief instrument of cultural change."[38]

In sum, pragmatism's antifoundationalist core appears to provide Rorty two important aspects of his discussion of progressive social change: the way in which he "justifies" the substance of his chosen prophecy, and his account of the processes by which his suggested means will effect progressive social change.

## II. Legal Scholars Respond

In addition to being intrinsically interesting, the above analysis of Rorty's discussion of progressive social change sheds important light on two popular responses by legal academics to Rorty's views. Scholars have applauded Rorty's concern for "marginalized people."[39] They have also, however, frequently criticized Rorty for offering a "complacent pragmatism,"[40] for providing a conservative "reaffirmation of liberal institutions and practices."[41] This section shows that both of these responses may be problematic if they fail to distinguish among the prophetic, processual, and antifoundationalist aspects of Rorty's views on progressive social change.

Legal scholars interested in pragmatism have explicitly or implicitly praised Rorty for his statement that "[w]e should stay on the lookout for marginalized people—people whom we still instinctively think of as 'they' rather than 'us'."[42] Joseph Singer, for example, has stated that "Rorty is right to advise all of us to be on the lookout for people who are oppressed."[43] And scholars such as Mari Matsuda and Margaret Jane Radin have suggested that pragmatism could be improved by explicitly incorporating a concern for oppressed persons.[44] It thus seems important to understand Rorty's statement in the context of his views on progressive social change.

Rorty's exhortation concerning marginalized people is only one of his many suggestions about how to make our world better, "much less cruel for a lot of people."[45] In *Contingency, Irony, and Solidarity*, for example, Rorty describes his "liberal utopia" at substantial length. And elsewhere, he suggests that schools should assign students books that will help them "learn about what it has been like (and often still is like) to be female, or black, or gay."[46]

Whether one views Rorty's suggestions for a better world as signs of his political radicalism or conservatism, it is important to keep straight the fact that these suggestions are not entailed by his antifoundationalism, they are merely consistent with it. Rorty makes these proposals as a prophet, not as an antifoundationalist. He is simply setting forth his vision of a better world and suggesting how it might be realized. Should any of Rorty's suggestions be tried and found useful, we will have evidence that Rorty is a useful prophet—not evidence that Rorty is a good antifoundationalist or that antifoundationalism is useful. Similarly, when Matsuda and Radin suggest improving pragmatism by explicitly incorporating a concern for marginalized people, they would be best understood as providing a prophecy for the realization of which antifoundationalism may or may not prove useful.

Although legal scholars have praised Rorty for his concern for the oppressed, they have also criticized him for his seeming political conservatism. For example, Joseph Singer writes that Rorty's "vision of pragmatism is inherently conservative because it equates 'democracy' and 'freedom' with established institutions."[47] And Allan Hutchinson accuses Rorty of being so "[c]onsumed in his efforts to argue that liberal institutions can eradicate [patriarchy, racism, economic inequality, and the continual threat of nuclear holocaust and environmental destruction, that he] fails to note that they have helped to create it."[48]

From their perception of Rorty as a defender of existing American political institutions and a proponent of "liberalism," these scholars have concluded that he is a complacent apologist for the social and political status quo.[49] To be sure, Rorty does explicitly advocate "the protection of something like the institutions of bourgeois liberal society,"[50] and he does repeatedly describe himself as a "liberal."[51] But his critics importantly overlook the larger context in which Rorty makes these statements.

The preservation of existing American political institutions is neither the substantive focus of Rorty's utopian vision nor is his advocacy of the preservation of those institutions evidence that he has no utopian vision. Rather, those institutions are a mechanism for the realization of his vision, which Rorty has chosen largely by default. Rorty's dream is of a society in which suffering and cruelty are minimized, freedom is maximized, and "chances for fulfillment of idiosyncratic fantasies will be equalized."[52] His prophecy includes "the institutions of bourgeois liberal society"[53] for three reasons. First, Rorty reads "the historical facts" to suggest that without the protection of something like those institutions, a society moves farther away from realizing his three hopes.[54] Second, he believes that the institutions of "contemporary liberal society" will affirmatively enable that society to improve itself in the direction of his vision.[55] Third, Rorty feels he can suggest no alternative to those institutions that would better enable society to move in the direction of his vision.[56]

Thus, the existing American political institutions play a role in Rorty's dream ultimately by default. Indeed, Rorty repeatedly expresses a willingness to reexamine the value of those institutions in light of "practical proposals for the erection of alternative institutions."[57] And he further concedes that his own failure to generate such a practical proposal is simply due to his own lack of prophetic imagination.[58] Or, perhaps more accurately, Rorty's quite substantial prophetic imagination simply does not extend this far.

Critics have also misunderstood Rorty's seeming praise and advocacy of "liberalism." Rorty does not mean the term to signify a complacent acceptance of the political status quo (or the unquestioning adoption of an extant political ideology), but typically uses it as a shorthand with regard to certain aspects of his prophecy. The society that realizes Rorty's hopes regarding freedom, cruelty, and poeticization is one that he terms "a liberal utopia" or "an ideal liberal society,"[59] not simply a "utopia" or "ideal society." Rorty also uses "liberal" to describe people who share the hopes at the core of his prophecy. "[T]hat cruelty is the worst thing we do," for example, he repeatedly describes as "the liberal's claim."[60]

Most importantly, however, Rorty uses the term "liberal" to help establish the historical roots of his own dream of an "ideal liberal society."[61] Rorty considers his three hopes for society to be importantly consistent with "a historical narrative" about existing institutions and customs that he also describes as "liberal": "the institutions and customs which were designed to diminish cruelty, make possible government by the consent of the governed, and permit as much domination-free communication as possible to take place."[62] Rorty's critics, however, may be confusing this antifoundationalist historicism and acknowledgment of contingency with political conservatism.

In discussing the three hopes at the core of his prophecy, Rorty repeatedly acknowledges his inability to escape the past entirely. Rorty reminds us, invoking Neurath's image, that we are people on a ship at sea who are constrained in the realization of our most radical visions of a new and better ship by our inability to replace all of the existing ship's planks at once.[63] Prophetic imagination freed completely from history is perceived as madness. Thus, any effective prophecy, including

Rorty's, is necessarily the product of varying degrees of both imagination and history.

It is in this context that one must understand Rorty's acknowledgment that "the contingencies of history" make it difficult for him (and us) to "see the kind of individual freedom which the modern liberal state offers its citizens as just one more value."[64]   Similarly, Rorty attributes his (our) ideal of a society in which pain and cruelty are minimized to his (our) historically contingent socialization process and "the sense of human solidarity which the development of democratic institutions has facilitated."[65]   But the past neither wholly determines nor wholly constitutes Rorty's prophecy.  History simply provides the inescapable roots of Rorty's own imaginative flower of a "poeticized" culture.[66]

### III. The Relationship Between Prophecy and Antifoundationalism

In their haste to mistakenly criticize Rorty for being a complacent defender of the status quo, legal scholars have failed to raise a potentially much more devastating issue.  They have never undertaken to evaluate, *by Rorty's own pragmatist terms*, his claims for a postmetaphysical culture in the context of progressive social change.   What use is antifoundationalism for achieving progressive social change as Rorty defines it?   Or, in other words, what is the relationship between prophecy, which Rorty suggests is necessary for progressive social change, and the antifoundationalism that he advocates?   Despite the centrality and importance of this issue, Rorty, like his critics, seems never directly to confront it.

Certainly, the fact that a society has given up metaphysics for antifoundationalism would not eliminate its need for progressive social change (or, therefore, for prophets such as narrators and separatist group leaders).  To suggest otherwise would be to hold out antifoundationalism as the Truth toward which the world has been converging—and Rorty, as an antifoundationalist, explicitly rejects the metaphysical notion that the world is "converg[ing] toward an already existing Truth."[67]

Would the postmetaphysical culture that Rorty advocates have any advantages over our current metaphysical one for achieving progressive social change?  To begin, there are several pertinent differences between an antifoundationalist culture, as Rorty describes it, and the existing metaphysical one. First, members of an antifoundationalist culture would understand   that   everything—"our   language,   our   conscience,   our community"—is a product of contingency, of time and chance.[68] They would therefore be "people who combined commitment with a sense of the contingency of their own commitment."[69] Second, their pervasive sense of contingency would make them skeptical that any status quo was either necessary or the best possible world.[70]

Third, members of an antifoundationalist culture would not employ, or be receptive to, foundationalist vocabulary and forms of argument.[71] They would not use words like "truth," "nature," "reality," and "reason" as warrants for certitude the way we often do at present. And their "arguments" would therefore more often be suggestions that one simply try thinking of things a different (and hopefully more useful) way, or suggestions that it might be more useful simply to stop doing certain things and do something else.[72] Fourth, a postmetaphysical culture will have made "a general turn against theory and toward narrative."[73] According to Rorty, "[s]uch a turn would be emblematic of our having given up the attempt to hold all the sides of our life in a single vision, to describe them with a single vocabulary."[74] Finally, members of an antifoundationalist culture would have a conception of progressive social change as an endless process of "the realization of utopias and the envisaging of still further utopias."[75]

Assuming *arguendo* that a postmetaphysical culture will have the characteristics Rorty attributes to it, what will that mean for progressive social change? Consider first the members of the society in which a prophet, such as a narrator or a separatist group leader, will be working. Will living in a postmetaphysical culture make that society more likely than at present to join with a prophet in realizing her vision of a less cruel world, more likely than at present to be moved by a narrator toward increased human solidarity? There seems little reason to believe so, despite Rorty's inconsistent, but often hopeful, claims.

At his most optimistic, Rorty asserts that for "the preservation and progress of democratic societies" an antifoundationalist vocabulary ("which revolves around notions of metaphor and self-creation") is preferable to a metaphysical vocabulary (which revolves around "notions of truth, rationality, and moral obligation.")[76] Indeed, he claims that this latter vocabulary of Enlightenment rationalism "has become an impediment" to social progress.[77] In a similarly positive vein, Rorty asserts that "reformulat[ing] the hopes of liberal society in a nonrationalist and nonuniversalist way" will "further their realization better than older descriptions of them did."[78]

At other times, however, Rorty's claim for an antifoundationalist culture is substantially weaker and more tentative. Rorty states, with regard to progressive social change, that an antifoundationalist culture (in which the "nonintellectuals" are "commonsensically nominalist and historicist") could "be every bit as self-critical and every bit as devoted to human equality as our own familiar, and still metaphysical, liberal culture—if not more so."[79] He then assures us that the general adoption of antimetaphysical, antiessentialist views in the public at large at least will do no harm: It will not "weaken and dissolve liberal societies."[80] Less optimistic still, Rorty asserts that individuals whose lives are given meaning by "the sort of social hope which characterizes modern liberal societies"—"that life will eventually be freer, less cruel, more leisure, richer in goods and experiences, not just for our descendants but for everyone's descendants"[81]—are unlikely to be interested in, much less adversely affected by, philosophers who are questioning metaphysics. "The idea that liberal societies are bound together by philosophical beliefs seems to me ludicrous,"[82] Rorty explains. At his least hopeful, Rorty concedes that "[i]t is possible that [the shift to an antifoundationalist culture] would weaken and dissolve liberal societies."[83]

Rorty never supports his more optimistic claims for antifoundationalism with explanations of how or why antifoundationalist vocabulary and reformulations of social hopes will be *superior* to metaphysical ones for achieving progressive social change. Is there nonetheless any reason to believe that antifoundationalism will be more useful than metaphysics for achieving progressive social change, as Rorty defines it? One possible advantage of an antifoundationalist culture that Rorty seems to imply is its potentially greater revisability. In the present culture, metaphysics anchors the bulk of our beliefs, some of which may impede social progress. So, eliminating those metaphysical anchors might yield a more "revisable" culture.

There are several problems with this argument. First, greater "revisability" alone does not increase the likelihood that any changes that occur in the society will be in the direction of progress. Revisability, after all, is as much a precondition for a society moving *away* from Rorty's vision of a better world as it is for moving *toward* it. Second, any metaphysical notion, such as religion or truth, which might impede progressive social change, might also expedite it. Martin Luther King, for example, shared Rorty's utopian vision. That he was a minister and frequently invoked religious concepts when advocating social change did not diminish his influence as a prophet, but rather was much of the source of it. Similarly, an antifoundationalist society may be *less* inclined to follow a prophet who can promise only a "contingent vision of a better world" than a metaphysical society is to follow a prophet who asserts that moral truth or God is on his side. For the latter prophet may be relatively better at inspiring and motivating, at capturing the imagination of his society. Thus, it is not clear that an antifoundationalist culture would be more revisable in the direction of social progress, that it would have more, or more influential, prophets who would share Rorty's vision of a better world.

In the end, Rorty persuades one only of that for which no persuading was necessary: An antifoundationalist culture (*by definition*) will be different from our foundationalist one. Notwithstanding his general claim that a postmetaphysical culture would be desirable, Rorty does not convince one that such a culture would be more useful than a metaphysical culture for purposes of alleviating oppression in American society. Rorty cannot—and does not—argue that a shift to antifoundationalism will eliminate America's need for progressive social change, that antifoundationalism is the Truth toward which our society has been converging. Nor does he persuade one that a cultural shift to antifoundationalism would be advantageous for realizing even his own utopian vision.

## IV. Pragmatic Prophets

If our culture does not move from foundationalism to antifoundationalism, would subscribing to the latter nonetheless be of greater use to prophets than a belief in metaphysics? Throughout his writings, Rorty's answer to this question seems to waver between "no" and "yes, quite a bit."

At one extreme, Rorty has stated that pragmatism has nothing to offer the prophet, the person with a vision for progressive social change: "[I]t seems to me that if you had the prophecy, you could skip the pragmatism."[84] In addition, Rorty has described pragmatism in the context of progressive social change as "something comparatively small and unimportant, a set of answers to philosophical questions—questions which arise only for people who find philosophical topics intriguing rather than silly."[85] Thus, with regard to pragmatism's "critical bite," Rorty notes that "pragmatism bites other philosophies, but not social problems as such—and so is as useful to fascists like Mussolini and conservatives like Oakeshott as it is to liberals like Dewey."[86]

At the other extreme, however, is the bulk of Rorty's recent Tanner Lecture, "Feminism and Pragmatism." There he states that feminist prophets—persons such as Catherine MacKinnon and Marilyn Frye who have a vision of a better world—"might profit from thinking with the pragmatists."[87]    With seeming modesty Rorty claims that "*All* we [antifoundationalists] can do is to offer feminists a few pieces of special-purpose ammunition—for example, some additional replies to charges that their aims are unnatural, their demands irrational, or their claims hyperbolic."[88]    Rorty goes on, however, to detail three much more important ways that he believes antifoundationalism might be useful to feminist prophets.  First, it provides a way for them to conceptualize the process of progressive social change and therefore, their job.[89]  Second, and related, antifoundationalism provides a rhetoric—a vocabulary and form of argument—for use with those one is trying to persuade.[90] Third, antifoundationalism can provide prophets a kind of moral support.[91]

Rorty's rather extreme positions cannot both be correct.  When his discussion is examined closely, a belief in antifoundationalism appears useful only to especially intellectual prophets who get into philosophical or    theoretical    quagmires.         Neither    the    visionary    nor    the persuasive/political parts of every prophet's job appears to be aided by a belief in antifoundationalism.  As Rorty defines her, a prophet has two chief characteristics:    a vision of a "better" world, and a voice to describe that dream.[92]    Already implicit in Rorty's notion of the prophet's dream are two of the things that a belief in antifoundationalism might be able to provide:  skepticism about the status quo, and the understanding that social progress is not about reasoning from first principles, but about responding to human needs, about "what works" (or might work).

In addition, a belief in antifoundationalism would not seem to be either necessary or sufficient for having a vision of a better world, for being a prophet who advocates progressive social change.  Even Rorty disclaims its necessity:  "Prophets are wherever you find them.  The great heroes—the prophetic leaders—in eastern Europe now are a faceless bureaucrat, Gorbachev, and a playwright, Havel. . . . I don't know who our [American] analogues of Havel and Gorbachev are going to be.  But I doubt very much that they will take their inspiration either from  deconstruction  or  from  neopragmatism."[93]    And  being  an antifoundationalist is not sufficient for becoming a prophet who advocates progressive social change because not all of the existing self-proclaimed pragmatists are prophets.

But is antifoundationalism useful in the three important ways Rorty suggested it might be when discussing feminist prophets?  It does not appear so. First, Rorty states that "pragmatist philosophy might be useful to feminist politics"[94] because of the way the former conceptualizes (redescribes) social progress: "by substituting metaphors of evolutionary development for metaphors of progressively less distorted perception," and by "drop[ping] the appearance-reality distinction in favor of a distinction between beliefs which serve some purposes and beliefs which serve other purposes."[95] Rorty adds that pragmatists "commend ourselves to feminists on the ground that we can fit [their claim that a new voice is needed] into *our* view of moral progress with relative ease."[96]

But is it really useful to prophets to conceptualize their own vision, the societal change they advocate, as being part of a larger, endless evolutionary process? Not necessarily. For such a conceptualization to be useful, it should somehow make the prophet's work more effective or easier. Rorty does not make a case that this conceptualization, without more, would be useful in this way—nor is such an argument easy to generate. Indeed, an antifoundationalist conception of social change as evolution may dilute both the prophet's belief in his own vision and his motivation to effect social change. It is one thing to believe (as a prophet, by definition, does) that the status quo is neither necessary nor the best possible state of affairs; but quite another to believe that the better world one envisions and would work toward achieving is also a contingency, a mere resting point in a larger evolution.

Rorty claims that the recognition of contingency that underlies the antifoundationalist conception of social change need not dilute the prophet's sense of conviction in his vision. He argues that "a belief can still regulate action, can still be thought worth dying for, among people who are quite aware that this belief is caused by nothing deeper than contingent historical circumstance."[97] Perhaps. But the question still remains as to whether this recognition of contingency makes the prophet *more* effective in any way. Rorty makes no case that it does.

According to Rorty, antifoundationalism offers feminist prophets rules of rhetoric consistent with an antifoundationalist conceptualization of social change. He suggests that feminists quit using words like "in truth" and "in reality," that they quit invoking "an ahistoricist realism," and instead see themselves as creating a new language through which they would simultaneously be creating what they did not before have: "a moral identity *as* women."[98] Rorty promises that with new linguistic practices come "new social constructs."[99] In addition to abandoning their old universalist and realist rhetoric, Rorty suggests that feminists should use substantively different arguments in attempting to persuade others to their view. Feminists, he argues, should "drop the notion that the subordination of women is *intrinsically* abominable, drop . . . the claim that there is something called 'right' or 'justice' or 'humanity' which has always been on their side, making their claims true."[100] Instead, they should "just make invidious comparisons between the actual present and a possible, if inchoate, future."[101] This is the only form of argument left, Rorty notes, when "one sees the need for something more than an appeal to rational acceptability by the standards of the existing community."[102]

There are two problems with Rorty's suggestions. First, as Rorty himself acknowledges, antifoundationalism cannot provide prophets (or anyone else) a *method* for selling their visions (or doing anything else): "There is no method or procedure to be followed except courageous and imaginative experimentation."[103] Second, as Rorty also notes, the extent to which metaphysics holds sway in our world means that "practical politics will doubtless often require [prophets] to speak with the universalist vulgar. . . ."[104] Indeed, antifoundationalist rhetoric and arguments would seem to be of questionable use to prophets who are selling their vision to a foundationalist society.

Finally, Rorty would have feminist prophets who are feeling discouraged look to antifoundationalism for a kind of "moral support." Rorty claims that antifoundationalism and political radicalism, such as feminism, "are compatible and mutually supporting": "This is because pragmatism allows for the possibility of expanding logical space, and thereby for an appeal to courage and imagination rather than to putatively neutral criteria."[105] In addition, Rorty exhorts feminists to have faith in their prophecy, their vision: "Prophecy, as we [pragmatists] see it, is all that non-violent political movements can fall back on when argument fails."[106] To be sure, some (rather intellectual) feminist prophets may be bolstered by Rorty's exhortation. But will not antifoundationalism then have become for the prophet what Rorty has claimed, with some disdain, that metaphysical entities are for the realist and universalist: "something large and powerful" that is on one's side and enables one to keep trying.[107]

Despite Rorty's broader claims, he persuades one ultimately only that antifoundationalism might be useful to especially intellectual prophets who need to extricate themselves from philosophical or theoretical hassles. Rorty convinces one only that if highly intellectual feminists redescribe themselves and their project in antifoundationalist terms, they will free themselves from the "philosophical" demand for a "general theory of oppression."[108] More importantly, feminists will then no longer need to raise "unanswerable questions about the accuracy of their representations of 'woman's experience'. They would instead see themselves as *creating* such an experience by creating a language, a tradition, and an identity."[109]

## V. Conclusion

Notwithstanding the claims of many legal scholars, and sometimes Richard Rorty, pragmatism is of scant use in alleviating oppression in American society. Rorty's own discussion of progressive social change is deceptive on this score because it contains both a prophetic and a processual strand. And pragmatic antifoundationalism entails the substance of only the latter strand. Thus Rorty's exhortation to look out for marginalized people is best understood as dictated by his prophecy, not his pragmatism. In contrast, Rorty's seeming defense of existing institutions does not indicate the absence of a utopian vision, but is rather the result of his pragmatist historicism and acknowledgment of contingency in crafting a prophecy.

The central issue that neither Rorty nor his critics has confronted is whether, by Rorty's own pragmatist terms, he shows antifoundationalism to be useful in realizing his own utopian vision. Evaluating Rorty's claims for antifoundationalism by his own pragmatist criterion of "usefulness" points up two distinct strains within pragmatism: Antifoundationalism and instrumentalism. And there would not seem to be any necessary connection between these two strains.

In this chapter I have argued that Rorty does not support his more hopeful claims for an antifoundationalist culture with convincing explanations of how or why that culture will be more useful than our current metaphysical one for achieving progressive social change. Nor has he provided persuasive evidence that subscribing to antifoundationalism will be of greater use to prophets than a belief in metaphysics. As a good pragmatist, Rorty cannot therefore be sure that antifoundationalism is preferable to metaphysics for realizing his—or any other—utopian vision.

In the end, pragmatism appears to be useful in achieving progressive social change to the extent that one profits from statements such as, "There is no method or procedure to be followed except courageous and imaginative experimentation."[110] Or, as the Nike people say, "Just do it."

# Notes

I am grateful to Jessica Feldman, Ken Kress, Dan Ortiz, Dick Rorty, George Rutherglen, and Bill Weaver for challenging conversations and careful readings of earlier drafts.

1. See, for example, Allan Hutchinson, "The Three 'Rs': Reading/Rorty/Radically," *Harvard Law Review* 103 (December 1990), 563—566; Martha Minow and Elizabeth V. Spelman, "In Context," *Southern California Law Review* 63 (September 1990): 1601 (reprinted as Chapter 13 in this book); Margaret Radin, "The Pragmatist and the Feminist," *Southern California Law Review* 63 (September 1990): 1699—1700 (reprinted as Chapter 8 in this book); Mari Matsuda, "Pragmatism Modified and The False Consciousness Problem," *Southern California Law Review* 63 (September 1990): 1763—1764; Joseph William Singer, "Property and Coercion in Federal Indian Law:    The Conflict Between Critical and Complacent Pragmatism," *Southern California Law Review* 63 (September 1990): 1821—1822; Joseph William Singer, "Should Lawyers Care About Philosophy?" *Duke Law Journal* 1989 (December 1989): 1765—1766.

2. See, for example, Hutchinson, "Reading/Rorty/Radically," 566—573, 583—585; Minow and Spelman, "In Context," 1600—1601, 1609—1615, 1647—1652; Radin, "The Pragmatist and The Feminist," 1705—1719; Matsuda, "Pragmatism Modified," 1764—1768; Singer, "Property," 1822—1824, 1837—1841; Singer, "Should Lawyers Care," 1759—1766.

3. Richard Rorty, *Contingency, Irony, and Solidarity,* xv, cited in bibliography.

4. Ibid., 60 ("liberal society is one which has no purpose except freedom"); Rorty, *Consequences of Pragmatism,* 69—70, cited in bibliography (there is "no better cause" than "enlarging human freedom").

5. Ibid., 53.

6. Ibid., xiv.

7. Ibid., xv.

8. Ibid.

9. Richard Rorty, "Feminism and Pragmatism," *Michigan Quarterly Review* 30 (spring 1990): 242; *see also*, Richard Rorty, "Thugs and Theorists: A Reply to Bernstein," *Political Theory* 15 (November 1987): 565 ("There is nothing sacred about either the free market or about central planning; the proper balance between the two is a matter of experimental tinkering.")

10. Rorty, *Contingency,* xvi.  "[O]ur sense of solidarity is strongest when those with whom solidarity is expressed are thought of as 'one of us,' where 'us' means something smaller and more local than the human race." Ibid., 191.

11. Ibid., xvi.

12. Ibid., (emphasis added).

13. Ibid., 144.

14. Ibid., xvi.

15. Ibid., 93.

16. Ibid., xvi (emphasis in original).

17. Ibid., 192.

18. Ibid., xvi.

19. Ibid.

20. Rorty, "Feminism and Pragmatism," 240.

21. Ibid., 247.

22. Ibid.

23. Ibid., 248.

24. Ibid.

25. Ibid.

26. Ibid., 247.

27. Ibid.

28. Rorty, *Contingency*, 143.

29. Rorty, "Feminism and Pragmatism," 233.

30. Richard Rorty, "Two Cheers for the Cultural Left," *South Atlantic Quarterly* 89 (1990): 229.

31. Richard A. Posner, "What Has Pragmatism to Offer Law?," *Southern California Law Review* 63 (September 1990), 1660.

32. At a less specific level, Richard Posner has posited "three 'essential' elements" of pragmatism: (1) "a distrust of metaphysical entities . . . viewed as warrants for certitude"; (2) "an insistence that propositions be tested by their consequences, by the difference they make"; and (3) "an insistence on judging our projects . . . by their conformity to social or other human needs rather than to 'objective,' 'impersonal' criteria." Ibid., 1660—1661.

33. Rorty, *Contingency*, xv.

34. Ibid., 54.

35. Ibid., 54.

36. Ibid., 58.

37. Ibid., 9.

38. Ibid., 7.

39. Ibid., 196.

40. Singer, "Property," 1826.

41. Hutchinson, "Reading/Rorty/Radically," 564.

42. Rorty, *Contingency*, 196.

43. Singer, "Should Lawyers Care," 1766.

44. Mari Matsuda would "bend pragmatism toward liberation" in several ways. She would: (1) "weight the pragmatic method to identify and give special credence to the perspective of the subordinated"; (2) "add a first principle of anti-subordination"; and (3) "claim that the use of pragmatic method with a normative first principle is not inconsistent." Matsuda, "Pragmatism Modified," 1764.

Radin would use "feminist methodology and perspective" to remedy what she takes to be pragmatism's "problem of bad coherence." Radin, "The Pragmatist and the Feminist," 1708—1711. She asserts that "rootedness in the experiences of oppression makes possible the distinctive critical contribution that feminism can make to pragmatism." Ibid., 1708.

45. Rorty, "Two Cheers," 233.

46. Ibid., 233.

47. Singer, "Property," 1825.

48. Hutchinson, "Reading/Rorty/Radically," 564.

49. See, for example, Hutchinson, "Reading/Rorty/Radically," 563—573, 583—585; Minow and Spelman, "In Context," 1611—1612, 1650; Singer, "Property," 1825—1826; Singer, "Should Lawyers Care," 1759—1766.

50. Rorty, *Contingency*, 84.

51. See, for example, ibid., 47, 84, 198.

52. Ibid., xv, 53, 60.

53. Ibid., 84.

54. Ibid., 84—85.

55. Ibid., 63.

56. Ibid., 197; Rorty, "Two Cheers," 229; Rorty, "Feminism and Pragmatism," 253 n. 15.

57. Rorty, *Contingency*, 197; Rorty, "Feminism and Pragmatism," 253.

58. Rorty, "Feminism and Pragmatism," 253.

59. Rorty, *Contingency*, xv, 60.

60. Ibid., 197.

61. Ibid., 84.

62. Ibid., 68.

63. Richard Rorty, "Solidarity or Objectivity?", in *Objectivity, Relativism, and Truth* (Cambridge: Cambridge University Press, 1991), 29. "[W]e can *understand* the revolutionary's suggestion that a sailable boat can't be made out of the planks which make up ours, and that we must simply abandon ship. But we cannot take this suggestion seriously. . . . Our community—the community of the liberal intellectuals of the secular modern West—wants to be able to give a *post factum* account of any change of view. We want to be able, so to speak, to justify ourselves to our earlier selves. This preference is not built into us by human nature. It is just the way *we* live now." Ibid. (emphasis in original; footnote omitted).

64. Rorty, *Contingency*, 50.

65. Ibid., 197.

66. Ibid., 53.

67. Ibid., xvi.

68. Ibid., 22.

69. Ibid., 61.

70. Ibid., xv—xvi, 61.

71. Ibid., 7—9.

72. Ibid.

73. Ibid., xvi.

74. Ibid.

75. Ibid. This process would yield "a history of increasingly useful metaphors rather than of increasing understanding of how things really are." Ibid., 9.

76. Ibid., 44.

77. Ibid.

78. Ibid., 44—45.

79. Ibid., 87.

80. Ibid., 85.

81. Ibid., 86.

82. Ibid.

83. Ibid., 85.

84. "Afterword," *Southern California Law Review* 63 (September 1990), 1917.

85. Rorty, "Feminism and Pragmatism," 238.

86. Ibid., 255 n23.

87. Ibid., 237.

88. Ibid., 238.

89. Ibid., 233—236, 238, 240—241, 246—249.

90. Ibid., 236—242.

91. Ibid., 235—236, 241—242.

92. Ibid., 232.

93. "Afterword," 1917—1918.

94. Rorty, "Feminism and Pragmatism," 234.

95. Ibid.

96. Ibid., 236.   This is the advantage Rorty claims that pragmatists have over universalists and realists.

97. Rorty, *Contingency*, 189.

98. Rorty, "Feminism and Pragmatism," 236—237 (emphasis added).

99. Ibid., 236.

100. Ibid., 237.

101. Ibid., 242.

102. Ibid., 239.
103. Ibid., 242.
104. Ibid., 237.
105. Ibid., 242.
106. Ibid., 235.
107. Ibid., 254.
108. Ibid., 238.
109. Ibid.
110. Ibid., 242.

# 7

## The Limits of Neopragmatism

### Cornel West

The renascence of pragmatism in philosophy, literary criticism, and legal thought in the past few years is a salutary development. It is part of a more general turn toward historicist approaches to truth and knowledge. I am delighted to see intellectual interest rekindled in Peirce, James, and especially Dewey. Yet I suspect that the new pragmatism may repeat and reproduce some of the blindness and silences of the old pragmatism—most importantly, an inadequate grasp of the complex operations of power principally owing to a reluctance to take traditions of historical sociology and social theory seriously. In this article, my strategy shall be as follows. First, I shall briefly map the different kinds of neopragmatisms in relation to perspectives regarding epistemology, theory, and politics. Second, I shall suggest that neopragmatic viewpoints usually fail to situate their own projects in terms of present-day crises—including the crisis of purpose and vocation now raging in the professions. Third, I will try to show how my conception of prophetic pragmatism may provide what is needed to better illuminate and respond to these crises.

Much of the excitement about neopragmatism has to do with the antifoundationalist epistemic claims it puts forward. The idea that there are no self-justifying, intrinsically credible, or ahistorical courts of appeal to terminate chains of epistemic justification calls into question positivistic and formalistic notions of objectivity, necessity, and transcendentality.

In this sense, all neopragmatists are antifoundationalists; that is, the validation of knowledge-claims rests on practical judgments constituted by, and constructed in, dynamic social practices. For neopragmatists, we mortal creatures achieve and acquire knowledge by means of self-critical and self-correcting social procedures rooted in a variety of human processes.

Yet all neopragmatists are not anti-realists. For example, Peircean pragmatists are intent on sidestepping any idealist or relativist traps and therefore link a social conception of knowledge to a regulative ideal of truth. This viewpoint attempts to reject metaphysical conceptions of reality *and* skeptical reductions of truth-talk to knowledge-talk. In contrast, Deweyan pragmatists tend to be less concerned with charges of idealism or relativism owing to a more insouciant attitude toward truth. In fact, some Deweyan pragmatists—similar to some sociologists of knowledge and idealists—wrongly collapse truth-claims into warranted assertability-claims or rational acceptability-claims. Such moves provide fodder for the cannons of not only Peircean pragmatists, but also old-style realists and foundationalists. To put it crudely, truth at the moment cannot be the truth about things, yet warranted assertable claims are the only truths we can get. To miss the subtle distinction between dynamic knowledge and regulative truth is to open the door to metaphysics or slide down the slippery slope of sophomoric relativism. Yet the anti-foundationalists claims put forward by neopragmatists are often construed such that many open such doors or slide down such slopes. In short, epistemic pluralism degenerates into an epistemic promiscuity that encourages epistemic policing by realists and foundationists.

Neopragmatists disagree even more sharply in regarding the role of theory (explanatory accounts of the past and present). All neopragmatists shun grand theory because it smacks of metaphysical posturing. Yet this shunning often shades into a distrust of theory per se—hence a distancing from revisable social theories, provisional cultural theories, or heuristic historical theories. This distrust may encourage an ostrich-like piecemeal incrementalism that reeks of a vulgar anti-theoreticism. On this view, neopragmatism amounts to crude practicalism. The grand pragmatism of Dewey and especially C. Wright Mills rejects such a view. Instead, it subtly incorporates an experimental temper within theory-laden descriptions of problematic situations (for example, social and cultural crises). Unfortunately, the pragmatist tradition is widely associated with a distrust of theory that curtails its ability to fully grasp the operations of power within the personal, social, and historical contexts of human activities.

It is no accident that the dominant form of politics in the pragmatist tradition accents the pedagogical and the dialogical. Such a noble liberalism assumes that vast disparities in resources, enormous polarizations in perceptions, or intense conflicts of interests can be overcome by means of proper education and civil conversation. If persuasive historical sociological claims show that such disparities, polarizations, and conflicts often produce improper agitation and uncivil confrontation the dominant form of politics in the pragmatist tradition is paralyzed or at least rendered more impotent than it is commonly believed. One crucial theme or subtext in my genealogy on pragmatism is the persistence of the sense of impotence of liberal intellectuals in American culture and society primarily because of unattended class and regional disparities, unacknowledged racial and sexual polarizations, and untheorized cultural and personal conflicts that permeate and pervade our past and present. My view neither downplays nor devalues education and conversation; it simply highlights the structural background conditions of pedagogical efforts and dialogical events.

This leads me to my second concern, namely, the relative absence of pragmatist accounts of why pragmatism surfaces now in the ways and forms that it does. Such an account must situate the nature of pragmatist intellectual interventions—their intended effects and unintended consequences—in the present historical moment in American society and culture. I suspect that part of the renascence of neopragmatism can be attributed to the crisis of purpose and vocation in humanistic studies and professional schools. On this view, the recent hunger for interdisciplinary studies—or the erosion of disciplinary boundaries—promoted by neopragmatisms, poststructuralisms, Marxisms, and feminisms is not only motivated by a quest for truth but also activated by power struggles over what kinds of knowledge should be given status, be rewarded, and be passed on to young informed citizens in the next century. These power struggles are not simply over positions and curriculums but also over ideals of what it means to be humanistic intellectuals in a declining empire—in a first-rate military power, a near rescinding economic power, and a culture in decay. As Henry Adams suggests, the example of a turn toward history is most evident in American culture when decline is perceived to be undeniable and intellectuals feel most removed from the action. Furthermore, pragmatism at its best in James and Dewey provided a sense of purpose and vocation for intellectuals who believed they could make a difference in the public life of the nation. And it is not surprising that the first perceivable consequence of the renascence of neopragmatism led by Richard Rorty echoed James's attack on professionalization and specialization. In this sense, Rorty's *Philosophy and the Mirror of*

*Nature* not only told the first major and influential story of analytical philosophy, but was also a challenging narrative of how contemporary intellectuals have come to be contained within professional and specialized social spaces with little outreach to a larger public and hence little visibility in, and minimal effect on, the larger society. Needless to say, Rorty's revival of Jamesian anti-professionalism—not to be confused with anti-intellectualism or even anti-academicism—has increased intellectuals' interest in public journalism and intensified the tension between journalists and academics.

The crisis of purpose and vocation in humanistic studies and professional schools is compounded by the impact of the class and regional disparities, racial and sexual polarizations, and cultural and personal conflicts that can no longer be ignored. This impact not only unsettles our paradigms in the production of knowledge but also forces us to interrogate and examine our standards, criteria, styles, and forms in which knowledge is assessed, legitimated, and expressed. At its worst, pragmatism in the academy permits us to embrace this impact without attending to the implications of power. At its best, pragmatism behooves us to critically scrutinize this impact as we promote the democratization of American intellectual life without vulgar levelling or symbolic tokenism.

But what is this "pragmatism at its best"? What form does it take? What are its constitutive features or fundamental components? These questions bring me to my third point—the idea of a prophetic pragmatist perspective and praxis. I use the adjective "prophetic" in order to harken back to the rich, though flawed, traditions of Judaism and Christianity that promote courageous resistance against, and relentless critiques of, injustice and social misery. These traditions are rich in that they help keep alive collective memories of moral (that is, anti-idolatrous) struggle and nonmarket values (that is, love for others, loyalty to an ethical ideal, and social freedom) in a more and more historically amnesiac society and market-saturated culture. These traditions are flawed because they tend toward dogmatic pronouncements (that is, "Thus saith the Lord") to homogeneous constituencies. Prophetic pragmatism gives courageous resistance and relentless critique a self-critical character and democratic content; that is, it analyzes the social causes of unnecessary forms of social misery, promotes moral outrage against them, organizes different constituencies to alleviate them, yet does so with an openness to its own blindnesses and shortcomings.

Prophetic pragmatism is pragmatism at its best because it promotes a critical temper and democratic faith without making criticism a fetish or democracy an idol. The fetishization of criticism yields a sophisticated ironic consciousness of parody and paralysis, just as the idolization of democracy produces mob rule. As Peirce, James, and Dewey noted, criticism always presupposes something in place—be it a set of beliefs or a tradition. Criticism yields results or makes a difference when something significant is antecedent to it, such as rich, sustaining collective memories of moral struggle. Similarly, democracy assumes certain conditions for its flourishing—like a constitutional background. Such conditions for democracy are not subject to public veto.

Critical temper as a way of struggle and democratic faith as a way of life are the twin pillars of prophetic pragmatism. The major foes to be contested are despair, dogmatism, and oppression. The critical temper promotes a full-fledged experimental disposition that highlights the provisional, tentative, and revisable character of our visions, analyses, and actions. Democratic faith consists of a Pascalian wager (hence underdetermined by the evidence) on the abilities and capacities of ordinary people to participate in decisionmaking procedures of institutions that fundamentally regulate their lives. The critical temper motivated by democratic faith yields all-embracing moral and/or religious visions that project credible ameliorative possibilities grounded in present realities in light of systemic structural analyses of the causes of social misery (without reducing all misery to historical causes). Such analyses must appeal to traditions of social theory and historical sociology just as visions must proceed from traditions of moral and/or religious communities. The forms of prophetic praxis depend on the insights of the social theories and the potency of the moral and/or religious communities. In order for these analyses and visions to combat despair, dogmatism, and oppression, the existential, communal, and political dimensions of prophetic pragmatism must be accented. The existential dimension is guided by the value of *love*—a risk-ridden affirmation of the distinct humanity of others that, at its best, holds despair at bay. The communal dimension is regulated by *loyalty*—a profound devotion to the critical temper and democratic faith that eschews dogmatism. The political dimension is guided by *freedom*—a perennial quest for self-realization and self-development that resists all forms of oppression.

The tradition of pragmatism is in need of a mode of cultural criticism that keeps track of social misery, solicits and channels moral outrage to alleviate it, and projects a future in which the potentialities of ordinary people flourish and flower. The first wave of pragmatism foundered on the rocks of cultural conservatism and corporate liberalism. Its defeat was tragic. Let us not permit the second wave of pragmatism to end as farce.

# 8

## The Pragmatist and the Feminist

### *Margaret Jane Radin*

I want to discuss pragmatism and feminism. I undertake this project not because I have read everything considered feminist or pragmatist by its writers or readers, although I wish I had, but rather because I have discovered that in my own work I am speaking both of pragmatism and feminism. I desire to explore how pragmatism and feminism cohere, if they do, in my own thought, and I write with the hope that what I find useful will be useful for others as well.

I offer four interlinked short essays in which I think I am "doing" both pragmatism and feminism. Actually writing pragmatist-feminist analysis is one way to explore the question I pose, and perhaps it is the way most in the pragmatic spirit, or at least closest to the practice side of pragmatism. There is a theory side of pragmatism too, however, and I am interested in suggesting a broader theoretical connection between feminism and pragmatism as well.

### I. The Double Bind

I begin at the point it became clear to me that I was combining pragmatism and feminism. That point was in my thinking about the transition problem of the double bind in the context of contested commodification of sexuality and reproductive capacity.[1] If the social regime permits buying and selling of sexual and reproductive activities, thereby treating them as fungible market commodities given the current capitalistic understandings of monetary exchange, there is a threat to the personhood of women, who are the "owners" of these "commodities." The threat to personhood from commodification arises because essential attributes are treated as severable fungible objects, and this denies the integrity and uniqueness of the self. But if the social regime prohibits this kind of commodification, it denies women the choice to market their sexual or reproductive services, and given the current feminization of poverty and lack of avenues for free choice for women, this also poses a threat to the personhood of women. The threat from enforced noncommodification arises because narrowing women's choices is a threat to liberation, and because their choices to market sexual or reproductive services, even if nonideal, may represent the best alternatives available to those who would choose them.

Thus the double bind: both commodification and noncommodification may be harmful. Harmful, that is, under our current social conditions. Neither one need be harmful in an ideal world. The fact that money changes hands need not necessarily contaminate human interactions of sharing,[2] nor must the fact that a social order makes nonmonetary sharing its norm necessarily deprive or subordinate anyone. That commodification now tends toward fungibility of women and noncommodification now tends toward their domination and continued subordination are artifacts of the current social hierarchy. In other words, the fact of oppression is what gives rise to the double bind.

Thus, it appears that the solution to the double bind is not to solve but to dissolve it: remove the oppressive circumstances. But in the meantime, if we are practically limited to those two choices, which are we to choose? I think that the answer must be pragmatic. We must look carefully at the nonideal circumstances in each case and decide which horn of the dilemma is better (or less bad), and we must keep redeciding as time goes on.

To generalize a bit, it seems that there are two ways to think about justice. One is to think about justice in an ideal world, the best world that we can now conceive. The other is to think about nonideal justice: given where we now find ourselves, what is the better decision? In making this decision, we think about what actions can bring us closer to ideal justice. For example, if we allow commodification, we may push further away any ideal of a less commodified future. But if we enforce noncommodification, we may push further away any ideal of a less dominated future. In making our decisions of nonideal justice, we must also realize that these decisions will help to reconstitute our ideals. For example, if we commodify all attributes of personhood, the ideal of personhood we now know will evolve into another one that does not conceive fungibility as bad. The double bind, then, is a problem involving nonideal justice, and I think its only solution can be pragmatic.

There is no general solution; there are only piecemeal, temporary solutions.

I also think of the double bind as a problem of transition, because I think of nonideal justice as the process by which we try to make progress (effect a transition) toward our vision of the good world.[3] I think we should recognize that all decisions about justice, as opposed to theories about it, are pragmatic decisions in the transition. At the same time we should also recognize that ideal theory is also necessary, because we need to know what we are trying to achieve. In other words, our visions and nonideal decisions, our theory and practice, paradoxically constitute each other.

Having discovered the double bind in true pragmatic fashion, by working on a specific problem, I now see it everywhere. The double bind is pervasive in the issues we have thought of as "women's issues." The reason it is pervasive is to be sought in the perspective of oppression. For a group subject to structures of domination, all roads thought to be progressive can pack a backlash. I shall mention here a few other examples of the double bind: the special treatment/equal treatment debate, affirmative action, the understanding of rape, and the idea of marriage as a contract.

When we single out pregnancy, for example, for "special treatment," we fear that employers will not hire women. But if we do not accord special treatment to pregnancy, women will lose their jobs. If we grant special treatment, we bring back the bad old conception of women as weaker creatures; if we do not, we prevent women from becoming stronger in the practical world.[4] Feminist theory that tends toward the ideal, the visionary side of our thought about justice, has grasped the point that the dilemma must be dissolved because its framework is the conceptual framework of the oppressors (who define what is "special" and what is "equal"). But feminist theory that tends toward the nonideal practical side of our thought about justice has also realized that if the dominant conceptions are too deeply held at this time, trying to implement an alternative vision could be counterproductive. My personal view is that in the case of pregnancy, the time has come to convince everyone that both men and women should have the opportunity to be parents in a fulfilling sense, and that the old conceptions of the workplace now can begin to give way. But I think that each women's issue situation, such as pregnancy, workplace regulation to protect fetuses, and height and weight restrictions, will have to be evaluated separately, and continually reevaluated.

If there is a social commitment to affirmative action, in this nonideal time and place, then a woman or person of color who holds a job formerly closed to women and people of color is likely to be presumed to be underqualified.[5] More women and people of color will hold jobs, but few will be allowed to feel good about it. The dominant group will probably be able to make women and people of color meet higher standards than those applicable to white males, and yet at the same time convince everyone, including, often, the beneficiaries of affirmative action themselves, that as beneficiaries they are inferior. But what is our alternative? If there is no affirmative action commitment in place, far fewer women and people of color will hold these jobs; yet those who do, whatever vicissitudes they endure, will not endure this particular backlash. The pragmatic answer in most cases, I believe, is that backlash is better than complete exclusion, as long as the backlash is temporary. But if backlash can keep alive the bad old conceptions of women and people of color, how will we evolve toward better conceptions of the abilities of those who have been excluded?

Our struggle with how to understand rape seems to be another instance of the double bind. MacKinnon's view—or perhaps an oversimplified version of her view—is that under current conditions of gender hierarchy there is no clear dividing line between the sort of heterosexual intercourse that is genuinely desired by women and the sort that is unwelcome.[6] There can be no clear line because our very conception of sexuality is so deeply intertwined with male dominance that our desires as we experience them are problematic. Our own desires are socially constituted to reinforce patterns of male dominance against our own interest.[7] "Just say no" as the standard for determining whether rape has occurred is both under- and overinclusive. It is under-inclusive because women who haven't found their voices mean "no" and are unable to say it; and it is over-inclusive because, like it or not, the way sexuality has been constituted in a culture of male dominance, the male understanding that "no" means "yes" was often, and may still sometimes be, correct.[8] MacKinnon's view is painful. If there is no space for women to experience heterosexuality that is not suspect, what does that do to our self-esteem and personhood in a social setting in which sex is important to selfhood?

The other prong of the double bind—roughly represented by the views of Robin West—is that we should greet all of women's subjective experience with acceptance and respect.[9] That view is less threatening to personhood in one way but more so in another. How can we progress toward a social conception of sexuality that is less male-dominated if we do not regard with critical suspicion some of the male-dominated experiences we now take pleasure in?[10]

The last example of the double bind I want to mention is the conceptualization of marriage. Is marriage to be considered a contract in which certain distributions of goods are agreed to between autonomous bargaining agents? Upon divorce, such a conception of marriage makes it difficult for oppressed women who have not bargained effectively to obtain much. Or is marriage to be considered a noncontractual sharing status in which the partners' contributions are not to be monetized? Upon divorce, such a conception makes it difficult for oppressed women who have contributed unmonetized services to their husbands' advantage to obtain much. The idea of contractual autonomy may be more attractive in our nonideal world if the alternative is to be submerged in a status that gives all power to men. Yet the autonomy may be illusory because oppression makes equal bargaining power impossible. At the same time, the reinforcement of individualist bargaining models of human interaction is contrary to our vision of a better world and may alter that vision in a way we do not wish.[11]

Perhaps it is obvious that the reason the double bind recurs throughout feminist struggles is that it is an artifact of the dominant social conception of the meaning of gender. The double bind is a series of two-pronged dilemmas in which both prongs are, or can be, losers for the oppressed. Once we realize this, we may say it is equally obvious that the way out of the double bind is to dissolve these dilemmas by changing the framework that creates them. That is, we must dissolve the prevalent conception of gender.

Calling for dissolution of the prevalent conception of gender is the visionary half of the problem: we must create a new vision of the meaning of male and female in order to change the dominant social conception of gender and change the double bind. In order to do that, however, we need the social empowerment that the dominant social conception of gender keeps us from achieving.

Then how can we make progress? The other half of the problem is the nonideal problem of transition from the present situation toward our ideal. Here is where the pragmatist feminist comes into her own. The pragmatist solution is to confront each dilemma separately and choose the alternative that will hinder empowerment the least and further it the most. The pragmatist feminist need not seek a general solution that will dictate how to resolve all double bind issues. Appropriate solutions may all differ, depending on the current stage of women's empowerment, and how the proposed solution might move the current social conception of gender and our vision of how gender should be reconceived for the future. Indeed, the "same" double bind may demand a different solution tomorrow from the one we find best today.

## II. The Perspective of Domination
## and the Problem of Bad Coherence

*Women's standpoint is not an ossified truth that some feminist academicians have chiseled in stone for all women to worship; rather, it is a kaleidoscope of truths, continually shaping and reshaping each other, as more and different women begin to work and think together.*

—Rosemarie Tong[12]

*It was when I said,*
*"There is no such thing as the truth,"*
*That the grapes seemed fatter.*
*The fox ran out of his hole.*

*You... You said,*
*"There are many truths,*
*But they are not parts of a truth."*
*Then the tree, at night, began to change,*
*Smoking through green and smoking blue.*

—Wallace Stevens[13]

Over the past few years I have been continually struck with some points of resonance between the methodology and commitments of many who call themselves feminists and those of certain important figures in the new wave of pragmatism. It now seems to me that the points of resonance between feminism and pragmatism are worthy of some exploration.

I begin with an awareness that there is something problematic about my ambition to talk theoretically about pragmatism and feminism together. I want to avoid the type of exercise that tries to define two "isms" and then compare and contrast them. Insomuch as they are lively, these "isms" resist definition. There are a number of pragmatisms. At least there are distinctive strains stemming from Charles Sanders Peirce, William James, and John Dewey, and the new wave may be considered a fourth pragmatism. There are also a number of feminisms. One recent survey of feminist thought lists them as liberal, Marxist, radical, socialist, psychoanalytic, existentialist, and postmodern.[14]

One way to frame the investigation I have in mind would be to start with the question, Is feminism "really" pragmatism? (Or, is pragmatism "really" feminism?) If this is the question, one way to respond to it—a way I think would be both unpragmatic and unfeminist—is to ask what commitments or characteristics are common to all the pragmatisms we are certain are pragmatisms, and ask what commitments or characteristics are common to all the feminisms we are certain are feminisms. We would then see whether the feminist list includes both the necessary criteria for being pragmatist and enough or important enough criteria to be sufficient for being pragmatist, or whether the pragmatist list includes the necessary and sufficient criteria for being feminist. This definitional response is a blueprint of conceptualist methodology, an abstract exercise in reification that promises little of interest to a pragmatist or a feminist.

In a more pragmatic and feminist spirit of inquiry, we might ask instead another question. Of what use might it be to think of feminism and pragmatism as allied, as interpenetrating each other? In this and the next essay I will pursue this question in various ways. In order to do so I still have to engage in some problematic cataloguing, but at least it will be easier to deal with the inescapable incompleteness of that way of seeing matters. I can explore how in some ways it might be useful to consider pragmatism and feminism together, without having to have a definite answer to the (to a pragmatist inapposite) question of what pragmatism and feminism "really are." Feminism and pragmatism are not things; they are ways of proceeding. The pragmatists were famous for their theory of truth without the capital T—their theory that truth is inevitably plural, concrete, and provisional. John Dewey wrote, "Truth is a collection of truths; and these constituent truths are in the keeping of the best available methods of inquiry and testing as to matters of fact."[15] Similarly, William James wrote:

> Truth for us is simply a collective name for verification processes, just as health, wealth, strength, etc., are names for other processes connected with life, and also pursued because it pays to pursue them. Truth is *made*, just as health, wealth and strength are made, in the course of experience.[16]

Pragmatism and feminism largely share, I think, the commitment to finding knowledge in the particulars of experience.[17]   It is a commitment against abstract idealism, transcendence, foundationalism, and atemporal universality; and in favor of immanence, historicity, concreteness, situatedness, contextuality, embeddedness, narrativity of meaning.

If feminists largely share the pragmatist commitment that truth is hammered out piecemeal in the crucible of life and our situatedness, they also share the pragmatist understanding that truth is provisional and ever-changing.   Too, they also share the pragmatist commitment to concrete particulars.   Since the details of our life are connected with what we know, those details matter.   Thus, the pragmatist and the feminist both arrive at an embodied perspectivist view of knowledge.

It is not surprising that pragmatists have stressed embodiment more than other philosophers,[18] nor that feminists have stressed it even more. Once we understand that the details of our embodiment matter for what the world is for us (which in some pragmatist views is all the world is), then it must indeed be important that only one half of humans directly experience menstruation, pregnancy, birth, and lactation.   So it is no wonder that feminists write about prostitution, contract motherhood, rape, child care, and the PMS defense.   It is not just the fact that these are women's issues that makes these writings feminist—they are after all human issues—but specifically the instantiation of the perspective of female embodiment.

Another pragmatist commitment that is largely shared by feminists is the dissolution of traditional dichotomies.   Pragmatists and feminists have rejected the dichotomy between thought and action, or between theory and practice.   John Dewey especially made this his theme; and he also rejected the dichotomies of reason and feeling, mind and body, nature and nurture, connection and separation, and means and ends.[19] In a commitment that is not, at least not yet, shared by modern pragmatists, feminists have also largely rejected the traditional dichotomy of public (man) and private (woman).   For these feminists, the personal is political.[20]

One more strong resonance between the pragmatist and the feminist is in concrete methodology.   The feminist commitment to learning through consciousness raising in groups can be regarded as the culmination of the pragmatist understanding that, for consciousness to exist at all, there must be shared meaning arising out of shared interactions with the world.   A particularly clear statement of this pragmatist position is found in Dewey's *Experience and Nature*.

Dewey's treatment is suffused with the interrelationship of communication, meaning, and shared group experience. In one representative passage, Dewey says:

> The heart of language is not "expression" of something antecedent, much less expression of antecedent thought. It is communication; the establishment of cooperation in an activity in which there are partners, and in which the activity of each is modified and regulated by that partnership.[21]

The modern pragmatists' stress on conversation or dialogue stems from the same kind of understanding.

The special contribution of the methodology of consciousness raising is that it makes new meaning out of a specific type of experience, the experience of domination and oppression. In order to do so, it must make communication possible where before there was silence. In general, rootedness in the experiences of oppression makes possible the distinctive critical contribution that feminism can make to pragmatism. Feminist methodology and perspective make it possible to confront the problem of bad coherence, as I will now try to explain.

Pragmatists have tended toward coherence theories of truth and goodness.[22] Coherence theories tend toward conservativism, in the sense that when we are faced with new experiences and new beliefs, we fit them into our web with as little alteration of what is already there as possible. James said that "in this matter of belief we are all extreme conservatives."[23] According to James, we will count a new idea as true if we can use it to assimilate a new experience to our old beliefs without disturbing them too much.

> That new idea is truest which performs most felicitously its function of satisfying our double urgency. It makes itself true, gets itself classed as true, by the way it works; grafting itself then upon the ancient body of truth, which thus grows much as a tree grows by the activity of a new layer of cambium.[24]

James also said that truth is what is good in the way of belief,[25] meaning that we should, and do, believe those things that work best in our lives.

To those whose standpoint or perspective—whose embodied contextuality—is the narrative of domination and oppression, these coherence theories raise a question that is very hard for the pragmatist to answer. Is it possible to have a coherent system of belief, and have that system be coherently bad?[26] Those who have lived under sexism and racism know from experience that the answer must be yes. We know we cannot argue that any given sexist decision is wrong simply because it does not fit well with all our history and institutions, for the problem is more likely that it fits only too well. Bad coherence creates the double bind. Everywhere we look we find a dominant conception of gender undermining us.

But how can the pragmatist find a standpoint from which to argue that a system is coherent but bad, if pragmatism defines truth and good as coherence? Inattention to this problem is what makes pragmatism seem complacent, when it does. One answer to the problem of bad coherence, which the pragmatist will reject, is to bring back transcendence, natural law, or abstract idealism. Another answer, which the pragmatist can accept, is to take the commitment to embodied perspective very seriously indeed, and especially the commitment to the perspective of those who directly experience domination and oppression.

What this leads to, first, is either an expansive view of coherence that leaves room for broad critique of the dominant understandings and the status quo, or else, perhaps, to denial that pragmatism espouses coherence theory.[27] Its other consequences need exploring. It seems that a primary concomitant of the commitment to perspectivism might be a serious pluralism. "We" are looking for coherence in "our" commitments, but the most important question might be, Who is "we"? A serious pluralism might begin by understanding that there can be more than one "we." One "we" can have very different conceptions of the world, selves, communities, than another. Perhaps, at least practically speaking, each "we" can have its own coherence. Dominant groups have tended to understand themselves without question as the only "we," whereas oppressed groups, simply by virtue of recognizing themselves as an oppressed group, have understood that there can be plural "we's." Perhaps, then, we should understand the perspective of the oppressed as making possible an understanding that coherence can be plural.

A serious pluralism must also find a way to understand the problem of transition, as the "we" of an oppressed group seeks to change dominant conceptions in order to make possible its own empowerment.[28] One important problem of transition is false consciousness. If the perspective of the oppressed includes significant portions of the dominant conception of the world, and of the role of the oppressed group in it, then the oppressed perspective may well be incoherent, rather than a separate coherence to be recognized as a separate "reality." If this is a useful way to view the matter, then we can say that the perspective of the oppressed struggles to make itself coherent in order to make itself real.

What leads some pragmatists into complacency and over-respect for the status quo is partly the failure to ask, Who is "we"? And what are "our" material interests? Why does it "work" for "us" to believe this? It is not necessary for pragmatists to make this mistake. Dewey, especially, understood the connection between truth, goodness, and liberation.[29] He argued cogently that many of philosophy's earlier errors, such as belief in eternal abstract forms, were expressions of the social position of philosophers as an elite leisure class.[30] But the mistake is tempting for a pragmatist whose perspective is that of a member of the dominant group, because from that perspective it seems that one has "the" perspective. I suggest that feminism, in its pragmatic aspect, can correct this complacent tendency. The perspective of domination, and the critical ramifications it must produce once it is taken seriously, seem to be feminism's important contribution to pragmatism.

### III. A Mediating Way of Thinking?

In *Pragmatism: A New Name for Some Old Ways of Thinking*,[31] William James asked us to recognize a distinction between two opposing philosophical temperaments or ways of construing the world. He labeled these characteristic habits of thought as "tender-minded" and "tough-minded." In *In a Different Voice: Psychological Theory and Women's Development*,[32] Carol Gilligan asks us to recognize a distinction between two opposing conceptions of morality or paths of moral development. She labels these characteristic moral personalities as ethics (or ideologies) of "care" and of "justice." Gilligan associates the ethic of care with the moral development of mature women, and the ethic of justice with the moral development of mature men. The ethic of care is the "different voice" of women.

For those who are struck with the parallels between pragmatist and feminist thought, it is tempting to associate feminism with the tender-minded prong of James's dichotomy. It is also tempting, in view of Gilligan's striking findings and our subsequent reflection upon women's culture, to associate feminism with the ethic of care prong of Gilligan's dichotomy. Both of these tempting assimilations are mistaken. Moreover, there is a great deal to be learned from understanding the way in which they are mistaken.

In order to see why it is tempting to think of feminist thought as tender-minded, consider how we might schematically understand the characteristics of the moral conceptions labeled caring and justice. The following list probably summarizes the way we think of the distinction:

| *Ethic of Care* | *Ethic of Justice* |
|---|---|
| nonviolence | equality |
| needs, interests | fairness, rights |
| contextual | universal |
| responsibility, nurture | desert, rights |
| attachment, connection, community | separation, autonomy, individualism |
| interdependence | independence |
| cooperation | competition |
| concrete, embedded, perspectival | abstract, universal, principled |
| narrative | systematic |
| intuitive | logical |
| emotional | rational |
| web | hierarchy |

Concentrate for a moment on the part of the justice list that characterizes this conception as abstract, universal, principled, systematic, logical. In contemporary intellectual culture we are inclined to regard logic as cold and hard, and to regard universal, systematic, all-encompassing structures as intellectually rigorous and appropriately rational. (Those who associate the justice list with men would say that this inclination reflects the fact that contemporary intellectual culture is masculine.) On the other hand, important aspects of the care list—feeling, responsiveness to needs and interests, nurturing, interconnectedness, intuition—are regarded as soft, mushy, unrigorous, and sentimental in contemporary intellectual culture. Cold, hard, rigorous: in other words, tough. Soft, sentimental, nurturing: in other words, tender.

If this is what James meant by tough-minded and tender-minded, Immanuel Kant and John Rawls would be the quintessential examples of tough-minded thinkers.[33] Perhaps G. E. Moore, or perhaps Søren Kierkegaard or Jean-Paul Sartre, would be tender-minded. If this is what James meant, it is easy to see the correlation between tough-mindedness and the conventionally masculine, and tender-mindedness and the conventionally feminine. We would be tempted to add other ways of thought to the tough, masculine list, such as market rhetoric, cost-benefit analysis, rigid entitlements, and going by rules rather than situated judgment.  Richard Posner would be tough because he can countenance baby selling if it enhances efficiency,[34] and Richard Epstein would be tough because he can countenance abject poverty and homelessness for the same reasons.[35]  Robert Nozick would be tough because he can countenance one person dying of thirst if water rights are owned by another.[36]  But this is not at all what James meant.  In the intellectual culture in which he drew up his lists, he meant to contrast idealist rationalism with skeptical empiricism.  Here are the opposing traits as James presented them:

| *The Tender-Minded* | *The Tough-Minded* |
|---|---|
| rationalistic (going by "principles") | empiricist (going by "facts") |
| intellectualistic | sensationalistic |
| idealistic | materialistic |
| optimistic | pessimistic |
| religious | irreligious |
| free-willist | fatalistic |
| monistic | pluralistic |
| dogmatical | skeptical[37] |

For James, the tender-minded are those who need the reassurance of a systematic, all-encompassing ideal structure.  They need the security of believing that the world is one; that it is, and must necessarily be, good; that there is a perfect, absolute reality behind the imperfect appearances in which we live; and that all things necessarily tend toward perfection and the salvation of the world.  The tender-minded need formal systems, principles, a priori reality, and complete rationality. The tough-minded, on the other hand, do not need to postulate a better and more unified world above, beyond, or beneath the messy and conflicting particulars in which we live—the facts as we know them. The tough-minded have the temperamental wherewithal to live with incompleteness, openness, uncertainty, skepticism, and the nonideal.  For us today, universal logic and systematicity are cold, hard, and crystalline.  But for James, they—that is, the need for them—evidenced vulnerability and tenderness.

It is evident that the quintessential tender-minded thinker to which James opposed his radical empiricism must be G.W.F. Hegel.  Indeed, he mentioned two contemporary turn-of-the-century strands of tender-minded philosophy, the more important of which is "the so-called transcendental idealism of the Anglo-Hegelian school."[38]  Among its exponents he included T. H. Green, Edward and John Caird, Bernard Bosanquet, and Josiah Royce.

If we try to be true to James, perhaps the foremost tender-minded thinker of today would be Roberto Unger. His work is thoroughly systematic, and it is neo-Hegelian. Even though John Rawls is not a transcendental idealist and is neo-Kantian rather than neo-Hegelian, we would probably also have to think of Rawls as tender-minded rather than tough-minded, because neo-Kantianism, no less than neo-Hegelianism, tries to find all-encompassing first principles and to build ideal theories systematically upon them. Perhaps indeed James's distinction would lead us to consider tender-minded all theorists who need universal, ideal, abstract, algorithmic structure.

What we have seen so far is that our current philosophical culture, perhaps including a conventionally accepted complex of traits divided into the masculine and feminine, tempts us to misunderstand what James meant by his distinction between tough-minded and tender-minded theories and temperaments. Although it is important to understand this, it is more important to understand that James introduced the distinction not to embrace one of its prongs, but rather to try to dissolve it or bridge it.

James offered pragmatism as a "mediating way of thinking."[39] Pragmatism is a way of understanding our simultaneous commitments to optimism *and* pluralism, to concrete empiricism *and* principles, to an incomplete and dynamic universe *and* to the possibility of perfection that our ideals impel us unceasingly to hope for and work for. It was important for James that pragmatism allow us to retain a religious commitment, though not the kind of religion characteristic of the tender-minded. Indeed, although James's sympathies are in many ways with the tough-minded—he is interested foremost in the pluralistic and incomplete nature of the world, the never-ending variety and crisscrossing conflict and interconnectedness of facts—he tells us that pragmatism must include all ideas that prove best for people to hold (the most useful, the ones that work the best). This means that pragmatism includes some of the commitments of tender-mindedness:

> One misunderstanding of pragmatism is to identify it with positivistic tough-mindedness, to suppose that it scorns every rationalistic notion as so much jabber and gesticulation, that it loves intellectual anarchy as such and prefers a sort of wolf-world absolutely unpent and wild and without a master or a collar to any philosophic classroom product, whatsoever. I have said so much in these lectures against the over-tender forms of rationalism, that I am prepared for some

misunderstanding here, [but] I have simultaneously defended rationalistic hypotheses so far as these redirect you fruitfully into experience.[40]

Pragmatism does not prefer a wolf-world because that is not a world that would be good for human beings. That is not a human world, not a conception of the world that works for us, and not one that makes us flourish as best we can. For James pragmatism is capacious:

On pragmatic principles we cannot reject any hypothesis if consequences useful to life flow from it. Universal conceptions, as things to take account of, may be as real for pragmatism as particular sensations are. They have indeed no meaning and no reality if they have no use. But if they have any use they have that amount of meaning. And the meaning will be true if the use squares well with life's other uses.

Well, the use of the Absolute is proved by the whole course of men's religious history. The eternal arms are then beneath.[41]

So James finds that we have used the idea of the absolute because we need to fall back and float upon the eternal arms.

James's own solution does not favor any such floating. His religion of pragmatism is neither optimistic (tender-minded: the world's salvation is inevitable and we need do nothing about it) nor pessimistic (tough-minded: there is no salvation and we cannot do anything about it). Instead, it is "melioristic"—the world's salvation is possible, and *it depends upon what we do about it*. Whether or not we follow James and choose to think of it as religious, this is one of the deepest commitments of pragmatism, its commitment to the interconnection, indeed the inseparability, of theory (vision) and action (practice). "In the beginning was the Act,"[42] wrote Goethe at the dawn of the romantic era, and perhaps this commitment of pragmatism to the significance of our actions is what it retains of romanticism. It seems so in passages such as this:

Does our act then *create* the world's salvation . . . ? Here I take the bull by the horns, and in spite of the whole crew of rationalists and monists, of whatever brand they be, I ask *why not*? Our acts, our turning-places, where we seem to ourselves to make ourselves and grow, are the parts of the world to which we are closest, the parts of which our knowledge is the most intimate and complete. Why should we not take them at their face-value? Why may they not be the actual turning-places and growing-places which they seem to be, of the world—why not the workshop of being, where we catch fact in

the making, so that nowhere may the world grow in any other kind
of way than this?[43]

The optimism of pragmatism is not the static and secure optimism of the
world in which everything is already fixed, could we but know or
understand it, but rather the dynamic and risky optimism of a "workshop
of being" in which reality is always incomplete and always dependent
upon our practice.

James did not argue that we should accept pragmatism because it is
a more rational system. Rather, he argued pragmatically that we should
be pragmatists because when we look at our various commitments and
practices we should recognize that pragmatism fits them best, that
pragmatism will work best for us. If we accept everything on either the
tender-minded or the tough-minded list, we are forced to deny, for the
sake of supposed philosophical consistency, things on the other list that
are very real and important to us.

When we see feminism in its pragmatic aspect, I think it will be easy
to conclude that feminists should not easily relinquish what are important
attributes of the ethic of justice because of the present conventional
association with a version of masculinity that needs to be transcended.
When we see feminism pragmatically, we may be impelled, rather, to
affirm both lists, suitably metamorphosed. Perhaps feminism, as well as
earlier pragmatism, can be a middle way.

In the wake of Gilligan's work, many feminists did affirm that there
is something essentially female about the moral structure characterized
in the care list. These feminists also affirmed that this female morality
is good, indeed that women's "different voice" is not just different from,
but better than, male morality, and should be the guide to moral and
political progress.[44] It did not take long for other feminists to point
out, however, that this simple identification with the care list might be
a bad mistake.[45]

Rather than a window into an essentially female form of character
and development or female kind of knowing and acting, the ethic of care
in our current world might be an artifact of coping with oppression. It
might be the expression of what is most useful for a group that exists in
bondage, in victimhood.[46] If so, it is the expression of
"femininism,"[47] not feminism, and its moral significance is complex.
Its traits will be a mixture of cooptation with defiance, and sycophantism
with subtle subversion. It will not be something either to affirm
wholeheartedly or to reject out of hand.

Certainly, it seems that male ideology invented the polarities of
rationality and just deserts versus emotions and nurturing, and then found

the rational pole to be dominant, suitable for the market and the public world, and the emotional pole to be subordinate, suitable for the family and the private world. Much of the eighteenth- and nineteenth-century rhetoric about the nature of womanhood makes this clear. To exalt the ethic of care leaves the polarities intact. It just reverses their signs. As others have pointed out, a group that seeks liberation from a dominating system of thought should be very suspicious of adopting its categories.[48]

What would a feminist middle way look like? It might recommend that all of us, women and men, are morally inclined toward both care and justice, and that neither women nor men should impoverish themselves with the conventional categories of femininity and masculinity. The feminist middle way would not want to relinquish the concrete knowledge that women have gained through living, working, creating, and surviving under male domination. This is a perspective that is unique and important for humanity. The actions and commitments of those who struggle to find room for themselves, and ultimately to free themselves, in a world whose formulating conceptions are not of their making, are indeed indispensable in the pragmatic "workshop of being." As I argued earlier, this perspective is the best way for pragmatism to confront the complacent tendency to be satisfied with coherence with the past. But neither would the feminist middle way want to deny women the right or the ability to engage in the theoretical joys of cold, hard logic and of rational system building, nor to deny women the practical power of standing at the top of a hierarchy, in a position of authority, and meting out just deserts.

The feminist middle way cannot be understood, however, as some kind of synthesis between the two lists. It would be unpragmatic, and perhaps incoherent, to seek some overarching universal conception or set of principles that could harmonize "attachment, connection, community" with "separation, autonomy, individualism," or "cooperation" with "competition," or the concrete with the abstract, or the intuitive with the logical, or the narrative with the systematic. Instead, the pragmatist middle way recommends two things for feminism: (1) We should recognize that sometimes one of the opposing modes of thought is appropriate, and sometimes the other, and no theory—only situated judgment—will tell us which one to adopt and when; (2) we should recognize that the traditional conceptions of the modes of thought on each list are inadequate insofar as they are part of a universal world view that denies the modes on the other list.

It could be that both the ethic of care and the ethic of justice are caricatures of morality. These caricatures have seemed plausible because to some extent they fit with contemporary conventions of femininity and masculinity. It could be that human beings, whether male or female, need both ethics to function morally. If we are pragmatists, we will reject static, timeless conceptions of reality. We will prefer contextuality, expressed in the commitment of Dewey and James to facts and their meaning in human life, and narrative, expressed in James's unfolding "epic" universe and Dewey's historicism. If we are pragmatists, we will recognize the inescapability of perspective and the indissolubility of thought and action. Indeed, as I have said, these pragmatist commitments are shared by many feminists, and they make it useful to think of many forms of feminism as sharing a great deal with pragmatism.

These pragmatic commitments nevertheless do not compel us to affirm the ethic of care and deny the ethic of justice, even if the realities of the narrative epic as it has so far unfolded have produced these contrasting ethics as the salient conventions of our day. James thought that if we reflected hard and honestly about our experiences and ideals, and our hopes and commitments, we would be neither tender-minded nor tough-minded, but would find a middle way that is truer to ourselves. So too today, it may be that we need not exalt either the characteristics of conventional femininity or conventional masculinity, but rather that we can define a middle way that is truer to ourselves, including what we hope to become.

## IV. The Struggle Over Descriptions of Reality and Its Consequences for Legal Discourse

One useful consequence of putting pragmatism and feminism together is that we need not deny that certain philosophical commitments are distinctively feminist just because they seem to be pragmatist too. Joan Williams writes that "the attempt to claim the new epistemology for women is unconvincing simply because the new epistemology has been developed largely by men."[49] By "the new epistemology," Williams means the "view of truths as necessarily partial and contextual," which she associates with "philosophers from Friedrich Nietzsche and the American pragmatists to Martin Heidegger and Ludwig Wittgenstein."[50] I think Williams moves too quickly here. Of course, it is correct that pragmatism, with its commitment to perspectivism, is not the exclusive province of females. But I have argued that the commitment to perspectivism finds its concrete payoff in the perspective of feminism and in the perspectives of oppressed people generally. Rather than affirming that there is no specific feminist perspective because men have espoused perspectivism, it is pragmatically better, as I have argued above, to affirm that the standpoint of people who have themselves been dominated and oppressed makes it possible to see and confront the problem of bad coherence. Their standpoint therefore assumes a crucial importance.

For the legal actor who accepts the significance of the perspective of the oppressed, the important issues must be: (1) How can we recognize bad coherence in our legal institutions? and (2) How can we use this recognition to change those institutions? In order to approach these issues for pragmatist-feminist legal theory, I suggest we can start with a distinction between two kinds of coherence. Like all pragmatic distinctions, this one is not meant to be hard and fast.

There seem to be two ways to construe coherence, which I will call conceptual and institutional. If traditional pragmatism is best understood as expressing a coherence theory, its thrust is primarily conceptual. James's conservatism about belief was connected with what conceptions we should hold to be true, especially in light of recalcitrant experience (to use W.V.O. Quine's later phrase).[51] On the other hand, complacent pragmatists are tempted to focus on existing institutions and not just conceptions. These different ways of construing coherence have ramifications for the problem of bad coherence. As I shall explain, dominant forms of legal pragmatism have been especially conservative because they have embraced institutional, not just conceptual, coherence.

If our world view exhibits bad coherence at the conceptual level, then we are unable to formulate and think about any opposing views. Indeed, it does not make any sense to speak of bad coherence at the time, for we can only see it in retrospect if we change our conceptions and come to see our past understandings as bad. This might have been the situation with slavery in the ancient world. It might have been unthinkable to conceive of human beings in such a way that there could be any plausible argument that all people are equal and that slavery is wrong. Some pragmatists might say that in this situation we have no standpoint from which to say that slavery is bad, and hence that it is meaningless, except in retrospect, to think of this situation as "bad" coherence. (This need not be a complacent or skeptical view. Pragmatists who adopt conceptual coherence as the test of truth need not be conservative about all institutions. When their view of coherence is expansive, taking in all our ideals and critical visions, they may find institutions unjust. Nor need an instance of conceptual meaninglessness be static. The methodology of consciousness raising is one way people can emerge from the unthinkable (silence) to an alternative conception of the world (voice). Perhaps that is the point at which it becomes meaningful to speak of bad coherence.)

With institutional bad coherence the situation may be different. If our social world exhibits bad coherence at the institutional level but not at the conceptual level, then our institutions uniformly exhibit the bad conception of things, but it is possible for at least some of us to conceive that things might be otherwise. This might have been the situation in the last days of coverture. All our legal institutions treated women as subordinate to their husbands, yet it was possible for some women to think of themselves otherwise, and to envision a legal regime that would recognize their changed self-conception. If bad coherence exists only at the institutional level, then the possibility of transition opens up. How can a newly conceivable alternative conception find the power to make inroads into the coherent legal order held in place by the dominant conception of the world?

The problem of institutional bad coherence is the point where the enlightened pragmatist, the pragmatist-feminist, can make the most significant contribution to legal theory. The unenlightened, complacent pragmatist tends to argue that since "truth" about the world is found in conceptual coherence, legal "truth" should be discerned by reference to institutional coherence. The enlightened pragmatist must counter this conservative non sequitur by finding a way to transform alternative conceptual possibilities into legal realities. She must find a way that "the law" can be understood to include the conceptions of the oppressed as they are coming to be, even if the weight of legal institutions coherently excludes them. In other words, the transition problem in this guise is how to make thinkable alternatives into institutional commitments.

Dworkin's Hercules can be understood as a complacent pragmatist judge.[52] This reading of Dworkin might not represent his real views, if we were to ask him. Yet I think it is a fair picture of how a reader might understand his work, taken as a whole. Although Dworkin confusingly, and I think irresponsibly, gerrymanders the word "pragmatism" to mean crass instrumentalism,[53] it is clear that he is a pragmatist of sorts. Pragmatism is reflected in his commitment to the ubiquity of interpretation, and his concomitant commitment to finding meaning in assembling concrete events (institutional coherence and fit), rather than to measuring correspondence with abstract truth or justice.

Hercules is conservative because Dworkin accepts the flawed analogy between truth as conceptual coherence and legal truth as institutional coherence. Hercules, the ideal interpreter, must find the interpretation that coheres best with all that has gone before in the legal system. He is not allowed to say that the web of previous precedent is coherently wrong,[54] or, in his chain novel analogy, that the narrative to which he must add is a bad story so far.[55]

Of course, Hercules is allowed to find that some of our institutional history, as embodied in concrete decisions, is mistaken. Any adherent of coherence theory must allow some of the old commitments to be given up when confronted with a new problem. Dworkin argues conservatively that the proper theory of mistake is to give up as little as possible. He does not even provide any serious discussion about how every once in awhile a paradigm shift must come about, to parallel the avenue pursued by conceptual pragmatists in science.

For the oppressed this means the status quo must change very slowly, if at all. For example, how would Hercules deal with *Plessy v. Ferguson*, in which the Supreme Court affirmed the doctrine of separate but equal?[56] Dworkin argues that at the time of *Brown v. Board of Education*,[57] *Plessy* should not have been treated as compelling precedent, but he stops short of arguing that *Plessy* was wrong at the time it was decided.[58] Nor could he do so, it seems, since he admits that *Plessy* cohered well with its contemporary institutional legal, moral, and political universe. Toward the end of *Law's Empire*, Dworkin makes a distinction between the integrity required by justice and the integrity required by all of the virtues that the legal system must balance.[59] Perhaps he might argue that the integrity of justice would have recommended that *Plessy* was wrong at the time, even though institutionally coherent with its surroundings. Since Dworkin appears in the end to measure justice by the same kind of institutional coherence, it seems to me that such an argument would fail.

Of course, Dworkin does argue that things have changed and that it was coherently right by 1954 to ignore *Plessy*. But how did things change? Not, it appears, with any help from the legal system. In Dworkin's conservative theory the legal system was required to hold fast to the old description of the world,[60] composed by the dominant order and expressed in its institutions, until extra-legal forces dislodged it. Moreover, if Dworkin cannot argue that *Plessy* was wrong at the time it was decided because in his theory there is no foothold from which to argue that the system was institutionally coherently bad, then he has no room to admit the possibility that in some ways our system is coherently bad today. All he can say is that some of the coherent things we are doing today will probably seem wrong in retrospect, not that they are wrong now. That is small consolation to the oppressed.

In contrast to complacent legal pragmatists are the legal writers who have stressed the crucial importance of the perspective of the oppressed and its consequences for a serious pluralism. These writers, such as Robert Cover, Frank Michelman, and Martha Minow,[61] are essentially at work on the particular transition problem posed by institutional bad coherence—that is, the problem of institutional bad coherence in the context of excluded but conceivable alternatives.

In his resolutely anti-statist view of law, Robert Cover wanted to make us aware of how in our commitments we create and inhabit a *nomos*. He wanted to make us concretely aware of the way meaning, including legal meaning, is inseparable from commitment and action. Reversing the old positivist slogan that judges should apply, not make, the law, Cover argued that the role of judges, like the roles of all who interpret authoritative texts for those who are committed to them, is rightly "jurisgenerative."[62] Cover drew attention in particular to the "hermeneutic of resistance,"[63] because he wanted us to see the deep and all-encompassing significance of the standpoint of those who are dominated and oppressed.

In many ways consonant with the work of Cover, both Minow and Michelman plead with us to drop the prevalent conception of the judicial role as one in which our hands are tied by abstract rules laid down.[64] Minow and Michelman urge that the best role for the judge in our legal system is to try to grasp the world from the perspective of the dominated, to hear the outsiders who have been silent and are now trying to speak, and to make concrete our deepest ideals of inclusion when the conventions of our day—"our" dominant perspective—run counter to them. In other words, Minow and Michelman ask us to allow the transitional possibilities opened up by the developing perspectives of the oppressed to infiltrate the dominant institutional coherence.

Minow "links problems of difference to questions of vantage point."[65] In "urg[ing] struggles over descriptions of reality,"[66] Minow echoes James's call for a workshop of being, but adds the perspective that only concrete participation in struggle can give. Michelman argues that pluralism is necessary for the evolutionary self-reflection appropriate to our best self-development, and that pluralism depends upon listening to the perspectives of the oppressed. He also argues that "judges perhaps enjoy a situational advantage over the people at large in listening for voices from the margins."[67] If they are willing to be sympathetic, judges, with their concrete knowledge of legal history and institutions and of their malleable character are perhaps better situated to conduct a sympathetic inquiry into how, if at all, the readings of history upon which those voices base their complaint can count as interpretations of that history which, however recollective or even transformative, remain true to that history's informing commitment to the pursuit of political freedom through jurisgenerative politics.[68]

Minow and Michelman embrace pluralism through taking seriously the perspective of the oppressed. This allows them to find, unlike Dworkin, that courts can take the lead sometimes in the search for better justice. Dworkin's Hercules does not admit the perspective of the oppressed. He cannot, because his task is to find coherence with existing institutions, and the oppressed have not made those institutions. They are outsiders. Perhaps through consciousness raising, or through struggle over descriptions of reality, they have created a thinkable perspective, but their perspective is not represented in the institutional artifacts of the power structure.

Even without the search for the excluded perspectives, Hercules would be truer to the critical spirit of pragmatism if Dworkin were attentive to the ways pluralism is built into our system of legal interpretation. Hercules has no colleagues in making his decisions, and this picture is quite untrue to our practice. After all, as Michelman points out, there is a reason why appellate courts decide things in groups, why they deliberate and why they issue plural opinions even when their deliberation is done.[69] The reason is that conversation and dialogue in appellate decisionmaking represent judges' interaction in the context of commitment, for the decisions of courts matter to people's lives, and no judge is unaware of this. This judicial interaction is crucial to our idea of what might be the best result.

A serious pluralism makes possible an understanding of the deep role of discourse in the way conceptions and practices are made and remade, and thus makes possible a commitment to dialogue among alternative conceptions. Even the occasional conceptual paradigm shift can only find the old dominant description of the world to be wrong in retrospect. It cannot help us find that today's dominant description is wrong. For that, we must realize that another perspective is always possible. The best critical spirit of pragmatism recommends that we take our present descriptions with humility and openness, and accept their institutional embodiments as provisional and incompletely entrenched. Pragmatism recommends this openness in the only way pragmatism can—because it seems to work best for human beings. It is time for the openness and critical spirit of pragmatism to infiltrate pragmatist legal theory. Feminism can lead the way.

## Notes

1. See entries in bibliography under Radin.

2. See Radin, "Justice and the Market Domain," 175—186.

3. See Radin, "Market-Inalienability," 1875—1876; Radin, "Reconsidering the Rule of Law," 816—817.

4. For an overview of the special treatment/equal treatment debate, see Herma H. Kay, "Text Note: Ensuring Non-Discrimination," in *Text, Cases and Materials on Sex-Based Discrimination*, 3rd ed., (Saint Paul, Minn.: West, 1988), 566—572.

5. See Margaret Jane Radin, "Affirmative Action Rhetoric," *Social Philosophy and Policy* (spring 1991): 130—149.

6. See entries in bibliography under MacKinnon.

7. MacKinnon, "Feminism, Marxism, Method, and the State," 533—542; MacKinnon, *Feminism Unmodified*, 85—92.

8. Nevertheless, in our current nonideal circumstances, "just say no" may be the best legal standard to adopt. See Susan Estrich, *Real Rape* (Cambridge, Mass.: Harvard University Press, 1987), 29, 38, 101.

9. See Robin West, "The Difference in Women's Hedonic Lives," *Wisconsin Women's Law Journal* 3 (1987): 81—145.

10. A related instance of the double bind is our attitude toward battered women. Are they weak-willed victims of false consciousness? If so, we view them as degraded selves, so how will they find the self-esteem to free themselves? Or (the other side of the double bind) do we view their situation as one that they are choosing? If so, do we risk trying to bring about empowerment by pretending it is already present? See Littleton, "Women's Experience and the Problem of Transition: Perspectives on Male Battering of Women," *University of Chicago Legal Forum* 23 (1989).

11. See Radin, "Justice and the Market Domain," 244. Also see Clare Dalton, "An Essay in the Deconstruction of Contract Doctrine," *Yale Law Journal* 94 (April 1985): 1106—1113.

12. Rosemarie Tong, *Feminist Thought: A Comprehensive Introduction* (Boulder, Colo: Westview Press, 1989), 193.

13. Wallace Stevens, "On the Road Home," in *The Collected Poems of Wallace Stevens* (New York: Knopf, 1954), 203.

14. Rosemarie Tong, *Feminist Thought: A Comprehensive Introduction*, 1. Cf. Alison M. Jaggar, *Feminist Politics and Human Nature* (Brighton: Harvester, 1983), 8, 10 (categorizing feminisms as liberal, Marxist, radical, and socialist).

15. John Dewey, *Experience and Nature*, 2nd ed., (New York: Dover, 1929), 410.

16. William James, *Pragmatism*, ed. Fredson Bowers, (Cambridge, Mass.: Harvard University Press, 1975), 104.

17. There is a strain of essentialist feminism that might be an exception. Some feminists, often labeled as "radical," tend to think there is a real nature of women, linked to female biology, that has been obscured but not shaped by the patriarchy. See Alison M. Jaggar, *Feminist Politics and Human Nature*, 93—98.

18. See, for example, John Dewey, *Experience and Nature*, 245—297.

19. See Dewey, *Experience and Nature*, ix.

20. See, for example, MacKinnon, *Toward a Feminist Theory of the State*, 191.

21. Dewey, *Experience and Nature*, 179.

22. This statement is subject to dispute. Hilary Putnam, for example, espouses "internal realism" or "pragmatic realism." See Hilary Putnam, *The Many Faces of Realism* (La Salle, Ill.: Open Court, 1987), 17. Putnam takes this view to be both characteristically pragmatic and a rejection of coherence theory. Others take the pragmatic test of truth to be coherence, often referring to W.V.O. Quine's famous assertion that "our statements about the external world face the tribunal of sense experience not individually but only as a corporate body." W.V.O. Quine, "Two Dogmas of Empiricism," in *From a Logical Point of View*, 2nd ed., (Cambridge, Mass.: Harvard University Press, 1980), 42.

Perhaps the controversy over whether pragmatism espouses coherence theory is fueled by a loose use of the term *coherence*. If coherence refers just to the totality of existing practices and institutions, then a sophisticated pragmatist would not want to use it as the measure of truth because on this view coherence becomes mere conventionalism: It does not take into account the ideals and critical visions that also properly belong to the totality of our circumstances. On the other hand, if coherence does include all of our ideals and critical visions, all of our possible meanings, then perhaps a sophisticated pragmatist would espouse it as amounting to the broadest form of immanent holistic understanding.

In this expansive understanding of coherence, it would perhaps be problematic to speak of bad coherence, as I do in the text, because the field over which coherence is supposed to organize understanding already includes whatever ideals and critical visions we would use for judging a situation bad. I use the term, however, to point out that some pragmatists at least implicitly adopt the narrow view that collapses coherence into conventionalism, and hence tend to find truth or goodness in the status quo. These complacent pragmatists are indeed vulnerable to the criticism that there is no room in their scheme to find the status quo on the whole bad or unjust. See below.

23. William James, *Pragmatism*, 35.

24. Ibid., 36 and 104 (where James elaborates on how we choose what theories to class as true).

25. Ibid., 42.

26. If the notion of coherent badness causes philosophical difficulties, see note 22 above, then we could speak here of integrity in badness or merely consistency in badness. The point is that we can experience a situation in which almost everything about the status quo—our language, our social priorities, our law—reflects and expresses racism or sexism. We need a way to recognize that this situation is bad or unjust, indeed worse or more unjust than a situation that is on the whole just and has only small pockets of injustice that can be seen to lack coherence (or integrity, or consistency) with the whole.

27. See note 22 above.

28. Indeed, there is a transition problem in the very commitment to take seriously the perspective of oppressed groups, because attention to the group qua group risks reinforcing the old categories of subordination. See Scott Brewer, "Pragmatism, Oppression, and the Flight to Substance," *Southern California Law Review* 63 (September 1990): 1753—1763; "Afterword," *Southern California Law Review* 63 (September 1990): 1922—1924.

29. See, for example, Hilary Putnam, "A Reconsideration of Deweyan Democracy," *Southern California Law Review* 63 (September 1990): 1681—1683. Reprinted as Chapter 12 in this book.

30. See Dewey, *Experience and Nature*, 119—120.

31. James, *Pragmatism*, 13.

32. See entry in bibliography under Gilligan.

33. I am referring to John Rawls as most readers saw him when *A Theory of Justice* was published. His later work invites pragmatist reinterpretation of his theory. See, e.g. "Justice As Fairness: Political Not Metaphysical," *Philosophy and Public Affairs* 14 (1985).

34. See, for example, Richard Posner, "The Regulation of the Market in Adoptions," *Boston University Law Review* 67 (January 1987): 59—73.

35. See Richard Allen Epstein, *Takings: Private Property and the Power of Eminent Domain* (Cambridge, Mass.: Harvard University Press, 1985), 315—323.

36. See Robert Nozick, *Anarchy, State and Utopia* (Oxford: Oxford University Press, 1972), 180—181.

37. James, *Pragmatism*, 13.

38. Ibid., 16.

39. Ibid., 26.

40. Ibid., 128.

41. Ibid., 131.

42. "*Im Anfang war die Tat.*" Johann Wolfgang von Goethe, *Faust*, ed. Calvin Thomas (Boston: Heath, 1892), Part I, line 1237. This is to be understood, of course, as countervailing the Gospel of St. John, "In the beginning was the Word." Pragmatists traditionally are wary of emphasis on words without action or without commitment to actual results in the world. Perhaps Richard Rorty's stress on conversation or dialogue can prove uncomfortable for pragmatism, if conversation becomes a category apart from practical action.

43. James, *Pragmatism*, 138.

44. See, for example, Ruddick, "Preservative Love and Military Destruction: Some Reflections on Mothering and Peace," in Joyce Trebilcot, *Mothering: Essays in Feminist Theory* (Totowa, N.J.: Rowman, 1983), 231—249.

45. See, for example, Joan Williams, "Deconstructing Gender," *Michigan Law Review* 87 (February 1989): 797—845.

46. See, for example, Catharine Wells (formerly Hantzis), "Is Gender Justice a Completed Agenda?" (Book Review), *Harvard Law Review* 100 (January 1987): 700—703.

47. I learned this word from Kathleen M. Sullivan. "Femininism" connotes the misunderstanding of today's conventional femininity as some kind of real woman's nature.

48. See, for example, Audre Lorde, "The Master's Tools Will Never Dismantle the Master's House," in *Sister Outsider* (Freedom, Calif.: Crossing Press, 1984), 112—129.

49. Williams, "Deconstructing Gender," 806.

50. Ibid.

51. See W.V.O. Quine, "Two Dogmas of Empiricism."

52. Ronald Dworkin introduces Hercules, "a lawyer of superhuman skill, learning, patience, and acumen," to represent the ideal judge. Ronald Dworkin, *Taking Rights Seriously* (Cambridge, Mass.: Harvard University Press, 1977), 104—105. Hercules plays the same role in Dworkin's *Law's Empire* (Cambridge, Mass.: Harvard University Press, 1986), 239.

53. See Dworkin, *Law's Empire*, 95, 151—164.

54. Dworkin, *Taking Rights Seriously*, 115—118.

55. Dworkin, *Law's Empire*, 225—232.

56. 163 U.S. 537 (1896).

57. 347 U.S. 483 (1954).

58. Dworkin, *Law's Empire*, 379—389.

59. Ibid., 404—407.

60. See Wallace Stevens, "The Latest Freed Man," in *The Collected Poems of Wallace Stevens*, 204. ("Tired of the old descriptions of the world / The latest freed man rose at six and sat / on the edge of his bed."). On the affinity of Stevens and pragmatism, see Thomas Grey, *The Wallace Stevens Case: Law and the Practice of Poetry* (Cambridge, Mass.: Harvard University Press, 1991). See also Margaret Jane Radin, "After The Final No There Comes A

Yes": A Law Teacher's Report," *Yale Journal of Law and Humanities* 2 (summer 1990): 253—266.

61. I think of these writers because of my own situatedness in the discourse of legal theory. It is equally important to think in this context of "critical race theory." See entries in bibliography under Bell, Delgado, and Matsuda. We should also look to the emerging perspective of gay and lesbian writers. See, for example, Patricia A. Cain, "Feminist Jurisprudence: Grounding the Theories," *1989 Berkeley Women's Law Journal*, 191—214.

62. See entry in bibliography under Cover.

63. Ibid., 48-53.

64. See entries in bibliography under Michelman and Minow.

65. Minow, "Justice Engendered," 13—14.

66. Ibid., 16.

67. Michelman, "Law's Republic," 1537.

68. Ibid.

69. Michelman, "Traces of Self-Government," 16—17.

# 9

## Rorty, Radicalism, Romanticism:
## The Politics of the Gaze

*Joan C. Williams*

Perhaps it is fitting that Richard Rorty, who has made a career defending perspectivalism,[1] should find himself signifying diametrically opposed things to different people. In roughly half of my conversations about Rorty, someone ultimately dismisses his "radical relativism." "Of course," I've been told innumerable times, after a long discussion of ethics or epistemology, "I don't go as far as *Rorty*."

Then I have to admit I do. Consequently, I value Rorty's elegant and influential explorations of nonfoundationalism.[2] The notion that there exists no absolute truth, no privileged text, no God's-eye point of view[3] has labored under a severe burden of perceived implausibility since its invention. Said Clifford Geertz in 1984: "To suggest that 'hard rock' foundations . . . may not be available is to find oneself accused of disbelieving the existence of the physical world, thinking pushpin as good as poetry, regarding Hitler as just a fellow with unstandard tastes.[4]

The felt implausibility of nonfoundationalism has been exacerbated by the aestheticist style of many of its advocates. A good example is Friedrich Nietzsche, who argued that once God was dead, morality came tumbling after, leaving only the raw exercise of power.[5] Perhaps the most influential contemporary practitioner of the aestheticist style is Jacques Derrida, with his vivid sense of the melodramatic, his abandonment of conventional philosophical prose, and his irresistible desire to *épater les bourgeois* by presenting the consequences of the death of "metaphysics" in a shocking and stylish way.[6]

The aestheticist celebration of found freedom is profoundly threatening if it signals the freedom to torture innocents. To make nonfoundationalism plausible in ethics, Rorty's resuscitation of pragmatism holds much greater promise. While aestheticists focus on what's gone once God is dead, pragmatists focus on what's left. Aestheticists aim to shock; pragmatists to reassure. Pragmatists' central message is that the critique of absolutes is not so threatening, after all. We *can* function without absolutes, they argue; in fact, we always have. Words were tools even when we thought they were mirrors.[7] The mere admission that they are no more than tools will not cause them suddenly to break.[8]

Rorty's work has helped explain how we can abandon foundationalism without becoming disoriented, immoral, mute, and without disbelieving in the physical world or dismantling our traditions. Pragmatism taps Americans' love of straight talk and useful thought, and avoids the antiintellectualism awakened by Derrida's extravagant density and verbal dazzle. Derrida's style may garner cultural power in France; in America, it places nonfoundationalism at a severe persuasive disadvantage.[9]

Despite Rorty's commitment to pragmatism, he often melds a pragmatist with an aestheticist tone. This worked well when Rorty limited his focus to epistemology and other technical philosophical issues. Now that Rorty's attention has turned to political and moral philosophy, however, his use of an aestheticist tone threatens to jeopardize his project of making nonfoundationalism seem a plausible and desirable way to think: Nonfoundationalism seems unappealing if the death of God signals the freedom to torture innocents. I therefore begin this essay by explaining in a consistently pragmatist tone how nonfoundationalism can be reconciled with the widespread sense that ethical certainties exist.

I then shift to a different perspective, and we meet a very different Richard Rorty. For while half my conversational partners dismiss Rorty as too threateningly radical, the other half roll their eyes at how reactionary he is. These encounters echo the rough sledding that has resulted from publication of his recent work, culminating in 1989 with *Contingency, Irony, and Solidarity*. This work has been called "myopic, smug, and insensitive,"[10] "complacent"[11] "somewhat placid and world weary;"[12] Rorty has been accused of "reinforc[ing] existing power relations that illegitimately oppress and exclude large segments of the population."[13]

Though I share the uneasiness that underlies these criticisms, they have an odd quality that stems from the fact that Rorty himself is neither complacent nor conservative. He is an egalitarian, a feminist, and social democrat. Why the impression created by his recent work?

complacent nor conservative. He is an egalitarian, a feminist, and social democrat. Why the impression created by his recent work?

The trouble, I argue in the second part of this essay, is Rorty's apparent unawareness of the ways that our institutions and patterns of thought currently render his egalitarian principles unattainable. Rorty could benefit from one of the key insights of feminism: that much of what we like about ourselves, notably our culture's definition of self-creation, is deeply intertwined with patterns of oppression.[14] Rorty's recent work is built around a Romantic idea of self-creation that serves to deflect his gaze from ingrained patterns of gender, class, and race inequities. For Rorty to integrate his egalitarian intentions with his other concerns, he must first come to terms with the political implications of his focus on making the world safe for strong poets.

## I. Innocents and Aztecs:
## Rorty's Epistemological Radicalism

*What, then, can the pragmatist say when the torturers come?*
                                                      —Jeffrey Stout[15]

The imagery of tortured innocents has played a central role in the intellectual history of nonfoundationalist thought. In this section, I first sketch the historical links between distrust of nonfoundationalism and people's sense that moral certainties exist. I then argue that these certainties reflect not objective truth, but the grammar of what it means to be us. The torture of innocents is wrong because it violates our culture's celebration of the individual and our sense of the essential dignity and equality of human beings. I conclude by exploring some of the benefits to be gained from redefining our moral certainties as cultural rather than as reflective of eternal truth.

Edward Purcell's excellent book, *The Crisis of Democratic Theory*, documents how the spectre of ethical relativism deflected Americans from their initial encounter with the critique of absolutes in the first half of the twentieth century.[16] Purcell incisively documents how the growing certainty of Nazi evil led to a rejection of nonfoundationalism in the social sciences and the law. When Ruth Benedict argued in 1934 that such elemental acts as murder and suicide were judged differently in different cultures and "relate to no absolute standard,"[17] the point seemed provocative and innocent enough; ten years later such ethical "relativism" seemed at once a serious threat to national purpose and intuitively, "obviously" wrong.

Today, the fear of "nihilism" still leads some scholars back to absolutes on the grounds that the alternative is relativism of the most standardless sort.[18]    Another common contemporary response is to embrace nonfoundationalism while preserving access to a few objective, moral certainties.[19] A recent notable example is Jeffrey Stout, who adopts a nonfoundationalist approach to ethics.    Stout's work is pragmatist in spirit, yet he reverts to objectivity to explain why slavery and the torture of innocents are wrong.[20]

In pragmatist ethics, objective moral certainties are both undesirable and unnecessary.  Objectivity is undesirable for a very simple reason. As the other contributions to this volume show, forging some coherency for neopragmatism will be difficult.  If pragmatism is to prove more than "generosity of spirit in search of something to say,"[21] we as pragmatists ought to agree on a vigorous nonfoundationalism.  Not only is objectivity undesirable; it also is unnecessary to explain our sense of certainty about torture and other horrors.  What follows is an attempt to reassure that, to the extent nonfoundationalism offers us ethical space, it is ethical space we have always handled and can handle in the future.

Why is the torture of innocents wrong?  A Wittgensteinian strategy provides the most direct response.  The torture of innocents is wrong because of the grammar of the sentence.[22]  If someone is "innocent," then by definition she should not be punished: by calling her innocent the speaker presupposes that conclusion.  And "torture"?  Let us begin by noting that, within our contemporary language of morality, torture provides the touchstone of moral bankruptcy.[23]  Whatever Evil Ones did to their Innocents, if Amnesty International can successfully label it as torture, it has won the battle for moral condemnation.  A successful charge that someone has tortured innocents ends the discussion: Torture's status as a trump card signals its central ideological role as the reference point of immorality.

Why does torture play this role in our form of life?  For a subtle, detailed and elegant answer see Charles Taylor's brilliant analysis of the sources of modern identity.[24]  I will strive for a less subtle but perhaps more widely accessible explanation, using the Aztecs as a heuristic.

What I know about Aztecs consists of vague impressions from Mexican museums.  They were a highly developed society with advanced astronomical knowledge.  They were great administrators and fierce warriors who built up a vast empire.  They believed the universe would run down without a steady stream of human sacrifice, and they killed lots and lots of people by ripping out their hearts.

To us, the Aztecs are not an attractive people. Their notions of human sacrifice seem senseless, cruel, and profligate in the extreme. How can we say other than that they were wrong? Do we "relativists" really claim that human sacrifice was as "right" for the Aztecs as respectful praying is for us? Rather than answer this question, I hope to unpack the assumptions behind it.

Let us begin by asking why we find the Aztec religion so repulsive. First of all, we don't believe in it, so we see the human sacrifice as unnecessary. We do not, for example, feel the same level of purified outrage at the fact that Americans boil some people's brains inside their heads until their eyes bulge and often pop out. Electrocution is unfortunate, but, in the common view, necessary.[25] But if we *really believed* that the world would end without human blood, the gore of human sacrifice would look to us more like the gore of our own highly ritualized executions. Undesirable, perhaps, but a given of adult life.

At a deeper level, we cry, we'd never stand for human sacrifice: we'd risk the lives of every one of us rather than allow the slaughter of innocents. During the Civil War, for example, Southern troops made a particular point of slaughtering black Union troops while taking their white comrades prisoner. Confederates, moreover, didn't waste their bullets: They clubbed and bayoneted even soldiers who had surrendered. Eventually, the North threatened to stop all prisoner exchanges unless the South agreed to treat black and white prisoners of war equally. The South refused. All prisoner exchanges stopped, and many Union soldiers died of starvation and disease as prisoner-of-war facilities became so overcrowded they turned into death camps.[26]

White men died rather than sacrifice the principle that all human life is sacred, that all human beings must be accorded equal dignity. This is the core principle that makes Aztec sacrifice incomprehensible, and it is (to me) the single most precious principle of our tradition. It is encapsulated in the Equal Protection Clause of the Constitution and in the Declaration of Independence: "All men are created equal."[27] But these are only its recent, secularized formulations: the principle goes back much, much further. It is a core principle of Christianity,[28] and of the Judaic tradition before it: Some think the story of Abraham and Isaac marks the end of human sacrifice in the Hebraic tradition.[29] The modern notion that people are equal—a notion closely linked with earlier notions of equal dignity of souls before the Lord—is a cornerstone of the Western tradition.

    This is the perspective from which we can understand our revulsion with Aztec sacrifice. That practice was deeply antithetical to our sense that each human being has an equal right to live, to create a full life, and to strive for happiness. Presumably, the Aztecs held some variant of a quite different vision, one in which human beings are seen as more like cells in a body, so that one feels no compunction about excising a breast to let the body (politic) live. To the extent that sacrificial victims were prisoners of war, the Aztecs also presumably drew sharp limits around their sense of kinship with other human beings and chose to identify as "like us" only those of their own group.

    Is Aztec sacrifice wrong? To us, of course it is. Does this mean it violated some eternal moral truth? No. It means that we could not be ourselves and be other than repulsed by the image of human hearts held up to the sun. We can see how the Aztecs acted as they did—they lived without a central principle that defines our identity. Saying the Aztecs were wrong simply means we do not want to change in the ways required to make their practices understandable. We have no wish to abandon the notion of the equal dignity of souls.

    Let's move from Aztecs to closer cultural villains: to Nazis, Iraqis, and abortion. The Nazis so threaten our imagination because they were part of our tradition—that's why they hid the death camps instead of making them arenas for ritual celebration. The Nazis are so frightening because they were Western Europeans acting like Aztecs, killing innocents without compunction in pursuit of an illusion of the common good. Iraqis did likewise when they used twelve-year-old boys as mine-sweepers during the Iran-Iraq war, a disgusting development from the standpoint of the Western principles that human life is sacred and that each human being has the right to a "full" life. The action made sense, though, from the framework of an older theological tradition that viewed human life as but an opportunity to maneuver oneself into heaven. From that perspective, the boys' sacrifice was also an opportunity; letting them grasp it left everyone better off.[30]

    This is the sense in which ethical thought is ethnocentric, not universal. A key move is to ask, when faced with an ethically troubling act, what would life have to look like to make this a justifiable choice? Then the second, crucial question: Do I want to change in the ways I would have to in order to adopt this novel point of view?

    This procedure explains not only Aztecs and innocents, but abortion. I, for example, am convinced, absolutely convinced without hesitation, that woman's access to abortion must be guaranteed.[31] And yet I can see how the conclusion that seems so obvious to me can seem foreign, even repulsive to (a) an idealistic celibate priest who has no incentive to think through what denial of abortion will mean in the lives of actual women, and every motivation to engage imaginatively with the drama of fetal life; or (b) a middle-aged Mormon mother of five who believes that a woman's vocation is to marry, that the purpose of marriage is procreation, that sex outside of marriage is wicked, and that the wicked shall be punished.

Neither the priestly nor the Mormon lifestyle seems to me an indefensible choice. And I can readily see how, from those perspectives, abortion seems indefensible. Yet I still believe that both my hypothetical characters are wrong about abortion and that I am right. This conclusion reflects not my more accurate mirror of ultimate realities but a coherent social-political-intellectual outlook that includes my beliefs about the role of women, about the impact of income disparities in this country, and about the duty of human beings to acknowledge responsibility for choices in human situations in which all available options involve inescapable tragedy.

Ethical choices offer not opportunities for appeal to absolutes, but the chance to find out who we are and who we want to be.[32] The torture of innocents functions as an absolute because no fully socialized American could help but condemn Nazis, Iraquis (in the context noted), and Aztecs. About abortion we are not so sure: Abortion brings us back from platitudes to the much broader range of contexts where we simply don't agree.

Once we redefine absolutes in this way, we can explain our sense of certainty about the torture of innocents without a God's-eye point of view. This refusal to appeal *in any context* to objective moral certainties has, in my view, more than epistemological significance. It offers us a chance to step back and examine the structure of our form of life, to assess the hidden costs of our ideals. It allows us to see that the ideal of universal brotherhood is inevitably hemmed in by the arbitrary lines that people draw to define, and ultimately to limit, the scope of their moral responsibility.[33]

To capture this arbitrariness, I turn to a brilliant series of articles by intellectual historian Thomas Haskell.[34] Haskell examines how Europeans after 1750 reached the "obvious" truth that slavery is evil. My discussion thus far suggests that our certain sense of slavery's evil signals that opposition to slavery is central to our ethical identity; for us, slavery violates the grammar of what it means to be human. Yet opposition to slavery is relatively recent. Before 1750, "slavery was routinely defended and hardly ever condemned outright, even by the most scrupulous moralists."[35]     Haskell traces development of a "humanitarian sensibility" that led to the "obvious" truth that slavery is immoral.  He begins with a thought experiment:

> Let us call this the "case of the starving stranger."  As I sit at my desk writing this essay, and as you, the reader, now sit reading it, both of us are aware that some people in Phnom Penh, Bombay, Rangoon, the Sahel, and elsewhere will die next week of starvation. They are strangers; all we know about them is that they will die.  We also know that it would be possible for any one of us to sell a car or a house, buy an airline ticket, fly to Bombay or wherever, seek out at least one of those starving strangers, and save his life, or at the very least extend it.  We could be there tomorrow, and we really could save him.  Now to admit that we have it in our power to prevent this person's death by starvation is to admit that our inaction—our preference for sitting here, reading and writing about moral responsibility, going on with our daily routine—is a necessary condition for the stranger's death.[36]

Haskell acknowledges that our inaction is only one of a number of interacting causes.  "But the troubling fact remains that *but for* our inaction this evil event would not occur."[37]  He continues:

> Why do we not go to his aid?  It is not for lack of ethical maxims teaching us that it is good to help strangers.  Presumably we all subscribe to the Golden Rule, and certainly if we were starving we would hope that some stranger would care enough to drop his daily routine and come to our aid.  Yet we sit here.  We do not do for him what we would have him do for us.  Are we hypocrites?  Are we engaged in self-deception?  Do we in any sense *intend* his death?[38]

To say we intend his death "stretch[es] the meaning of intention way beyond customary usage."[39]  Haskell's central point is not to argue about issues of causation or intent, but to point out that we have to draw the limits of moral responsibility *somewhere*, and that "somewhere" will always exclude much pain and suffering we could alleviate.  Necessarily so: Even if we drop our pens and go to Bombay, we will have to choose to begin by saving person A or person B.

Haskell's thought experiment aptly dramatizes the now-traditional nonfoundationalist assertion that the limits we draw in ethics are a matter of convention.[40]  Haskell's thesis is that the growth of opposition to slavery was part of a rather sudden widening of Europeans' sense of responsibility to strangers.  He points out that medieval minstrels sang joyfully, without apparent feelings of distress, of hearing the vanquished cry for help.[41]  Those slaughtered fell outside the Europeans' ambit of responsibility; so did slaves until about 1750.  Only after slaves were reconceptualized as human beings "like ourselves" did slavery seem clearly immoral rather than a necessary evil.

Haskell's dramatization of the conventional nature of our ambit of responsibility has extraordinary power if we turn it back to Aztecs, Nazis, and abortion.  The Aztecs and the Nazis did not feel morally implicated in the death of their victims because they felt those victims were outside the ambit of responsibility—much as nonvegetarians today define animals as outside the range of creatures to whom they owe the right to life.[42]  Haskell's analysis suggests that the abortion debate can be understood as a controversy about whether (or, more correctly, when) to include the developing fetus within our ambit of responsibility.[43]  Pro-life advocates often preserve the traditional assumption that our ambit of responsibility is incontestable rather than a matter of convention; or else they think that a refusal to identify with a fetus the size of a lima bean[44] does more moral damage than refusal to feed a starving adult: I disagree.  Once we view the scope of our moral responsibility as a matter of convention, it may become clearer why women—faced with grossly disproportionate physical, psychological, and economic burdens of raising children and extraordinarily high cultural standards of what it means to raise a child "well"—choose to place some fetuses outside their ambit of responsibility.

However much we disagree about abortion, one thing is clear.  A defining characteristic of ourselves is our commitment to the ideal of identifying with all humanity at least to the extent of refusing to kill or torture people by means of positive actions.  That's what makes the actions of the Nazis and the Aztecs seem so indisputably unconscionable.

Haskell's analysis highlights the conventional, limited, and historically contingent nature of our moral definitions.  We are repulsed by the torture of innocents, but we still choose to kill Iraqis, animals, starving strangers, criminals, infants,[45] and victims of defective products and environmental contamination.  We define these deaths as necessary evils, using much the same distancing procedures as the Aztecs might have used to absolve themselves of moral responsibility.

Pragmatists should object to the notion of moral absolutes not because we want people to be free to torture or enslave, but because using the language of absolutes lets us evade the troubling fact that our moral choices fall on a continuum on which we set limits far short of our power to intervene. This theme of self-responsible freedom is a key theme in pragmatic thought.[46]

Although pragmatists and aestheticists agree that nonfoundationalism offers greater scope for human will, the projects they sketch out are very different. Aestheticists greet this final Galilean revolution with celebrations of found freedom. A pragmatist tone is less exuberantly playful. The pragmatist notes that we've always had the freedom to create ourselves, and, while we've used it remarkably well to a certain extent, genocide and starvation are also made by human hands.

Dewey combined this weighty sense of responsibility with a sunny American optimism about the power of a reforming spirit. These are qualities that make pragmatism precious in a troubled world. A neopragmatism more chastened and historical than Dewey's can help cure a key drawback of Western moral life, that serene sense of moral exceptionalism that pervades our tradition.[47] Haskell's parable points out the troubling structure of our morality: overly ambitious, designed to have us fail to attain our high ideas. To quote Charles Taylor:

> We have somehow saddled ourselves with very high demands of universal justice and benevolence. Public opinion, concentrating on some popular or fashionable "causes" and neglecting other equally crying needs and injustices, may apply these standards very selectively. . . . Or we can while approving them neutralize them as a distant ideal. . . . Some degree of this latter is probably necessary to keep our balance.[48]

Is a morality high-minded but inevitably honored in the breach inherently better than an approach less ambitious but implemented more consistently? The answer is unclear, but this is not the crucial issue. The key issue is that questions of this sort virtually never are discussed, despite their crucial importance in our particular, contingent moral universe.

To summarize: We as pragmatists do not need *any* absolutes to account for our sense of moral certainties. We should refuse to link our certainties to absolutes because in doing so we lose the opportunity for insight into the grammar of what it means to be us. Understanding the arbitrariness of our "absolutes" can help us grasp some of the hidden costs implicit in our current, contingent self-definition.

## II. The Politics of the Gaze:
## Rorty's Conservatism

In recent years, for every conversation I have had with someone decrying Rorty's radicalism, I have had a matching one decrying him as a slavish defender of the status quo. Earlier in his career Rorty was attacked for tearing down the treasures of Western civilization; now he is attacked as one of its most uncritical proponents. Cornel West led the way in 1985:

> Rorty's neopragmatism only kicks the philosophical props from under bourgeois capitalist societies; it requires no change in our cultural and political practices. What are the ethical and political consequences of adopting his neopragmatism? On the macrosocietal level, there simply are none. In this sense, Rorty's neopragmatism is, in part, a self-conscious post-philosophical ideological project to promote the basic practices of bourgeois capitalist societies while discouraging philosophical defenses of them.[49]

As mentioned earlier, subsequent critics have agreed in increasingly unbuttoned language.[50] Jeffrey Stout, for instance, associates Rorty with "smug approval of the status quo."[51] Stout continues:

> My point is not that Rorty is himself a myopic, smug or insensitive man. I am talking about the impression created by his writings; an impression I believe he regrets but has had trouble disowning or undoing. In fact, when Hilary Putnam says it would be "facile" to accuse Rorty of "conservatism," I wholeheartedly agree. "Rorty," Putnam writes, "is as 'wet' a liberal as they come." And yet, Putnam goes on to say, "If Rorty is not conservative, he does, at times, seem ever so slightly decadent."[52]

Stout and Putnam highlight the important oddness of Rorty's current situation: He is a feminist[53] and egalitarian[54] who condemns "greedy and stupid conservatives" (170) and "greedy and shortsighted capitalists" (175). Why is he being accused of complacent conservatism?

Rorty's recent work is built around the Romantics' ideal that associates self-creation with mastery, autonomy, and masculinity.[55] While Rorty attempts to distance himself from the masculinist and elitist elements within Romantic thought, he fails to appreciate how his model of self-creation subtly but systematically deflects his gaze away from his egalitarian aspirations. Rorty encapsulates his ideal in the notion of the "strong poet," whom Rorty celebrates as "humanity's hero" (26), "the vanguard of the species" (20).  "In my view," Rorty notes, "an ideally liberal polity would be one whose culture hero is [Harold] Bloom's 'strong poet' rather than the warrior, the priest, the sage, or the truth-seeking, 'logical,' 'objective' scientist" (53).  Bloom is famous for his analysis of the "anxiety of influence": the Romantics' view that poets are driven by a "horror of finding [themselves] to be only a copy or replica" (24).  Rorty notes the strong poet's "fear that one might end one's days in . . . a world one never made, an inherited world."[56]  One can avoid this fate by offering a "metaphorical redescription" (28) that "impress[es] one's mark on the language" (24).  "[T]o have figured out what was distinctive about oneself," Rorty says, would be to "*demonstrate* that one was not a copy or a replica.  One would have been as strong as any poet has ever been, which means as strong as any human being could possibly be" (24).

To understand how Rorty's focus on strong poets deflects his gaze from his egalitarian goals, one must place the strong poet in the context of Romantic thought.  Marlon Ross explores in elegant detail the masculinist bias in Romantic imagery.[57]  Ross concludes that the Romantics used gendered imagery to establish the moral and intellectual authority of the strong poet.  One strategy entailed associating poets with potency and strength—the latter association picked up by Harold Bloom in his image of the "strong" poet and by Rorty in his assertion that strong poets are "as strong as any human being could possibly be" (24).  Bloom and Rorty carry on an intellectual tradition that began with Wordsworth, who identified poeticizing as a (the?) quintessential expression of masculine maturity.[58]  Wordsworth did this consciously and explicitly; Rorty does so implicitly by associating success in life with unstoppable strength.

Ross explores the cultural background for the Romantic poet's obsessive insistence on their virility.  He reminds us of the stereotypes of pale, emasculated male writers[59] and points out that male poets' sexual anxiety may have intensified in the Romantic period because of the emergence of an influential group of women writers.[60]  The original Romantics felt a particular need for masculinized metaphors because their project was to celebrate the emotions—an arena traditionally the province of women.  The "Wordsworthian agenda of transforming the vulnerability of passive emotion into the power of manly heroic action"[61] transformed "unmanly vulnerability into manly self-control."[62]

Mastery and autonomy were key themes in the Romantics' celebration of the strong poet.  The Romantic focus on autonomy reflected the assumption that self-creation entailed (to quote Wordsworth) "a song of myself."[63]  This celebration of self is traditionally interpreted as evidence of Wordsworth's contribution in unleashing subjectivity; Ross stresses instead the peculiarly masculine assumption that self-realization involves the solitary autonomy of the quest.[64]  The Romantics persistently used themes of quest and conquest—of the Alps,[65] of other poets,[66] of the reading public.[67]  Wordsworth's persistent association of the poet with conquerors and empire builders of the past[68] reflected the masculinist assumption that influence over others involves mastering them.[69]  Wordsworth and his successors sought, and succeeded in, the mastery of the reading public by establishing the norms that ensured their greatness.  By associating greatness with the mastery and autonomy of the strong poet, the Romantics used masculine gender ideology to exclude women.

Definitions of self that stress autonomy and mastery are the norm within our culture, but they were (and to a substantial extent remain today) unacceptable for women.[70]  Thus the strong Romantic association of poetry with songs of masculine selves ensured that women poets would have difficulty conforming to the Romantic norms of greatness. The female poets who competed with the Romantics were pioneers in a traditionally masculine realm; to mute the cultural sense that "woman poet" was a category mistake, they wrote poetry that reassured readers of their essential femininity.  Their emphasis on emotion gently modulated and socialized, and on affiliative responsibilities rather than radical autonomy, effectively precluded women's poetry from "greatness" as that term came to be defined by the norms set by the Romantics.[71]  Rorty is attracted to the figure of the strong poet in part because he is fighting a battle for masculine authority that originated with the Romantics: the battle between the poet and the scientist.  The Romantic poets were born into a world in which the accepted repositories of male authority were the soldier, the industrialist, and the scientist. They responded both by analogizing themselves to, and by claiming to supersede, these traditional cultural icons.  Rorty, in his effort to decenter the scientist, adopts the Romantic strategy of associating poets with traditionally male attributes as a way of supporting their claim to cultural authority.  Yet Rorty's unselfconscious adoption of masculinized imagery subtly deflects his gaze from his own feminist and egalitarian goals.  To understand how requires close attention to his discussion of self-creation.

In some passages, Rorty adopts the model of the strong poet virtually intact.  He consistently associates self-creation with autonomy (xii, xiv,

141, 144)[72] and adopts as well the idea of creating the intellectual universe that will ensure the greatness of its creator (24, 29, 40). Once he adopts these tenets, though, he is left face to face with the Romantic notion of a mastering genius and a mastered public. Here's an example: "Autonomy is not something which all human beings have within them and which society can release by ceasing to repress them. It is something which certain particular human beings hope to attain by self-creation, and which a few actually do" (65). In thus equating autonomy with self-creation, this passage appears to limit self-creation to a few strong poets.

Elsewhere Rorty is careful to distance himself from the genius/rabble syndrome in Romantic thought. He starts by recommending Freud over Nietzsche because "he does not relegate the vast majority of humanity to the status of dying animals" (35). Freud "shows us how to see every human life as a poem," Rorty continues. This makes the intellectual "just a special case—just somebody who does with marks and noises what other people do with their spouses and children, their fellow workers, the tools of their trade, the cash accounts of their businesses, the possessions they accumulate in their homes, the music they listen to, the sports they play or watch, or the trees they pass on their way to work. Anything from the sound of a word through the color of a leaf to the feel of a piece of skin can, as Freud showed us, serve to dramatize and crystallize a human being's sense of self-identity. Any seemingly random constellation of such things can set the tone of a life" (37).

As is evident from Rorty's cry of "every life a poem," this passage still starts from the paradigm of the strong poet. Then Rorty veers to avoid the elitism implicit in Romantic thought. In the process, he changes his conception of self-creation in two crucial ways. First, he abandons the notion that successful self-creation necessarily involves mastery. Instead, he greatly widens out the cultural expressions he considers apt expressions of healthy self-creation, to include not only mastery (through economic power), but also the experience of beauty, a sense of vocation about one's work, and affiliative ties with lovers, spouses, children, fellow works, team mates, and fellow sports fans. Once freed from the exogenous skeleton of masculine gender ideology, self-creation is no longer flattened into one-sided mastery of other people. Nor does it focus solely on autonomy. Indeed, many of the things that spring to Rorty's mind when his thoughts about self-fulfillment are unfettered by Romanticism involve affiliative bonds.

Feminists' usual point is that masculinized notions such as that of the strong poet make women feel left out. They do, in two ways. First, to the extent most women identify with the norms of femininity, they will feel alienated, silenced, passed over, if self-creation is described in terms that they could not adopt and still feel like well-adjusted, "feminine" women.[73] Second, masculinist norms that equate self-creation with autonomy alienate many women not only because gender ideology *tells* them that successful self-creation is not premised on autonomy alone; most women's adult lives *show* them that a full adulthood is not characterized solely by autonomy. To the extent that women want to have children (and most do), a "full life" for women is defined in terms of affiliative bonds *as well as* in terms of autonomy. (This is in part, of course, because well-socialized men feel justified in deflecting their children's needs onto their women—thereby preserving for themselves a much broader range of autonomy than that enjoyed by those women.)

Those points are important ones, though I have been careful to express them a little differently from the way they usually are expressed. This usual formulation is to say that equating self-creation with mastery and autonomy leaves out women's voice, because women define themselves in terms of relationships. Note how this not only perpetuates—by feminizing—the devaluation of affiliative bonds; it also recreates a culture in which men of good faith will literally *fail to see* that they, too, value affiliative bonds as key elements in a successful adult life. Masculinist ideology is destructive not only because it leaves out women, but because it blinds both men and women to the full range of their concerns and aspirations. The full results of this are rarely recognized: It leads to a particular, and undesirable, construction of the political.

Rorty sharply constricts his definition of the public sphere in order to make the world safe for strong poets. "[A]n ideal liberal society is one which . . . has no purpose . . . except to make life easier for poets and revolutionaries while seeing to it that they make life harder for others only by words, not deeds" (61).[74] This suggests a construction of the political much narrower than Rorty's earlier work implied. That earlier work presented the polity in a positive light. Rorty's essay on "Solidarity or Objectivity?" is replete with complimentary references to "our community."[75] "Solidarity" (comradely overtones intact) is recommended as the only antidote to epistemological chaos. Rorty locates in communal life the only truth we've got or can hope to achieve. Integral to this description is a focus on the democratic process of forging truths from amongst the welter of contested certainties within American culture. Rorty's imagery of solidarity carries a Deweyan sense of purpose about the intellectual's role in helping to forge new social

truths.   It melds the social theory of knowledge with Americans'
romance with democracy.

Though *Contingency, Irony, and Solidarity* preserves the language of
human solidarity, it sharply constricts its sphere.   Rorty still views as
important the project of forging solidarity from contested and contingent
truths, but he now wants to construct a wall between the private pursuit
of perfection and one's duty as a citizen.   In the final pages of
*Contingency, Irony, and Solidarity*, he notes:

> [A] central claim of this book, which will seem . . . indecent to those
> who find the purity of morality attractive, is that our responsibilities
> to others constitute only the public side of our lives, a side which
> competes with our private affections and our private attempts at
> self-creation, and which has no automatic priority over such private
> motives. . . . Moral obligation is, in this view, to be thrown in with
> a lot of other considerations, rather than automatically trump them.
> (194).

This division into public and private reflects Rorty's fear of a
voracious morality that demands automatic priority over private
self-creation.   We have seen this morality before: Its voraciousness is
that of the Golden Rule, which defines an ambit of responsibility so wide
we are threatened with self-obliteration.   Either we live with a guilty
sense of hypocrisy or we join Mother Theresa in Calcutta.

Rorty attempts to solve this problem with a wall between public and
private.   It is a wall he does not need.   Haskell suggests a much simpler
solution: to acknowledge that—given the insane ethical ambitiousness of
our form of life—we must necessarily draw a line beyond which we will
not act on the mandate to love others as ourselves and to accept that line
as an artificial one.   Once we accept our responsibility for choosing our
truths, we must accept our responsibility for deciding at which point we
will fail to live up to our sweeping and illimitable ideals.   This is exactly
the kind of acceptance, though, that pragmatism can help us achieve.
Pragmatism's recognition of the contingency of our ideals, and its theme
of self-responsible freedom, can help us accept the inevitability of
arbitrary lives in the context of our particular form of life.   To
exaggerate only a little, my sense is that Rorty's line between public and
private stems from his concern to protect Marcel Proust.   Rorty notes the
central role of Proust in structuring his argument that "the ironist's final
vocabulary can be and should be split into a large private and a small
public sector, sectors which have no particular relation to one another"
(100).   Although I am no expert on Proust, I shall reinterpret Rorty's

interpretation of Proust in a way that eliminates the need for a wall between a narrow public and a broader private sphere. Proust, I shall argue, was involved not in the mere pursuit of private perfection, but in a cultural project with profound public consequences.

Proust's work is designed, first, to remind us that there is no God's-eye point of view. His project was a contribution to nonfoundationalist thought, not a mere frolic of his own. Proust's project was public in a second way as well. He wished to draw from this nonfoundationalist premise a point of profound political importance, namely, that people who present themselves as authorities can be de-divinized by redescribing them as simply people. No man's a hero to his valet; Proust turned this truism into a strategy for undercutting authority figures by reducing the conceptual distance between leaders and ordinary people. If we take this argument as far as the assertion that political power is everywhere, we see it as an explicitly political argument. Proust presents his concern as involving only *private* life, but ultimately Proust's project was part of a broader reconceptualization of political power.

In addition to Proust's contributions to philosophical and political thought, *Remembrance of Things Past* helped construct the ethical consciousness of the Western world. Proust's detailed description of the experience of eating a cookie carried profound ethical messages. Proust's close attention to the experience of a small child signaled, first, the antihierarchical judgment that a small boy's experience could help adults define what it means to be a human being. Proust's focus on sense experience followed the Romantics in redeeming sensuality in the face of Christianity's traditional distrust. The ordinariness of the experience reinforced a major theme in Western ethics, one Charles Taylor calls the affirmation of ordinary life.[76] In prior periods, Taylor notes, family life was viewed as important primarily because it provided the infrastructure for men's pursuit of ethical goals in the "higher" sphere of public life. Taylor documents the shift that made ordinary family life seem central to what makes a life worthwhile.[77] Taylor also argues persuasively that Proust's book carried crucial modern messages about the fragmentation of self and about the need in the modern world to construct a centered self through exercise of will.

I could go on, but perhaps this is enough to explain Proust's contributions to ethical and political life. It is these contributions that show us why Rorty needs no wall between public and private to protect Proust or anyone else. Given the scope of Proust's (severe) personal limitations, he defined his ambit of responsibility very broadly—in fact he served his fellows far better than most of us manage to do. This is not to justify the life of every self-proclaimed genius who claims to serve humanity by sitting in a padded room. For most of us, Proust's form of service is not available or not enough. We need to include our fellow humans in our projects of self-creation in quite different, much more direct ways.

Rorty's fears for Proust bring him face to face with a central challenge of our ethical tradition: how to live in peace with a voracious Golden Rule. It can, first, remind us to take a step back from our form of life, to remind ourselves that ours isn't the only way to organize the universe. This, in turn, can give us a steady appreciation for the limitations as well as the strengths of our approach, humility we urgently need in an imperialistic world. It can also help us to forgive ourselves, with the knowledge that our particular set of ideals is structured so that most adherents cannot reach them. Pragmatism holds the promise of serenity.

Rorty correctly senses that any egalitarian must approach the Golden Rule with a certain sense of resignation, with the certain knowledge that our commitment to the equal dignity of others will entail an arbitrary line beyond which we simply fail to love our neighbors as ourselves.

All this, however, evades the harder question of where we should draw that line. Rorty is ambiguous on the topic though he defines the key public goal of liberal society as avoiding cruelty. But the scope of this mandate is unclear because his definition of cruelty is ambiguous. At the center of Rorty's field of vision is the cruelty of inflicting physical pain (35, 36). If the key goal of a liberal polity is to eliminate the torture of innocents, then the scope of the public sphere is narrow indeed. But Rorty quickly widens out his notion of cruelty to include actions that "produce that special sort of pain which the brutes do not share with the humans—humiliation" (92). Once he does so, the floodgates quickly open wider and wider.

> [T]he best way to cause people long-lasting pain is to humiliate them by making the things that seemed most important to them look futile, obsolete, and powerless. Consider what happens when a child's precious possessions—the little things around which he weaves fantasies that make him a little different from other children—are described as "trash," and thrown away. Or consider what happens when these possessions are made to look ridiculous alongside those of another, richer child. (90)

What happens indeed?[78] If a defining goal of liberals is their desire "that the humiliation of human beings by other human beings may cease" (xv), and if poverty is recognized as a key source of personal humiliation, then the scope of the public sphere is wrenched wide open. Once poverty is defined as cruelty, redistribution becomes a moral mandate.

One of the most distasteful and unconvincing aspects of models of self-creation that extol autonomy and mastery is their assumption that true self-fulfillment lies solely in sustained pursuit of self-interest. The Romantic model of the strong poet is part of a much larger family of cultural images that flatten out our sense of what enriches human life. If we include in our notion of self-creation our mutual interdependence not only with those with whom we share affiliative ties—children, lovers, sports fans—but also with a broader range of strangers; if "we have a moral obligation to feel a sense of solidarity with all other human beings" (190); if we liberals "are people who include among [their central beliefs and desires] their hope that suffering will be diminished, that the humiliation of human beings by other human beings may cease" (xv), then we can't adopt a notion of self-creation that defends people's right to be as "privatistic, 'irrationalist,' and aestheticist as they please so long as they do it on their own time—causing no harm to others and using no resources needed by those less advantaged" (xiv). Or—to be more precise—we can, so long as we recognize that the conditions after the dashes are not met today. We live in a society in which white households typically have ten times as much wealth as black households,[79] in which over half of black children live in poverty[80] and one-quarter of young black males are involved in the corrections system;[81] in a society where women are one and one-half times as likely to be impoverished as men,[82] and as many as one-half of all women report domestic violence;[83] in a society in which one-fourth of all children live in poverty[84] while one percent of all households hold one-third of the personal wealth. These facts depict a society with deep patterns of systematic brutality. If our goals are egalitarian, making progress on race, class, and gender inequities is necessarily part of our personal projects of self-creation.[85] Moreover, if "the core of liberal society is a consensus that the point of social organization is to let everybody have a chance at self-creation to the best of his or her abilities . . ." (84), then we liberals need to focus on the humiliation of poverty and the existence of a large and growing underclass of Americans whose virtually only avenues of self-creation are teenage pregnancy[86] and the sale or use of drugs.[87]

I am not arguing for the priority, much less the *automatic* priority, of public responsibilities over private goals. Quite the contrary: For me, the message of pragmatism—particularly when combined with feminism—is that I can contribute to my "public" goals in the conduct of two of my chief private obsessions: my children and my writing.

Children first. For me, as for most of us in this troubled and introspective age, raising kids is a chance at personal redemption. Like my parents before me, I want to give them what I never got. If I do, I will consider it one of the chief accomplishments of my life. To a certain extent I refer to psychological goods, but I also view my childrearing as the start of a new America, a new world of gender relations. For me the personal is political every day in very concrete ways.

Writing second. Let me quote a passage from Dewey often quoted by neopragmatists (one Rorty quotes as well):

> When it is acknowledged that under disguise of dealing with ultimate reality philosophy has been occupied with the precious values embedded in social traditions, that it has sprung from a clash of social ends and from a conflict of inherited institutions with incompatible contemporary tendencies, it will be seen that the task of future philosophy is to clarify men's ideas as to the social and moral strifes of their own day.[88]

One of the attractions of pragmatism is its promise of a public role for intellectual work. Without absolutes, anything is possible, but everything remains difficult. This is particularly true if one remains committed to proceeding democratically, for any change (particularly a radical one) will be deeply contested. To the extent that what is needed to win elections is exactly the opposite from what is needed to achieve transformative goals, we need less to win elections than to produce deep cultural change (though the two are by no means mutually exclusive).

This is a pragmatist theme over a century old. Though it has sobering implications for the possibility of change, one key attraction is its implication that intellectual life holds the potential for inspiring political action. "The most [human beings] can do is to manipulate the tensions within their own epoch in order to produce the beginnings of the next epoch," as Rorty notes (51), but that is not so very little. I have argued in another context that this entails a close study of intellectual history to examine rhetorics that persuade Americans of the need to take their egalitarian instincts much more seriously.[89] It also, I have argued here, involves delving much deeper into the ways apparently neutral concepts (like the Romantic notion of self-creation) in fact create "a certain blindness in human beings."[90] Though one blindness will be replaced by another, it is time to try a new one whose blind spots do not align so eerily with pervasive patterns of oppression.

## III. Conclusion

In this paper I have made two different points. I have first warned nonfoundationalists of the pitfalls of an aestheticist tone when the discussion is one of ethics. If nonfoundationalism is to have any hope of overcoming its severe burden of implausibility, nonfoundationalists need to adopt a reassuring pragmatic tone when addressing ethical issues.

My second goal has been to challenge Rorty's advocacy of a world carved up into a small public and a large private sphere. Rorty feels compelled to adopt that vision, I suggest, by his desire to defend a notion of self-creation better deconstructed and discarded.

## Notes

Grateful thanks to James X. Dempsey, Peter A. Jazi, Dorothy Ross, Ann C. Shalleck, and Martha Woodmansee for help and advice; Tracy Hauser and Melissa Vogrin for research assistance; and to Robert Kelso and Rosemarie Pal for word processing.

1. Perspectivalism is another term for nonfoundationalism that stresses that, without absolutes, we cannot achieve a "view from nowhere." (The phrase is from Thomas Nagel's *The View from Nowhere*, cited in the bibliography.) According to William James, "What we say about reality . . . depends on the perspective in which we throw it." William James, *Pragmatism*, cited in bibliography and quoted in Joseph William Singer, "Property and Coercion in Federal Indian Law: The Conflict Between Critical and Complacent Pragmatism," *Southern California Law Review* 63 (September 1990): 1840. Note that other nonfoundationalists have used visual metaphors of blindness and gazing. See for example, Allan Megill, *Prophets of Extremity: Nietzsche, Heidegger, Foucault, Derrida* (Berkeley and Los Angeles: University of California Press, 1985), 217, 243; William James, *Talks to Teachers*, cited in bibliography.

2. See Richard Rorty, *The Linguistic Turn: Recent Essays in Philosophical Method* (Chicago: University of Chicago Press, 1967); Richard Rorty, *Philosophy and the Mirror of Nature* and *Consequences of Pragmatism* (full citations in bibliography).

3. This phrase is drawn from Hilary Putnam's *Reason, Truth, and History* (Cambridge: Cambridge University Press, 1981), 49.

4. Clifford Geertz, "Distinguished Lecture: Anti Anti-Relativism,"*American Anthropologist* 86 (June 1984): 263.

5. For a recent application of this interpretation of Nietzsche, see Thomas L. Haskell, "The Curious Persistence of Rights Talk in the 'Age of Interpretation,'" *Journal of American History* 74 (December 1987) 984—1012; for a critique, see Megill, *Prophets of Extremity*, 29—64.

6. This interpretation of Derrida's work is quite different from the one I discussed in "Critical Legal Studies: The Death of Transcendenceand the Rise of the New Langdells," cited in bibliography. There I was tracking the application to law by critical legal scholars of the Yale critics' interpretation of Derrida. Allan Megill offers a much more sympathetic and persuasive interpretation of Derrida. See Megill, *Prophets of Extremity*, 257—337.

7. For an exploration of the mirror metaphor, see Richard Rorty, *Philosophy and the Mirror of Nature*; for discussion of the tool metaphor, see Richard Rorty, *Contingency, Irony, and Solidarity*, 11—13 (cited in bibliography).

8. Cf. Clifford Geertz, "Anti Anti-Relativism," 264. The text's formulation presents the "tool" metaphor as superior to the traditional "mirror" metaphor. This is the sense in which nonfoundationalism presents a new theory of knowledge (of which the tool metaphor is an integral part). See James Kloppenberg, *Uncertain Victory* (New York: Oxford University Press, 1986), 64—94.

9. Rorty has almost single-handedly resuscitated interest in the American pragmatists John Dewey, William James, and Charles Peirce. See Cornel West, *The American Evasion of Philosophy*, 199 (cited in bibliography). For an example of open derision of Derrida's style by an eminent American intellectual historian, see Thomas Haskell, "The Curious Persistence," 992 n. 15.

10. Jeffrey Stout, *Ethics After Babel* (Boston: Beacon Press, 1988), 230.

11. Joseph William Singer, "Property and Coercion in Federal Indian Law," 1826.

12. Thomas Grey, "Hear the Other Side," 1577 (cited in bibliography).

13. Joseph William Singer, "Should Lawyers Care About Philosophy?" *Duke Law Journal* 1989 (December 1990): 1759.

14. See Joan C. Williams, "Virtue and Oppression," in *NOMOS 33: Yearbook of the American Society of Political and Legal Philosophy*, ed. John W. Chapman and William A. Galston (New York: New York University Press, forthcoming).

15. Stout, *Ethics After Babel*, 256.

16. Edward A. Purcell, Jr., *The Crisis of Democratic Theory* (Lexington: University of Kentucky Press, 1973).

17. Ibid., 70, 158.

18. Another common approach is to adopt nonfoundationalism, but to reaccess nigh-objective certainties by linking them to consensus within a given culture. For a critique of this approach, see Joan C. Williams, "Culture and Certainty: Legal History and the Reconstructive Project," *Virginia Law Review* 76 (May 1990): 713—744.

19. See, for example, P. Foot, "Moral Relativism," in *Relativism: Cognitive and Moral*, ed. J. Meiland and M. Krausz (Notre Dame, Ind.: Notre Dame University Press, 1982), 163.

20. Stout, *Ethics After Babel*, 225, 245.

21. This phrase originally was applied to republicanism. See Larry G. Simon, "The New Republicanism: Generosity of Spirit in Search of Something to Say," *William and Mary Law Review* 29 (Fall 1987): 83. I am grateful to my colleague Mark Hager for this citation.

22. Ludwig Wittgenstein, *Philosophical Investigations*, 371—373 (full citation in bibliography).

23. Cf. Ludwig Wittgenstein, *On Certainty*, trans. and ed. G.E.M. Anscombe and G. H. von Wright (New York: Harper and Row, 1969), 94, 357—358, 410.

24. Charles Taylor, *Sources of the Self: The Making of Modern Identity* (Cambridge: Cambridge University Press, 1989).

25. Public opinion polls show that 70—80% of the American public supports the death penalty. *Boston Globe*, July 28, 1990, 18.

26. I should note that, in wartime, the decision to spend the lives of some in order to save the lives of others is an everyday occurrence. This fact's inconsistency with the basic structure of our ethics is glossed over with rhetoric of duty and bravery. The North's refusal to tolerate

the South's attacks on African-American soldiers in the context noted reflected the fact that the equality of blacks and whites had become a key contested issue in the war.

27. Whether the Preamble of the *Declaration of Independence* considered "women" to be created "equal" is, of course, less clear.

28. See Charles Taylor, *Sources of the Self*, 287.

29. See George A. Buttrick, *The Interpreter's Bible* (Oxford: Abingdon-Cokesbury Press, 1952), vol. 1, 164.

30. During the concluding plenary of the Conference on Pragmatism in Law and Politics at the University of Virginia, November 7—9, 1990, the Iraqis' reported use of boys as mine sweepers during the Iran-Iraq War was cited as evidence that objective certainties exist.

31. This discussion tracks Joan C. Williams, "Abortion, Incommensurability, and Jurisprudence," *Tulane Law Review* 63 (June 1989): 1669—1670.

32. Who are "we"? Richard Rorty's notion of North Atlantic culture is useful here. See Richard Rorty, "Habermas and Lyotard on Postmodernity," 33 (cited in the bibliography).

33. This point is dramatized by the fact that we have no ungendered way to capture the serene, inspirational overtones of the phrase "universal brotherhood."

34. Thomas L. Haskell, "Capitalism and the Origins of the Humanitarian Sensibility, Part 1," *American Historical Review* 90 (April 1985): 339—362; Thomas L. Haskell, "Capitalism and the Origins of the Humanitarian Sensibility, Part 2," *American Historical Review* 90 (June 1985): 547—567. Haskell's articles have proved controversial on a number of grounds. See, for example, John Ashworth, "The Relationship Between Capitalism and Humanitarianism," *American Historical Review* 92 (October 1987): 813—829. See also David Brion Davis, "Reflection on Abolitionism and Ideological Hegemony," *American Historical Review* 92 (October 1987): 797—813; Thomas L. Haskell, "Convention and Hegemonic Interest in the Debate over Antislavery: A Reply to Davis and Ashworth," *American Historical Review* 92 (October 1987): 829—879.

35. Haskell, "Capitalism and Humanitarian Sensibility 1," 339.

36. Ibid., 354—355.

37. Ibid., 355 (emphasis in original).

38. Ibid.

39. Ibid., 349.

40. Friedrich Nietzsche, *The Will to Power* (New York: Russell & Russell, 1964), 224; Friedrich Nietzsche, *On the Genealogy of Morals and Ecce Homo*, trans. and ed. Walter Kauffman (New York: Vintage Books, 1969), 77, 80.

41. Haskell, "Capitalism and Humanitarian Sensibility 2," 549 n. 5.

42. See Haskell, "Capitalism and Humanitarian Sensibility 1," 354.

43. The traditional law of "quickening" can be interpreted as reflecting a decision to include the fetus within the community's ambit of responsibility when the mother could feel the baby move. See J. Mohr, *Abortion in America: The Origins and Evolution of National Policy* (Oxford: Oxford University Press, 1978), 3—6.

44. This describes a seven-week-old fetus. Sheila Kitzinger, *The Complete Book of Pregnancy and Childbirth* (New York: Knopf, 1990), 65. A three-month-old fetus is 2 1/2 to 3 inches long and weighs 1/2 ounce. Arlene Eisenberg, Heidi Eisenberg Murkoff, Sandee Eisenberg Hathaway, *What to Expect When You're Expecting* (New York: Workman Publishing, 1984), 120. In 1981, over 90% of abortions were performed in the first three months of pregnancy. Patrick J. Sheeran, *Women, Society, the State, and Abortion* (New York: Praeger, 1987), 20.

45. The overall United States infant mortality rate is 10.4 (per 1,000 births). This is exactly twice as high as Japan's rate. *Newsday*, March 6, 1991, 99.

46. Charles Taylor traces the theme of self-responsible freedom back to Immanuel Kant and the Enlightenment. See Taylor, *Sources of the Self*, 366—367; 167—176. Related pragmatist themes stress a world still in the making, see John Dewey, *Essays in Experimental*

*Logic* (Chicago: University of Chicago Press, 1916), 305 and John Dewey, *Reconstruction in Philosophy* (New York: H. Holt, 1920), 186, and the transformative potential of democracy, see Richard Bernstein, "Dewey, Democracy: The Task Ahead of Us," in *Post-Analytic Philosophy*, ed. John Rajchman and Cornel West (New York: Columbia University Press, 1985), 48—63, and Hilary Putnam, "Reconsideration of Deweyan Democracy," *Southern California Law Review* 63 (September 1990) reprinted as Chapter 12 below.

47. The term "moral exceptionalism" is Charles Taylor's. See Taylor, *Sources of the Self*, 397.

48. Taylor, *Sources of the Self*, 397—398.

49. In slightly different forms, this passage recurs in Cornel West's essay in *Post-Analytic Philosophy*, (book is cited in n. 46), 267, and in his *American Evasion of Philosophy*, 206 (full citation in bibliography). Here I have combined his two versions.

50. See notes 11—13 above.

51. Stout, *Ethics After Babel*, 230.

52. Ibid., 230. Quoting Hilary Putnam's "Liberation Philosophy," *London Review of Books* 8 (March 1986), 5.

53. Richard Rorty, "Feminism and Pragmatism," *Michigan Quarterly Review* 30 (Spring 1991): 231-259.

54. Rorty, *Contingency, Irony, and Solidarity*, 84. Future references to this work are noted in parentheses in the text.

55. For an earlier feminist critique that points out the masculinist bias in Rorty's Romanticism, see Nancy Fraser, "Solidarity or Singularity? Richard Rorty between Romanticism and Technocracy," reprinted in Nancy Fraser, *Unruly Practices: Power, Discourse, and Gender in Contemporary Social Theory* (Minneapolis, Minn.: University of Minnesota Press, 1989), 93—110. For another's thoughts on the relationship of pragmatism and feminism, see Margaret Radin, "The Pragmatist and the Feminist," *Southern California Law Review* 63 (September 1990) reprinted as Chapter 8 in this book.

56. Can a poet, however strong, hope to avoid ending his days in an inherited world? Of course not, a fact that highlights the acute tension between Rorty's claims for the strong poet and nonfoundationalism's social theory of knowledge. Every rebellion assumes huge areas of uncontested agreement, cf., Ludwig Wittgenstein, *Philosophical Investigations*, 115, so every poet's self-creation occurs firmly within a background in which large areas of tradition are left intact. When Rorty gains some distance on his romance with the strong poet, he recognizes this. See Rorty, *Philosophy and the Mirror of Nature*, 46.

57. Marlon B. Ross, *The Contours of Masculine Desire: Romanticism and the Rise of Women's Poetry* (Oxford: Oxford University Press, 1989). Earlier studies include *Romanticism and Feminism*, ed. Anne K. Mellor (Bloomington: Indiana University Press, 1988); Sandra M. Gilbert and Susan Gubar, *The Madwoman in the Attic: The Woman Writer and the Nineteenth Century Literary Imagination* (New Haven: Yale University Press, 1984), 98—99, 219—220, 401—403, 460—462. I am grateful to Martha Woodmansee for bringing Ross's book to my attention.

58. Ross, *The Contours of Masculine Desire*, 22, 87—186.

59. Ibid., 39.

60. Ibid., 51.

61. Ibid., 54.

62. Ibid., 31, 34, 50.

63. Ibid., 22.

64. One could add that a Wordsworthian exploration of self is the prerogative of the powerful: It rests on the assumption that the self-discoverer's emotions should be important to those around him. Critical race theorists have pointed out that neither slaves nor women have

had this luxury. In a sense the male Romantic's insistence that emotions form part of the objective reality of those around them entails the exercise of a new form of masculine power.

65. Ibid., 38.

66. Ibid., 87—111.

67. Ibid., 37—39, 49—51.

68. Ibid., 41.

69. Ibid., 49.

70. A contemporary example of this phenomenon is the popular sentiment that labels "working mothers" as "selfish" to the extent they do not continue to shoulder child-rearing responsibilities. Implicit in this view is the notion that adult women, but not adult men, should subordinate their desire for autonomy and career fulfillment to the needs of their children.

71. Ross, *The Contours of Masculine Desire*, 158—167, 187—316.

72. Indeed, Rorty's description of successful self-creation sometimes sounds like Jake, the paradigmatic male voice described by Carol Gilligan. Carol Gilligan, *In a Different Voice*, 24—38 (cited in the bibliography). I would argue that this is because the paradigm of maturity Gilligan critiques shares with the Romantics' "strong poet" the assumption that maturity means autonomy. Both these images are part of a larger pattern in which men are associated with the values celebrated within liberalism. See Joan C. Williams, "Domesticity as the Dangerous Supplement of Liberalism," *Journal of Women's History* 2 (1991): 69—88.

73. See Williams, "Domesticity as Dangerous Supplement," 74—76.

74. Rorty's belated addition of utopian revolutionaries to his list of humanity's heroes is unexplained. Why does he suddenly add the revolutionary? What makes the revolutionary a culture hero? See Rorty, *Contingency, Irony, and Solidarity*, 52, 60.

75. Richard Rorty, "Solidarity or Objectivity?" in *Post-Analytic Philosophy*, ed. John Rajchman and Cornel West (New York: Columbia University Press, 1985), 12, 13, 15.

76. Taylor, *Sources of the Self*, 211—302.

77. Ibid., 292.

78. Perhaps the reason Rorty does not answer this question is that, in this passage, he is discussing irony and redescription, not cruelty.

79. Robert Pear, "Rich Got Richer in the 80's: Others Held Even," *New York Times*, January 11, 1991, A1, col. 2.

80. Delores Kong, "Funding, Political Will Crucial To Saving Babies' Lives," *Boston Globe*, September 13, 1990, 1.

81. One in four African-American men between 20 and 29 is in jail, prison, on parole, or on probation. *Christian Science Monitor*, July 23, 1990, 20.

82. See Goldin, *Understanding the Gender Gap: An Economic History of American Women* (New York: Oxford University Press, 1990), 212.

83. Martha Mahoney, "Legal Images of Battered Women: Redefining the Issue of Separation," *Michigan Law Review* 90 (October 1991) (forthcoming).

84. This estimate is from Dr. Michael Weitzman, quoted in Kong, "Funding, Political Will Crucial to Saving Babies' Lives," 1. Other sources place the figure at 19%. In 1979, 19% of American children were raised in poverty. In New York City today, approximately 40% of children are raised in poverty. *Christian Science Monitor*, May 18, 1990, 7.

85. Pear, "Rich Got Richer in the 80's: Others Held Even," A20.

86. See Regina Austin, "Sapphire Bound!" *Wisconsin Law Review* (1989), 539—578; Anonymous, "Having a Baby Inside Me Is the Only Time I'm Really Alive," in *Black Women in White America: A Documentary History*, ed. Gerda Lerner (New York: Vintage Books, 1973): 313—314.

87. William Finnegan, "Out There," *The New Yorker*, September 10, 1990, 51; September 17, 1990, 60.

88. John Dewey, *Reconstruction in Philosophy* (Boston: Beacon Press, 1948), 26 (quoted in Rorty, *Contingency, Irony, and Solidarity*, 50).

89. See Joan C. Williams, "Virtue and Oppression."
90. William James, *Pragmatism*, 134.

# 10

## Civic Identity and the State: From Hegel to Jane Addams . . . and Beyond

*Jean Bethke Elshtain*

*I was convinced that disinterested action was like truth or beauty in its lucidity and power of appeal.*

—Jane Addams

What have G.W.F. Hegel and Jane Addams to do with pragmatism in law and society? This may seem a bit of a stretch but, indeed, it is not. American political and social thought, including pragmatism, and Hegelianism were no strangers to one another. Josiah Royce, the early John Dewey, and, most notably and dramatically, George Herbert Mead embody the Hegelian turn, or at least strong Hegelian moments, in the American tradition. Jane Addams, who will be the subject of this chapter, is not only a representative of the American Hegelian strand of pragmatism, but the liver of an exemplary life shaped and ongoingly fed by her social and political philosophy. One might call her philosophy social liberalism. I mean here to signify the Christian social hope tied to a social ontology strong in its egalitarianism that shaped her reformist thought and action.

For Addams, a life of incessant self-insistency was an impoverished life as was a life of self-capitulation and both these poles tended towards harshness and cruelty to self and others. By contrast, hers was a life of action *and* self-surrender, not capitulation, by which I mean the giving of oneself over to the passions of one's time. She insisted we must begin where we are, in a world that is there and that we neither made nor willed. In addition, quotidian concerns, an immersion in concrete

*181*

histories, in the tones, textures, and tempos—the sheer bewildering messiness of life—invites, or should, a certain humility in all activists and social philosophers. Thus she countered the unbearable lightness of liberalism in its excessively procedural and atomistic variants. Human identity is embodied and embedded—yet one can shape the particulars of a life into a story and become the protagonist of a meaningful tale. Here she countered universalists and relativists alike with her insistence on equity, reciprocity, on recognition of that concrete other who faces one as opponent or supporter, enemy or friend, foreigner or neighbor, and so on. With that I begin.

Jane Addams is a familiar name to students of American history. Though her once great fame has faded, we continue to learn of "Jane Addams of Hull House" and the era of Progressive reform of which she was a leading exemplar. But few scholars pay much attention to Addams as a social and political theorist.[1] The name Hegel, on the other hand, conjures up the intimidating picture of a world-historic thinker, a philosopher whose works are synonymous with grand, imposing systematicity. Yet Hegel and Addams meet on the ground of shared concerns—at least that is the argument I shall make. If we look at some of the problems each thinker was trying to solve or a few of the questions by which each thinker was vexed in turn, startling similarities emerge.

Hegel writes of "family, civil society, and the state"; Jane Addams of "the family claim" and "the social claim." Both struggled with the nature and purpose of the state and the relation of the human being, as "self" and "citizen" to the public world. From the point of view of an abstract idealist metaphysic, however, Addams and Hegel are lodged in embodiment and particularity. Neither fits tidily with the liberal tradition, broadly defined, though Hegel's project makes necessary reference to Kant and Addams's to American liberal culture in and through its exemplary texts and political figures. But there is an important difference in how each has been received and appropriated: Hegel is rightly celebrated as a theoretical giant. But Addams, though she was given her day as an activist, has yet to receive her due as a thinker. Taking the measure of Hegel and Addams's responses to the historic forces at work in their respective epochs, including the coming into existence of the centralized nation-state and modern nationalism, for Hegel, and the double-edge of nation and state in the twentieth century, for Addams, helps us to think about men, women, and the civic identity in our own era.

## I. Hegel and Our Age

It is impossible to approach anything like completeness in a brief discussion of Hegel. I shall stay with the central lineaments of his theory. Hegel's "self" emerges in a particular historic situation and this self reflects—or has the power to reflect—on that situation. Self-knowledge must always be cast in historical form. Experience must be earned, in a sense, and made one's own. Self-identity is ongoing and changes over time. At any given moment we as human subjects both "are" and "are not," simultaneously affirm and negate if we are open to the battle of reason and to the ambiguous disclosures of lived life. Thinking proceeds through negation, through a complex dynamic that enables us to absorb particular, concrete reality into a more systematic and complete formulation and understanding.

This no doubt says both too little and too much: too little for those who already have at least passing familiarity with Hegel and too much for those for whom he is obscure and unknown. But it must do for now. One point that must be stressed is that Hegel's is no "passive" account of mind and knowledge. He challenges the presumptions of common sense empiricists or, in our day, simple behaviorists who believe understanding proceeds from and rests upon observable facts and data-as-such. If facts do not exist "as such" for Hegel neither does the human subject or self. His is a complex depiction of the human subject's capacity for consciousness and self-consciousness as the mind works actively and purposively upon material given to it through the senses.[2]

The salient features of Hegel's social thought, for the purpose of this discussion, revolve around the three *moments* or aspects of ethical life (*Sittlichkeit*) in Hegel's system. These are the family, the sphere of ethical particularity; civil society, or ethical life in its division and appearance; and the state, the sphere of universal altruism and freedom.[3] It is with his understanding of the inner meaning or content of each of these spheres that Hegel brilliantly articulates a vision and structures dilemmas that later thinkers have had to contend with in their own reflections on liberal civil society, private life, and the state.

In contrast to classic liberalism, Hegel refuses to reduce either the family or the sphere of the state to the point of contract. His repudiation of contract theories of marriage is explicit for in the complex dialectic of love, one finds one's "self" only through absorption in the "other." The individual is not unchanged with the unfolding of this ethical moment. The family is not a series of exchanges between preposited social atoms but a many-faceted social form that fulfills basic human needs—for sustenance, for sexuality, for intimacy irreducible to the sum of these commingled parts. One cannot capture the family as a sphere of ethical life under any description that takes one part (say, sexuality or the legal contract that inaugurates marriage) for the whole thing.

Within the natural ethical realm of the family, women are in their preeminent domain. Women are the ethically particular beings *par excellence*. The "law of the family is her inherent implicit inward nature," Hegel writes.[4] Concerned with the philosophical meaning of family and love, Hegel finds the family necessary for its reciprocal identifications, its unity based on feeling, and as a kind of civic training ground: Rousseau's republican mother hovers in the background. The relations of the sphere of ethical particularity are required, indeed they make possible, an eventual civic identity and solidarity with the wider community ("itself an individuality")—at least for the male who alone is a citizen.

The family as moral ideal and social reality (however imperfectly actualized in Hegel's sense) cannot from itself guarantee the emergence of autonomous moral agents or individuals with a commitment to freedom, reflective self-understanding, and citizenship. But such developed human qualities cannot flourish in societies, real or theorized, in which "the family" as moral ideal and social reality has been eliminated or has disintegrated.

Hegel would find "proof" of his argument in the histories of twentieth-century totalitarian societies. For absolutist states without exception have taken various steps to eradicate the family as an autonomous social sphere, a locus for identity, and an arena of concrete loyalties. From Plato's plans to abolish "private families" for his Guardian class (in the interest of making "the city" as one) to the relentless policies of the Nazi German state designed to shred private loyalties and to turn the family into just another cog in the wheel of the Reich, thinkers and political leaders who demand total loyalty and who fear plurality, multiplicity of associations, and diversity of purposes *must* destroy the family. They must eradicate "the family," in Hegel's sense, as the sphere of ethical particularity as well as families in the sociological sense as sources of meaning, purpose, and commitment at least somewhat outside the dominant order and ideology.

On all these issues Hegel's discussion of the family is notable for its richness and complexity. But there are irritants in the image if one works from a perspective informed by Jane Addams's concern for an active civic life *for* women. Hegel dubs womankind "the everlasting irony [in the life] of the community." Woman, he argues, changes "by intrigue the universal activity into a work of some particular individual, and perverts the universal property of the state into a possession and ornament for the Family."[5] Women are petty-minded, in his view, and corrosive of a wider universal purpose and spirit. The woman is too individualistic—predatory on behalf of her own. (The individualism Hegel condemns is not synonymous with the abstract individualism of classical liberalism but represents, instead, a familial insularity.) She attains vicarious victories (Hegel suggests) through the "power of youth," her son. But it is a pyrrhic victory for the "brave youth in whom woman finds her pleasure . . . now has his day and his worth is openly acknowledged"—in War (capitalized by Hegel).

Family insularity, the heavy-hand of Mother, may impede the young man's transition to citizenship by goading him into premature individualism within civil society. Liberal society itself ongoingly creates a disease by bringing into being both the *necessary* particularity of the family and that sphere of triumphant self-interest, bourgeois civil society. The only "cure" for the disease is the State and the State's most potent medicine is War. Otherwise one finds only familial particularity and atomized contractualism. These two alone or taken together are insufficient to instantiate freedom and universal ethical life.[6]

As sketched this sounds rather nasty, and certainly my highly condensed version does not do justice to Hegel's complete argument. Hegel is trying to get at dynamics he finds at work in the modern world. That world is complicatedly at odds with itself but in ways that contain possibilities for resolution. For example: We require families. Without these relations life would be Hobbes's nasty, brutish, and short nightmare. But families insure separatism, division into independent entities "presided over by womankind." For civilization to triumph, for the sphere of reason to enlarge its reign, the family must be interfered with and individual self-consciousness dissolved. Women are thus essential and yet "an internal enemy," a view similar to points in Rousseau and to several of Freud's remarks in *Civilization and Its Discontents*. Necessary to . . . but not an essential part of . . . that is the irony of woman's situation as Hegel sketches it.[7]

Hegel's is a grand vision of the state. It is, to recall Aristotle's characterization of the *polis*, the "final and perfect association"—in Hegelian language the "actuality of the ethical idea." As a state-identified being, I am fulfilled only so long as I live through my communion with other citizens. My freedom is dependent on that of others, hence a supersession of the rapacious and individualistic freedom of civil society. The state transcends both familial insularity and the competitive anomie of civil society. The dynamic of civil society is an incessant machine, in Hegel's view, that transforms human needs and creates expectations it cannot, from itself, satisfy. It is a cauldron unceasingly producing conflicts, dehumanization, and disparities of wealth and poverty.

Enter the state and a way, first, to meet those human needs left unsatisfied by the competitive individualism of civil society and, second, to transcend the conflict endemic to that sphere. The state is that arena calling upon and sustaining the individual's commitment to universal ethical life, satisfying these yearnings through sacrifice on "behalf of the individuality of the state."[8] For with the state comes not simply the possibility but the inevitability of war. The human work of courage plays itself out in "the genuine, absolute, final end, the sovereignty of the state."[9] The modern world guarantees this end by transforming personal bravery into something impersonal, for "thought has invented the gun, and the invention of this weapon, which has changed the purely personal form of bravery into a more abstract one, is no accident."[10]

War transcends material values. The individual reaches for a common end. Solidarity and the power of association find a sphere of action. This solidarity is immanent within the state form. But it and the nation come to life with war. Peace poses the specific danger of sanctioning the view that the atomized world of civil society is absolute.[11] In war, however, the state as a collective being is tested and, in addition, the citizen recognizes the state as the source of all rights. Just as the individual emerges to self-conscious identity only through a struggle, so the state must struggle to attain recognition—to pass, in a sense, the definitive test of political manhood.[12]

War is also a reminder of the finiteness of individual existence. The awesome power of negativity, of death, makes itself manifest as we are drawn out of ourselves into a larger purpose. Of course, men and women are "drawn out" differently. The woman gives up her son. The man becomes what he in some sense is "meant" to be by being absorbed in the larger stream of life—war and the state.[13] In all this, Hegel does not glorify war. But he declares it a necessity, insisting it plays and has played vital historic functions. He prods us to ask why people, men and women, seem to like war so much—even as they hate it. Perhaps one reason men and women often recall wartime with fondness is for the reasons Hegel notes: They are a part of something larger than themselves; they are absorbed more fully in a communal, not simply an individualistic, freedom. They play their part in an effort requiring solidarity with their fellows. Life seems larger, somehow, and even more precious because it is threatened. This is a reverberating theme in memories and memoirs of war.[14]

The lure of war—its embodiment of the State in a grand sense and its assurance of group cohesion—forms one of the intractable poles in the life and work of Jane Addams. Addams emerged in a heady time in American life, politically and intellectually. To call her, as most do, a pragmatist after the manner of John Dewey is accurate but incomplete. Addams and Dewey drew upon a complex background including Hegel's philosophy as transmitted and Americanized in the work of Josiah Royce, who stressed the social bases of self and morality, and George Herbert Mead, the greatest American theorist of self/other.

Mead's Hegelianized argument holds that the self can be an object to itself and that the self cannot arise outside social experience nor exist in independence from an other.[15] Mead insisted, with Hegel, that consciousness of one's own self-consciousness needs recognition by others to exist. But we are not so entirely dependent on the social group in its relation to the self (Mead's word for the social whole is the "generalized other") that we must be swept up automatically, or nearly so, in group enthusiasms. Mead offers some space for an individual to brave the disapproval of the generalized other by setting up "a higher sort of community that in a certain sense outvotes the one we find," thus having a voice which "is more than the voice of the community."[16] Mead's account of ethical life finds a sphere of reason and freedom beyond the state, indeed higher than the state—a community of conscience. It is this moralized version of a yet-to-be-realized community that helps us to understand Addams's social thought and to interpret the diverse ways in which she struggled with the problems Hegel unearthed so cannily. These problems include the ethical duty to family but its limited particularity; the corrosive effect of civil society on social relations and community, yet its role in historicizing and transforming needs and springing individuals "loose" from particular ties; and the modern state and our identification *with* its universally cast purposes. How, then, does Jane Addams resolve the struggles of self/other and citizen/state in her social theory?

## II. A Return to Hull House:
## Jane Addams and Social Thought

Mistrusting systematic, highly abstract theory, and understanding how such thinking invites dogmatism, Jane Addams's approach to thought bears little resemblance to the grand Hegelian edifice. Addams's is a story-shaped life constituted in and through narrative. Her favorite mode of expression was autobiography. But she shares with Hegel the conviction that the self cannot define itself outside complex social relations. Rather than grasping these truths through overpowering language and logic, Addams begins with empathy and experience. She agrees with Rousseau: One starts with feeling. To truly understand *any* individual or feature of social life, one must enter sympathetically into the self-understanding of the other and ways of being different from one's own. Her essays, speeches, and longer autobiographical accounts revolve around stories; she generalizes universal imperatives from thickly described particular dilemmas and events.

The world in which young Jane Addams grew up was a world in transition. Dominated by the rise of the market and the radically transforming forces of capitalist accumulation, older primary relations of family and clan, small town and village, came under what was to be decades of relentless pressure. Urban centers grew up and out of control. Thousands of immigrants flooded into cities unprepared to deal with this influx of humanity. Crime, poverty, illness, unsanitary conditions, unemployment, prostitution: The image of a pastoral democracy became a Jeffersonian dream of the past. Hegel, of course, had marked the nature of civil society well. And he had attempted to work out dialectically interrelated but separate spheres of "influence," including the family and the state as well as the realm of *Homo economicus*. But women, in and through all of this, remained the "everlasting irony."

For Jane Addams, one of the first generation of college women, the world presented a picture not so much of inescapable irony as, to her mind, transformable dependencies and interdependencies. Her "solution" to the Hegelian dilemma of the woman in the home was neither to keep her there, an everlasting "irony" in the community, nor to spring her wholesale into the competitiveness of civil society, but to transform the woman into a civic being, leading an active life, who acknowledges both "the family claim" and "the social claim" and complexly mediates the legitimate obligations and possibilities flowing from each.

In her essay, "Filial Relations," which appeared in the collection *Democracy and Social Ethics*, Addams described the conflict between familial duties and dependencies and the responsibilities of the individual to the larger social whole as one both necessary and tragic. "The collision of interests, each of which has a real moral basis and a right to its own place in life, is bound to be more or less tragic. It is the struggle between two claims, the destruction of either of which would bring ruin to ethical life."[17] Hegel would not disagree. But Addams and Hegel part company on how these respective moments of ethical life, each with its "right to its own place in life" can be best preserved—can be held in some fructifying tension with one another rather than becoming paralyzing and destructive to individuals and, thereby, corrosive of the social good.

Addams understood, as Hegel did not, that women could not ongoingly play out the drama of ethical life in the private sphere or family alone. Eventually the structure will collapse (even with Hegel's terms this seems likely). Just as the public world predominates and gives meaning to the private, for Hegel public identity is central. In serving the state, the man serves a purpose larger than his own life, yet one that is the ground of his identity. But surely it is not only males whose identities are tied to the public world if we take seriously Hegel's insistence that language is essential to a shared way of life and that public and private experiences and imperatives are in some sense linguistically structured.[18] Man becomes alienated if public experiences are drained of meaning. But such alienation must be woman's lot as well, at least in part, because even if women cannot act within the public world, they can act, or believe they are acting for or in the interests of that world. Sending off sons to die in war is one grim example.

The corrosive effects of civil society cannot be forestalled indefinitely. Addams understood this and she understood as well that, deprived of responsibility to and for the state, of a civic identity, women were less capable of imparting a capacity for civic virtue to others, specifically to their children. Addams raises to an explicit concern questions of female identity and political purpose—the conflicts in which Hegel's women find themselves irrevocably stuck, unable to do other than what they have "always" done. Women, too, must undergo a struggle for identity and self-consciousness. They, too, must wrestle with dependencies and enter a wider realm of action if they are able to sustain the civic order and to serve the cause of freedom. That, at least, is Addams's hard-won conclusion. Although she asserted the "ultimate supremacy of moral agencies," she linked these to a reflective female awareness.[19] Women—the sister as well as Hegel's "brother"—experience a need to be "useful" and a part of life's larger adventure. Never wavering from the conviction that women are different from men and have a particular sensibility to offer to the greater good, Addams called upon women to enter the world yet not to abandon their own emotional and ethical lives. The family claim *is* a claim: We are duty-bound to answer. But it is not the only claim and cannot absorb the whole of us. To truly enter into ethical life, Addams argues, one must resist grand claims couched in universal abstractions and bring matters down-to-earth. Hers is a moral egalitarianism that feeds her democratic commitments. Addams insists that we not "kick off" the particular as we reach for universal understandings or imperatives. To keep one's feet on the ground, she proposes a secular version of the "imitatio Christi." For example: She charted her own life by measuring herself up against "Mr. Lincoln," a figure with whom she self-consciously identified.

Addams describes moral life and existence by filtering it *through* particular individuals and relations. For truth "may be discovered by honest reminiscence."[20] No social abstraction has authenticity, she argued, unless it is rooted in concrete human experience. Her immersion in the particular, her ability to articulate wider social meaning through powerful depictions of individual suffering or joy, hope or despair, sets her apart from those who write abstractly about moral life. One example will illustrate the suffering the early wage-labor system trailed in its wake. Addams pens an unforgettable word portrait of a single suffering woman, one human story beneath—or beyond—Hegel's theoretical characterizations of the sphere of civil society and the poor that society necessarily (in Hegel's view) creates:

> With all the efforts made by modern society to nurture and educate the young, how stupid it is to permit the mothers of young children to spend themselves in the coarser work of the world! It is curiously inconsistent that with the emphasis this generation has placed upon the mother and upon the prolongation of infancy, we constantly allow the waste of this most precious material. I cannot recall without indignation a recent experience. I was detained late one evening in an office building by a prolonged committee meeting of the Board of Education. As I came out at eleven o'clock I met in the corridor of the fourteenth floor a woman whom I knew, on her knees scrubbing the marble tiling. As she straightened to greet me, she seemed so wet from her feet up to her chin, that I hastily inquired the cause. Her reply was that she left home at five o'clock every night and had no opportunity for six hours to nurse her baby. Her mother's milk mingled with the very water with which she scrubbed the floors until she should return at midnight, heated and exhausted, to feed her screaming child with what remained within her breasts.[21]

This is very powerful stuff—a potent anthropological description meant to arouse moral feeling, to call forth compassion. Addams was convinced that only a tug upon our human sympathies and affections can draw us into an ethical life and keep us there in contrast to Kantian categorical imperatives and Hegelian systematizing, and her stories exemplify this belief. "Pity, memory, and faithfulness are natural ties with paramount claims," she writes.[22] But in this vignette we see those claims—the "family claims"—being run roughshod over by the requirements of an economically rapacious, socially irresponsible order. The scrubwoman is the actuality of the family claim and the wider social claim. And her situation, Addams assures us, is not unique but representative of the life of the immigrant poor.

Endorsing a life of action, articulating a social ontology that was Christian in its origins and tilted toward the poor and downtrodden, Addams became a state enthusiast. Although she insisted upon the need for individual effort, she joined other reformers in looking to the state, as an embodiment of a social ethic of care, as a way to ameliorate the dislocations produced by bourgeois civil society. That she was overoptimistic in her commitment to the beneficent state is no doubt true. With other Progressives she was a meliorist who sought "adjustment" to the new industrial order and its inevitable alienations. But she and the state came to a dramatic parting of the ways, and this break highlights her most dramatic disassociation from Hegel's political thought.

The rupture for Addams is World War I. Hegel's theory of war, remember, is of an activity limited in its aims and means, a uniting struggle for recognition calling citizens into a shared effort. Such war is the agent of reason and freedom. For Addams such *talk* is an errant capitulation to murder, an embrace of the state as a terrible engine of death. For one who had long associated herself with the buoyant certainty that the world was slowly but surely progressing towards ever more inclusive and benign forms—towards international cooperation, interdependence, and peace, "an inevitable historical advance," the war was a terrible blow. Breaking with such Progressive colleagues as John Dewey, who reconciled themselves to the war, Addams insisted that war coarsened human relations and posed a threat, in both the short and long runs, to democratic institutions. Hegel's solidarity is bought, for Addams, at too high a price.

She writes: "Some of us had suspected that social advance depends as much upon the *process* through which it is secured as upon the result itself."[23] Of course, she was stirred by the self-sacrificing response of youth, by their patriotism and sense of duty. Courage and a sense of devotion are always admirable. But surely we can enlist these enthusiasms in some grand cause that does not involve killing or being killed? Disillusioned by the transformation of the state into an engine of war, Addams's ideal of the democratic state as a sure and certain avatar of justice collapsed. She continued to hope the state could be turned to benign purposes. But she never took up—in any cogent way—Hegel's challenge that unity of state purpose is not possible in a liberal, individualist society unless the nation is at war.

Speaking from the point of view of "woman," defined not as an everlasting irony but as the sorrowing mother of the dislocated and dead, Addams evoked images of women as creators of nonstatist social forms. In a passage that would only confirm Hegel's view of women as mired in the particular, Addams writes:

> Undoubtedly women were then told that the interests of the tribe, the diminishing food supply, the honor of the chieftain, demanded that they leave their particular caves and go out in the wind and weather without regard to the survival of their children. But at the present moment the very names of the tribes and of the honors and the glories which they sought are forgotten, while the basic fact that the mothers held the lives of their children above all else, insisted upon staying where the children had a chance to live, and cultivate the earth for their food, laid the foundations of an ordered society.[24]

In celebrations of selfless male action in wartime, Addams sees a centuries-old trail of tears. She also alerts us to how difficult it is to stand against the "generalized other," the state-at-war, for one is "starved of any gratification of that natural desire to have [his own] decisions justified by his fellows."[25] To combat war enthusiasms, for Hegel was right about the solidarity they require and inspire, identity with a nonstatist ethic is needed. Addams found it in a civil religion indebted to Protestant Christianity and in a network of activists, most of them women, some of them pacifist. Family, civil society, and the state, she insists, do not suffice as bases for ethical life. One also requires communities of conscience, associations and movements, many plural possibilities. Otherwise, especially in times of social upheaval, the state will be all that remains standing and we will be compelled to love it—as Simone Weil once chillingly wrote—because nothing else exists.

During her lifetime, Jane Addams saw the state in which she reposed such high ethical hopes become a calculating engine of mass slaughter.[26] She did not go as far in her disillusioned critique as Randolph Bourne, another member of the Progressive intelligentsia, but never again could she entertain high Hegelian hopes. For Bourne's devastating refrain, in his unfinished 1919 fragment, "War is the health of the state," though a vulgarization, comes harrowingly close to Hegel's theory of war and the state. Writes Bourne: "Citizens are no longer indifferent to their Government, but each cell of the body politic is brimming with life and activity. We are at last on the way to full realization of that collective community in which each individual somehow contains the virtue of the whole. In a nation at war, every citizen identifies himself with the whole, and feels immensely strengthened in that identification."[27] It is this certainty that represents, for Hegel, a vital, necessary moment of ethical life. But Jane Addams sees civic tragedy, the reaffirmation of force, and the crushing of lives and hope. Between these two positions there can be no resolution.[28]

## III. From Sacrifice to Responsibility

It would be comforting to conclude on so bold a claim, so uncompromising a judgment. Alas, this is not possible. For underneath the alternative constructions of Hegel and Addams lies a vision of the citizen in relation to the state that either valorizes or calls into question the *sacrifice* of the self on behalf of others in war. Addams backs off the sacralization of war-time sacrifice, touched as she is by the preparedness of young soldiers to die for their country. But this repudiation is a simultaneous affirmation of an alternative image of civic responsibility, of living both in truth and in service to others. Recall, if you will, the dimensions of Addams's understanding of human identity and the capacity of human beings to live ethically. Ethics, she insists, is "but another word for 'righteousness,' that for which many men and women of every generation have hungered and thirsted and without which life becomes meaningless."[29] This hunger and thirsting forges desires and forms habits of the heart given her theory of child development, the story of the child becoming an adult, as a *Bildung* of a very special sort. Blind appetite, she insists, transforms into psychic impulsions informed by moral motives. If the child is early neglected, the man, and woman, will remain impervious to the gentler aspects of life. Adults must not force the moral nature of the child beyond that of which she is capable but neither should they expect so little that the child's hunger and thirsting are dissatisfied, becoming a font of cynicism, even despair. Discipline, yes; tyrannical impression, no. Truth and experience must be linked for child and adult alike. The mnemonic traces of early sympathetic understandings remain an ever present source of later, knowing propulsion into social life, into service to others.

Addams's is not an aspiration to autochthony, towards a rational self-consciousness that suppresses the familial and the female.[30]  No, she recognizes the tugs and strains of a life as lived.  Thus she remained open to the lure of war-induced nationalism; she understood the appeal, but she was also capable of resisting it, of bringing alternative strains and claims to bear.  For Addams a life of service need not be a life that claims, more or less automatically as a condition of civic membership for young males, the "highest sacrifice" in time of war.  Her politics shifts the focus of political loyalty and identity from sacrifice (actual or in situ) to responsibility.  I want to be very careful here.  She accepted, as do current democratic protesters and theorists in Central Eastern Europe, the fact that there are causes worth suffering and dying for.  But such sacrifice should not be sacralized; should not be deified as in Hegel's demanding vision of the *Kriegstaat*.

With Vaclav Havel, she ties human identity to responsibility.  And the development of responsibility requires a rich, "thick" social base.  It was, for Addams, a "monstrous absurdity" for society to refuse to recognize the contributions of parents, especially mothers, and to force them into situations that compromise *both* the family and the social claim.  Addams understood that the nation-state is a phenomenon that cannot be imagined or legislated out of existence.  But she aimed to tame and to limit state demands even as she enormously enhanced the legitimate aims and claims of citizens.  She would share wholeheartedly Havel's insistence that politics is a form of practical morality, of humanly measured care for our fellow human beings.

To serve is to be dutiful, not as a servant to a master but as a free citizen to her willingly acknowledged and accepted civic responsibilities.  To be responsible is to be capable of fulfilling an obligation or trust, to be reliable, and of good credit and repute.  Sacrifice that takes the form of blood offerings to various gods of war whenever and wherever the call goes out—that she rejects, but not civic responsibility and duty.  My hunch is that she would find in much contemporary postmodern or deconstructive discourse too thin an account of the self, hence, too labile a structure for the formation of civic identity.  As a result there would be no basis from which to either reject war-time sacrifice or to construct some alternative notion of living in service to others as a central feature of civic identity.  For Addams civic life is no carnival of difference in which Dionysus reigns supreme, but a rich tapestry, perhaps a State Fair.  We come together, not to celebrate "the different" per se—a hopelessly abstract injunction in any case—but to reveal ourselves and our works to others who share with us some general purposes and some of whom are in a position to offer judgments and understandings that may be challenged the next time 'round.

Unlike many contemporary pragmatists who are too jolly by far, as well as past and present Hegelians who oppress with their systematic stuffiness, Addams looked to a future mindful of the terrible wreckage of the past. Not quite Walter Benjamin's mordant meditation on Paul Klee's painting, "*Angelus Novus*" in which the angel of history is driven into the future "while the pile of debris before him grows toward the sky. That which we call progress is this storm."[31] Addams's view of the future is nevertheless one acquainted with spooks in the night, yet ever open to the dream and promise of American democracy.

## Notes

1. Christopher Lasch is an important exception. He discusses Addams at length in his *New Radicalism in America, 1889—1963* (New York: Vintage, 1965), 3—37, and in his edited collection of excerpts from her writings, published as *The Social Thought of Jane Addams* (Indianapolis: Bobbs-Merrill, 1965). This chapter incorporates and goes beyond a discussion in my now out-of-print book, *Meditations on Modern Political Thought* (New York: Praeger, 1986).

2. For this discussion I draw upon G.W.F. Hegel, *Phenomenology of Spirit*, trans. A. V. Miller (London: Oxford University Press, 1977) as well as on my own previous interpretations in *Public Man, Private Woman* (Princeton, N.J.: Princeton University Press, 1981).

3. The key text here is G.W.F. Hegel, *Philosophy of Right*, trans. T. M. Knox (Oxford: Oxford University Press, 1967). A highly condensed and lucid advanced introduction to Hegel's understanding of ethical life and theory of the state remains Shlomo Avineri, *Hegel's Theory of the Modern State* (Cambridge: Cambridge University Press, 1972).

4. Hegel, *Phenomenology*, 476. Cf. Hegel, *Philosophy of Right*, par. 166, pp. 114—115.

5. Hegel, *Phenomenology*, 488.

6. This should sound familiar if one remembers Tocqueville's apprehensions concerning the characteristic vice toward which bourgeois civil society pushes—social fragmentation, the break-down of association, and so on.

7. See also Hegel's discussion of *Antigone* in *Phenomenology* and in *Philosophy of Right* and contrast it with my article, "Antigone's Daughters," *democracy* (April 1982): 46—59.

8. Hegel, *Philosophy of Right*, 210.

9. Ibid., 211.

10. Ibid., 212.

11. See Hegel, *Philosophy of Right*, 278.

12. If one surveys briefly just the wars fought in the post-World War II era, most have been wars of "national liberation," wars to create and to gain recognition for one's nation. Hegel would certainly see this as evidence for his thesis.

13. Avineri's chapter on "War" in *Hegel's Theory of the Modern State* is provocative and detailed.

14. Hegel does warn that protracted war may backfire, may have debilitating effects, as does any war that is total rather than limited, fueled by rapaciousness rather than the struggle for recognition.

15. George Herbert Mead, *Mind, Self and Society* (Chicago: University of Chicago Press, 1962), 140.

16. Ibid., 167—168, 189.

17. Jane Addams, *Democracy and Social Ethics* (New York: Macmillan, 1902), 76—77.

18. I draw here upon portions of the discussion of Hegel in *Public Man, Private Woman,* 180.

19. Jane Addams, *The Long Road of Woman's Memory* (New York: Macmillan, 1916), 129.

20. Jane Addams, *Second Twenty Years at Hull House,* in *Forty Years at Hull House,* (New York: Macmillan, 1935), 6.

21. Jane Addams, *Twenty Years at Hull House* (New York: Macmillan, 1968), 174—175.

22. Ibid., 247.

23. Jane Addams, *Peace and Bread in Time of War* (Boston: G. K. Hall, 1960), 132.

24. Addams, *Long Road,* 126—127.

25. Addams, *Peace and Bread,* 150.

26. For example, in the first day of the Battle of the Somme, July 1, 1916, 110,000 British men got out of the trenches and began to walk forward along a thirteen-mile front. They had no visible enemy to fight; they wore number tags around their necks; 60,000 were dead by the end of the day. This is the modern soldier not as a warrior but as cannon fodder, an observation Addams made over and over again of the tragedy of World War I.

27. Randolph Bourne, *The Radical Will, 1911—1918* (New York: Urizen, 1978), 361.

28. Perhaps, horrifyingly, the possibility of nuclear war literally explodes Hegel's theory of war. For nuclear war cannot end in mutual state-recognitions but, instead, in mutual state obliterations, thus defeating the major purpose of war fighting. As well, because nuclear war is total and indiscriminate it does not allow for solidarity and commitment; rather, as social atoms, we are all potential victims and there are no warriors.

29. Jane Addams, *Democracy and Social Ethics* (Cambridge, Mass.: Harvard University Press, 1964), 1.

30. See Martha Nussbaum's discussion in *The Fragility of Goodness* (Cambridge: Cambridge University Press, 1986), 40.

31. Cited in Susan Buck Morss, *The Dialectic of Seeing* (Cambridge, Mass.: MIT Press, 1989), 95.

# 11

## Punishment and Legitimacy

### *Milton Fisk*

### I. The State and Legitimacy

I shall speak about punishment as the inflicting of harm that is properly authorized by state institutions. I shall, then, ignore harm that results from extralegal state activity. This limits my discussion to only one form of state repression, the one that is often taken to be a legitimate exercise of its power. The question I want to raise is how such properly authorized harming can be legitimate.

This question is part of a much broader one about the legitimacy of the state itself.[1] Legitimacy goes beyond acceptance out of fear; it involves acceptance based on a variety of possible responses to the state. Associated with the liberal theory of the state is the requirement that the legitimate state achieve acceptance through being in accord with fundamental moral principles.[2] I shall speak of this view as one that calls for moralizing the state. As applied to punishment, it is the view that legitimate punishment can be moralized. Punishments for crimes would then be in accord with fundamental moral principles.

Punishment makes the case for state legitimacy a tough one. First, when it punishes, the state, which is presumably to protect its citizens, uses its power against them. Naturally, those who see themselves as protected when the state uses power against offenders will be less likely to find a problem here. But those against whom the state uses its power will be more likely to question the state's legitimacy. If they are to accept the state, its punishment of them must make sense in terms that refer beyond the interests of those who are protected. But is there a way to surmount the differences between the protected and the punished that will lead the latter to accept the state?

Second, there are deep divisions in the society over whether and how much punishment to apply. According to their different interests, different groups in the society will have different conceptions of what is punishable and what the sanctions should be. A state that is not neutral in regard to these differences will establish only a tenuous legitimacy within the groups it sides against.[3] We face again the question as to how the state can surmount these differences to achieve legitimacy. Since the state is still in part a "body of armed men," punishment must be legitimated for there to be overall state legitimacy.

Difficulties of this sort abound, making the search for a moral justification of state punishment, on the basis of fundamental moral principles, a futile one. After establishing its futility in what follows, I shall cast doubt on the whole procedure that seeks first to legitimate punishment in order then to avoid a problem with the legitimacy of the state as a whole. The logic of legitimacy takes an unexpected turn here. Punishment comes on the scene not to be legitimated itself but in order to legitimate the state of which it is a part. It is not just that punishment makes citizens fear the state. It is rather that punishment generates respect for the legal order that is vital, at least to the liberal state on which I shall focus.

## II. Internal and External Legitimation

Punishment is, to be sure, not merely a legitimator; it is also legitimated, but only in an internal way. That is, it is legitimated by being called for by courts of law in response mainly to what the state has come to call crimes against the public. In saying that this is an internal legitimation of punishment I do not wish to imply that the procedures of the courts, the criminalization of certain behavior, and the setting of limits on sanctions are determined in a political vacuum. They reflect, of course, popular demands either for moderation or for greater harshness, either for a greater burden on the state in making its case or for a lesser burden for the prosecution. The state itself cannot remain legitimate while systematically ignoring such demands.[4]

This internal legitimacy is not, then, purely formal; it does not derive simply from the consistency of punishment with the requirements of the legal/penal system, without regard to whether that system is responsive to popular demands. Nonetheless, this legitimacy of punishment is internal to the state to the extent that the state does not simply adopt popular demands as they are presented. If it did this the contradictions within it would become so pronounced that the state would be incapacitated, for those popular demands have different origins and thus conflict sharply with one another. Thus the state fashions its response to these demands by selecting from among them and modifying them. It puts its imprint on them and to that extent the legitimacy of punishment derives from norms fashioned from within the state.

This internal legitimacy contrasts with the alleged legitimacy provided by agreement with fundamental moral principles. These principles are supposed to be outside the state; they either originate directly in the moral base of the society or else have a transcendent status. Given the cohesiveness even of societies with deep divisions, there is some prospect that fundamental moral principles originate directly within society. Yet it would be a mark against the project of moralizing punishment if it had to resort to the transcendent, with all its attendant metaphysical problems. I shall then pursue the matter of external legitimacy from only the social perspective.

The important thing about the project of moralizing punishment is that it takes up a critical attitude toward an aspect of the state from a perspective within society. A separation of state from society is assumed by this critical attitude. One might object that because the state has an influence on everything in society such a separation is dubious, and hence even a critical attitude is influenced by the state. But the critical attitude and the principles it is based on are not state attitudes and principles, as was the case with norms the state adopts in the face of popular demands. Instead, they have the potential, despite being influenced by the state, for generating a condemnation of the state that the internal procedures and norms of the state itself could not generate. However much it may be influenced by the state, the critical standpoint in the society toward punishment is still not the standpoint of the state.[5] The critical attitude is a political necessity for those whose position in society makes them most vulnerable to punishment. Others, whose position is less vulnerable, may be satisfied with punishment's internal legitimacy. For them it is enough that punishment by their state not be arbitrary; it is enough, that is, that it be reasonably consistent and is occasionally responsive to popular demands for reform, however conflicting these responses might be.

The question formulated by those who take the critical attitude is as follows: On what basis does the state define some of our actions and omissions as criminal with a view to punishing us for them? This question might be challenged by those who adopt the pragmatic perspective that only internal questions are acceptable, for how can one pretend to raise a question about the legitimacy of state practices from outside the state? If, as I believe, the state is only relatively autonomous from the society, then the state's rootedness in the society is sufficient to allow this question to be raised about it from within the society. If, though, the state were fully autonomous, it could reasonably be argued that critical questions about it could only be raised from within it, for societal norms would not automatically be relevant to an autonomous state. I cannot then accept a form of pragmatism that limits questions of legitimation to ones purely internal to the state.[6] This limitation would make sense only for a fully autonomous state.

However, accepting the critical question does not presuppose there is an acceptable basis for punishment. The question is legitimate even though it receives a negative reply. I will, in fact, be arguing that moralizing punishment by the liberal state fails. There is no moral basis in the society for defining criminality and punishing the criminal. If this is correct, there is a pull in the other direction: Instead of seeking an external legitimation for punishment, one seeks a legitimation of the state by punishment. Though punishment would then admit of nothing more than internal legitimation, efforts to moralize it would continue because they would usefully conceal the fact that punishment is only a legitimator.

As far as the liberal state goes, my view has the same practical result as the pragmatic view: There is only an internal justification of punishment. There are, though, circumstances, differing from those associated with the liberal state, that might allow a legitimation of punishment from a standpoint outside the state. However, such circumstances would involve a reduction in the antagonistic social divisions associated with the liberal state. By eliminating the critical question, pragmatism overlooks the possibility of successfully moralizing punishment in such a case.

## III. Retributivism

Punishment is moralized in two ways. One of them is the retributivist way. Its popularity among theorists today coincides with the rise of a retributivist attitude in the society. The reemergence of capital punishment in the United States in the 1980s is the popular symbol of this retributivism in a liberal setting. The other way is the futurist way; I call it this since it moralizes punishment in terms of its ability to create a better future. Making people suffer—whether by beating, incarceration, fines, or mandatory attendance at therapy sessions—is justified only by its future effect. The futurist way of moralizing punishment includes a concern for the reform of those who commit offenses, but it is compatible with the recognition of irreformable offenders, whose punishment is then geared merely to protecting society from them.

Retributivism is the dominant tendency now, so I shall focus on it.[7] But first it will be important to sketch how the results of my general argument will apply to the futurist way as well. The futurist way depends on the assumption that the state can say what a better future is and that its conception of the reformed offender is a good one. So we can pose the critical question: On what basis is the state a judge of what is good, or what is better, for offenders and for the society?

It cannot judge simply on the basis of what some group in the society wants for the future. That would ignore the other groups and compromise state legitimacy. The state will have to look behind such disagreements for principles on which diverse groups can agree, principles we have already called fundamental moral principles. But this is just what we sketched out in Section 2 as a requirement for moralizing punishment generally. It is then a requirement for both the retributivist and the futurist approaches to moralizing punishment. I show below that the retributivist approach fails due to the absence in a divided society of a consensus on a system of fundamental moral principles. The kinds of principles needed for the futurist approach may have a different content, but in a divided society it will be no less likely that there will be a consensus on them. So my argument against the retributivist approach will tend to undermine the futurist approach as well. But to reach that argument against retributivism I shall first move through some intermediate stages.

The theory of the criminal law is usually cast against a background of retributivism. It is assumed that those who do wrong deserve punishment.[8] The question this theory addresses is an important but quite a different one from the above. It is about insuring a fair match of punishment with the accused, not about whether punishing anyone can be fair. The theory addresses the matter of the rights of the accused when faced with the possibility of a sentence that would punish them for an alleged wrong. It is about how to be sure the accused deserves the punishment. The relevant questions become: Can the accused be sentenced in the absence of a clear law; for thought instead of action; for thoughtless negligence; when no harm has resulted; for action that is causally remote from a harm; or when the wrong was necessary to avoid a greater harm?

There are two issues that need to be looked at here. The first concerns the claim that (A) in certain cases, doing wrong implies being deserving of punishment; (B) at least in some cases, being deserving of punishment implies that the state is to sentence the wrongdoer and administer the punishment. The question in each case is whether the claim can possibly be substantiated in other than a blatantly ideological way. Liberal retributivism needs to give us some nonideological reason for thinking that both of these claims can be justified. Otherwise, the legitimacy of state punishment itself remains unsubstantiated.

One might try to get this chain of implications—(A) "doing wrong → deserving punishment" and (B) "deserving punishment → being punished by the state"—justified with the device of appealing to fundamental moral principles that make certain behavior wrong. This would, though, not be enough. For there doesn't seem to be any case of wrongful behavior from which it can be inferred, just from its being wrong, that it is punishable or punishable by the state. To be sure some wrongs are punished, whereas others, like denying affection to your child or voting for a racist measure, are not, at least outside Hell or Purgatory. How, though, do we distinguish between those that are punishable, on earth, and those that aren't?

In addition to the chain of implications we need fundamental moral principles including those that specify not just wrong behavior, but also punishable behavior. Any such principles would, though, be difficult to justify to everyone's satisfaction in view of the constant changes in what is deemed punishable. We used to perform a charivari when older men married younger women, but they are no longer thought deserving of punishment.[9] Changing conceptions of humanity doubtless lie behind such changes in our conceptions of punishable actions. But within any society today there will be several passionately held conceptions of humanity, each with its own implications for what is punishable. This situation leads, on the one hand, to there being many who think they are made subjects of punishment because of an unwarrantedly broad view held by others of what wrongs are punishable, and on the other hand, to there being many who think that those who offend them will not be punished because of an unwarrantedly narrow view held by others of what wrongs are punishable. People who might think abortion is wrong differ, in view of their differing conceptions of what is humane, over whether pregnant mothers and their doctors should be punished for voluntary abortions. Another failure of agreement on principles of punishability occurs when the state does not, whereas certain others do, consider punishable many practices associated with ownership that kill or disable people. Preventable workplace hazards, though wrongs of some sort, are not considered murderous or criminally negligent by the state; otherwise the state might have to agree with many workers that work for wages is forced rather than freely consented to. Similarly, as Cora Diamond has noted, victims of various forms of sexual abuse would consider those abusing them deserving of punishment, even though those committed to male domination would object or at least argue for less severe punishment.[10] So even in cases where many people find a wrong has occurred, there may still be strong opposition to punishment.

The job is no easier when we turn to the second implication in the chain, the one from the existence of certain kinds of punishable behavior to its being within the state's domain to sentence and punish the offender. The problem here is that when the state punishes, it is not the victim nor does it seek to compensate the victim or those close to the victim by forcing the offender to pay damages. The state is an interloper forcing the victim aside in order to deal with the offender directly. There are of course crimes against the state itself, such as treason, in which the state is both victim and judge. But these crimes remain artifacts of the state until such a time as the state becomes legitimate itself. But to legitimate it one must first legitimate its power to punish when it is not the victim.

A response to this anarchistic-sounding line of criticism might be that, as the punishment is deserved on the basis of fundamental moral principles, a reliable authority like the state must take on the task of punishment to insure it gets done. The fact is, though, that it does get as reliably done by other hands, both by individuals and institutions. As punishment, fathers disinherit wastrel children and institutions fire members guilty of gross improprieties. It would be difficult to get around this fact by claiming that, still, there is a basic difference between the cases of wrong where the state is needed to punish and these other cases. The line between state and private jurisdictions for punishment is too shifting and uncertain to support such a claim.

In addition, the state's reliability is hardly such that it insures punishment is done. The bias of the state is notorious in regard to punishment; neither the laws nor their administration are evenhanded. Its agenda of promoting the dominant conception of the society—until social pressures, as in the case of the black movement of the 1960s, chip away at its agenda as well as at that dominant conception—makes this inevitable rather than an accident of the corruption by power of certain officials. Members of the lower classes and of certain oppressed groups have fewer defenses against the state. Those in dominant groups, despite notorious wrongs, tend to escape punishment or get lighter sentencing. Attacks on minorities by racists and on women by those intent on sexual abuse   often leave the victims of such attacks with little hope of punishment for the attackers.   The state prefers to sue upper-class lawbreakers in civil court rather than to treat the wealthy as criminals. Though crimes of the poor against property cost the public less than white-collar crime, the sentencing for crimes of the poor is stiffer.[11] We can't then base much on the reliability of the state in punishing wrongdoers. Instead, we could look to the power of the state in order to have some chance that punishment will be systematically, though perhaps not fairly, carried out in our complex society. But this would be a frankly amoral concern on our part, one turning on efficiency in handling lots of alleged offenses with no guarantee that wrongdoers would be punished.

I will say no more about implication (B), that process from punishable wrong to state sentencing.   It suffices to have raised a question about its familiar justification in terms of the reliability of the state as a punisher.   Instead I will concentrate on implication (A), that process from wrong to punishment. We must look more closely at the basis for the fundamental moral principles that might justify this first implication.

## IV. Community Consensus

In his *Law's Empire* Ronald Dworkin places the question of state legitimacy in the context of a communitarian theory of morality. He takes fundamental moral principles to arise from the history of a community rather than from individual choices of principles.  These principles can then be the source of the legitimacy of the state, and of punishment, if the state's actions can be seen as flowing from them. Going back to such principles is important for legitimacy because a state whose actions represent compromises between different pressure groups will sacrifice integrity—acting on principle—to the strongest pressure of the moment.  And without integrity there is no reason for those the state happens to decide against to support its decision rather than to undermine it.

Dworkin assumes that the principles of justice, fairness, and due process from which a state's actions might actually flow are those of a community.   Its members view themselves as guided by common principles. They and their forebears have worked them out in debate. This is not a community either of strangers or of antagonistic groups; such communities would be guided by artificial compacts and compromises needed to avoid conflicts rather than by common underlying principles. Dworkin calls his model of community, in which members are guided by common principles, the model of principle. As in contract theory, the legitimacy of the state depends on a "theater of debate," but unlike contract theory, individualist assumptions are jettisoned in Dworkin's model of community. He calls the model in which antagonistic groups agree on rules to avoid conflict the rulebook model. A state in a rulebook community could not claim moral legitimacy, and no moral legitimacy could be claimed for its power to punish. The reason is that the rules arrived at within such a community and its state are a result of a power struggle between competing social forces. And power cannot moralize the state or punishment. Only principle can.

If we go only this far with Dworkin, his argument seems to yield the conclusion that punishment cannot be legitimated in today's liberal democracies. For the model of principle seems distant from, whereas that of the rulebook seems closer to, actually existing communities. But this would be to miss the point of Dworkin's project. He is intent on legitimating the liberal state in general—with its representative democracy, its separation of powers, and its support for the market—and that of the United States in particular. Thus he is committed to holding that in the United States the model of principle applies sufficiently well, despite need for improvement, to allow for moralizing its state. He offers little to substantiate this claim and makes no attempt to show that the rulebook model is not a better approximation.[12]

It would be a mistake to limit ourselves to the alternatives Dworkin provides. The rulebook model is a bit too stark to illuminate the reality of communities. But it touches on something that needs to be recognized in a more adequate model. The model of principle is also wide of the mark; its fraternal members may experience the divisiveness of class and oppression but Dworkin is not concerned lest this impede their progress to moral unity.[13] Still, the note of unity the model of principle catches is worth preserving in a modified form in a more adequate model; there is in fact a submission to shared values in most communities, a submission the rulebook model of community is simply too stark to capture.

But there are several qualifications on this submission to shared values that prevent us from equating it with the submission to common principles in the model of principle. First, although there are members of opposed groups who submit to these so-called common principles, enough do not submit to make dissent an important factor alongside consent. This is precisely where the need for shared values to paper over deep divisions on principles comes in. Those who consent to what are thought to be principles are not a permanent majority, but a majority with a fluctuating membership. To govern, the state cannot ignore the fluctuating group of dissidents. For them, and for those whose consent is compatible with support for some of their causes, rulebook measures must be devised. That is, compromises that may even flaunt principle will be a necessity for legitimacy. But this will no longer be a moral legitimacy of the kind the liberal had hoped for. Nonetheless, the state will appeal to certain value slogans to paper over the compromises.

Second, these value slogans promoted by the state become the shared values that decent citizens are guided by, and hence these shared values have little in common with fundamental moral principles reached by consensus in open debate. (I call them shared values rather than common principles simply to keep straight the fact that they aren't the common principles reached in open debate within the society.) An accurate picture of these shared values gives a central place to the state itself in forming the consensus on them among decent citizens. The different groups in a community are, as in the rulebook model, too preoccupied with protecting their own turf to build a society-wide consensus around a group of principles. In Gramscian terms, they are too preoccupied with their own "corporate interests" to build a moral hegemony.[14] Once, however, someone takes on the job of ruling and sentencing to punishment, there is a need to build such a consensus just in order to rule. The state must then devise its own legitimation in face of the centrifugal forces of opposed social groups. To do this it should be at least relatively autonomous from that divided society. For if it is an arena of debate that merely reflects the divisions in the society, that debate will yield pragmatic compromises without shared values.

So we see that there is a third model, showing better credentials for application to existing communities than either of Dworkin's. Let's call it *the mixed model* since it mixes antagonistic groups with a unity in the form of shared values. Where does the mixed model leave us with the problem of moralizing punishment? The liberal problem of moralizing the state and punishment was conceived as one with a solution outside the institutions of the state itself. There was to be a moral standard either transcendent to society or immanent in it that the state could be held to and legitimated by. Now, with the mixed model, we reach a supposed solution that is only outside the state as a result of the state putting it there. To hold the state to this standard is to hold it to its own device for generating a consensus on values where there is division.[15] To say that this device moralizes the state is to take the notion of morality in an ideological sense, that is, it represents what is in the special interest of some—in this case those who govern—as being in the general interest.

There are, then, difficulties with the approach taken by Dworkin to moralizing the state. On the one hand, the state must resort to compromises that will be at the expense of principles in order to secure at least a truce with the large number in any society who are effectively outside the circle of consent on common principles. Thus it is that there are not just laws but also decisions of the courts that cannot easily be illuminated by a common set of principles, as the Critical Legal Studies school has attempted to point out.

On the other hand, the damage done by compromises necessitated by divisions in the society goes even deeper. Compromises eventually go against the state-promoted values intended to obscure the fact that they are compromises. Equality is one of the values associated with numerous limited, legal protections of equality, from the constitutional equal-protection clause, to giving workers a chance to press demands with owners through unions, and then to 1960s civil-rights legislation. Yet the value of equality is undercut as further compromises are made. Racial equality is undercut when, as now, the burden of proof in regard to discriminatory job practices is placed, not on the employer, but on the potential employee. And economic equality is undercut when employers are free to replace strikers immediately in economic disputes.[16] In bending one way to react to one social vector and at a later date another way to react to yet another social vector, the state undercuts the values with which it has so painstakingly created the circle of consent. There are, of course, ways to conceal the fact that together these compromises clash with the state-made consent. But in the end, cynicism about the state replaces consent; it is doubted that it was ever serious about the shared values around which it built its ability to govern.

## V. From Morality to Power

There is something fundamentally wrongheaded about the moralizing approach of liberal theory to punishment. That approach starts with the assumption that punishment within the well-run liberal state should admit of a moral legitimation. This approach has deep roots in the desire to get beyond the abuses of the absolute state of late feudalism and of the one-party states of Fascism and Communism. The moral rhetoric used in criticism of those abuses has made liberal theory resistant to recognizing the fact that power rather than universalist morality is also a root of the modern liberal state. As Reinhold Niebuhr put it, the most significant moral characteristic of the modern state remains its hypocrisy.[17] Its moralizing covers its use of power.

Retribution cannot, as we saw, be given moral legitimacy by basing it on values imposed by the state for the purpose of unifying the society. By similar reasoning, the futurist view of punishment cannot be given moral legitimacy by basing it on values for constructing a better society that are also imposed by the state in the interest of its own governability. Having then no luck with moralizing punishment, we might try taking a look at the role of punishment in the political arena.

There is doubtless no one role, but certain alleged roles merit our suspicion. For example, it is said that punishment is for stopping crimes. But as Foucault wryly notes, crimes are usually defined so there can be punishment.[18] The savings-and-loan companies scandal in the United States illustrates his point nicely. Congresspeople, in responding to outrage among voters, have proposed harsher sentences for criminal actions believed to have led to S&L insolvency. Punishing more harshly would allow the state to appear outraged by a crisis for which in fact it bears considerable responsibility. This legitimating role of punishment should not be overlooked in favor of its alleged deterrent role.

A popular outcry at certain abuses often leads the state to consider criminalizing a new category or imposing harsher punishment for other categories. Such consideration is a response to a retributivist attitude in the population, but the state itself responds to this attitude, not for parallel reasons of retribution but for reasons of governability. Governability is a matter of the power to continue ruling. Even in the absence of a public outcry at certain abuses, the state may punish to remind the populace of its power when its laws, decrees, or procedures are defied.

In whatever cases we choose, the state promotes, or attempts to promote, through the threat of punishment an awe for its laws, decrees, and procedures. The political psychology of this awe is a complex one. Some of the elements in that psychology are the following. First, there is the element of force, a force normally able to overcome any opposition to the administration of punishment. Second, there is the magnitude of the harms inflicted by punishment, harms often greater than those private citizens are allowed to inflict on one another. Third, there is the omnipresence of the state, making it virtually inescapable for the offender. Fourth, there is the seeming fairness of the state in the legal/penal process, a fairness coming from the fact that popular pressures, rather than a single will, have had an influence on the laws and on procedures of their application.

In the awareness of the innocent citizen these elements combine to generate a feeling of awe. In isolation, though, they are incapable of generating more than fear before extraordinary power or a sense of nonarbitrariness before a responsive process. Taken together they generate not the fear that makes one cringe, but a feeling of wonder at and respect for a state order that while responsive to popular pressures is implemented with overwhelming power. Even if one has one's doubts about the justness of some of the laws or decrees of the state, the fact that their violation is such a grave matter in the eyes of the state makes one discount one's doubts in order to be reconciled with the state.[19] Of course, if one thought that the laws, decrees, and procedures were arbitrary, that is, that they were reflections of the interests of one person or of one group at the expense of the rest, then the great power manifested in surveillance and punishment would occasion cringing or outrage without awe.

Awe is a link that leads us from the internal legitimacy of the state to its external legitimacy, but here this external legitimacy is of the nonmoral sort. As noted in Section 2, internal legitimacy rests not just on consistently following certain laws and procedures but also on there being a popular element in these laws and procedures that keeps them from being arbitrary. As we saw, this popular element is not external because the state selects what it wants from it. Beyond this there must be something apart from the state that is the basis for external legitimacy. I am suggesting that the awe felt by the citizen confronted with the state's punitive role is at least one of the external legitimators. Machiavelli had it almost right when he wrote:

> And men have less scruple in offending one who makes himself loved than one who makes himself feared; for love is held by a chain of obligation which, men being selfish, is broken whenever it serves their purpose; but fear is maintained by a dread of punishment which never fails. Still, a prince should make himself feared in such a way that if he does not gain love, he at any rate avoids hatred; for fear and the absence of hatred may well go together, and will be always attained by one who abstains from interfering with the property of his citizens and subjects or with their women.[20]

This fear without hatred, which is close to legitimacy, cannot, we are being told, be based on arbitrary sanctions. It is limited by popular pressures, the chief of which Machiavelli took to be pressures against the confiscation of property and the violation of women by the state. But fear without hatred need not, in my view, be sufficient for acceptance of the state; for that, the more complex awe at the order of the state is needed.

Punishment, then, does serve to legitimate the state through making the state awesome. By criminalizing behavior the state takes advantage of the possibility this holds out for legitimizing the state. In prestate societies there was no comparable need to legitimize, so notables with a special position in regard to holding the society together did not, in general, criminalize categories of behavior and hence did not punish offenders.[21]

But didn't their role as judges and counselors actually demand for them a legitimation of the very kind that punishment could provide? To answer, we need to consider what the demands of legitimacy in a homogeneous society such as theirs would be. These demands are minimal, at least when behavior is narrowly defined by custom. In comparison the demands of legitimacy are much greater in a society divided by class and various oppressions and where trends rather than customs are the norms of behavior. We need to add to this the practical fact that in a prestate society there was often no concentration of power sufficient for the administration of punishment throughout the society.

Let us take account of where we are. In the last section I did not quite show that it is impossible to justify punishment morally. I showed only that it would be impossible on a double assumption. First, I assumed that the justification would be social in nature, being based on the community it takes place in. Second, I assumed that a realistic model of the kind of community we live in is a model with antagonistic subcommunities. In this section I have tried to show that, in addition, it is no surprise that the moral justification of punishment is in doubt. I have done this by asking how punishment functions within the state. If I am right that it functions to legitimate the state by awe at the power involved in punishment, then in defining criminality and in administering punishment the state's concern is not with the morality of crime and punishment—beyond, of course, their consistency with internal state norms—but with their efficacy in legitimating the state.

It is then utterly contingent that punishment should admit of moral justification. The need of the state, even of the liberal state, for legitimation may take it beyond what can be morally justified by a community-wide consensus toward a reliance on its power. It is punishment's effect in sustaining state power, and not its morality, that counts for the state. (The only requirement beyond sustaining power is that punishment appear nonarbitrary in the ways indicated.) It is wrongheaded, then, to expect that, if a liberal state is legitimate, there has to be a moral justification for its use of punishment. To repeat, this is so for a double reason. First, as I showed in this section, the state does not need its punishment to be morally justified because it can satisfy its need for a legitimator through awe rather than moralizing. Second, as I showed in the last section, there will be no consistent set of fundamental moral principles, which can be used to justify punishment, emerging from the conjunction of antagonistic subcommunities making up the kind of society the liberal state rules.

## VI. A Progressive Approach

I am not a pacificist-anarchist. I would hold that for the foreseeable future there will be a need for punishment, and there will be a need for the state. There will be wrongs we wish to protect against, and punishment, perhaps of a less frequent and less brutal sort, will probably be part of any program for protection against them.[22] Antagonistic divisions will, though hopefully attenuated, remain characteristic of society, and make the state, in some hopefully less autonomous form, a needed instrument of social organization.

Thus I do not propose, as part of any medium-term agenda for social change, a full devolution of punishment from the state to the people. Nor do I propose that the cultivation of a cooperative republic, to replace our competitive republic, will altogether end the need for criminalization.

Instead, the program I propose as a progressive one starts with the idea of reducing the need for the state to be awesome in order to be legitimate. The point of this is that punishment would begin to have quite another dominant role in the state than that of legitimating the state through awe. It could begin to serve either a retributivist or a futurist role or even both. As such punishment would no longer be chosen because it legitimates the state, but because it plays a defensible role within a political morality. Its morality is no longer made contingent and precarious by its first having to play a role in bolstering the state.

How could we arrive at an appropriate political morality? Haven't we shown how difficult it is to get moral backing for punishment? Yes, but we showed it in the context of the assumption that the state ruled a divided society. The divisions in the society would have to be attenuated if there is to be a reduced need for awe in legitimating the state.[23]

This need for awe results from the state's being saddled with the contradictory task of, on the one hand, keeping a society running in which some groups dominate others, and on the other hand, keeping the dominated groups from feeling that the society is being ruled at their expense. To paper over the contradictions involved in this task, it needs to resort to political psychology. It needs to awe those who might otherwise respond negatively to the way it navigates through these contradictions. So attenuating the antagonisms in a divided society frees it from the necessity of resorting to awe in order to reconcile supporting group domination with legitimacy.[24]

Only when the society is made over with the end in view of freeing the state from this contradictory task does the possibility emerge that people could form what Dworkin called a community on the model of principle. Then there could be a certain basic set of moral principles that have a social origin but that legitimate punishment. What I called the mixed model of community would begin to be less applicable. In the mixed model, the state itself generates agreement on shared values, whereas in the model of principle, community dialogue is the basis for such agreement.

I would like to contrast my progressive approach with what normally goes under the heading of a progressive approach to the legal/penal system. It is assumed under what normally goes by this name that the problem with the legal/penal system is inadequate protection of human and civil rights within it. Cruel and unusual punishment is to be avoided; people aren't to be sacrificed for the good of the community; dissent should not be outlawed. The difficulty with this "rights approach" is that, though commendable in detail, it is myopic in regard to the whole. It fails to face the problem as to how punishment itself can be successfully moralized in a society of exploitation and oppression.

This normal progressive approach, which contrasts with the more radical one I've proposed, has a response to the charge of myopia that confirms my suspicions. The response is that there is a right to punish for authorized agents of the state, and that this right is upheld by the common sense of those living in states. Admittedly, the reply continues, only against the background of this common sense about the right to punish does it make sense to struggle to secure the rights of the accused and the convicted. I would not want to deny any of this, but it needs to be asked whether this common sense about the right to punish owes its origin to awe in face of the power of the state or to something else. If indeed the state is crucially part of the source of this common sense, then the state's right to punish has more to do with its manipulation of attitudes through punishment than with a pristine common sense. So the charge has to stand that the normal progressive approach is myopic since its concern for punishing in the right way overlooks whether externally punishment itself is right.

It is a political and not just a theoretical mistake to think that punishment can be moralized in contemporary states. The liberal theory, with its emphasis on moralizing the state, makes this political mistake. The political mistake is that by assuming the liberal state and its punishment can be moralized that theory gives the go-ahead to the state's use of a powerful tool—refined in a context in which some groups are dominant—against the nondominant elements in the society. That tool is a combination of armed force with laws that makes effective protest punishable. The state's restrictions of labor provide a case in point. Outlawing the secondary boycott in the United States undermined the usefulness of the strike as a means by which unions can protest unfair conditions.

Theories of civil disobedience, devised to deal with this objection within the liberal theory of punishment, proceed from the assumption of the moral legitimacy of the liberal state and of its general right to punish.[25] They thus make an exception for protest within what is assumed to be a morally acceptable state system. But it is little consolation to nondominant groups that they are morally permitted to contravene state regulations when the state, with the blessing of moral legitimacy, has little compunction in punishing such dissidents. The political damage done by the view that modern liberal democracies can be morally legitimated is not undone by the right to civil disobedience.

Why, one might ask at last, is there an effort to moralize what, in the circumstances, cannot be moralized? The answer could be oversight: The theorist simply fails to take into account that the circumstances are those of divided societies. It could be loyalty: The theorist is simply so devoted to the values of liberal democracy that this attitude is transformed into the belief that liberal democracies have the moral legitimacy to punish. Or it could be deception: The theorist, recognizing that the governance of divided societies cannot be moralized, proceeds, in order to conceal this consequence of division, to devise a moral legitimation within some standard framework. I suspect that a bit of each of these motives is present, in differing degrees, in most liberal theories of punishment.

My motive is different.  In arguing that the project of giving moral legitimation to state punishment can be carried out only with the attenuation of a divided society—of class, gender, race, age, and national oppressions—I am starting with a concern about the harm these oppressions do.  I register a further concern when to this harm is added that of punishment used to quell protest and distributed unevenly against the oppressed.  The normal progressive approach, though, does not change the green light that allows the state to repress dissident activity on the basis of what it would call a moral consensus.  Yet such dissident activity, over and above the protections internal to the legal/penal process as advocated by the normal progressive approach, may be needed to make punishment morally legitimate.

# Notes

1. See, for example, Alan Wolfe, *The Limits of Legitimacy* (New York: Free Press, 1977), Chapter 10.

2. The moralizing tendency is not the only one in liberalism; see C. B. Macpherson, *The Life and Times of Liberal Democracy* (New York: Oxford University Press, 1977), Chapter 4.

3. See, for example, Catharine A. MacKinnon, "Feminism, Marxism, Method, and the State," cited in bibliography.

4. Milton Fisk, *The State and Justice* (New York: Cambridge University Press, 1989), Introduction and Chapter 7.

5. Robert W. Gordon, "Critical Legal Histories," *Stanford Law Review* 36 (January 1984): 57—125.

6. "We should see allegiance to social institutions as no more matters for justification by reference to familiar, commonly accepted premises—but as no more arbitrary—than choices of friends or heroes."  Richard Rorty, *Contingency, Irony, and Solidarity*, 54.  Cited in bibliography.

7. The trend is manifest in the broad acceptance of H.L.A. Hart's retributivist rebuttal of Barbara Wootton's futurist position in his *Punishment and Responsibility* (New York: Oxford University Press, 1976), Chapter 8.

8. Douglas N. Husak, *Philosophy of the Criminal Law* (Totowa, N.J.: Rowman and Littlefield, 1987), Chapter 8.

9. E. P. Thompson, "'Rough Music': Le charivari anglais," *Annales: Economies sociétés civilisations* 27 (1972): 285—312.

10. Cora Diamond's comment on my paper at the Conference on Pragmatism in Law and Politics held at the University of Virginia, 7—8 November 1990.

11. Jeffrey Reiman, *The Rich Get Richer and the Poor Get Prison*, 3rd ed. (New York: Macmillan, 1990), Chapter 3.

12. Ronald Dworkin, *Law's Empire*, 211—215. Cited in bibliography.

13. This lack of concern with divisions in society not only gives Dworkin's effort an air of unreality but also affects the work of other communitarian thinkers, including Michael Sandel and even Michael Walzer.  See the collection of communitarian writings by these and

other thinkers in *Liberalism and Its Critics*, ed. Michael Sandel (New York: New York University Press, 1984), Part 2.

14. Nicos Poulantzas, *Political Power and Social Classes* (London: Verso, 1978), 130—141.

15. Roberto Unger puts this point in a different perspective when he says that, in societies with domination, shared values are experienced as precarious and contingent precisely because they depend on domination. See his "Liberal Political Theory," in *Critical Legal Studies*, ed. Allan C. Hutchinson (Totowa, N.J.: Rowman and Littlefield, 1989), 35.

16. The National Labor Relations Act (1935) outlaws the discharge of striking workers, but in *NLRB v. MacKay Co.* (1938) the Supreme Court established a permanent strike replacement doctrine that in the late 1980s became the backbone of union-busting.

17. Reinhold Neibuhr, *Moral Man and Immoral Society* (New York: Scribner's, 1932), 95.

18. From Michel Foucault's *Discipline and Punish* in *The Foucault Reader*, ed. Paul Rabinow (New York: Pantheon, 1984), 171—172.

19. Walter Bernes argues for capital punishment on the ground that it is essential for creating this awe; see his *For Capital Punishment* (New York: Basic Books, 1979).

20. Niccolò Machiavelli, *The Prince*, trans. Luigi Ricci (New York: Mentor, 1952), Chapter 17.

21. The situation is naturally more complex. Among Alaskan Eskimos a single murder is a private affair to be avenged by kinsmen, but repeated murder is a public crime to be punished by death at the hands of an agent of the band. See Lawrence Krader, *Formation of the State* (Englewood Cliffs, N.J.: Prentice-Hall, 1968), Chapter 2.

22. Where criminalization of behavior can have no other basis than to prop up state power, a broad program of decriminalization is a priority, even if many kinds of behavior remain criminalized. See Harold E. Pepinsky and Paul Jesilow, *Myths That Cause Crime* (Washington, D.C.: Seven Locks Press, 1984).

23. Jeffrie G. Murphy, "Marxism and Retribution," *Philosophy and Public Affairs* 2 (Spring 1973): 218—243.

24. This is a quite different way of putting the contradiction the state must deal with than is current in the Critical Legal Studies movement, where the contradiction is the more elusive Rousseauian one between order (brought by law) and freedom (of the individual).

25. See John Rawls, *A Theory of Justice*, Sections 55—59, and Ronald Dworkin, *Taking Rights Seriously*, 184—205 (full citations in bibliography).

# 12

## A Reconsideration
## of Deweyan Democracy

*Hilary Putnam*

### I. Introduction

I want to discuss a philosopher whose work at its best illustrates the way in which American pragmatism (at *its best*) avoided both the illusions of metaphysics and the pitfalls of skepticism: John Dewey. While Dewey's output was vast, one concern informed all of it; even what seem to be his purely epistemological writings cannot be understood apart from that concern. That concern is with the meaning and future of democracy. I shall discuss a philosophical justification of democracy that I believe one can find in Dewey's work. I shall call it *the epistemological justification of democracy* and although I shall state it in my own words, I shall deliberately select words which come from Dewey's own philosophical vocabulary.

The claim, then, is this: Democracy is not just a form of social life among other workable forms of social life; it is the precondition for the full application of intelligence to the solution of social problems. The notions from Dewey's vocabulary that I have employed are, of course, *intelligence* (which Dewey contrasts with the traditional philosophical notion of *reason*) and *problem solving*. First, let me say a word about the sense in which such a claim, if supported, can be called *a justification* of a form of social life.

In a recent book,[1] Bernard Williams draws a very useful distinction between two senses in which one might attempt to justify ethical claims. One is an Utopian sense: One might try to find a justification for ethical claims that would actually convince skeptics or amoralists and persuade them to change their ways. (This is like finding a "proof" that Hitler was a bad man that Hitler himself would have had to accept.) Williams rightly concludes that this is an unrealistic objective.

> When the philosopher raised the question of what we shall have to say to the skeptic or amoralist, he should rather have asked what we shall have to say about him. The justification he is looking for is in fact designed for the people who are largely within the ethical world, and the aim of the discourse is not to deal with someone who probably will not listen to it, but to reassure, strengthen, and give insight to those who will. . . . If, by contrast, the justification is addressed to a community that is already an ethical one, then the politics of ethical discourse, including moral philosophy, are significantly different. The aim is not to control the enemies of the community or its shirkers but, by giving reason to people already disposed to hear it, to help in continually creating a community held together by that same disposition.[2]

Here Williams's conception of moral philosophy seems to be exactly Dewey's conception. Yet Williams ignores not only the historical figure John Dewey, but the very possibility of Dewey's particular justification. Instead, Williams considers just two ways in which ethical claims could "objectively" be justified, and associates these two kinds of justification with Aristotle and Kant, respectively.[3] Even though Williams considers Kantian and Aristotelian strategies of justification to be the only possible ones, he might still have left room for a discussion of Dewey. Some commentators have seen a sense in which Dewey might be an Aristotelian, even though he was much more of an empiricist than Aristotle.[4] But when Williams discusses Aristotelian strategies—strategies of justification based on conceptions of human flourishing—something very strange happens. "Human flourishing" is defined in an entirely individualistic sense. Thus, after repeating the remark that "the answer to Socrates' question [How should one live?] cannot be used by those who (from the perspective of the rest) most need it,"[5] Williams goes on to say:

> Still, this does not cast us to the opposite extreme, that the answer is simply meant to keep up the spirits of those within the system, give them more insight, and help them to bring up their children. The answer does that, but not only that. On Aristotle's account a virtuous life would indeed conduce to the well-being of the man who has had

a bad upbringing, even if he cannot see it. The fact that he is incurable, and cannot properly understand the diagnosis, does not mean that he is not ill.[6]

An *Aristotelian* justification, in the only sense that Williams considers, is one that can be given to each nondefective human being (each human being who is not "ill"). In short, the only hope for an objective foundation for ethics[7] that Williams considers is what might be called a "medical" justification—an "objective" justification for ethics that would show, in some sense of "ill" that does not beg the question, that the amoral or immoral man is ill. Moreover, the only place that such a justification could originate, according to Williams, is in "some branch of psychology."[8] Williams is skeptical about that possibility, although he says that "[i]t would be silly to try to determine a priori and in a few pages whether there could be such a theory."[9] The aim mentioned earlier, "not to control the enemies of the community or its shirkers but, by giving reason to people already disposed to hear it, to help in continually creating a community held together by that same disposition"[10]—has been radically reinterpreted.

However, when Williams explains why it is unlikely that there will ever be a "branch of psychology" that will provide us with "objective" foundations for ethics, he makes a very interesting remark:

Any adequate psychology of character will presumably include the truth, in some scientifically presentable form, that many people are horrible because they are unhappy, and conversely: where their unhappiness is not something specially defined in ethical terms, but is simply basic unhappiness—misery, rage, loneliness, despair. That is a well-known and powerful fact; but it is only one in a range of equally everyday facts. Some who are not horrible, and who try hard to be generous and to accommodate others' interests, are miserable, and from their ethical state. They may be victims of a suppressed self-assertion that might once have been acknowledged but now cannot be, still less overcome or redirected. There is also the figure, rarer perhaps than Callicles supposed, but real, who is horrible enough and not miserable at all but, by any ethological standard of the bright eye and the gleaming coat, dangerously flourishing. For people who want to ground the ethical life in psychological health, it is something of a problem that there can be such people at all.[11]

Williams does go on to question whether the latter sort of people really exist, or whether it is simply an illusion that they do. What I want to call your attention to here is not the worry about whether such people really exist, but the reference to "any ethological standard of the bright eye and the gleaming coat."[12] Apparently, an "objective" standard of human flourishing would regard us as if we were tigers (or perhaps squirrels)! Williams describes a standard of human flourishing that ignores everything that Aristotle himself would have regarded as typically human. Dewey, on the other hand, thought of us primarily in terms of our capacity to intelligently initiate action, to talk, and to experiment.

Not only is Dewey's justification a social justification—that is, one addressed to the community as a whole rather than to each member of the community—it is also an *epistemological* justification, and this too is a possibility that Williams ignores. As I stated earlier, the possibility that Williams considers is a "medical" justification; a proof that if you are amoral then you are in some way "ill." If we tried to recast Dewey's justification in such terms, then we would have to say that society which is not democratic is in a certain way ill; but the medical metaphor is, I think, best dropped altogether.

## II. The Noble Savage and the Golden Age

Although John Dewey's arguments are largely ignored in contemporary moral and political philosophy, his enterprise—the enterprise of justifying democracy—is alive and well. John Rawls's monumental *A Theory of Justice*,[13] for example, attempts both to produce a rationale for democratic institutions and a standpoint from which to criticize the failures of those institutions. This could also serve as a description of Dewey's project. But there are scholars in disciplines other than philosophy, and to some extent even scholars of philosophy, who consider the very enterprise of justifying democracy a wrong-headed one. One objection comes from anthropologists and other social scientists,[14] although it is by no means limited to them.[15] These relativist social scientists are sometimes also radicals when it comes to their own cultures, but they strongly oppose any attempt by members of liberal democratic cultures to prescribe change for traditional societies. In the most extreme case (the case I have in mind is an essay by a radical economist, Stephen Marglin[16]) they reject the idea that we can criticize traditional societies even for such sexist practices as female circumcision. Marglin defends his point of view in part by defending an extreme relativism,[17] but I think there is something else at work—something which one finds in the arguments of many social scientists who are not nearly as sophisticated as Marglin: Not to be too nice about it, what I think we are seeing is the revival of the myth of the Noble Savage.

Basically, traditional societies are viewed by these thinkers as so superior to our own societies that we have no right to disturb them in any way. To see what is wrong with this view, let us for the moment focus on the case of male chauvinism in traditional societies.

One argument that is often used to justify a relativistic standpoint is virtually identical to an argument that is used by reactionaries in our own culture, and it is surprising that these social scientists fail to see this. At bottom, the idea is that people in traditional societies are "content"—they are not asking for changes and we have no right to say that they should be asking for changes, because in so doing we are simply imposing a morality that comes from a different social world. It is important in discussing this to separate two questions: the question of paternalistic intervention on one hand, and the question of moral judgment, moral argument, and persuasion on the other. It is not part of Dewey's view, for example, that benevolent despots should step in and correct social ills wherever they may exist. It is time to let Dewey speak for himself:

> The conception of community of good may be clarified by reference to attempts of those in fixed positions of superiority to confer good upon others. History shows that there have been benevolent despots who wished to bestow blessings on others. They have not succeeded except when their actions have taken the indirect form of changing the conditions under which those lived who were disadvantageously placed. The same principle holds of reformers and philanthropists when they try to do good to others in ways which leave passive those to be benefited. There is a moral tragedy inherent in efforts to further the common good which prevent the result from being either good or common—not good, because it is at the expense of the active growth of those to be helped, and not common because these have no share in bringing the result about. The social welfare can be advanced only by means which enlist the positive interest and active energy of those to be benefitted or improved. The traditional notion of the great man, of the hero, works harm. It encourages the idea that some "leader" is to show the way; others are to follow in imitation. It takes time to arouse minds from apathy and lethargy, to get them to thinking for themselves, to share in making plans, to take part in their execution. But without active cooperation both in forming aims and in carrying them out there is no possibility of a common good.[18]

The true paternalists are those who object to *informing* the victims of male chauvinism, or of other forms of oppression, of the injustice of their situation and of the existence of alternatives. Their argument is a thinly disguised utilitarian one. Their conception of the good is basically "satisfaction" in one of the classic utilitarian senses; in effect they are saying that the women (or whoever the oppressed may be) are satisfied, and that the "agitator" who "stirs them up" is the one who is guilty of creating *dissatisfaction*. But Dewey is no utilitarian. (He was a consequentialist, but he was no utilitarian.) The fact that someone feels satisfied with a situation means little if the person has no information or false information concerning either her own capacities or the existence of available alternatives to her present way of life. The real test is not what women who have never heard of feminism say about their situation; indeed, it is hard to see how the situation of a chauvinist woman in India is different from the situation of a chauvinist woman in this country thirty years ago who had never been exposed to feminist ideas. Such women might well have answered a questionnaire by saying that they were satisfied with their lives; but after realizing the falsity of the beliefs on which the acceptance of their lives had been based, the same women not only felt dissatisfied with those lives, but they sometimes felt ashamed of themselves for having allowed such a belief system to be imposed upon them. One of Dewey's fundamental assumptions is that people value growth more than pleasure. To keep the oppressed from learning so that they remain "satisfied" is, in a phrase originated by Peirce, to "block the path of inquiry."

What the radical social scientists are in fact proposing is an "immunizing strategy," a strategy by which the rationales of oppression in other cultures can be protected from criticism. If this is based on the idea that the aspirations to equality and dignity are confined to citizens of Western industrial democracies, then the events of Tien-an-men Square in the spring of 1989 speak a more powerful refutation of that view than any words I could write here.

At the other extreme, at least politically, from the "Noble Savage" argument against attempting to justify democratic institutions is an argument found in the recent writings of Alasdair MacIntyre.[19] MacIntyre gives a sweeping philosophical resumé of the history of Western thought which endorses the idea that one system of ethical beliefs can "rationally defeat" another system and insists that there can be progress in the development of world views. MacIntyre's argument, however, is haunted by the suggestion that such progress fundamentally stopped somewhere between the twelfth and fourteenth centuries, and that we have been retrogressing ever since. MacIntyre's conception of rationality is based largely on the work of Thomas Kuhn[20] but with certain interesting omissions. Like Kuhn, MacIntyre believes that world views such as Confucianism, or Aristotelianism, or utilitarianism cum empiricism are often incommensurable. At the same time, MacIntyre believes that the adherents of a world view can incorporate elements from another world view, or even in exceptional cases, scrap their world view and go over to another by a kind of wholesale conversion. What makes such a wholesale conversion rational is that the new paradigm dissolves difficulties that the old paradigm is unable to escape either by straightforwardly answering the questions, or by showing why and how they are not genuine questions at all. Moreover, the new paradigm solves problems in a way that an honest adherent of the old paradigm must acknowledge as superior to anything his or her paradigm can supply.[21] Of course, the new paradigm must not at the same time lose the ability to answer what its adherents must admit are genuine questions that the old paradigm could answer.

MacIntyre makes one application[22] of this idea that startled me. According to MacIntyre, the great Scholastic synthesis of Aquinas and his successors was rationally superior, in this sense, to Aristotelian philosophy.[23] What is startling about this is that, according to MacIntyre, a key ingredient which enabled Scholastic philosophy to handle problems and internal difficulties that the Aristotelian system could not solve was the notion of original sin![24]

What makes this startling is that if the new system *could* solve or dissolve problems that the old system could not, it also purchased difficulties that the old system did not face. Christianity took over from Judaism the notion of a Fall, but it interpreted that notion in a way in which traditional Judaism, for the most part, refused to do. The specifically Christian notion of original sin is unintelligible apart from the Christian notion of a Redeemer. That is, no religion would or could hold that we are compelled to sin or that our nature is so fundamentally corrupt that we cannot help sinning, unless it was prepared to provide a Redeemer to help us (or at least *some* of us) out of this predicament. I don't mean that this was the only option open to Christianity as a matter of logic, but it was the only option open to Christianity as a matter of its own history and traditions.

MacIntyre speaks[25] of the great medieval synthesis of Revelation and Greek philosophy which requires both the notions of original sin and of a triune God. If Christianity is to be viewed as the resolution of a set of problems and difficulties that a scientific or metaphysical system may be called upon to explain, dissolve, or reformulate, then surely the question of the *intelligibility* and the *logical coherence* of its fundamental notions must arise. Of course, if we view Christianity in a different way, for example, as Kierkegaard viewed it,[26] as not something that we accept on the basis of reason at all, then the problem does not arise in the same way (or the notion of "intelligibility" becomes a very different one).

The fact is that the methodological conceptions that MacIntyre defends are deeply flawed. I said that MacIntyre leaves certain things out of Kuhn's account of paradigm change in science. What he leaves out, in fact, is simply *experiment.* But the pragmatists recognized the value of experimentation. Dewey, of course, comes from the pragmatist tradition, and while the founder of pragmatism, Charles Sanders Peirce, eventually repudiated both the label "pragmatism" and much that William James and Dewey associated with that word, the two famous articles that Peirce published in *Popular Science Monthly* in 1877 and 1878, "The Fixation of Belief" and "How to Make Our Ideas Clear,"[27] remain the founding documents of the movement to the present day. In the first of those articles, Peirce discusses a methodology closely related to the one that MacIntyre proposes. He calls that the methodology of "What Is Agreeable to Reason."[28] Peirce tells us, I think rightly, that what we have learned—learned by trying that method, and trying again and again throughout the long history of our culture—is that it simply does not work. The method of "What Is Agreeable to Reason" by itself, without fallibilism, without experimentation, has never been able to lead to the successful discovery of laws of nature, nor has it been able to lead to resolutions of metaphysical disputes that would command the consensus of intelligent men and women. In place of the method of "What Is Agreeable to Reason" (and the other failed methods that Peirce calls the methods of "tenacity" and "authority"),[29] Peirce proposes the "scientific method." By employing the scientific method Peirce does not mean following some rule book, say John Stuart Mill's, or Francis Bacon's, or Rudolf Carnap's. What he means is testing one's ideas in practice, and maintaining an attitude of fallibilism toward them. To judge ideas simply on the basis of their ability to resolve difficulties without putting them under strain, without testing them, without trying to falsify them is to proceed prescientifically. Peirce would agree with MacIntyre that rational decision between paradigms requires reflection and discussion. More than any scientific philosopher of his time, Peirce stressed that scientific method is not just a matter of experimentation, but experimentation and testing remain crucial in the formation of rational beliefs about matters of fact.

I know that MacIntyre will say that this criticism passes him by. Far from claiming that rationality is just "out there," available to all properly trained human minds, as traditional rationalists did, MacIntyre insists that rationality (but not truth) is relative to one's paradigm.[30] No historical or universalistic account of rationality can be given at all, he insists. And, he argues, rejecting claims to unrevisable possession of truth makes one a fallibilist. The charm of MacIntyre's writing lies precisely in displaying how such a "postmodern" mind can come to such traditional conclusions! But I cannot accept this defense for two reasons. First, although rationality is relative and historical (perhaps *too* relative and historical!), in MacIntyre's view, there is a fixed principle governing rational discussion *between* paradigms, which allows one paradigm to sometimes "rationally defeat" another. It is in the application of *this* principle that MacIntyre is forced back upon what amounts to "What Is Agreeable to [MacIntyre's] Reason." The claim that he is only conceding what any "honest" adherent of the defeated paradigm would have to concede is a bit of persiflage that, in a different context, MacIntyre would be the first to see through. Second, fallibilism in the sense of giving up the a priori is not all there is to Peirce's sense of fallibilism. Peirce's fallibilism requires that one see experimentation, in the widest sense of that term, as the decisive element in rational paradigm change. MacIntyre might reply that reliance on experimentation is only rational "relative to" the contemporary scientific paradigm. But if that were his reply, then this is just where MacIntyre and pragmatism decisively part company.

If I am disturbed by the suggestion haunting MacIntyre's writing that we have been retrogressing ever since the late Middle Ages (a suggestion that has been put forward much more blatantly in Allan Bloom's best seller, *The Closing of the American Mind*),[31] it is because the politics which such views can justify are nothing less than appalling. As many historians have reminded us, the Roman Catholic Church practiced torture through much of its long history. There was a total contempt for what are today regarded as human rights (of course, MacIntyre knows this), and there was terrible persecution of religious minorities. As a Jew, I am particularly worried by the possibility that the sufferings that the Church inflicted upon Jews could someday be "justified" as exercises of a paradigm which had "rationally defeated" the Jewish world view.

What the defenders of the Noble Savage and the defenders of the Golden Age have in common is that their doctrines tend to immunize institutionalized oppression from criticism. The immunizing strategies are different, but they have this in common: They give up the idea that it would be good for the victims of oppression to know of alternative ways of life, alternative conceptions of their situation, and to be free to see for themselves which conception is better. Both Noble Savagers and Golden Agers block the path of inquiry.

### III. Dewey's Metaphysics (or Lack Thereof)

From what "premises" does Dewey derive the claim that I imputed to him,[32] that is, that democracy is a precondition for the full application of intelligence to solving social problems? As we shall shortly see, the underlying premises are some very "ordinary" assumptions. Stanley Cavell, who in the preface to his recent *Carus Lectures*[33] has pointed out a number of interesting similarities and differences between Dewey and Wittgenstein, speaks of the "intermittent appeal to the ordinary"[34] in Dewey. Cavell is right about the presence of such an appeal as well as its intermittence in Dewey's writing, but the appeal goes further, in Wittgenstein as well as in Dewey, than just a sensitivity to the music of ordinary words. To Cavell, what it means to appeal to the ordinary is, in part, to acknowledge the language, the community, and the world as one, in all their entanglement with one another. This is something that I think (and I believe Cavell also thinks) that Dewey—at his best—knew very well. But part of what makes "the appeal to the ordinary" intermittent in Dewey is that he at times[35] feels the need for something like a metaphysical story about the difference between being valued and being valuable. The story is very sketchy, however, and I regard it as a concession to the philosophical style of his (and our) contemporaries. Roughly, Dewey proposes to identify the valuable with what maximizes, or better "unifies," not satisfactions or pleasures, but consummatory experiences[36] which are the product of intelligent experimentation, reflection, and discussion. We are to "unify" appraised and intelligently brought about consummatory experiences.

It is pretty clear that consequentialism (that is, the doctrine that the good must be what maximizes something) is all this story adds to the claim that intelligence is applicable to the solution of moral problems. This is, in my view, a defect. Moreover, the metaphysical story is deeply problematic: even if a consummatory experience has been "appraised," it is not necessarily valuable, since, in Dewey's own story, all appraisals are corrigible. It is always possible that the intelligently brought about and appraised consummatory experiences will, on reappraisal, turn out not to have been valuable after all. In part, Dewey meets this problem by speaking of resolutions of problematical situations (for example in his *Logic*), but a metaphysician would say the use of the word "resolution" here begs all the questions.

Nevertheless, Dewey believes (as we all do, when we are not playing the skeptic) that there are better and worse resolutions to human predicaments—to what he calls "problematical situations."[37] He believes that of all the methods for finding better resolutions, the "scientific method" has proved itself superior to Peirce's methods of "tenacity," "authority," and "What Is Agreeable to Reason." For Dewey, the scientific method is simply the method of experimental inquiry combined with free and full discussion—which means, in the case of social problems, the maximum use of the capacities of citizens for proposing courses of action, for testing them, and for evaluating the results. And, in my view, that is all that Dewey really needs to assume.

Of course, a conventional analytic metaphysician would not hold this view. In analytic philosophy today, one cannot simply assume that intelligent people are able to distinguish better resolutions to problematical situations from worse resolutions even after experimentation, reflection and discussion; one first must show that better and worse resolutions to problematical situations exist. This is, for example, what bothers Bernard Williams. For Bernard Williams there could only be facts about what forms of social life are better and worse if such facts issued from "some branch of psychology."[38] Lacking such a "branch of psychology" (and Williams thinks it very unlikely there will ever be one), we have no basis for believing that one form of social life can be better than another except in a relativist sense, that is, unless the judgment of better or worse is explicitly made relative to the principles and practices of "some social world or other."[39] For Williams the distinction between facts which are relative in this way and facts which are "absolute" is omnipresent; there can not be "absolute" facts of the kind Dewey thinks intelligent people are able to discover.[40] Dewey, as I read him, would reply that the whole notion of an "absolute" fact is nonsensical.

However, it is a fact that, while at one time analytic philosophy was an antimetaphysical movement (during the period of Logical Positivism), it has recently become the most pro-metaphysical movement. And from a metaphysician's point of view, one can never begin with an epistemological premise that people are able to tell whether A is better or worse than B; one must first show that, in "the absolute conception of the world," there are such possible facts as "better" and "worse." A discussion of what is better than what. In my view, Dewey's great contribution was to insist that we neither have nor require a "theory of everything," and to stress that what we need instead is insight into how human beings resolve problematical situations. But again, it is time to let Dewey speak for himself:

> [Philosophy's] primary concern is to clarify, liberate and extend the goods which inhere in the naturally generated functions or experience. It has no call to create a world of "reality" *de novo*, nor to delve into secrets of Being hidden from common sense and science. It has no stock of information or body of knowledge peculiarly its own; if it does not always become ridiculous when it sets up as a rival of science, it is only because a particular philosopher happens to be also, as a human being, a prophetic man of science. Its business is to accept and to utilize for a purpose the best available knowledge of its own time and place. And this purpose is criticism of beliefs, institutions, customs, policies with respect to their bearing upon good. This does not mean their bearing upon *the* good, as something itself attained and formulated in philosophy. For as philosophy has no private score of knowledge or of methods for attaining truth, so it has no private access to good. As it accepts knowledge of facts and principles from those competent and inquiry and discovery, so it accepts the goods that are diffused in human experience. It has no Mosaic or Pauline authority of revelation entrusted to it. But it has the authority of intelligence, of criticism of these common and natural goods.[41]

Here Dewey uses the notion of "intelligence." This notion, however, is not meant to be a metaphysical notion. Dewey contrasts this notion of intelligence with the traditional philosophical notion of reason. Intelligence, for Dewey, is not a transcendental faculty; it is simply the ability to plan conduct, to learn relevant facts, to make experiments, and to profit from the planning, the facts, and the experiments. The notion is admittedly vague, but we do have the ability to determine whether persons are more or less intelligent with respect to the conduct of their activities in particular areas. In a number of places Dewey connects intelligence with the ability for developing new capacities for acting effectively in an environment with what he calls "growth."

## IV. Habermas's and Apel's Epistemological
## Justifications for Democracy

If Deweyan insights and argumentative strategies have been largely ignored by analytic philosophers in recent years, they have in a sense been rediscovered, although with a difference, in recent continental philosophy. Both Jürgen Habermas[42] and Karl-Otto Apel[43] give epistemological justifications for democracy that have a definite relation to Dewey's arguments. I think we can better understand Dewey's view by comparing it with their epistemological justifications for democracy.

Both Habermas and Apel present arguments that are at least in part "transcendental arguments," but the term must be taken with caution. Neither Apel nor Habermas believes in the possibility of a transcendental deduction of a system of categories which will give the a priori structure of the world of experience, in the style of Kant. For Apel and Habermas, "transcendental argument" is simply inquiry into the presuppositions of things that we do—for example, the presuppositions of the activity of arguing about whether something should or should not be done. Their work cannot be simply assimilated to the philosophical work of pragmatists like Dewey (which may be a good reason to compare and contrast it with that work), for it rests on the notion of internal relations between concepts (that is, the notion of analytic truth). Dewey was extremely leery of such a notion, and he certainly would not have given it a prominent place in any exposition of his views. Moreover, Apel, in particular, seems to view philosophy as consisting entirely of transcendental argument (although Habermas allows both "transcendental" and empirical considerations to play a role), and Dewey would certainly have rejected such a conception.

In Apel's presentation of the argument,[44] the act of stating something has certain formal presuppositions: The speaker implicitly or explicitly claims that what he is saying is true (if the statement is descriptive) or normatively right (if the statement is normative), or possesses still other kinds of validity (in the case of other kinds of statements).[45] The speaker implicitly or explicitly claims to be sincere: "I say that p, but I am not sincere in saying this" is self-defeating, if intended as a "constative" speech act (an act of asserting that p). The speaker implicitly or explicitly claims to be able to give reasons: in most circumstances, "I claim that p, but I can give no reason" will fail in a rational discussion. And there are still other conditions of this kind that need not concern us in this sketch of the position.[46]

Apel and Habermas further explain that the idea of a fully justified statement is that the statement can withstand tests and criticism. This is implicit in the practice of discussing whether or not a given statement really is fully justified. At the same time, they draw on the work of Peirce and the later work of Wittgenstein to argue that the idea of a statement whose complete and final warrant is wholly available to the speaker him- or herself—who neither needs nor can profit from the data of others—is an empty and fallacious idea. The idea of a statement which is true (or normatively right) or one which can withstand tests and criticism, is empty unless we allow any statement claimed to be true to be tested by an ongoing community of testers, or at any rate, critics. The upshot is that if I am a participant in a rational discussion (or wish to be, and therefore refrain from pragmatically contradicting my declared intention to participate in such a discussion), then I am committed to the idea of a possible community of inquirers.

So far this may not seem to have anything to do with democracy, although it does concern pragmatist models of inquiry, Wittgenstein's private language argument,[47] and other philosophical models. But what sort of community must the ideal community of inquirers be? A community which is competent to determine what is true and false (or any other sort of validity that can be rationally discussed) must be such that anyone in that community can criticize what is put forward knowing that his or her criticism will be heard and discussed. If some criticisms are simply ignored, then the possibility of an "immunizing strategy" rears its ugly head; we are back at the method of "What Is Agreeable to Reason," or worse, the methods of "tenacity" or (still worse) "authority."[48] In short, the community must be one which respects the principles of intellectual freedom and equality.

Although the argument just summarized has clear points of agreement and overlap with Dewey's view, there are strong differences. Habermas and Apel claim to show that the moral obligations fundamental to democratic politics can be derived from the obligation not to perform "pragmatically contradictory" speech-acts. That is, they would claim, each member of the community of inquirers has the obligation to make only statements which are (as far as one knows) true, sincere, and supported by reasons. But such a derivation, even if correct, surely is backward. We are not concerned with the ethical or democratic life only or even primarily because we have to live that way in order to discover and tell the truth, be sincere, and have reasons; rather, being sincere and telling the truth are among the obligations that we sometimes undertake in connection with the ethical life. Moreover, the obligation to discover and to tell the truth is a defeasible obligation. For example, we should not try to discover any more truths about better ways to make bacteriological weapons or nerve gasses. Indeed, if the whole human race could agree not to try to discover any more truths about better ways to make atom bombs, that would be a good thing. I don't mean that it would be a good thing if we stopped doing physics altogether, and I recognize that pursuing pure physics will undoubtedly lead to discoveries that can be used to make weapons. But the fact remains that there is a difference between trying to discover fundamental laws of nature and trying to discover specific engineering applications. Refusing to discover specific engineering applications is, after all, refusing to even try to discover some truths that human beings are capable of discovering and that have bearing on rational arguments. Yet the decision that, for weighty moral reasons, we are better off not knowing certain things is at times perfectly justified. Indeed, someone who thought that we had an obligation to discover the most effective ways to torture people and a further obligation to publicize that knowledge would be a monster.

But this observation seems to undercut much of the force of Habermas's and Apel's arguments. After all, the anti-democratic despot need not be insincere when saying what he or she believes to be the truth. He or she may honestly believe that an authoritarian society is the best society. He or she may refuse to allow that belief to be put to the test because the despot believes that the moral cost of such a test would be much too high. If, for example, the despot is convinced that trying democratic modes of social organization would lead to enormous amounts of suffering, he or she may feel that while not allowing them to be tried, or even discussed, is unfortunate epistemologically, and prevents his or her beliefs from having as much warrant as they might otherwise have, not trying them is not only morally justified, but morally required. The problem with the arguments of Habermas and Apel is that what is required for the optimal pursuit of truth may not be what is required for human flourishing or even for human survival.

Apel's reply to this objection is that when the anti-democratic despot puts forward this argument, then, by the very act of offering an argument, he or she undertakes to listen to reasons on the other side. If this is right, the despot's behavior is pragmatically self-contradictory. But I do not see the force of this reply at all. Avoiding "pragmatic self-contradiction" in this highly sophisticated sense can hardly be the supreme maxim governing human life!

It seems to me that Dewey does have an answer to this kind of objection, but it is not a "transcendental" answer. Dewey believes, and he recognizes that this is an empirical hypothesis, that it is simply not true that democratic societies (and Dewey was a democratic socialist) cannot survive without producing massive unhappiness, or that ordinary people are not capable of making the decisions and taking the responsibilities that they must make and take if democracy is to function effectively. As a matter of empirical fact, the arguments offered by the despot and by all who defend special privilege are rationalizations, that is, they are offered in what is, at bottom, bad faith. I quote:

> All special privilege narrows the outlook of those who possess it, as well as limits the development of those not having it. A very considerable portion of what is regarded as the inherent selfishness of mankind is the product of an inequitable distribution of power—inequitable because it shuts out some from the conditions which direct and evoke their capacities, while it produces a one-sided growth in those who have privilege. Much of the alleged unchangeableness of human nature signifies only that as long as social conditions are static and distribute opportunity unevenly, it is absurd to expect change in men's desires and aspirations. Special privilege always induces a stand pat and reactionary attitude on the part of those who have it; in the end it usually provokes a blind rage of destruction on the part of those who suffer from it. The intellectual blindness caused by privileged and monopolistic possession is made evident in "rationalization" of the misery and cultural degradation of others which attend its existence. These are asserted to be the fault of those who suffer; to be the consequence of their own improvidence, lack of industry, willful ignorance, etc. There is no favored class in history which has not suffered from distorted ideas and ideals, just as the deprived classes suffered from inertia and underdevelopment.[49]

The critical thrust of this discussion is unmistakable. Democracy may, as Winston Churchill said, be "better than all the other systems which have actually been tried," but it by no means provides full opportunity for the use of "social intelligence" in Dewey's sense. For the use of "social intelligence," as Dewey makes clear, is incompatible, on the one hand, with denying the underprivileged the opportunity to develop and use their capacities, and, on the other hand, with the rationalization of entrenched privilege. Dewey's justification is a critical justification of democracy, one that calls as much for the reform of democracy as for its defense. But what I wish to call attention to here, by contrasting Dewey's argument with Habermas's and Apel's arguments, is its thoroughgoing dependence on empirical hypotheses. For Dewey, the justification of democracy rests at every point on arguments which are not at all transcendental, but which represent the fruit of our collective experience. Deweyan philosophy exemplifies the very methodology for which it argues.

## V. Dewey and James

While Dewey's social philosophy seems, as far as it goes, entirely correct, his moral philosophy is less satisfactory when we try to apply it to individual existential choices. To see why, consider the famous example of an existential choice that Jean-Paul Sartre employed in *Existentialism and Humanism.*[50] It is World War II, and Pierre has to make an agonizing choice. He has to choose between joining the Resistance, which means leaving his aging mother alone on the farm, or staying and taking care of his mother, but not helping to fight the enemy. Dewey's recommendation to use intelligently guided experimentation in solving ethical problems does not really help in Pierre's case. Pierre is not out to "maximize" the "good," however conceived; he is out to do what is right. Like all consequentialists, Dewey has trouble doing justice to considerations of what is right. This is not to say that Dewey's philosophy never applies to individual existential choices. Some choices are just dumb. But Pierre is not dumb. Neither of the alternatives he is considering is in any way stupid. Yet he cannot just flip a coin.

There are, of course, problems of individual choice which can be handled just as one should handle social problems. If, for example, I cannot decide which school my child should attend, I may decide to experiment. I may send the child to a school with the idea that if it doesn't work out, I can take her out and put her in a different school. But that is not the sort of problem that Pierre faces. Pierre is not free to experiment.

What some philosophers say about such a situation is that the agent should look for a policy such that, if everyone in a similar situation were to act on that policy, the consequences would be for the best. He or she should then act on that policy. Sometimes that is reasonable, but in Pierre's situation it isn't. One of the things that is at stake in Pierre's situation is Pierre's need to decide who Pierre is. Individuality is at stake; and individuality in this sense is not just a "bourgeois value" or an Enlightenment idea. In the Jewish tradition one often quotes the saying of Rabbi Susiah, who said that in the hereafter the Lord would not ask him, "Have you been Abraham?," or "Have you been Moses?," or "Have you been Hillel?," but "Have you been Susiah?" Pierre wants to be Pierre; or as Kierkegaard would say, he wants to become who he already is.[51] And this is not the same thing as wanting to follow the "optimal policy"; or perhaps it is—perhaps the optimal policy in such a case is, in fact, to "become who you are." But doing that is not something that the advice to use "the scientific method" can help you very much with, even if your conception of the scientific method is as generous as Dewey's.

There are various possible future continuations of Pierre's story, no matter what decision he makes. Years afterward, if he survives, Pierre may tell the story of his life (rightly or wrongly) depicting his decision (to join the Resistance or to stay with his mother) as clearly the right decision, with no regrets or doubts, whatever the costs may have turned out to be. Or he may tell his story depicting his decision as the wrong decision, or depicting it as a "moral dilemma" to which there was no correct answer.[52] But part of the problem Pierre faces at the time he makes the decision is that he doesn't even know that he faces a "moral dilemma."

William James somewhere quotes an aphorism of Kierkegaard's (whom he could not have read, since Kierkegaard had not been translated into any language James read) to the effect that "We live forward but we understand backward."[53] That is exactly Pierre's situation. Dewey's advice to consider "consummatory experiences" is of no use in this case, even if we restrict ourselves to consummatory experiences which are intelligently brought about and "appraised." For if Pierre considers only his own consummatory experiences, then he is horrendously selfish, but if he tries to consider all relevant consummatory experiences, then he is involved with a hopelessly vague question. This is often the case when we try to think like consequentialists in real life.

It was precisely this sort of situation that William James was addressing when he wrote the famous essay "The Will to Believe"[54] (which James later said should have been titled "The Right to Believe"). Although this essay has received a great deal of hostile criticism, I believe that its logic is, in fact, precise and impeccable, but I will not try to defend that claim here. For James it is crucial for understanding situations like Pierre's that we recognize at least three of their features: that the choice Pierre faces is "forced," that is, these are the only options realistically available to him; that the choice is "vital"—it matters deeply to him; and that it is not possible for Pierre to decide what to do on intellectual grounds. In such a situation—and only in such a situation—James believes that Pierre has the right to believe and to act "running ahead of scientific evidence."[55] The storm of controversy around "The Will to Believe" was largely occasioned by the fact that James took the decision to believe or not to believe in God to be a decision of this kind. Because religious (and even more anti-religious) passions are involved, most of the critics do not even notice that the argument of "The Will to Believe" is applied by James and is meant to apply to all existential decisions.[56] Most critics also have not noticed that it is meant to apply to the individual's choice of a philosophy, including pragmatism itself.[57]

James believed, as Wittgenstein did,[58] that religious belief is neither rational nor irrational but arational. It may, of course, not be a viable option for those who are committed atheists or committed believers. But those for whom it is a viable option may be in a situation completely analogous to the one Sartre imagines (or so James believed). For James, however, the need to "believe ahead of the evidence" is not confined to religious and existential decisions. It plays an essential role in science itself. Although this is hardly controversial nowadays, it was what caused the most controversy when the lecture, "The Will to Believe," was repeated for the graduate students at Harvard University.[59] James's point—which anticipated an idea that historians of science have documented very well in recent years—was that the great innovators in science (as well as their partisans) very often believe their theories despite having very little evidence, and defend them with enormous passion.

The scientific community's acceptance of Einstein's theory of relativity provides a very nice example of James's point. By way of background, let me explain that Max Planck was an early convert to Einstein's theory of special relativity. He played a crucial role in bringing that theory to the attention of elite physicists.[60] At that time, however, Einstein's theory appeared to lead to exactly the same predictions as Poincaré's theory, which also incorporated Lorentz transformations. (In Poincaré's theory there is still an absolute rest that cannot be detected experimentally because of the Lorentz contractions.) According to Gerald Holton, who recently related the story to me, the physicists in Berlin met with Planck on one occasion and drove him to the wall by demanding that he provide an experimental reason for preferring Einstein's theory over Poincaré's. Planck could not do this. Instead he said, "*Es ist mir eigentlich mehr sympatisch*" (it's simply more sympatico). Einstein himself had an equally passionate belief in his own general theory of relativity. When asked what he would have said if the eclipse experiment had turned out the wrong way, Einstein responded, "I would have felt sorry for the Lord God."

James made a point not just about the history of science, although he was quite right about that. His claim—a claim which the logical positivists paradoxically helped to make part of the conventional philosophy of science with their sharp distinction between context of discovery and context of justification—was that science would not progress if scientists never believe or defend theories except on sufficient evidence. When it comes to the institutional decision, the decision made by academically organized science, to accept a theory or not, then it is important to apply the scientific method; in "the context of justification" (although James did not use that jargon) James was all on the side of scrupulous attention to evidence. Even before logical positivism appeared, however, James recognized that there is another moment in scientific procedure—the discovery moment—during which the same constraints cannot be applied.

Perhaps even the positivists might not have gone as far as James. Even the positivists might have said that in the context of discovery it is all right to think of a theory, and propose it for testing without sufficient evidence, but even the individual scientist should not become a believer in his or her theory before it has been fully tested. To this, James would say, in company with many historians and sociologists of science nowadays, that if scientists took that advice, too many good theories would never get tested at all. Enormous numbers of theories are proposed everyday, and only a very small number really are eventually tested. The willingness of individuals to "believe ahead of the evidence" thus plays a crucial role in empirical science itself.

The situation with respect to religion is, of course, quite different. Even though the physicist or the molecular biologist who invents a theory, or the advocates who find the theory "*sympatisch*," may believe the theory ahead of the evidence, the eventual acceptance by the scientific community depends on public confirmation. In the case of religious belief however—*pace* Alasdair MacIntyre—there is never public confirmation. Perhaps the only one who can "verify" that God exists is God Himself.[61] The Pierre case, moreover, is still a third kind of case.[62] In that case, as I already remarked (following an observation by Ruth Anna Putnam[63]), Pierre may come to feel afterward that he made the right choice (although he will hardly be able to "verify" that he did), but there is no guarantee that he will "know" later whether he did. James would say that in each of these cases it is valuable, both from the point of view of the individual and of the public, that there should be individuals who make such choices.

James thought that every single human being must make decisions of the kind that Pierre had to make, even if they are not as dramatic (of course, this was Sartre's point as well). Our best energies, James argued, cannot be set free unless we are willing to make the sort of existential commitment that this example illustrates. Someone who only acts when the "estimated utilities" are favorable does not live a meaningful human life. For instance, even if I choose to devote my life to a calling whose ethical and social value is certain, say, to comforting the dying, helping the mentally ill, curing the sick, or relieving poverty, I still have to decide, not whether it is good that someone should do that thing, but whether it is good that I, Hilary Putnam, do that thing. The answer to that question cannot be a matter of well-established scientific fact, no matter how generously "scientific" is defined.

This existentialist note is unmistakable in the quotation from Fitzjames Stephen[64] with which James ends "The Will to Believe":

> What do you think of yourself? What do you think of the world?
> . . . These are questions with which all must deal as it seems good
> to them. They are riddles of the Sphinx, and in some way or other
> we must deal with them. . . . In all important transactions of life we
> have to take a leap in the dark. . . . If we decide to leave the riddles
> unanswered, that is a choice. If we waver in our answer, that too is
> a choice; but whatever choice we make, we make it at our peril. If
> a man chooses to turn his back altogether on God and the future, no
> one can prevent him. No one can show beyond reasonable doubt that
> he is mistaken. If a man thinks otherwise, and acts as he thinks, I do
> not see how any one can prove that he is mistaken. Each must act as
> he thinks best, and if he is wrong so much the worse for him. We
> stand on a mountain pass in the midst of whirling snow and blinding
> mist through which we get glimpses now and then of paths which
> may be deceptive. If we stand still, we shall be frozen to death. If
> we take the wrong road, we shall be dashed to pieces. We do not
> certainly know whether there is any right one. What must we do?
> "Be strong and of a good courage." Act for the best, hope for the
> best, and take what comes. . . . If death ends all, we cannot meet
> death better.[65]

The life of Rudolf Carnap is a beautiful example of James's point. No doubt Carnap thought that his entire adult life was based on rational principles, and that at each point he could cogently and rationally justify what he did. This includes his commitment to socialism, as well as his commitment to logical positivism (which he called "the scientific conception of the world" in a famous manifesto[66]). He believed in logical positivism not only for what he considered its intrinsic correctness, but also as a means to "social transformation." Yet those of us who look back on Carnap's life can see that he was making exactly the "leaps in the dark" that Fitzjames Stephen described.

James's existentialism is all the more remarkable because he had not read a single existentialist writer (except Nietzsche, whom he pitied[67] and read without any sensitivity). At the same time, James never failed to see the need for a check on existential commitment. For James, my right to my own existential commitments stops where it infringes upon the similar right of my neighbor. Indeed, James described the principle of tolerance ("our ancient national doctrine of live and let live") as having "a far deeper meaning than our people now seem to imagine it to possess."[68] If reason (or "intelligence") cannot decide what my ultimate commitment should be, it can certainly decide from long and bitter experience that fanaticism is a terrible and destructive force. James always tempered a sympathetic understanding of the need for commitment with a healthy awareness of the horrors of fanaticism.

If Dewey is less sensitive than James to the limits of intelligence as a guide to life, it is perhaps because of Dewey's dualistic conception of human goods. For Dewey there are fundamentally two, and only two, dominant dimensions to human life: the aesthetic dimension and the social dimension, which for Dewey meant the struggle for a better world, a better society, and for the release of human potential. Dewey was criticized for seeing all of life as social action; he could and did always reply that on the contrary, in the last analysis he saw all "consummatory experience" as aesthetic. The trouble with this answer is that a bifurcation of goods into social goods, which are attained through the use of instrumental rationality, and consummatory experiences, which are ultimately aesthetic, too closely resembles a similar positivist or empiricist division of life into the prediction and control of experiences and the enjoyment of experiences. James, I think, succumbs less than Dewey to the temptation to offer a metaphysics of terminal goods.

## VI. Conclusion

If, in spite of these criticisms, I still take John Dewey as one of my philosophical heroes, it is because his reflection on democracy never degenerates into mere propaganda for the democratic status quo. It is true that Dewey's optimism about human potential is not something which has been proven right beyond all doubt, nor does Dewey claim that it has. As Dewey emphatically reminds us, however, neither has pessimism about human potential been proven to be right. On the contrary, to the extent that previously oppressed groups have been given the opportunity to develop their capacities, those capacities have always been surprising.

I would like to close by saying a little more about this critical dimension of Dewey's thought. When Dewey speaks of using the scientific method to solve social problems, he does not mean relying on experts, who, Dewey emphasizes, could not solve social problems. For one thing, experts belong to privileged classes and are affected by the rationalizations of which Dewey spoke. As an elite, they are accustomed to telling others how to solve their social problems. For Dewey, social problems are not resolved by telling other people what to do. Rather, they are resolved by releasing human energies so that people will be able to act for themselves.[69] Dewey's social philosophy is not simply a restatement of classical liberalism; for, as Dewey says,

The real fallacy [of classical liberalism] lies in the notion that individuals have such a native or original endowment of rights, powers and wants that all that is required on the side of institutions and laws is to eliminate the obstructions they offer to the "free equipment of individuals." The removal of obstructions did not have a liberating effect upon such individuals as were antecedently possessed of the means, intellectual and economic, to take advantage of the changed social conditions. But it left all others at the mercy of the new social conditions brought about by the freed powers of those advantageously situated. The notion that men are equally free to act if only the same legal arrangements apply equally to all—irrespective of differences in education, in command of capital, and that control of the social environment which is furnished by the institution of property—is a pure absurdity, as facts have demonstrated. Since actual, that is effective, rights and demands are products of interactions, and are not found in the original and isolated constitution of human nature, whether moral or psychological, mere elimination of obstructions is not enough. The latter merely liberates force and ability as that happens to be distributed by past accidents of history. This "free" action operates disastrously as far as the many are concerned. The only possible conclusion, both intellectually and practically, is that the attainment of freedom conceived as power to act in accord with choice depends upon positive and constructive changes in social arrangements.[70]

We too often forget that Dewey was a radical. But he was a radical democrat, not a radical scoffer at "bourgeois democracy." For Dewey, our democracy is not something to be spurned, nor is it something with which we should be satisfied. Our democracy is an emblem of what

could be.  What could be is a society that develops the capacities of all
its men and women to think for themselves, to participate in the design
and testing of social policies, and to judge the results.  Perhaps for
Dewey education plays the role that revolution plays in the philosophy
of Karl Marx.  Not that education is enough.  Education is a means by
which people can acquire capacities, but they have to be empowered to
use those capacities.  In the above passage, Dewey lists a number of
things that stand in the way of that empowerment.  Nevertheless,
education is a precondition for democracy if democracy is a precondition
for the use of intelligence to solve social problems.  The kind of
education that Dewey advocated did not consist in a Rousseauistic belief
in the native goodness of every child, or in an opposition to discipline in
public schools, or in a belief that content need not be taught.  As
Dewey's writings on education show, he was far more hard-headed and
realistic than the "progressive educators" in all of these respects.  Dewey
did insist, however, that education must not be designed to teach people
their place, or to defer to experts, or to accept uncritically a set of
opinions.  Education must be designed to produce men and women who
are capable of learning on their own and of thinking critically.  The
extent to which we take the commitment to democracy seriously is
measured by the extent to which we take the commitment to education
seriously.  In these days, saying these words fills me with shame for the
state of democracy at the end of the twentieth century.

## Notes

1. Bernard Williams, *Ethics and the Limits of Philosophy* (London: Fontana, 1985).

2. Ibid., 26—27.

3. Ibid., 29.

4. See, for example, James Gouinlock, "Introduction" to *The Moral Writings of John Dewey*, ed. James Gouinlock (New York: Hafner, 1976), xxiii.

5. Williams, *Ethics and the Limits of Philosophy*, 40.

6. Ibid.

7. Although Williams also considers the Kantian strategy, he concludes that it is unworkable and that if any objective justification could be given—which he doubts—it would have to be along Aristotelian lines.

8. Williams, *Ethics and the Limits of Philosophy*, 45.

9. Ibid.

10. Ibid., 27.

11. Ibid., 45—46.

12. Ibid., 46.

13. John Rawls, *A Theory of Justice* (Cambridge, Mass.: Harvard University Press, 1971).

14. See, for example, Frédérique A. Marglin and Stephen A. Marglin, eds., *Dominating Knowledge* (Oxford: Clarendon Press, 1990).

15. See, for example, Michael Walzer, *Interpretation and Social Criticism* (Cambridge, Mass.: Harvard University Press, 1987). In his recent work, Walzer seems to be searching for a middle path between relativistic social scientists and moral philosophers like John Rawls.

16. Stephen Marglin, "Towards the Decolonization of the Mind," in *Dominating Knowledge*, 1—29.

17. Ibid.

18. John Dewey and J. H. Tufts, *Ethics*, rev. ed. (New York: Holt, 1936).

19. See entries under Alasdair MacIntyre in bibliography.

20. See entry under Kuhn in bibliography.

21. Here MacIntyre's thinking resonates more with Stephen Toulmin's than with Kuhn's.

22. MacIntyre, *Whose Justice? Which Rationality?*, Chapters 9—11.

23. MacIntyre, *After Virtue*, 205.

24. Ibid., 181.

25. Ibid., 152.

26. See Søren Kierkegaard, *Concluding Unscientific Postscript*, trans. David F. Swenson (Princeton, N.J.: Princeton University Press, 1941).

27. Charles Sanders Peirce, *The Fixation of Belief*; Peirce, *How to Make our Ideas Clear*, reprinted in *Writings of Charles S. Peirce*, ed. Christian J. Kloescl (Bloomington: Indiana University Press, 1986), 3.242—276.

28. Peirce, *Fixation*, 256.

29. Ibid., 250, 251.

30. MacIntyre, *After Virtue*, 9—10.

31. Allan Bloom, *The Closing of the American Mind* (New York: Simon and Schuster, 1987).

32. See Williams, *Ethics and the Limits of Philosophy*.

33. Stanley Cavell, *Conditions Handsome and Unhandsome* (Chicago: University of Chicago Press, 1990).

34. Ibid.

35. See John Dewey, *The Quest for Certainty: A Study in the Relation of Knowledge and Action* (New York: Minton, Balch, and Company, 1929).

36. John Dewey, *Experience and Nature*, 2nd ed. (La Salle, Ill.: Open Court, 1958).

37. John Dewey, *Logic* (New York: Holt, 1938), 280.

38. Williams, *Ethics and the Limits of Philosophy*, 45.

39. Ibid., 150.

40. For a discussion of William's metaphysical views, see Hilary Putnam, "Objectivity and the Science/Ethics Distinction," in *The Quality of Life*, ed. M. Nussbaum and A. Sen (forthcoming).

41. John Dewey, *Experience and Nature*, 407—408.

42. See entries in bibliography under Habermas.

43. See entry in bibliography under Apel.

44. Ibid. Habermas refers to this argument repeatedly in *The Theory of Communicative Action*, but it is not given explicitly at any one place in that book. One can, nevertheless, get a pretty clear view of how Habermas understands the argument from the set chapter of Volume 1 of that work and from Habermas's own statement of the argument that appears in Jürgen Habermas, "Wahrheitstheorie," in *Wirklichkeit und Reflexion*.

45. It may be noticed that even though Habermas and Apel are, like Dewey, "cognitivists" in ethics, they accept a dichotomy between normative and descriptive statements that Dewey would have regarded as an untenable dualism.

46. While I would of course agree with these other conditions, I would not attach weight to the claim that they express "internal relations," that is, that they are analytic. But neither would I attach much weight to the fact that they are not (in my view) analytic. The important thing is that they are "necessarily relative to our present body of knowledge." Hilary Putnam, *Philosophical Papers: Mathematics, Matter and Method* (Cambridge: Cambridge University Press, 1976), 1.237—249. Although American analytic philosophers, who have been disabused of the notion of analyticity by Quine, will be quick to point out that a "paradigm shift" might someday lead us to abandon the very notions of truth and statement making in favor of we-know-not-what "successor notions." Furthermore, they will argue, the fact that we do not as of this time know what it would be like to have such "successor concepts" makes such talk empty, even if the claim that there are not "analytic" truths in this area is correct.

47. Ludwig Wittgenstein, *Philosophical Investigations*, trans. G.E.M. Anscombe (New York: Macmillan, 1953), 243—326.

48. See Peirce, *The Fixation of Belief*, 29.

49. Dewey and Tufts, *Ethics*, 385—386.

50. Jean-Paul Sartre, *Existentialism and Humanism*, trans. P. Mairet (London: Methuen, 1948).

51. Søren Kierkegaard, *Concluding Unscientific Postscript*, 116.

52. See also Ruth Anna Putnam, "Weaving Seamless Webs," *Philosophy* 62 (April 1987): 207—220. Ruth Anna Putnam uses as an example of a "moral dilemma" the predicament of a pacifist who must decide whether and to what extent he or she is willing to participate in the war effort, for example, by serving in a non-combat capacity. As she says, "sometimes only within the frame of a whole life, and sometimes only within the frame of the life of a whole community, can these decisions be evaluated." Ibid., 216.

53. William James, *Pragmatism*, 107. For full citations of William James's work, see bibliography.

54. William James, *The Will to Believe and Other Essays in Popular Philosophy*.

55. Ibid., 29.

56. This conclusion is clear not only from the essay itself, but from many other essays in which James offers similar arguments.

57. See James, *Pragmatism*, 281 ("[W]hether the pragmatic theory of truth is true really, they [the pragmatists] cannot warrant—they can only believe it. To their hearers they can only propose it, as I propose it to my readers, as something to be verified ambulando, or by the way in which its consequences may confirm it."); William James, *The Meaning of Truth*.

58. Wittgenstein's views can be found in twenty printed pages of notes taken by some of his students on his lectures on religious belief. Reprinted in Ludwig Wittgenstein, *Lectures and Conversations on Aesthetics, Psychology and Religious Belief*, ed. Cyril Barrett (Oxford: Blackwell, 1966).

59. See Edgar Arthur Singer, Jr., *Modern Thinkers and Present Problems: An Approach to Modern Philosophy Through Its History* (New York: H. Holt, 1923), 218—20.

60. Planck was also responsible for publishing Einstein's paper in the journal Planck edited.

61. This is not to say that religious belief is unwarranted. I believe that it is "warranted," although not by evidence. This stance is intimately connected with a sense of existential decision.

62. See Jean-Paul Sartre, *Existentialism and Humanism*.

63. See Ruth Anna Putnam, "Weaving Seamless Webs."

64. See entry in bibliography under Stephen.

65. Quotation from James Fitzjames Stephen in William James, "The Will to Believe," in *The Will to Believe and Other Essays in Popular Philosophy*, 33.

66. Rudolf Carnap, Hans Hahn, and Otto Neurath, "The Scientific Conception of the World: The Vienna Circle," in *Empiricism and Sociology*, ed. Marie Neurath and Robert S. Cohen (Boston: Reidel, 1973), 300—319.

67. See William James, *Varieties of Religious Experience*, 296—297 (referring to "poor Nietzsche").

68. William James, *Talks to Teachers on Psychology and to Students on Some of Life's Ideals*, 5. The entire concluding paragraph of the preface, from which this quotation is taken, is a paean to tolerance and an attack on "the pretension of our nation to inflict its inner ideals and institutions *vi et armis* upon Orientals" (James was referring to the colonization of the Philippines).

69. An example that comes to mind is the energies that were released when Polish workers formed Solidarity.

70. John Dewey, "Philosophies of Freedom," in *Freedom in the Modern World*, ed. Horace Meyer Kallen (New York: Coward-McCann, 1928), 249—250.

# PART TWO

# Pragmatism, Judicial Decisionmaking, and Constitutional Interpretation

# 13

## In Context

*Martha Minow and Elizabeth V. Spelman*

A call to consider context unites the work of early twentieth-century pragmatists[1] and late twentieth-century feminists and critical race theorists.[2]

We have noticed three contrasting uses of the phrase "in context" in contemporary theoretical debates. The first refers to the historical and social situation of writers and thinkers, such as the drafters of the United States Constitution. By calling for an examination of their context, critics seek to challenge the claim that the texts stand free of the situation in which they were produced, or to challenge the asserted universality of the norms and rules they articulate. The reference to the context of the drafters is not designed to reduce the texts to the identities and self-interests of the drafters, but is posed as an effort to render comprehensible the contrasts between the drafters' language of universality and the particular, and at times discriminatory effects of their words as applied.[3]

A second possible meaning of the phrase "in context" in contemporary debates over political philosophy and legal theory focuses on the context of the reader or critic who examines texts and understands them within a context not envisioned by the author. For example, Joyce Appleby has written evocatively of the contests in Constitutional interpretation between those who defend "a conservative, sometimes literal, reading of the Constitution and those articulating a more radical, underlying meaning."[4] She argues that the Constitution represented a victory by some interests over others, but that its language permits continued struggle by the "disinherited" to replace biblical and common law traditions with legal rights against hierarchy. Based on their own experiences, white women, people of color, members of religious and ethnic minorities, and others who have been "disinherited" by prevailing legal and cultural documents thus claim authority to use those very documents and argue for social and political change.

Yet the phrase "in context" can also carry a third meaning. Here, especially when addressing actions and decisions, people emphasize "context" in order to highlight the importance of the particular details of a problem. For example, as one philosopher maintained, "Ethical problems arise in the changing contexts of persons and events within which we live. We make our choices and act . . . in situation. [We must be] sensitive to the special characteristics and requirements of each problematic situation, to the distinctive needs of the persons involved."[5] Moral decisions cannot be reached adequately by simply figuring out what moral rule applies to the situation at hand; that situation is too specific and its particularities too numerous and too complex to be covered by a rule whose very abstractness has been made possible by erasing contextual details.

All of these meanings of context may, however, wrongly imply that we can ever escape a context. We are always in some context, as are the texts that we read, their authors and readers, our problems, and our efforts to achieve solutions. Typically, therefore, when people advocate looking or deciding "in context" they advocate a switch from one context to another—from one level of analysis to another, or from a focus on one set of traits or concerns to focus on another set. In many contemporary arguments for context, what people in fact urge is greater attention to factors of race, gender, or class. Perhaps paradoxically, then, the call for context represents a call to consider structures of power in society that extend far beyond the particularities of a given situation. The call for context itself tacitly signals both that the selection of some context is unavoidable, if only by default, and that the selection of one context over another implies a preference for one set of analytic categories rather than another. Against the background assumptions of liberal political and legal theory that treat principles as universal and the individual self as the proper unit of analysis, a call for contextual interpretation may well defend switching from one set of analytic categories to another that only seems more "contextual" because it emphasizes group-based traits of individuals. In the late 20th century in the United States, those who urge contextual interpretation often point to the harmful effects of legacies of expulsion based on race, gender, class, or other group trait. They imply new normative directions for legal and political life.

Objections can be raised against the contexualism that abounds in contemporary legal and philosophical arguments. We consider here several such objections and offer responses to them.

## I. Objections to Contextualism

A central concern is the risk of incapacitating ourselves as moral and political critics. Attention to context in all three senses is attention to the contingencies of a situation—the particular cultural and historical background of the speakers or writers, the interpretative framework of the hearers and readers, the particular and peculiar details of the issue at hand. But given this commitment to the importance of contingency, how is judgment possible within a particular situation? Moreover, even if such judgment is possible, how could any judgment specific to a situation bear any implications beyond itself?

These worries actually translate into two different concerns. The first criticizes the commitment to context for denying the very possibility of foundations which ground moral and political judgment. The second objects to the tendency of contextual approaches to emphasize the uniqueness of each individual situation, person, and culture—thereby undermining the possibility of criticism across situations, persons, and cultures. Although these two concerns converge at many points, the first may be associated more with concern for tradition and authority, while the second emanates from the impulse to justify moral and political transformations. Some are concerned that if context becomes pre-eminent, all that remains is pure politics; others are convinced on the contrary that emphasis on context makes politics possible.

## A. *Objections Based on the Belief in Foundations*

If texts should be interpreted by looking to the situations of their authors, and if even these interpretations are contingent once we consider the situation of the interpreters, then there seem to be no bases for knowing or judging the meanings or values of a given text. Similarly, if a particular moral or political dilemma can be understood and evaluated only in light of the specific details of the circumstances, then we risk abandoning or refusing to acknowledge foundations for moral and political judgment that endure through time. These kinds of objections to the calls for knowing and judging "in context" can lead to charges of relativism and to defenses of traditional criteria for interpretation and judgment.

These objections may stem from defenses of reason and the rule of law; contextual approaches become targets of attack because they seem to deny the possibility of trustworthy and legitimate foundations for the exercise of judgment and thereby leave power and politics standing bare.[6] Thus, those who claim that the original intent of the drafters of the United States Constitution can be discerned and that it in turn should guide and constrain contemporary interpretations at the same time reject arguments that the historical situations of the text's authors, their distance from the situations of contemporary observers, and the contingency of meaning itself on historical circumstances, are relevant for contemporary adjudication.[7] Even among those who reject the search for original intent, there are advocates of rational conventions for interpretation. These conventions are defended because they are real, palpable, and even discoverable, if used over time.[8] Similar objections more generally attack an emphasis on the perspectives of authors and readers in literary criticism, historiography, and epistemology for raising doubts about meaning and knowledge and for challenging established criteria for judging meaning and truth.[9]

Whether the subject is law, literature, history, or philosophy, the objections reflect several implicit assumptions. First, some foundations for knowledge and for judgment exist beyond a given situation. Second, these foundations can be discovered, even if there may be some debate about them. Third, the call for contextual approaches undermines the search for foundations and also the justifications for knowledge and judgment. Fourth, absent foundations, knowledge and judgment reflect mere power and politics; the results risk not merely intellectual chaos and incoherence, but also social and political disorder and violence.[10] Absent foundations for knowledge and judgment, there are no bases for holding those who wield power to account, much less for constraining their own political preferences and prejudices.

What, though, are these foundations, allegedly jeopardized by the call for context? On one view, foundations pre-exist human judgment—they stem from divine authority or from nature. Arguments based upon natural law are a persistent version of this view. Conflicts over interpretation of law, in this view, have the status of conflicts over interpretation of the physical universe. People in a given time may be mistaken about the truth that will later be affirmed through self-revising and self-correcting methods of analysis successively applied to better approximate the pre-existing truth. The contrasting and probably more widely held contemporary view is that the foundations emerged from deliberate human efforts to invent them—through the social contract, deliberately constructed devices to assure participation, or customs tested by time.[11]

Thus, John Rawls's *Theory of Justice* suggests a heuristic device, the original position behind the veil of ignorance, through which he and his readers can construct a theory of justice that stands outside of the particular situations of any of the individuals.[12] Jürgen Habermas has advocated methods for broad participation, and preconditions to that participation, drawing from a theory of human communication to provide a new foundation for moral and political judgments.[13] One example of customs invented by humans, tested through time, is the common law;[14] another would be the customs developed by participants in commercial markets;[15] a third would be the conventions devised by constitutional lawyers over the course of many decades for interpreting the text of the Constitution.[16] Whether justified by reference to the divine, or nature, or instead to methods invented by humans for transcending subjectivity and power, foundations for knowledge and judgment can be discerned and cited to give legitimacy to decisions.[17] Under either view, there is more to knowledge and moral reasoning than the situations of the observed and observer.

Connected to each view of the origins of foundations for knowledge and judgment are particular conceptions of the sovereign rational subject, the distinction between objectivity and subjectivity, the source of knowledge and morality in either natural order or natural languages and cultural development, and the possibility and verifiability of human progress. Contextual approaches assault each of these conceptions. A contextualist casts doubts on the possibility of sovereign reason, removed from historical situations, and even questions any idea of human individuality that assumes an ahistorical human core. The foundationalist maintains that the contextualist risks blurring the distinction between objectivity and subjectivity critical to gaining understanding of the world and to forging legitimate judgments.[18]

As an example, consider the basic problem of interpreting a contract after one party claims the other has breached it. If the situation of all authors conditions the meanings of the texts they produce, then the judge has no authoritative basis for interpreting the language of the contract itself. Indeed, since the two parties occupy different situations, the meaning of the contract could well differ for each of them, blending into their subjective desires. How, then, is the judge to pick between them?[19] At the same time, if the judge herself cannot interpret except by bringing in aspects of her own situation, then subjectivity infects the entire process of judgment.

Finally, if interpretation is conditioned upon the multiple contexts of the producers of governing texts, their interpreters, and the individuals affected by the dilemma at hand, the possibility of universal norms for knowing and judging grows increasingly remote. Indeed, it seems dubious or irrelevant that there are sources of morality in either nature or culture and it becomes impossible to gauge human progress or to condemn human venality. The call to context thus endangers reason and the legitimate exercise of power. As a result, judgment is incapacitated, moral argument undermined, and the bases for social order discarded or exploded.

Alasdair MacIntyre explores such consequences in his noteworthy book, *After Virtue*. There he suggests that the Enlightenment project—to move morality from Christian and Aristotelian foundations to secular, rational foundations—has washed up against the critiques of Nietzsche and others who claim that the language of objective reason merely masks power and prejudice. If these critiques prevail, however, and there are no impersonal, objective criteria for reasoned appeals, then all human relations become merely manipulative. Having only incommensurable arguments, reflecting shards of broken foundations for morality, people are left with their own preferences and their own struggles for power. With whim and power laid bare as the sole explanation for why people argue and conclude what they do, there is no longer even any shared language for moral judgment.

In addition to this basic objection to context as a threat to judgment and order, some may argue that the call to context allows people to duck hard questions, to avoid reaching generalizations or decisions that can be assessed by others or applied elsewhere. Perhaps most telling, however, is the objection that the contextualist cannot even defend the call to context as a better method for understanding or reaching judgments. Having kicked free of the foundations for describing and evaluating, having rejected grounds for objective judgment transcending particular situations, the contextualist has nothing to point to in advocating context over foundations or indeed any other way of knowing and judging.[20]

## B. Objections Based on a Fear of Losing Politics

A second kind of objection stems from recognition that an emphasis on context in all three senses is an emphasis on the uniqueness of persons and events and thus on the importance of the differences among them. After all, the move to context is a move meant to counteract the effect of abstracting away from the details of a situation peculiar to it: the writer isn't just a writer—he is a white Brit whose daily bread comes from working for his country's overseas offices; the reader isn't simply a reader—she is someone whose literary conventions allow her to squeeze orange juice out of what according to an ancient author's literary conventions is an apple; the situation isn't just one in which one is asked to weigh the relative importance of property and life—it is one in which decisions and actions have quite particular meaning and consequences for the particular people in the particular situation.

The move to context, then, is an attempt to shift the location of significance: writers emphasizing context have done so out of a sense that the significance of particular facts about persons and events was being obscured by the processes of abstraction necessary for the formulation of general empirical statements or universally applicable moral rules. Those focusing on the forest cannot see the trees.

But, the objection might go, one cannot emphasize contextual details without undermining the importance of commonality of persons and events. Tree-gazers can't really see the forest. And political movements need foresters: they need understandings of the structural similarities in people's apparently different situations. This has been insisted upon in a variety of ways by those interested in the possibility of social change.

Forty years ago, Simone de Beauvoir wondered about why women had not engaged in more political activity in their own behalf.[21] Part of her explanation was that, for a number of reasons,[22] women have been unable to see beyond their own quite particular situations: too often we have lacked "the sense of the universal" and taken the world to be "a confused conglomeration of special cases."[23]

This concern about the inability to see a plurality of cases as lumped together in anything but an unconnected, confused, and contingent way is expressed by some contemporary Black feminists who are not likely to claim de Beauvoir as a political mother. In "A Black Feminist Statement," the Combahee River Collective describe part of the genesis of Black feminism as "the political realization that comes from the seemingly personal experiences of individual Black women's lives."[24] This political realization is hard earned, the Collective argues, because racism "did not allow us, and still does not allow most Black women, to look more deeply into our own experiences and, from that sharing and growing consciousness, to build a politics that will change our lives and inevitably end our oppression."[25] The interests of white supremacy, the

Collective suggests, are served when Black women are *not* able to see and name the forces and institutions to which all of them are subject no matter the differences in their lives. Though the Collective does not explicitly say this, their work surely implies that anything that makes less legitimate the processes of abstraction by which they came to be able to see and name what they had in common thereby pulls the rug out from under their motivation for and hopes for political change.

A final example of this kind of concern about depoliticizing effects of an emphasis on context can be found in the work of that quintessential political text of the 1960s, Herbert Marcuse's essay "Repressive Tolerance."[26] Marcuse worried about what he saw as the disastrous political consequences of "doing your own thing": in the name of the importance of each individual's own special desires and needs, and in the name of an individual freedom which would allow one to express those desire and fill those needs, so-called liberationists were in fact encouraging the loss of political will—the loss of attention to, and will to resist, the mighty forces of destruction all around us, such as the grotesque growth of United States military power and the rampant and well-fed compulsion to consume goods produced with ever shorter half-lives. In reaction to a fear about "monkey-see, monkey-hear, monkey-do" conformity, we may be inclined to insist not only that we ought not to see, hear, and act like others, but that we *cannot* see, hear, or act like others. We are all too different from one another to be reduced to a common denominator, whether that be a description of our common condition or a prescription for a common political aim. Though Marcuse doesn't talk about context in the senses we have laid out, he clearly is deeply concerned about the consequences of insisting on the radical plurality of differences in people's consciousness, desires, and needs. He is particularly worried about the presentation of what he sees as a wholly regressive politics of individual difference in the guise of a politics of liberation. Attention to context can be seen as a crucial means of such illusion and deception: in the name of retrieving crucial unique details, it invites or even requires us to remain blind to politically significant similarities.

Attention to context involves not only the loss of political vision and political will; it makes political judgment, and other important kinds of judgment, seem impossible. We cannot learn anything from a particular event if we focus only on those details unique to it, for if it has no significant similarity to any other event, it has no implications for any other. The development of judgment in at least one sense has to do with being able to tell whether acts of certain kinds will have certain characteristics or consequences; if I am to assume ahead of time that each new act I come upon is irredeemably distinct from any other, I have no grounds on which to predict or estimate anything about it. Indeed the possibility of even describing an event as a particular event gives rise to a certain extreme version of contextuality: Most of the nouns and verbs in our language do not operate like proper nouns—they do not name a single person or thing or event. "Chair" and "medicine" have the kind of uses they do in English precisely because they are applicable to an indefinite number of things which are numerically distinct but have relevant characteristics in common. So we cannot use language properly to describe a situation without abstracting to a certain extent from the particular context of use. Those two chairs are chairs even though one is blue and one is green; those two blue chairs are blue chairs even though one is azure and one is navy.

At the evaluative level, to judge an act as good or bad, politically progressive or regressive, involves perceiving it as a certain kind of act and thereby and to that extent in abstraction from its particular context. It would be very hard to understand what "good" and "bad," "right" and "wrong," mean if it were the case that what made an action deplorable in one situation had nothing at all to do with what made another action deplorable. Has our judgment about the horror of the atrocities committed by Hitler no connection at all with our judgments about other cases? This is not to say that Hitler's crimes were not in some important sense unique; it is to say that our judgment of them as crimes has a lot to do with our judgment of other cases. If terms of moral and political approbation are not to be seen simply as complicated ways of saying "I like that" or "I don't like that," that is, if what we say has any normative status at all, then we are invoking a standard against which a person or an act is measured, a standard which may in principle be appropriately invoked in other relevantly similar situations.

In sum, those wishing to present social and political criticism as grounded in something other than personal fancy or passing interest may see the move to context as deeply depoliticizing: The normative claims at the heart of serious social and political challenges cannot make sense on the assumption that each person's condition and each political situation is *sui generis*.

## II. Responding to the Objections: In Context

Although joined in opposition to the call to context, some may object that contextual analysis blasts away foundations in reason for moral and political claims and leaves brute political power, while others may object that contextual analysis eliminates generalizations and the possibility of politics. The two views converge in suggesting that contextual approaches disable judgment and produce relativism. These are essentially consequentialist arguments: they are objections that the move to context will have bad consequences.

But there are also two converging internal criticisms of the call to context. One is that the contextualist cannot reasonably advocate contextualism after rejecting all grounds for preferring one way of knowing and one set of judgments over others. The second is that the contextualist cannot meaningfully talk of context without using categories that simplify, in at least some respects, the particularities under examination.

Although we ultimately support many of the moves to context, for reasons we will elaborate, we begin our response to the objections by accepting these internal criticisms as correct (though, as will soon become apparent, such criticisms end up having an important bearing on the views of the objectors as well). Indeed, we believe that these internal criticisms usefully demonstrate a defect in the usual rhetoric of contextualism: The usual rhetoric mistakenly implies a binary distinction between abstraction and context, when at best there are constant interactions between them.

### A. *Reasons for Contextualism*

There are several reasons why the binary distinction between abstraction and context misdescribes the arguments either for or against "contextual" reasoning. The first is that those who advocate contextualism do not do so from mere whim or chance. They invoke a rhetoric or injunction, such as "it all depends on the context" or "you must consider this in context." Thus, Justice Powell noted that "when a defendant contends that a prosecutor's question rendered his trial fundamentally unfair, it is important 'as an initial matter to place th[e] remar[k] in context.'"[27] Similarly, dissenting opinion may often criticize a majority for failing to read a particular term or phrase in context.[28]

Proponents of contextual analysis reflect at least implicitly a moral theory, a political theory, and a theory of knowledge in preferring a focus on the context of authors, readers, or problems in the course of interpreting texts and resolving dilemmas. For example, Carol Gilligan describes the contrast between the ethic of justice and the ethic of care not only as the contrast between abstract conceptions of universal morality and contextual assessments of particular patterns of relationship, but also as a choice between two moral orientations—a choice that itself assumes moral dimensions. She advocates the ethic of care because of a theory about its own moral consequences: "The reconstruction of the dilemma in its contextual particularity allows the understanding of cause and consequence which engages the compassion and tolerance repeatedly noted to distinguish the moral judgments of women. Only when substance is given to the skeletal lives of hypothetical people is it possible to consider the social injustice that their moral problems may reflect and to imagine the individual suffering their occurrence may signify or their resolution engender."[29] Attention to detail inspires compassion, tolerance, and respect for the dignity of each individual.[30] Indeed, Gilligan emphasizes that the subjects of her interviews who use the ethic of care speak in terms of a moral injunction to notice and respond.[31]

Similarly, for Cornel West, a focus on context reflects a political theory: He is interested in pragmatism as a philosophic method that points to context because he believes it will enable forms of cultural criticism that can challenge hierarchical political arrangements that have harmed people of color, women of all races, and poor and working class peoples. At the same time, West himself is able to criticize leading figures in American pragmatism because of his own attention to the contexts of race, class, and gender arrangements that their work neglects. Here, context refers less to the unique, situated experiences of each individual than to the structures of experience influenced by historic discrimination along lines of race, gender, and class. Both kinds of context enable authors to challenge political theories that speak in terms of abstract individual rights with the friction produced by insistent contact with situated experiences.

But if advocates of context must draw on visions beyond particular situations in their very call for attention to context, exponents of abstraction are themselves situated in particular ways of knowing that limit their understandings. This is another version of the defects in viewing context and abstraction as sharply distinguished. As summarized by Thomas Nagel's phrase, there is no "view from nowhere."[32]

Arguments and principles presented as if they came from no situation still sit within the contexts of their authors and readers; the absence of overt clues that those contexts exist does not eliminate them nor overcome the inevitable limitations of their circumstances. Even rationalists such as Plato and Kant, in different ways, recognize that as long as we are embodied, historical beings, we are limited by our partial view—and they each prescribe arguments and disciplines to help us struggle against those limits. For modern critics of such rationalists, such as Dewey and Nagel, the only chance for moving beyond one's own limited perspective comes from acknowledging it and trying to incorporate an understanding of those limitations in one's next effort to understand the world. But absent such attention to the partiality or perspective framed by each viewer's situation, claims of knowledge carry mistaken implications of comprehensive understanding.

Abstract theories are in some sense rooted in particular contexts and operate within context with real and particular effects that often benefit some people more than others. At the same time, contextual approaches are in some sense expressive of abstract theories. The contextualist has moral, political, and epistemological theories for preferring contextual approaches. Moreover, the contextualist uses categories to select what particular details matter. Those categories can be generalized. The binary distinction between abstraction and contextualism is not only mistaken, but also obscures these important points of interdependence between them.

## B. The Principled Choice of Contexts

A second reason for rejecting the distinction between abstraction and contextualism also provides a response to the charge that contextual approaches undermine the possibility of moral judgments beyond the particular situation at hand. The call to look at context typically represents a call to focus on some previously neglected features. It does not, however, mean focusing on all possible features. As human beings, we simply cannot hold in our heads all possible sensory inputs. Thus, we may say, "but don't forget the historical context," but we do not then mean, "don't forget to look at all possible features of the historical moment and its place in the chronology of history." Perhaps even more obviously, many calls to look at context specifically refer to the traits of race, gender, and class that have been ignored by a more general statement.

Thus, once the pretended distinction between context and abstraction is discarded, the important question becomes which context should matter, what traits of aspects of the particular should be addressed, how wide should the net be cast in collecting the details, and what scale should be used to weigh them? Whether you prefer to be called a contextualist or a devotee of principled reason, you make choices about what features of context to address.

It is for this reason that contextualists do not merely address each situation as a unique one with no relevance for the next one. The basic norm of fairness—treat like cases alike—is fulfilled, not undermined, by attention to what particular traits make one case like, or unlike, another. Here, a useful contrast can be drawn between the notions of universality and generality. Both "Thou Shall Not Kill" and "Thou Shall Not Kill Except in Self-Defense" have a universal form: They are meant to apply to everyone—their form tells us "This means YOU, whoever you are." So however "Thou Shall Not Kill" and "Thou Shall Not Kill Except in Self-Defense" differ, both make unconditional demands on everyone—their form is meant to tell us that they apply to us whatever our particular historical and personal condition happens to be. There are no exceptions in the scope of their applicability to human beings.

But they are different, of course. The first says that all acts of killing are forbidden to all human beings; the second says that some acts of killing are not forbidden to all such beings. "Thou Shall Not Kill" is more general than "Thou Shall Not Kill Except in Self-Defense," in the sense that the scope of forbidden acts is broader in the first case than in the second. "Thou Shall Not Kill Except in Self-Defense" specifies that some acts of killing are not forbidden.

"Thou Shall Not Kill Except in Self-Defense" is no less *principled*—in the sense of determining similar outcomes for similar cases—than "Thou Shall Not Kill" just because it builds in a certain kind of exception. What determines whether one holds a principled position in this sense is whether one applies it to all situations so specified and not with how those situations are specified.[33]

The degree of specificity does not alter the fact of principle nor the injunction of universal application. This holds even if the norm read, "Thou Shall Not Kill Except If Thy Name Be Rambo and Thy Motives Be Inspiring to a Public Composed of Teen-Agers." Just in case there happens to be more than one person named Rambo, this rule would apply to more than one case; it is universal with respect to the situation so specified and its form reveals this intent to assure universal applicability.[34] When a rule specifies a context, it does not undermine the commitment to universal application to the context specified, it merely identifies the situations to be covered by the rule. Thus, universal applicability may still be indicated where a rule prescribes analysis of context—as in the rule directing application of the securities laws' antifraud provisions.[35] In *Landreth Timber Co. v. Landreth*, the Supreme Court endorsed prior decisions emphasizing the context of a transaction as a feature pertinent to the applicability of these provisions while reasoning that "the context of the transaction involved here—the sale of stock in a corporation—is typical of the kind of context to which the Acts normally apply."[36]

If we are no longer distracted by a confusion between the universal and the general, we avoid the mistaken view that increased attention to specific circumstances undermines commitments to universal normative judgments. And if we are no longer besieged by a simplistic distinction between context and abstraction, we may have to speak with more cumbersome phrases, but we can respond without difficulty to the objections raised against "contextual" approaches.[37]

## C. Defending Contexts

The first set of objections could be described as the fear of the barbarians at the gates[38] or else a fear of tyranny unrestrained by reason or law.[39] A critic of context could object that the principled qualities of legal interpretation are dislodged by a focus on the context giving rise to specific legal rules, such as the property interests of the Constitution's framers. Or a critic may charge that it is similarly improper to focus on the context of a text's interpreters; thus, it was wrong for members of the Supreme Court to interpret the collateral bar rule in 1967 as barring a challenge by Dr. Martin Luther King, Jr., to the city ordinance forbidding his 1963 protest march, if this judgment reflected white Americans' reactions to the urban riots in the intervening years.[40] Finally, a critic may reject a call to respond to the particular circumstances of a given person because this threatens principled decisionmaking.

We, too, would be concerned if power rather than principle prevailed. Principles such as equality, fairness, and freedom can be defended and even fulfilled in light of contextualized assessments of the limitations of particular rules, given the frames of references of their authors and their expositors, and given studies of the actual effects of rules on people. But past failures to attend to context have often permitted the imposition of a judgment precisely because it reflects the view of more powerful members of the society or of the given dispute. False claims of universality do not make a text or its application fair or a basis for restraining power.

Rather than assuming that application of a given rule treats like cases alike, attention to the three kinds of context can expose risks that people with greater power will have the chance to control definitions of "like" and "unlike" to work in their own favor. Exposing for debate the question of what differences should matter in discerning what makes cases like or unlike is not caving into tyranny, but is instead the best hope for challenging it.[41]

What about those who worry that a focus on context will produce paralysis and a loss of political direction? Eradicating the false distinctions between context and abstraction, especially by noting precisely which categories of particulars people signal when they call for contextual attention, can provide some reassurance to these critics. Even more explicitly, we would suggest that the call to context in the late 20th century reflects a critical argument that prevailing legal and political norms have used the form of abstract, general, and universal prescriptions while often neglecting the experiences and needs of women of all races and classes, people of color, and people without wealth. The attention to particularity that aims to highlight people subject to domination is not an unthinking immersion in overwhelming detail, but instead a sustained inquiry into the structure of domination in our society. People engaged in such an inquiry should remain open to proof that injuries to people occur randomly, but evidence to the contrary, evidence that tends to demonstrate that race, gender, class, and other traits of group membership become bases for injuries, can help mobilize political action and judgments, not undermine them.

If the evidence suggests that the categories of race, gender, and class are themselves too general, attention to context may help elucidate patterns of harms along more refined and specific lines. Age, region, sexual orientation, physical impairments and other traits may be recognized as significant factors explaining who risks injury in employment, credit, or other fields of endeavor.[42] Acknowledging these multiple patterns seems to complicate the task of mobilizing political groups. It can encourage greater resistance by people when faced with others who claim to speak for their interests. But perhaps the need to consult more people about how their interests differ, and how they converge, will produce more genuine, stronger political coalitions, based on fuller information and more honest mutual demands. Attention to particular backgrounds and foregrounds, situational details and complexities, can provide grounds for judgment of good and evil and for descriptions that enable judgments. Moreover, politics in a full sense becomes both inevitable and urgent if the contextual approach is taken seriously. For if you and I bring different understandings to bear on a situation because of our different contexts, then we must work together to forge solutions. We cannot presume that our differences can be dissolved by agreeing to a more abstract framework.

If the impulse to look at context stems from political concerns about oppression and exclusion, those concerns may only grow deeper with immersion in the context of people's actual experience. Consider the example of the American women's movement during the 1980s. For many feminists, securing and protecting rights to freedom of choice in reproductive decisions has been an important mission. Many white, middle-class feminists who decry the Supreme Court's decision in *Webster v. Reproductive Services*[43] have faced criticism for neglecting the earlier defeat of *Harris v. McRae*,[44] which did not restrict the abstract statement of the privacy right to an abortion but did confine it to those who could afford an abortion on their own. Moreover, to many women even the focus on abortion seems to emphasize the interests of some women while neglecting others. Thus, some cite sterilization as a larger, more pressing problem, especially for women of color, that has remained long neglected by the mainstream (that is, white and middle-class) women's movement.[45] Others object that the focus on reproductive rights of any sort has neglected their needs to have and raise children—needs that call for pre-natal care, childcare, increased minimum wages, safe housing, and other policies that would support family life. The question becomes, therefore, who will define the agenda for the women's movement? Some white and middle-class women may feel that a focus on the myriad contexts of women's lives in America dislodges their agenda for women's rights and disables their ability to organize a movement. But if the movement depends upon submerging some women's interests to the interests of those with more access to the leadership ranks, then the problem is not the focus on the context but the conflict between privilege and democracy.

## D. *Contextual Judgments, Not Relativism*

Relativism is the dreaded label so often foisted upon contextualism. The claim is that if we turn to context, not only do we lose our bearings, our principles, and our politics, we also endanger our very ability to know right and wrong and to object to what is wrong. According to some historians, the Legal Realists' pragmatism left them ill-equipped to respond to the rise of Nazism, and the skeptical movement in law ran into the sand.[46]

It is not hard to hear relativism in the statements of some of the people Carol Gilligan cites for her theory of the ethic of care. Consider, for example, a woman identified as Ruth. She illustrates what Gilligan describes as "the reticence noted in women's moral judgments," that is, their reluctance to judge.[47]

> I think that everybody's existence is so different that I kind of say to myself, "That might be something I wouldn't do," but I can't say that it is right or wrong for that person. I can only deal with what is appropriate for me to do when I am faced with specific problems.[48]

Ruth responds to a question about whether she is willing to "apply to others her own injunction against hurting."[49] "I can't say that it is right or that's wrong, because I don't know what the person did that the other person did something to hurt him."[50] Indeed, the "frame of reference" Ruth brings to moral problems leads her to say: "I don't even think I use the words *right* and *wrong* any more, and I know that I don't use the word *moral*, because I am not sure I know what it means. . . ."[51]

If Ruth cannot judge, perhaps she is a relativist. Yet, it may also be that Ruth, and others like her, reveal a rhetorical style more than an inability to judge. She states, "I can only deal with what is appropriate for me to do when I am faced with specific problems."[52] Presumably, then, she can reach decisions, although she refrains from concluding that her decisions carry any implications for anyone else. Indeed, upon close examination, Ruth's view includes the moral injunction *not* to pass judgment of others due to the risk that such judgments could wrongly cause hurt and due to her commitment to try to change what she perceives to be an unjust world.[53] Gilligan specifically interprets this view not as moral relativism, but instead as "a reconstructed moral understanding."[54]

There are several elements at work in Ruth's conception of morality: (1) a view that is both general and universal about the wrong involved in hurting others; (2) a view that society in general is unjust; (3) a view that she as an individual should try to change the injustice in the world; (4) a view that one important way to do this is to refrain from judging others, at least when she lacks specific information about them; and (5) a view that judgment may be more possible and justified in light of specific information about another. It is as if Ruth had said, "What keeps me from judging others is a moral view that it is wrong to form judgments in the absence of knowledge of their context. But if I had knowledge of their context, I could judge them." In addition, she expressly notes her own ability to form judgments about what is right and wrong for herself. If she knew enough about the contexts facing another person to discern whether similarities to her own situation predominated over differences, she could well conclude that her judgment about herself should apply to another. If the specific details of her own moral views are satisfied with reference to another, there is no reason to infer from her commitment to contextual knowledge a logical barrier to drawing universal implications of her normative views.

Whether Ruth's reluctance to judge (which, as we've seen, really is only a reluctance to judge about some things, not about others; and which may stem from her own misunderstanding of what judging involves) amounts to relativism depends upon what "relativism" means. Like most highly charged concepts living in close intimacy with hyperbolic pronouncements about "the end of civilization as we have known it" or real worries about "the dangers of cultural imperialism," "relativism" has a variety of meanings.

In its descriptive form, relativism is presented as based on observations about the different ways in which different people live, think, and experience, and evaluate the world.[55] For example, different groups of people seem to have different views about the value of the elderly among them or about how many genders there are. People within the same culture have different and incompatible beliefs about the morality of abortion. In this sense of relativism, Kant was a relativist, and so probably are we and our readers; no doubt Ruth is a relativist in this sense too. She probably does not expect there to be universal agreement about many moral concerns.[56]

A relativist in a second sense of "relativism" reflects on this irreducible variety of moral beliefs and concludes that they are so different as to render impossible any meaningful comparison between them. It is not that people in one culture ought not to judge those in another, according to this view, but rather that whether they want to or not, they cannot do so: It just does not make any sense. Such a relativist does not as such have anything to say about moral debates within a given culture; this relativist's "cultural relativism" has no bearing on how we are to think about actual moral differences but only on what we can count as meaningful moral differences. Ruth is not saying anything which bears on the question of whether she is a relativist in this sense.

A third kind of relativist thinks there are no logical or conceptual barriers to making comparisons among cultures or within them. Indeed, since this kind of relativist tells us that many comparisons ought not to be made, she or he surely believes that they are or can be made, logically speaking. But such a relativist enjoins us from making them on the grounds that it is wrong to do so. Perhaps such a relativist believes that people ought not to hold their own morality as a standard by which to judge others, or thinks that doing so only leads to unnecessary enmity among people, or because she thinks that we are all children of the same God and God tells us not to judge one another. As has been well remarked, this version of relativism has a very non-relativist cast to it: far from holding that no one *ever* has the right to judge another, it insists that we ought to judge those who judge others as wrong.

If Ruth is a relativist, she would more likely be this kind. When we look at some of her language, it certainly may look as if she is. While she is not reflecting on the possibility of making moral judgments across cultures, she is reflecting—here at the request of her interrogator—on the possibility of making judgments about other people within her own culture. And she is balking at the very possibility of doing so. But why? Is it because she thinks it wrong to do so? All she actually has allowed is that it is wrong to do so in the absence of the requisite knowledge. She expressly is not saying that if in their particular situation it seems right to them, it is right. Ruth does not regard further knowledge of the context of a situation as making it impossible for her to judge the person in that situation; on the contrary she speaks as if it is just that further knowledge she needs in order to reach a thoughtful and fair decision. Ruth is not without moral standards, as noted above: for example, she believes that people ought not to be hurt unnecessarily. That is why she does not want to hurt people unnecessarily, and why she then would not want anyone else to hurt others unnecessarily. Ruth's epistemological humility should not be taken—by her or by us—to entail moral relativism. Indeed, her relatively high standards for the knowledge necessary for moral judgment are part of her moral principles.

Ruth is "reticent" to make moral judgments not because she has no moral principles, but because by her moral lights the more knowledge she has of the particular details of a situation the more secure her moral bearings are and the more willing she is to see others as subject to those particular bearings. A moral relativist of the third sort would insist that one can never know enough about a situation to be entitled to make a judgment about it: short of being identical to that other person, one ought to keep one's moral principles to oneself. Ruth is hardly insisting that one can never know enough; she is worried, *on moral grounds*, about not knowing more than she does. Both the relativist in the third sense and Ruth resist the idea that we are never entitled to judge others. Some relativists, in the by now familiar paradoxical stance, are morally appalled at the idea that any one should judge anyone else. Ruth's largest concern is to guard against the danger that people may be hurt. It seems that such harms can be committed when people judge without paying attention to the patterns of injustice in the world, and that very inattention can reinforce those larger patterns of injustice.

### III. The Beginning of a Conclusion

As the early pragmatists suggested, some of the intellectual difficulties we encounter are actually obstacles we put in front of ourselves when we try to solve particular problems. If our goal is to reach conclusions that work for the many people affected, Dewey and James suggested that we should assume an experimental attitude, which requires us to immerse ourselves in the particulars of historical situations. Moreover, they suggested that we need to become more self-conscious about the processes of reasoning and judging we use so that we constantly subject our thoughts and plans of action to the challenging questions: Are these useful? Do they help us?

In this light, Dewey called attention to the varieties of contexts for human judgment. Dewey's work is now inspiring renewed attention to human intelligence—to the thinking, creating, responding parts of human beings, drawn out by the task of making decisions about how to live and treat others. Dewey urged discussion of intelligence, rather than "reason," in order to locate responses to moral problems in the context of lived experience. He wrote that "the primary significance of the unique and morally ultimate character of the concrete situation is to transfer the weight and burden of morality to intelligence." Moreover, the "nominal and esthetic worship of reason discourage[s] reason, because it hinder[s] the operation of scrupulous and unremitting inquiry."[57] Judgment, then, marks the use of human minds that keeps us very much in our many contexts while helping us become alert to their variety. Some followers of Kant would argue that the emphasis on reason identifies human commonality, but it is a commonality that submerges or renders invisible actual relations among concrete human beings.[58] In a fundamental sense, the contemporary call to context is a reminder of the human relationships within which we exercise our reason.

Consider the problem of whether children who allege that they are victims of child abuse must testify in open court, facing the alleged abuser, or whether instead alternative arrangements can be made to protect them from a potentially traumatic experience while still securing evidence to permit prosecutions. As it has been put in litigation, the question is whether a defendant's sixth amendment right to confront the witnesses against him precludes the use of a screen barrier to shield the child witness from seeing the defendant while testifying, or the use of videotape, closed circuit television, or other technological innovations designed for the same purpose.[59] Despite large increases in the reports of child abuse, especially child sexual abuse, advocates for children—including the American Bar Association—have pressed for modifications of the trial process to "protect victims from being abused a second time by the criminal justice system."[60] It seems inhumane to force a child to face the alleged perpetrator of abuse in open court; it also seems a process likely to deter children from testifying or to undermine their ability to do so. Few charges of child sexual abuse result in successful prosecutions.[61] Given this problem, how could considerations of context help decisionmakers reach closure on questions about the lawfulness of efforts to protect child witnesses in child abuse trials?

Our exploration of the meanings of context in contemporary political and legal debate suggests at least the following answers to this question. (1) The question about the legality of shielding child witnesses from face-to-face confrontation with the defendant will be decided in light of some context, whether the context chosen treats as significant or insignificant the particular fact that the witness is a child. The decision to consult Western literary and legal canonical texts that view face-to-face confrontation as a precondition for valid and truthful testimony is a decision about which context to favor just as much as is the decision to consult the rules of evidence permitting hearsay, which similarly lacks the safeguard of face-to-face.[62]

(2) Consideration of a "contextual" rule—a rule that directs decisionmakers to evaluate individual cases in order to assess whether to permit child testimony in the absence of direct face-to-face confrontation with the defendant—departs from an ideal of generality, but not from an ideal of universality, for the contextual rule itself can then be applied across the universe of possible cases, and the factors made relevant in

individual circumstances would be as relevant in any other particular case that presents them.

(3) There is thus no necessary connection between attention to particulars and the danger of relativism; attending to the particular reasons why a given child might be traumatized by confronting the defendant face-to-face or might be unable to speak in his presence demonstrates a refined sense of what factors should count in judgment, not an abandonment of the possibility of judgment. Developing a rule that departs from an absolute requirement of face-to-face confrontation is not abandonment of principle if it reflects commitments to multiple principles.

(4) The sense of an imperative that informs judgment can be strengthened by immersion in a variety of contexts that different people believe are relevant to a given problem; it may increase one's sense of the factors helpful to judging if one connects the permissibility of closed-circuit television, a one-way screen, or other devices to protect the child witness from viewing the defendant with (a) information about the accommodations permitted for adult victims who are witnesses in the criminal system; (b) information about what psychologists think is the experience of children who are victims; (c) information about what experts think are good techniques for testing the veracity and reliability of children's testimony; (d) exceptions to face-to-face confrontation permitted elsewhere in the rules of evidence; and (e) information about both the difficulties in securing prosecutions and convictions for child abuse and about the probable incidence of false allegations of child abuse.

(5) Looking at each of these contexts does not uproot a decisionmaker from a sense of moral moorings or other bases for judgment. Instead, the process can help a decisionmaker specify what considerations should matter in forming a judgment.

(6) Similarly, looking at each of these contexts does not depoliticize the problem of protecting child witnesses. Instead, we can examine in the particulars of each context the expression of larger patterns of power, domination, and exclusion. Children may well be the most likely victims of unequal power and of systems of control and judgment designed without their interests in mind, but concerns about power, domination, and exclusion also apply to criminal defendants. Close focus on particular contexts can enable assessments of the relative power and powerlessness of the child witness and the criminal defendant.

Implicit here is still another notion of context. Employing the conception of judgment developed by Hannah Arendt, a critical question for a judge is which imagined reference group the judge should seek to persuade.[63] Especially given the subject of child abuse prosecutions, are children inside or outside of the circle of contemplated agreement? Drawing on Kant's conception of aesthetic judgment, Arendt articulated the view that moral and political judgments must be made by individuals, in part by imagining the views of others about the issue.[64] In an important respect, this conception of judgment introduces a notion of context that is compatible with and yet still differs from many that we have discussed thus far. This notion emphasizes that human judgments take place in the contexts of social experiences and, even more to the point, in context of other human beings who have views on the subject. Rather than treating judgment as a task removed from human history and from social interactions, Arendt urges us to view judgments as an important expression of each person's connection with other, actual human beings.

Context, in this sense, represents the acknowledgment of the situatedness of human beings who know, argue, justify, and judge. Rather than a weakness or a departure from the ideal of distance and impersonality, acknowledging the human situation and the location of a problem in the midst of communities of actual people with views about it is a precondition of honesty in human judgments. Ultimately, the attention to the varieties of contexts for judgment helps to focus on human intelligence, the thinking, creating, responding parts of human beings, drawn out by the task of making decisions about how to live and treat others.

Our consideration of context has led us through several paradoxes. First, the call to make judgments in context often seems misleading if it implies that we could ever make judgments outside of a context; the question is always what context matters or what context should we make matter for this moment. Second, in many contemporary political and legal discussions, the demand to look at the context often means a demand to look at the structures of power, gender, race, or class relationships, or the effects of age and physical vulnerability on people's abilities to protect themselves. Rather than an injunction to immerse in the unique particularities of the situation, the emphasis on context often means identifying structures that extend far beyond the particular circumstance. But perhaps it is not so surprising that this should be named a contextual move against the backdrop—the context by default—created by Western liberal legal and political traditions that emphasize as ideals individual freedom, equality, universal reason, and abstract principles. Because persistent patterns of power, based on lines of gender, racial, class, and age differences, have remained resilient and at the same time elusive under traditional political and legal ideas, arguments for looking to context carry critical power. In this context, arguments for context highlight these patterns as worthy of attention and, at times, condemnation.

Attention to context implies no particular political agenda, but it does signal a commitment to consider and reconsider the meaning of moral and philosophical purposes in light of shifting circumstance.

## Notes

This is an abridged version of an article by the same name, appearing in *Southern California Law Review* 63 (September 1990): 1597—1675.

1. See Thomas Grey, "Holmes and Legal Pragmatism," cited in bibliography.

2. See, for example, Carol Gilligan, *In a Different Voice*, and Cornel West, *The American Evasion of Philosophy*, cited in bibliography. Also see "Symposium: Minority Critiques of the Critical Legal Studies Movement," *Harvard Civil Rights-Civil Liberties Law Review* 22 (1987): 297—447.

3. See, for example, Gordon Wood, *The Creation of the American Republic, 1776—1787* (Chapel Hill: University of North Carolina Press, 1969) and Alasdair MacIntyre, "The Relationship of Philosophy to History," in *After Virtue*, 2nd ed. (Notre Dame, Ind.: University of Notre Dame Press, 1984), postscript.

4. Joyce Appleby, "The American Heritage: The Heirs and the Disinherited," in *The Constitution and American Life*, ed. David Thelen (Ithaca, N.Y.: Cornell University Press, 1988), 148.

5. Charles E. Conover, *Personal Ethics in an Impersonal World* (Philadelphia, Penn.: Westminster, 1967), 48—49.

6. See the debate between Thrasymachus and Socrates in Plato's *Republic* (Cambridge, Mass.: Loeb Classical Library, 1918), 336b—347e.

7. For a discussion of the role of original intention in Constitutional interpretation, see chapters 15—18 by Sanford Levinson, Daniel Ortiz, Steven Knapp, and David Hoy, respectively.

8. See Ronald Dworkin, *Law's Empire*, and Owen M. Fiss, "Objectivity and Interpretation," *Stanford Law Review* 34 (April 1982): 739—763, and Thomas L. Haskell, "The Curious Persistence of Rights Talk in the 'Age of Interpretation,'" *Journal of American History* 74 (December 1987): 984—1012.

9. See James Clifford, *The Predicament of Culture: Twentieth Century Ethnography, Literature, and Art* (Cambridge, Mass.: Harvard University Press, 1988); Clifford Geertz, *Local Knowledge: Further Essays in Interpretive Anthropology* (New York: Basic Books, 1983); Peter Novick, *That Noble Dream: The 'Objectivity Question' and the American Historical Profession* (Cambridge: Cambridge University Press, 1988); Renato Rosaldo, *Culture and Truth: The Remaking of Social Analysis* (Boston: Beacon, 1989). For an overview of the subject, see Clifford Geertz, "Distinguished Lecture: Anti Anti-Relativism," *American Anthropologist* 86 (June 1984): 263—277.

10. For explorations of such assumptions, see Richard J. Bernstein, *Beyond Objectivism and Relativism* (Oxford: Blackwell, 1983), and Frank Michelman, "Foreword: Traces of Self-Government," cited in bibliography.

11. This formulation is Michael Walzer's in *Interpretation and Social Criticism* (Cambridge, Mass.: Harvard University Press, 1987), 1—32.

12. In work published subsequent to the book, responding to critics of the contextualist persuasion, Rawls has expressly qualified his claims to limit his argument to Western nations that share the tradition of liberalism. See John Rawls, "Justice as Fairness: Political not Metaphysical," cited in bibliography. But within this larger concession to contextualism, Rawls's schema maintains the possibility of judgments that transcend the particular situation of the individuals affected and the individuals doing the judging.

13. See Jürgen Habermas, *Communication and the Evolution of Society*, trans. Thomas McCarthy (Boston: Beacon, 1979). See Seyla Benhabib, *Critique, Norm, and Utopia: A Study of the Normative Foundations of Critical Theory* (New York: Columbia University Press, 1986), 253—279.

14. See Oliver Wendell Holmes, *The Common Law*, ed. Mark DeWolfe Howe (London: Macmillan, 1968).

15. See Zipporah Batshaw Wiseman, "The Limits of Vision: Karl Llewellyn and the Merchant Rules," *Harvard Law Review* 100 (January 1987): 465—541, esp. 493—519.

16. See, for example, Owen M. Fiss, "Objectivity and Interpretation"; Charles Fried, "Sonnet LXV and the 'Black Ink' of the Framer's Intention," *Harvard Law Review* 100 (February 1987): 751—760.

17. See, for example, Hans Kelsen, *General Theory of Law and State*, trans. Anders Wedberg (Cambridge, Mass.: Harvard University Press, 1949); Roscoe Pound, *Jurisprudence* (St. Paul, Minn.: West, 1949), 2.374; Lon L. Fuller, "American Legal Philosophy at Mid-Century," *Journal of Legal Education* 6 (1954): 457—485; H.L.A. Hart, "Positivism and the Separation of Law and Morals," *Harvard Law Review* 71 (February 1958): 593—629. But see Benjamin Cardozo, *The Nature of the Judicial Process*, 161—180, cited in bibliography.

18. Arthur Allen Leff, "Memorandum: Review of Roberto Unger, Knowledge and Politics," *Stanford Law Review* 29 (April 1977): 879—889 (criticizing view that there is any superhuman basis for judgment and action).

19. Further complications arise with the possibilities that the judge could find a unilateral contract or promissory estoppel. See Grant Gilmore, *The Death of Contract* (Columbus: Ohio State University Press, 1974).

20. See Thomas L. Haskell, "The Curious Persistence of Rights Talk in the 'Age of Interpretation,'" 343.

21. Simone de Beauvoir, *The Second Sex*, trans. H. M. Parshley (New York: Knopf, 1953), 580.

22. These reasons include the fact that most women live apart from one another and live instead with men and children. Another reason is the differences among women based on race and class.

23. Simone de Beauvoir, *The Second Sex*, 580.

24. See Combahee River Collective, *This Bridge Called My Back*, ed. Cherríe Moraga and Gloria Anzaldúa (Latham, N.Y.: Kitchen Table, 1983), 211.

25. Ibid., 212.

26. Herbert Marcuse, "Repressive Tolerance," in Robert Paul Wolff, Barrington Moore, and Herbert Marcuse, *A Critique of Pure Tolerance* (Boston: Beacon, 1965), 81—123.

27. *Greer v. Miller*, 483 U.S. 756, 765 (1987) (citing *Darden v. Wainwright*, 477 U.S. 168, 179 [1986]).

28. See, for example, *Philip Brendale v. Confederated Tribes and Bands of Yakima Indian Nation* et al., 109 S.Ct. 2994 (1989) (Blackmun, J., dissenting); *United States v. Monsanto*, 109 S.Ct. 2657 (1989) (Blackmun, J., dissenting).

29. Carol Gilligan, *In a Different Voice*, 100.

30. Attention to detail makes certain emotions morally relevant—not only compassion and tolerance, but also anger, etc. Those who may object to Gilligan's approach because it inclines toward tolerance rather than judgment or condemnation may not understand the full meaning of care. As Aristotle knew, care does not rule out seeing a situation in such a way that anger is the appropriate response.

31. Carol Gilligan, *In a Different Voice*, 100.

32. Thomas Nagel, *The View from Nowhere*, cited in bibliography.

33. A different meaning of principle that is sometimes used refers to the content of the norm quite aside from its scope or directive as to its application. Thus, some may call a norm principled only if it does not rest on arbitrary distinctions between people or situations, such as a law forbidding sales of residential property to people who are not Caucasian. Similar issues are raised in the debate over whether a general ban against abortion should encompass victims of incest and rape.

34. Similarly, an even more highly specific rule detailing the specific circumstances for its application can easily retain its intent to apply to anyone who satisfies its specific provisions. See Eric R. Emmet, *Learning to Think* (New York: Taplinger, 1985), 33.

35. See Marc I. Steinberg and William E. Kalubach, "The Supreme Court and the Definition of 'Security': The 'Context' Clause, 'Investment Contract' Analysis, and Their Ramifications," *Vanderbilt Law Review* 40 (April 1987): 489—541.

36. 471 U.S. 681 (1985).

37. As Frank Michelman has suggested to us, some people might argue that a norm can never be meaningful except when someone acts in reference to it, and in that case, the meaning of the norm depends importantly upon—indeed, is constituted by—the situated circumstances in which it is enacted. This position is not necessary for our defense of contextualism, although it raises intriguing problems for any pragmatic theory of meaning.

38. See Robert B. Reich, *Tales of a New America* (New York: Random House, 1987).

39. Hence the phrase, "the rule of law rather than the rule of men." See, for example, the debate between Socrates and Thrasymachus in Plato's *Republic*, 336b—347e.

40. See David Luban, "Difference Made Legal: The Court and Dr. King," *Michigan Law Review* 87 (August 1989): 2152—2224.

41. See, for example, Kenneth M. Stampp, *The Peculiar Institution* (New York: Random House, 1989), and Charles L. Black Jr., "The Lawfulness of the Segregation Decisions," *Yale Law Journal* 69 (January 1960): 421—432, esp. 424—425, on laughter as a response to Herbert Wechsler's argument about neutral principles.

42. National civil rights legislation has been designed to redress injuries along the lines of race, gender, and disability. See, for example, 42 USC 2000, 6000 (1982). Some localities have also addressed discrimination on the basis of sexual orientation. See, for example, *Madison, Wis., General Ordinances*, 3.36, 38.03 (1988).

43. 109 S.Ct. 3040 (1989).

44. 448 U.S. 297 (1980).

45. See generally Laurie Nsiah-Jefferson, "Reproductive Laws, Women of Color, and Low Income Women," *Women's Rights Law Reporter* 11 (Spring 1989): 15—38.

46. See, for example, Edward A. Purcell, Jr., *The Crisis of Democratic Theory* (Lexington: University of Kentucky Press, 1973).

47. Carol Gilligan, *In a Different Voice*, 101.

48. Ibid., 102.

49. Ibid.

50. Ibid.

51. Ibid.

52. Ibid.

53. See Ibid.

54. Ibid., 102—103.

55. For useful discussions of the distinction between moral and cognitive relativism, see *Relativism: Cognitive and Moral*, ed. Jack W. Meiland and Michael Krausz (Notre Dame, Ind.: Notre Dame University Press, 1982).

56. Yet even this position may assume some minimum points for moral argument on such points as napalming babies is bad. See Arthur Allen Leff, "Unspeakable Ethics, Unnatural Law," *Duke Law Journal* 1979 (December): 1229—1249.

57. John Dewey, *Reconstruction in Philosophy* (New York: H. Holt, 1920), 134.

58. See Seyla Benhabib, "The Generalized and the Concrete Other," in *Women and Moral Theory*, ed. Eva F. Kittay and Diana T. Meyers (Totowa, N.J.: Rowman Allenheld, 1987), 154.

59. See generally, Ellen Forman, "They Keep the Balance True: The Case of *Coy v. Iowa*," *Hastings Law Journal* 40 (1989): 437—456; Emily Campbell, "LB 90 and the Confrontation Clause: The Use of Videotaped and in Camera Testimony in Criminal Trials to Accommodate Child Witnesses," *Nebraska Law Review* 68 (Winter/Spring 1989): 372—409.

60. "The Supreme Court, 1987 Term—Leading Cases," *Harvard Law Review* 102 (November 1988): 151.

61. Only 24% of sexual abuse cases nationwide end in successful convictions. See Demetra John McBride, "Sexually Abused Children: The Best Kept Legal Secret," *New York University Law School Human Rights Ann*. 446.

62. Another context to consider is the emerging body of social science literature evaluating the credibility of children's testimony under varied circumstances. See, for example, *Perspectives on Children's Testimony*, ed. S. J. Ceci, et al., (New York: Springer-Verlag, 1989).

63. For a thoughtful exploration of this problem, see Frank Michelman, "Bringing the Law to Life: A Plea for Disenchantment," *Cornell Law Review* 74 (January 1989): 256—270, esp. 267—268.

64. Hannah Arendt, *Lectures on Kant's Political Philosophy* (London: Harvester Press, 1982), 42.

# 14

## Situated Decisionmaking

### Catharine Wells

#### I. Introduction: Situated Judgments

Increasingly, legal theorists are interested in problems of perspective. The idea that it is possible to make legal decisions in an atmosphere of judicial detachment has seemed less compelling in the face of an increasingly complex and diverse society. As this reality has sunk deeper into the collective unconscious, scholars have begun a reexamination of the phenomena of legal reasoning and legal judgment with a view towards understanding their "situated" character.[1] These theorists reject the notion that there is a universal, rational foundation for legal judgment. Judges do not, in their view, inhabit a lofty perspective that yields an objective vision of the case and its correct disposition. Instead, these scholars understand the role of judging more pragmatically; they recognize that all judges bring their own situated perspective to the case and do the best they can under all the circumstances to reach a fair and just disposition.[2]

These differing theoretical perspectives correspond roughly to the roles of agent and spectator as they are invoked in contemporary ethics and epistemology. How we think about questions like "What should I believe?" and "What should I do?" depends in part upon whether we confront them as an agent or as a spectator—as a real participant in the flow of human activity or as a philosopher. This consideration has led many philosophers to adopt agent-centered theories that are "situated" in the sense that the philosopher assesses the rationality of certain beliefs and values with reference not to an abstractly conceived philosophical foundation, but rather to a contingent web of experience and location that provides individual agents with their own particular point of view.

These philosophers describe themselves as "pragmatic" and find comfort in Ludwig Wittgenstein's famous phrase: "I have reached bedrock and this is where my spade is turned."[3]

When we turn from ethics and epistemology to the rendering of legal judgments, there seems to be an equally helpful distinction to be made between agents and spectators. Common sense tells us that those who are engaged in a controversy will judge its merits differently from those who stand apart. The law recognizes this distinction by requiring that judges recuse themselves from adjudicating any matter in which they have a significant interest.[4] But this requirement does not eliminate the problems that arise from judicial engagement. Judges are not spectators. The judicial role requires that they locate themselves within the situated sphere of activity if only to fulfill their function of rendering judgment. Thus, judging must be viewed as a second-order activity that is distinct from, and logically posterior to, the first-order activities that are the subject of judgment. With respect to first-order activities, judges are supposed to be spectators; with respect to the second-order activity of judging, they are agents. Judges are agents not only because they render particular judgments in particular cases, but also because they participate in the larger task of shaping the development of an adjudicatory tradition.

If we apply the roles of "agent" and "spectator" to the second-order activity of judging, we get two very different images of the judicial role. When we picture judges as "spectators," we expect that they will base their decisions upon a rational foundation of law; when we picture them as "agents," we recognize that they inevitably bring their own distinctive perspective to their consideration of the case. The argument between these two conceptions of judicial role occupies a central place in the history of American legal theory. Christopher Columbus Langdell, who conceived of a spectator-judge utilizing rational first principles and deductive logic has served as a lightning rod for attacks against the possibility of rational foundations.[5] The naive realist, on the other hand, has been accused of undermining the legitimacy of the legal system by introducing the agent-judge as an element of corruption and cynicism.[6] For reasons that have been amply stated in the ensuing debate, neither judicial stance gives an entirely satisfactory account of legal judgment. The notion of a rational foundation for law is attractive but intractably elusive; the notion of situated judgment is accessible but offends fundamental ideals of justice and fairness. In a diverse society, the agent-judge runs afoul of such important aspirations as treating like cases alike[7] and making official decisions that are a product of laws rather than persons.[8]

The renewed interest in pragmatism among legal theorists must be viewed in the context of these concerns about situated judging. Pragmatic legal theories reject traditional notions of judicial detachment and emphasize the situated character of legal judgments. They therefore encounter the same dilemma that challenged the realists—being a realist about judging seems to entail being a cynic or a skeptic about justice. The purpose of this article is to examine the concerns that surround situated judging and the central question to which they give rise: How can a situated judge render a just decision? On its face, the question appears to be both decisive and unanswerable. Upon deeper examination, however, we can see that the question relies upon a doubtful set of presuppositions about situated decisionmaking. It presupposes, for example, that situated decisionmaking is an entirely *ad hoc* and intuitive process. Further, it presupposes that there is an alternative method of decisionmaking that is capable of producing just and principled outcomes. Finally, the objection assumes that pragmatic judges engage in the first manner of decisionmaking and that nonpragmatic judges engage in the second.

In the course of this article, I will try to defend the pragmatic analysis of legal decisionmaking by casting doubt upon these assumptions. In Part II, I will develop two contrasting models of normative decisionmaking that represent the purported distinction between situated and non-situated decisionmaking. In Part III, I will argue that these two models do not represent two alternative decisionmaking procedures. Instead, I will suggest that they describe two interdependent and indispensable parts of any decisionmaking process. Finally, I will conclude that the pragmatic espousal of situated decisionmaking can be understood, not as a rejection of rationally structured decisionmaking procedures, but rather as an elucidation and appreciation of the contextual elements of all forms of deliberation.

## II. Two Models Of Normative Decisionmaking

Normative decisions require complex interactions of beliefs, attitudes and feelings. Deliberative styles are highly personal and, even in a specialized context like law, there are no standard protocols for making a decision. In this section, I will describe two distinct approaches to normative decisionmaking that define opposite ends of a continuum. At one end of the continuum is a highly structured procedure of investigation and interpretation that aims at resolving specific cases in accordance with previously established norms of judgment. At the other end is a less structured, more contextual exploration of the case that aims at prompting sound intuitive recommendations concerning its resolution. The first, in effect, transforms the case into an instance of a more general rule; the second recreates the case as an individual narrative that requires an outcome satisfactory to our sense of justice in this particular context. The first places legal structure in the foreground as a central organizing theme; the second brings background to foreground by focusing directly upon the "facts" of the case as they are experienced by the participants.

## A. Structured Decisionmaking

Structured decisionmaking treats each individual normative problem as a token that is to be understood in terms of its type. The facts of the case are compared to a general hypothetical type of situation, and the solution to the case is found by applying a rule, standard, or value that is generally recognized as the appropriate touchstone for resolving cases of this type. Factual inquiries are rigorously controlled by conceptions of relevancy that are built into the recognized classifications. Controversy about the case centers not upon the merits of the proposed solution in this particular case, but upon the appropriateness of the case's characterization as an instance of the chosen type. In short, normative questions are resolved by fitting the case into a preexisting classificatory scheme. Structured deliberations include the following steps:

*1. Selecting a Normative Theory.*[9] Deliberation begins with a decision as to what kinds of arguments should count in evaluating the circumstances presented by the case. For example, the decisionmaker might select a utilitarian theory and thereby decree that arguments will have weight to the extent that they demonstrate that the parties' conduct tends to the net benefit or detriment of society as a whole. The selection of such a background theory will often be tacit or will be seen as given by the nature of enterprise.

*2. Characterizing the Case in General Terms.*[10] The decisionmaker will investigate the case by paying particular attention to the factual issues that seem relevant under the normative theory (s)he has selected. (S)he will thus treat certain details of the situation as central to the normative problem and marginalize or disregard the remainder. For example, suppose the situation involves a deceptive representation made to a member of the green team by a member of the blue team. The decisionmaker could focus on the case either as an instance of a deception or as an instance of blue/green interaction. If the chosen normative theory permits clear conclusions about the utility of deceptive practices but does not speak clearly about the effects of favoring one team over the other, a structured approach requires treating the case as an instance of deceptive conduct rather than as a question of blue/green interaction.[11]

*3. Analyzing the Case in Accordance with the Chosen Normative Theory.* The decisionmaker might consider how to define the general circumstances under which deceptive conduct would promote or subvert the chosen normative goals.[12] For example, (s)he could decide that a certain amount of "puffing" is beneficial (perhaps it lubricates commerce), but that deceptive claims that are specific enough to induce reliance are detrimental (perhaps they subvert the gains that can be made by informed bargaining).

*4. Selecting a Rule That Will Decide the Case in Accordance with the Normative Theory.*[13] The decisionmaker might formulate rules of general application that identify practical criteria by which good or benign cases could be separated from undesirable cases.[14] For example, (s)he might use a distinction between misrepresentations as to matters of opinion and misrepresentations as to matters of fact to condemn harmful deceptions while maintaining a lawful place for harmless puffing.

*5. Applying the Rule to the Facts of the Cases.*[15] The decisionmaker might reexamine the original case to determine whether its facts fit the categories established in the formal rule. For example, (s)he could decide that the claim "goes from zero to sixty in thirty-five seconds" is a misstatement of fact whereas the claim "a speedy little sports car" is a matter of opinion. If there is no controversy concerning the actual words used by the salesperson and if these words fall neatly into one category or the other, then there is, under this approach, a clearly correct outcome for the case.

## B. Contextual Decisionmaking

Contextual decisionmaking treats a case as an individual set of circumstances that requires resolution upon its own terms. Rather than fitting the facts to preconceived categories of legal significance, the decisionmaker focuses upon the parties' own characterizations of what happened. Inconsistent responses will prompt deeper inquiries concerning viewpoint and perspective. Solution of the problem requires a reconstruction of the underlying circumstances in such a way that differing accounts form a coherent whole. Once the controversy is understood as a coherent whole, it prompts an intuitive response that specifies the appropriate outcome. Understanding a controversy in this way requires that it be experienced from several different perspectives as a developing drama that moves towards its own unique resolution.

A contextual decisionmaker undertakes a number of separate tasks. Typically, these tasks are not performed in any determinate order but are done and redone as the process unfolds. Contextual decisionmaking involves the following steps.

*1. Relatively Undirected Fact Gathering.* The decisionmaker begins by becoming familiar with the general outlines of the controversy. (S)he may speak to participants, to experts, and to anyone who has useful insights or information. (S)he may inspect the site, read documents, or consider extrinsic evidence. The object of this activity is to recreate in the decisionmaker's mind as much of the context and detail as possible.

*2. Reconstructing the Event from the Perspectives of the Various Parties.* The decisionmaker imagines the event as it may have appeared from the vantage point of each participant. By successively standing in the shoes of all the various players, (s)he seeks to reconstruct subjective appearances and motivations.

*3. Recreating the Incident as a Coherent Whole.* The decisionmaker constructs a story that is consistent with all the known details and accounts for each character's subjective experience and known motivations.[16] The story aims at plausibility; the actions of every character must be sufficiently supported by his or her goals, state of mind, and perception of the unfolding event.

*4. Forming an Intuitive Response to the Concrete Situation Taken as a Whole.* At any given point, the decisionmaker will have a point of view with respect to the relative praiseworthiness and blameworthiness of the various participants in the incident. Questions of relevancy will not be determined by a pre-selected normative theory. Instead, as the decisionmaker thinks about the case, some details will begin to emerge as particularly salient.[17] (S)he will base tentative conclusions not only upon an emerging grasp of the situation but also upon prior experience of similar matters and perhaps even upon certain preconceptions. Normative intuitions may be affected by all these items whether we regard them as consciously relevant or not.

*5. Self-Criticism: Correcting Intuitive Responses.* Having formed an initial response, the decisionmaker may entertain doubts about its correctness. These doubts arise by reflection upon the limitations that may be inherent in her point of view. Whether these doubts can be adequately or even partially resolved is open to question, but it is nevertheless clear, as a descriptive matter, that some process of self-criticism is frequently an important step in coming to a final judgment.

## C. Structured and Contextual Justification

Just as the structured and contextual models describe two very different conceptions of normative decisionmaking they each suggest two distinct forms of justification. With a structured decision, issues of justification center upon the normative theory that has been utilized in the deliberative process: Is the theory the appropriate basis for resolving disputes of this kind? Has it been properly applied to the facts of this case? A contextual decisionmaker, on the other hand, focuses upon the particular circumstances that have created the controversy. Thus, justification for her decision is less abstract and more circumstantial. For example, (s)he might describe her or his deliberative process as a way of showing that (s)he has reached a decision in a conscientious way. In effect, (s)he proclaims: "This is the best I could do under all the circumstances of this case." Such justification is inherently "pragmatic" in the sense that it recognizes that even good decisions are subject to the limitations of perspective and viewpoint.[18]

In the context of legal decisionmaking, the problem of justification is complicated by the demand that cases should be decided in accordance with law. Many structured judges, for example, justify their decisions by a two-step process: First, does the outcome result from a correct application of a correct legal rule and, second, is the legal rule justified by a larger normative theory.[19] Under this approach, legal theory seems to require increasingly abstract statements of "the law" and correspondingly abstract theories of justification. Contextual judges, on the other hand, resort to less universal forms of justification that may seem problematic in a legal context. While they rely upon their intuitions in reaching a decision, they justify their decisions by writing opinions that appeal to traditional sources of legal authority.[20] This has led many legal scholars to question the authenticity of contextual justification. Some scholars argue that it is inappropriate for a judge to cite reasons that (s)he does not herself find persuasive.[21] Others simply point out that nearly every legal outcome could be justified by this kind of *ex post* justification. Since the end of the realist movement, these arguments have been widely viewed as decisive with the vast majority of legal scholars, one group of legal scholars believing that legal decisions require structured justification and another group believing that all legal decisions are inherently arbitrary.[22]

In the context of this analysis, the pragmatist seems to embrace several contradictory positions. First, (s)he concedes that *ex post facto* justifications are not adequate justifications for legal outcomes. On the other hand, (s)he also believes that structured theories fail to provide the kind of timeless and universal justification that the theories themselves seem to require. But, despite the fact that the pragmatist rejects these two major forms of justification, (s)he also believes that justification for legal decisionmaking is both necessary and possible. In the remainder of this article, I will suggest that this position is not so contradictory as it seems. Rather, the contradiction seems fatal only in the context of a vastly oversimplified model of normative decisionmaking. By developing a more complex model of normative decisionmaking, we can begin to develop a notion of justification that has both structured and contextual elements.

### III. Legal Adjudication

As a descriptive matter, it seems clear that legal decisionmaking has both structured and contextual elements. The structured elements are highly visible in the simplest reconstructions of legal method. The contextual elements are less visible but can be seen in the common law preference for case-by-case adjudication, in relaxed standards of evidential relevance, and in the use of juries to resolve legal controversies.[23] In this section, I will develop the distinction between structured and contextual decisionmaking with a view towards showing that neither can operate independently of the other. Thus, the fact that legal adjudication displays elements of both models should not surprise us.

### A. *The Two Models Compared*

The two models of normative decisionmaking are sometimes contrasted by using words like "abstract," "rational," "universal," and "rule-bound" to characterize structured decisionmaking and opposing words like "concrete," "intuitive," "particular," and "case-specific" to characterize contextual decisionmaking. But these characteristics are misleading in several ways.

First, the difference between structured and contextual decisionmaking is not in the type of mental operations that they employ; both models require the use of abstraction, reason, and intuition. We cannot, for example, engage in contextual decisionmaking as I have described it without recreating the central events from several different viewpoints. This step requires the use of both abstraction and reason.[24] On the other hand, structured theorists frequently appeal to intuition[25] as a justification for certain parts of their analysis.[26]

Second, the two models are not adequately characterized by contrasting pairs of terms such as "general" and "particular" or "universal" and "concrete." These are relative terms.[27] A case may be described as "an auto accident," "a hit and run," "an accident on Main Street on December 3rd," "an accident between Mr. Smith and Ms. Jones," or even as, "an accident between Mr. Smith and Ms. Jones on Main Street on December 3rd," and it will still be a general description. Descriptions are always general and general terms are always necessary to describe "particular" facts. The "facts" of a legal case are inevitably only descriptions of fact,[28] and these descriptions are not identical with the concrete circumstances that gave rise to the case. On the one hand, we are able to talk about a "case" only if the descriptions are specific enough to pick out a unique set of circumstances. On the other hand, the "case" is not a specific occurrence but an amalgam of descriptions of the circumstances surrounding the occurrence. In thinking about contextual decisionmaking, it is important not to confuse the legal "case" with the concrete circumstances that generate it. Contextual decisionmakers may be more concerned with factual detail and complexity, but they are nevertheless entirely dependent upon general descriptions. Even a wealth of description will not recreate, except in a metaphorical way, the actual event being investigated.

Third, the use of terms like "rule-centered" and "case-specific" to describe these models is also misleading. On the one hand, it is true that the structured model focuses on categories and criteria while the contextual model focuses on specific circumstances. On the other hand, the conception of rule-centeredness itself is open to widely varying interpretations. Several generations of legal theorists have analyzed the role of legal rules in resolving individual cases. This considerable body of literature has generated a diverse array of understandings about what it means to decide a case in accordance with a legal rule. Are rules prescriptive statements of the form, "If x and y are true, rule in favor of the plaintiff"?  Or are they to be understood as a particular hierarchy of values?  Because there is no consensus surrounding the use of the word "rule," its meaning is often imprecise and it is therefore not very helpful in analyzing normative decisionmaking.  Furthermore, the designation "rule-centered" is deceptive in overlooking the diversity of legal theories that could be considered structured theories.  It is true that structured theories invoke rules, standards, or values as a part of their procedure, but that is not a full description of the strategy.  For example, Ronald Dworkin clearly does not believe that legal decisions result from applying a formal rule to the facts of a controversy; nevertheless, he pursues a structured approach to normative questions.  His Hercules begins with a political theory, a theory of legislation, and a theory of precedent, then, with "superhuman skill, learning, patience and acumen,"[29] fashions a result that accords with those theories.  In short, Hercules need never retreat to his own contextual judgment of the concrete case because "his theory identifies a particular conception of community morality as decisive of legal issues."[30]  Dworkin's Hercules may not be a simple rule follower, but his approach is clearly structured in the way outlined above.

## B. The Interdependence of Structured and Contextual Analysis

For the reasons discussed above, it is an oversimplification to think of the structured and contextual models as two separate ways of making a decision.  Instead, we can understand each model as describing a set of activities that are essential to normative decisionmaking.  In this respect, an analogy will be helpful.

Imagine that a traveller is lost in the middle of nowhere and that it is imperative that (s)he get home.  The structured approach resembles the approach we would use if (s)he could give us a signal that would locate her on a giant map.  In order to locate her specific position and direct her to her destination, it would be necessary to zero in on her by employing a series of maps that cover successively smaller territories.  The location on the large map would give us coordinates that we could use to select a more detailed but less extensive map that also contained the specific location.  The location would then be extrapolated onto the second map and new, more exact coordinates would be obtained.  The process would be repeated until a map was found with sufficient detail that we could identify the road on which our traveller stood and the exact location of her home.  The use of a structured approach to solve normative problems presupposes that we have a very large map (that is, a reason to prefer one normative theory to another) and that we are able to locate the traveller (define the problem) within the map (in terms of the theory) by means of coordinates (that is, morally relevant features) that are contained on the map (in the theory) itself. It assumes that both the maps and the signal that places the traveller on the map are accurate.

The contextual approach is the approach we would use if we could locate the traveller but had no map. We would join the traveller and begin to explore. We would try various roads, ask any people we met, and begin to construct our own tentative map of the immediate vicinity. In short, we would look for any clues that we could find until we were able to lead the traveller home. This process could be very time consuming or, with some luck, we might complete it relatively quickly. The use of a contextual method to solve normative problems presupposes that we have no map or only a partial one. The only means of investigating the problem is to exploit our potential connection with it. We can put ourselves in the traveller's shoes, but we cannot locate her in the larger universe.

The two approaches represent the difference between zeroing in on a spot from afar or starting with the spot and working our way outward. The virtue of the first approach is that it removes us from the traveller's subjective situation into an objective but abstract conception of her terrain. The strength of the second approach is that it brings us closer to the problem by placing us "on the spot." Despite these apparent differences, it is clear that the two approaches are strongly interrelated. The objectivity of the mapmaker's space is achieved by abstraction and reason, but abstraction and reason, by themselves, are not effective tools. Their usefulness depends upon the accuracy of the information that they analyze. Thus, making a map requires keen "on-the-spot" observation of real geographic areas. Similarly, the "situated" rescuer cannot rely solely upon observation. To be effective, (s)he must make at least some effort to map out, to record and interpret, what (s)he sees.

It is tempting to draw a distinction between maps and observations that is based on the idea that individual observations are situated while maps are not. On the one hand, individual observations are "situated" in the sense that they are each made relative to an individual viewpoint. On the other hand, maps seem to be less situated in that they are constructed from observations that have been obtained from more than one viewpoint. Even so, maps can never be entirely free of perspective. Consider two different maps: One is drawn by a giant who is hunting tigers; the other is drawn by a Lilliputian who is seeking a sunny place for a nap. Will these two maps look the same? Which one is more objective? Are footprints or rays of sunshine the objective features of this terrain?

The analogy between mapmaking and legal adjudication suggests two things about structured and contextual decisionmaking. First, it suggests that we should not view the structured and contextual analyses of legal adjudication as an either/or proposition. Instead, we should recognize that decisionmakers cannot create a particular structure unless there is a willingness independent of the structure to commit themselves to the correctness of some individual decisions in some individual cases. Thus, even the most abstract forms of deliberation ultimately rely upon contextual decisions. Second, the analogy suggests that even the structured elements of legal decisionmaking are themselves situated. Legal rules do not necessarily begin with first principles; they may begin, like mapmaking, with observations of what seems to be an appropriate response to an individual case. Thus, a legal analysis cannot be perspective free if the categories it uses arise from a decisionmaker's (or a group of decisionmakers') experience in adjudicating cases. Inevitably, what these decisionmakers come to regard as salient and objective features of the decisional terrain will depend upon their own particular situation. This means that the structures that are used to analyze cases are themselves situated in a particular history of adjudicating cases and in a particular set of purposes for engaging in adjudicatory activity.

## C. The Interdependence of Factual and Normative Judgment

Many theorists would deny that there is a useful analogy between the traveller's dilemma and the decision of a legal case. Their objection centers upon the nature of evaluative judgments. The traveller's problem, in their view, is factual and is therefore most readily solved by a combination of particular observation and accumulated knowledge. An evaluative judgment, on the other hand, differs from a factual one in that observations of, or intuitions about, concrete circumstances are inherently untrustworthy. It is clear, they argue, that individual normative responses undergo significant variations as a result of such subjective factors as mood, prejudice, and self-interest. Because of this variation, the argument continues, normative theory should be based upon rational arguments rather than contextual intuitions. Or, to put the point in terms of the mapmaking analogy, normative decisionmakers who place themselves "on the spot" are sure to lose their way in a tangle of unreliable and subjective impressions. Thus, the argument continues, reliable "maps" of normative terrain can be drawn only from a detached and objective stance.

The alternative to "on-the-spot" moral judgments are detached normative theories that begin with first principles and lead to conclusions about particular cases. Examples include the utilitarianism of Bentham and Mill, Kantian theories of deontic obligation, and Rawlsian conceptions of justice and fairness. These theories solve the problem of value by appealing either to self-evident principles such as the value of human utility or to principles that are derived from such worthy conceptions as personhood or justice. The consequent distinction between fact and value excludes the possibility that legitimate judgments of value can be made intuitively by simple observation of an individual case.

Despite the analytical clarity of this distinction between facts and values, the distinction is extremely problematic when we attempt to apply it to the normative decisionmaking of ordinary life. Intuitive normative judgments are an essential and pervasive feature of human experience. For example, we choose a particular route to get to work; we decide to spend more time with our children; we call a questionable tennis serve in or out; we work late so that we can do a better job; or we take time to help a person find something (s)he has lost. We are confronted hourly with demands upon our attention that we can ignore or to which we can respond. Sometimes we decide in accordance with previously articulated principles; most of the time we simply have a "feeling" about such situations.[31] On the basis of this feeling, we believe that certain things ought to happen; under certain circumstances, we are even moved to try to make them happen.[32] This feeling rarely comes to us as the result of conscious application of previously enunciated standards of judgment. Rather, it is a response to a situation taken as a whole—a signal of our "individual stance" with respect to that situation.[33] In responding, we see not only that certain things have been done but also that we favor or oppose those things. In short, we not only perceive an event but we develop an attitude towards the event that, in turn, focuses our attention and colors further perceptions.

When we examine experience in this way, it is clear that a sharp distinction between factual observations and normative judgments cannot be maintained. What we see and hear is filtered and interpreted within a cognitive framework that is constructed largely from our own individual temperament and prior experience.[34] Normative judgments in particular cases are strongly influenced by perceptions about the nature of the controversy within this larger framework. Thus, reality is not something that can be easily or naturally reported as a series of simple observations. Instead, we are enmeshed in scores of overlapping dramas, and our experience of the facts is shaped, in part, by the dramatic roles we play.

It is possible, of course, to make conscious efforts to cleanse our perceptions of their more obvious evaluative elements. We might, for example, say "John approached the group" rather than "John approached the group like a mean son-of-a-gun." But the most scrupulous efforts at impartiality will not restore the details lost as a result of selective attention nor will they permit us to come to a neutral judgment about the facts. I might recognize, for example, that my belief in X's truthfulness is a product of my bias. Nevertheless, this recognition will not necessarily lead to a less partisan view of "the facts." When I discount my estimate of X's credibility, I can't simply conclude that X is lying. Nor is it possible to measure the effect of my bias on the strength of my feelings and to reduce those feelings accordingly; I cannot simply order up a new and corrected sense of the situation. While recognition of bias may be an important step in improving our understanding of a situation, it will not necessarily provide us with a sanitized version of the facts of a case. This does not mean that we cannot make, under some circumstances, factual observations that are relatively untainted by our normative attitudes. We can, for example, make efforts to ensure that scientific observations in a controlled experimental setting are relatively factual.[35] But there is a natural limit to these kinds of efforts, and this is especially true when they are taken outside the laboratory.

In the legal context, the rules governing admissibility of testimony attempt to exclude the most obvious evaluative statements. Nevertheless, witnesses do not observe events under experimental conditions, and trials do not resemble scientific experiments. Controlled observation is not the experience of daily life nor is it the experience that legal testimony describes. Legal testimony is "histrionic" in the sense that it is the telling of a story by one who is a part of the story.[36] Witnesses may be minor characters, but they are nevertheless a part of the story; their view of the facts is as dependent upon their normative position as it is upon their physical viewpoint.

Considerations like these suggest that legal decisionmaking may well be like mapmaking after all. It is true that intuitive normative responses are somewhat unreliable, but it is equally true that they cannot be easily discarded in favor of rational first principles. It is also true that there can be no unbiased and sanitized version of *the* facts of a case to which such principles can be applied. Instead, the legal enterprise is a complicated endeavor that aims at reaching a considered normative judgment in the face of a confusing array of participant accounts. Such judgments are relative to a perspective; they are situated in prior experience and affected by normative attitudes. They are based upon complex, if not fully conscious, estimates of the relative soundness of each party's case.

## IV. Conclusion: Situated Structures

In this chapter, I have argued that normative decisionmaking requires the simultaneous operation of two distinct deliberative procedures. Each procedure is incomplete: Structured reasoning ultimately presupposes a variety of contextual judgments and contextual judgments, in turn, are not truly useful unless they are incorporated into a framework that imposes a structure on the surrounding terrain. Thus, a belief in situated decisionmaking does not entail the abandonment of structuring methods such as reason, generalization, and abstraction. Instead, it recognizes that there is more to legal decisionmaking than the mechanical application of these techniques and, for this reason, it sees all legal reasoning as "situated" in the sense that it operates within a structure that is constructed by the decisionmaker's own unique mode of participation in the ebb and flow of human events.

For the pragmatist, all theoretical structures must be understood in terms of the real world practices that generate them.[37] In addition—and this point needs emphasis—theoretical structures are not only relative to a practice but also relative to a certain subset of participants in the practice. What you observe and how you categorize depends, in part, on who you are and what you seek. Thus, the judgment that a given normative structure is "logical" or "useful" must be understood in relation to the purposes that render it so. For example, the practice of surrogate parenting has raised a variety of legal issues. Underlying these issues are differing assumptions about the essential nature of the surrogacy arrangement. This poses the question: With whose experience should we try to empathize when we are constructing a legal analysis of this controversial issue? From the point of view of a couple who provide a fertilized ovum to a surrogate mother, the practice might be described as the rental of a womb.[38] They "possess" a fetus and they are seeking to "rent" a place where it can grow. But the "rental" characterization will likely seem inadequate to the surrogate mother. Indisputably, she is pregnant. From her point of view, there is more going on than a commercial lease. She is engaging in genuine acts of mothering. The question—"Should surrogate parenting be described as womb rental or as a form of parenting?"—recalls a similar question about hunting tigers—"Should we describe the hunt from the hunter's point of view or from the tiger's?"

My point in all this is not skeptical. A pragmatist can recognize that judges do not render their judgments from "nowhere"[39] while still not denying that just outcomes are possible. The recognition that legal judgments are situated is the first step towards an authentic ideal of fairness. If our judgment is inevitably limited by our perspective, then consideration of the character of that perspective is the beginning of rational inquiry. The point of this inquiry is a form of justice that is not rooted in images of detachment and remoteness. Rather it is contained in two related commitments: first, a commitment to be scrupulously honest about the limits of one's own particular viewpoint and, second, a commitment to be genuinely open to understanding and respecting the viewpoint of others. These are serious commitments. To honor them, we must cultivate more flexible approaches to normative problems; we must abandon the pretense that our methods of analysis are universally correct; and we must learn to speak in ways that do not obscure the origins of our judgments in experience and desire. By recognizing the situated character of abstract reasons and structures, we make it possible to consider what reasons and structures are pragmatically appropriate to a particular decision and, in explicitly addressing this question, we move closer to fulfilling our aspiration for a genuinely just form of adjudication.

## Notes

1. See, for example, entries in bibliography under Cover, Kennedy, Michelman, and Minow. The concept of "situated judging" was also a recurrent theme in realist writing. See, for example, Benjamin Cardozo, *The Nature of the Judicial Process* (New Haven: Yale University Press, 1921); Arthur L. Corbin, "The Law and the Judges," *Yale Review* 3 (January 1914): 234—250.

2. See, for example, Patricia A. Cain, "Good and Bad Bias: A Comment on Feminist Theory and Judging," *Southern California Law Review* 61 (September 1988): 1945—1955; Judith Resnik, "On the Bias: Feminist Reconsiderations of the Aspirations for Our Judges," *Southern California Law Review* 61 (September 1988): 1878—1944.

3. Ludwig Wittgenstein, *Philosophical Investigations*, trans. G.E.M. Anscombe (New York: Macmillan, 1953), 217 (quoted in Hilary Putnam, *The Many Faces of Realism* (La Salle, Ill.: Open Court, 1988), 85.

4. See, for example, 28 U.S.C. 455 (1988).

5. The use of Langdell as a focus for attacks on formalism may not be entirely justified. See Thomas Grey, "Langdell's Orthodoxy," *University of Pittsburg Law Review* 45 (Fall 1983): 1—55.

6. See, for example, Max Lerner, "The Shadow World of Thurman Arnold," *Yale Law Journal* 47 (March 1938): 687—703.

7. Most realists recognize that situated conceptions of judging entail the inevitable conclusion that two judges may legitimately come to different results in the same case. See, for example, Benjamin Cardozo's remarks in *The Nature of the Judicial Process*, 12—13.

8. For a statement of this aspiration, see Ronald Dworkin's discussion of the doctrine of political responsibility in his *Taking Rights Seriously* (Cambridge, Mass.: Harvard University Press, 1977), 87. But see Margaret Radin, "Reconsidering the Rule of Law," *Boston University Law Review* 69 (July 1989): 781—823.

9. See, for example, Dworkin's description of a political theory in *Taking Rights Seriously*, 91.

10. Characterizing a case in general terms requires a theory of the case that emphasizes some facts while ignoring others. For example, the classificatory scheme in Blackstone's *Commentaries* provides a way of differentiating one general type of case from another. See Sir. William Blackstone, *Commentaries*, ed. James DeWitt Andrews, 4th ed. (Chicago: Callaghan, 1899), 1.37 and 2.3. As these differentiations are made, certain facts become central while others are relegated to an irrelevant residue of particularity.

11. Some critical theories do not reject a structured approach but, in effect, quarrel with the legal categories that determine which facts are relevant. For example, a theory that focuses upon hierarchies and disparate distributions of power may argue that categories relating to race, gender, or class are more central to the decision of a case than traditional legal categories. See, for example, entries in bibiliography under MacKinnon and Matsuda.

12. Many judges describe themselves as rule utilitarians. For a definition of rule utilitarianism see John Rawls, "Two Concepts of Rules," *Philosophical Review*, 64 (January 1955): 3—33. By describing themselves as rule utilitarians, they mean to say that they decide a case not by focusing on the best outcome for this particular case, but by adopting a rule that produces the best outcome if it is applied in all relevantly similar cases. See, for example, Roger J. Traynor, "Some Open Questions on the Work of State Appellate Courts," *University of Chicago Law Review* 24 (Winter 1957): 218.

13. This is perhaps the kind of move Jules Coleman and Jody Kraus have in mind in "Rethinking the Theory of Legal Rights," *Yale Law Journal* 95 (June 1986): 1335—1371.

14. The formal rules need not be "deduced" from the theory but may only be general formulations that seem sound given the underlying values recognized by the theory. For an example of an argument that justifies legal rules in terms of their loose connection with a particular underlying value (reciprocity), see George P. Fletcher, "Fairness and Utility in Tort Theory," *Harvard Law Review* 85 (January 1972): 537—573.

15. This procedure is the essence of structured accounts of legal method. It is well known to law students as the "A" term of the IRAC (Issue-Rule-Application-Conclusion) formula.

16. See Reid Hastie, Steven D. Penrod, and Nancy Pennington's description of the "Story Model" as a model that reflects a "juror's actual cognitive processing" in *Inside the Jury* (Cambridge, Mass.: Harvard University Press, 1983), 22.

17. David Wiggins has described this kind of deliberation in "Deliberation and Practical Reason," in *Essays on Aristotle's Ethics*, ed. Amelie Oksenberg Rorty (Berkeley and Los Angeles: University of California Press, 1980), 233.

18. The outcome of a contextual analysis may, of course, agree with the requirements of some normative theory, but this fact is incidental to the process of justification. In a conflict between what the theory seems to require and a decisionmaker's own intuitive sense, truly contextual decisionmakers follow their intuitions rather than the theory.

19. Some judges, of course, view themselves as simply following the law without regard to underlying normative considerations. They do not, however, lack a normative theory because they presumably believe that judges ought to follow whatever sources of law they have invoked to decide the case.

20. See, for example, Joseph Chappell Hutcheson, *Judgment Intuitive* (Chicago: Foundation Press, 1938), 20—34.

21. For a fuller discussion of this criticism, see Scott Altman, "Beyond Candor," *Michigan Law Review* 89 (November 1990): 299—352.

22. See, for example, Owen M. Fiss, "The Death of the Law?" *Cornell Law Review* 72 (November 1986): 1—16.

23. See Catharine Wells, "Tort Law as Corrective Justice: A Pragmatic Justification for Jury Adjudication," *Michigan Law Review* 88 (August 1990): 2348—2414.

24. One cannot compare what A saw with what B saw unless one is able to abstract the individual perceptions of A and B from their respective viewpoints.

25. The term "intuition" is used in many ways: It is sometimes used as I am using it to denote a nonstructured judgment about the merits of a particular case, but it is also sometimes used to denote a general claim for which reasons or proof need not be given. Proof may not be necessary for a number of reasons, the most common of which is an expectation that the listener's intuitions will not differ.

26. An example of such an appeal to intuition is when a theorist says, "My intuitions say that personal dislike does not justify murder," and so declines to treat personal animosity as an excuse for murder.

27. Or as Dworkin would say, a "distinction of degree." Ronald Dworkin, *Taking Rights Seriously*, 93.

28. Indeed, they are value-laden descriptions of fact. See Part III, Section C. below.

29. Ronald Dworkin, *Taking Rights Seriously*, 105.

30. Ibid., 126.

31. I use "feelings" in this context because I believe this is how it is ordinarily described. In using this term, I do not mean to commit myself to placing moral intuitions within any particular framework of perceptual or emotional judgments.

32. For a phenomenological description of this way of evaluating day-to-day decisions, see Charles Sanders Peirce, "Questions Concerning Certain Faculties Claimed for Man," in *The Collected Papers of Charles Sanders Peirce*, ed. Charles Hartshorne and Paul Weiss (Cambridge, Mass.: Harvard University Press, 1934), 5.213.

33. The pragmatists placed all normative decisionmaking within a context of beliefs, desires, and habits. In speaking of an "individual stance" with respect to a given situation, I mean to refer to such a context.

34. See Peirce's claim that "we see what we are adjusted for interpreting, though it be far less perceptible than any express effort could enable us to perceive; while that, to the interpretation of which our adjustments are not fitted, we fail to perceive although it exceed in intensity what we should perceive with the utmost ease, if we cared at all for its interpretation." Charles Sanders Peirce, "Pragmatism and Abduction," in *Collected Papers*, 5.185.

35. I say "relatively factual" because of the familiar problems of observer bias and experimental design. Some philosophers raise doubts about whether scientific results are even relatively factual. See, for example, entries in bibliography under Feyerabend and Kuhn.

36. "Histrionic" has two senses: (1) dramatic, emotional, affected, and (2) of or having to do with actors or acting. In choosing this term, I mean to invoke both connotations.

37. This is simply an application of the pragmatic maxim. See, for example, Charles Sanders Peirce, "How to Make Our Ideas Clear," in *Collected Papers*, 5.388.

38. See Richard Posner, "The Ethics and Economics of Enforcing Contracts of Surrogate Motherhood," *Journal of Contemporary Health Law and Policy* 5 (1989): 27. Note that other surrogate parents might see it differently. "Womb renters" are one kind of player. It is possible, of course, that there can be other kinds of players. For example, some couples may genuinely seek to engage in a practice of cooperative planning for a child. Against this is the difference between giants hunting tigers and Lilliputians seeking a sunny place for a nap. See Part III, Section B. above.

39. Thomas Nagel, *The View from Nowhere* (Oxford: Oxford University Press, 1986).

# 15

# A Multiple Choice Test: How Many Times Has the U.S. Constitution Been Amended? (A) 14; (B) 26; (C) 420±100; (D) All of the Above

*Sanford Levinson*

## I

The notion of a living constitution—especially when coupled with developmental or evolutionary notions—is one of our central metaphors, not to say cliches. It is hard to find anyone who is truly willing to reject it, given that the alternative seems to be a **dead** Constitution, an option which, so far as I know, has no explicit supporters. Still, as Chief Justice Rehnquist once said, "the phrase 'living Constitution' has about it a teasing imprecision that makes it a coat of many colors."[1] However, even he, whom some of us would identify with a rather deadly conception of constitutional interpretation, was happy (or at least willing) to quote Justice Holmes's famous comment from *Missouri v. Holland* about the framers of the Constitution having performed "a constituent act," "call[ing] into life a being the developments of which could not have been foreseen completely by the most gifted of its begetters."[2] The "organism" that was "created" in Philadelphia thus took on a life of its own. Not for Holmes—or his followers—is a sterile form of "originalism" that would limit constitutional meaning to the first order "intentions" of the framers, impervious to the later developments that require more expansive and generous interpretation than would have been thought likely by a framer. Interestingly enough, as the reference to Rehnquist suggests, it is hard to find someone who *does* reject this version of the Holmesian insight. Raoul Berger probably does, but

Robert Bork, for example, certainly does not, as witnessed by his insistent and presumably heartfelt argument before the Senate Judiciary Committee that *Brown v. Board of Education* was perfectly consistent with his "jurisprudence of original understanding."[3]

What the Chief Justice as well as Bork and former Attorney General Edwin Meese, who popularized the "jurisprudence of original intent," object to presumably is not the fact of organic development as such; rather, they oppose *de facto* creation of a *new* organism on the basis that the earlier one turns out to have defective genes. Similarly, even one willing to use developmental metaphors might nonetheless profess to be able to distinguish between, on the one hand, development that, however unexpected (and thus unforeseen), can be shown to have been generated by the organism's internal structure and, on the other, outright mutation generated by exogenous causes.

Thus I arrive at the central topic of this chapter, which is the meanings packed within the term "amendment." Americans, at least, confront the notion of amendment as contextualized by our commitment to a legal order presumptively structured by reference to some set of basic norms that are independent from the *ordinary* political process. The least acquaintance with the ordinary operations of our legal system makes us aware of the crucial contrast usually offered between ordinary development by "interpretation" and extraordinary development by "amendment." The former is, almost by definition, unexceptional; the latter signifies something out of the ordinary. The contrast between interpretation and amendment is akin to that between organic development and the *invention* of entirely new solutions to old problems. From this perspective "interpretations" are linked in specifiable ways to analyses of the text or at least to the body of materials conventionally regarded as within the ambit of the committed constitutionalist.[4] "Amendments" are something else.

Perhaps the simplest way of conceptualizing what we mean by an amendment is to describe it as a legal invention not derivable from the unamended law. Consider in this context James Madison's plaintive argument to the First Congress, while attacking the legitimacy of chartering the first Bank of the United States, that the Constitution must be interpreted within an ideological framework that accepts as "[t]he essential characteristic of the Government" its composition only from "limited and enumerated powers." By way of exemplifying his view that "no power, therefore, not enumerated could be inferred from the general nature of Government," he stated that "[h]ad the power of making treaties . . . been omitted, however necessary it might have been, the defect could only have been lamented, or supplied by an amendment of the Constitution." Assuming one needs it, additional proof of the sincerity[5] of Madison's strong distinction between what can legitimately be inferred from the Constitution and what would require amendment for its realization comes in his 1817 veto of a bill providing for internal improvements. Though acknowledging "the great importance of roads and canals" and the "signal advantage to the general prosperity" of their improvement, he nonetheless saw it as beyond the enumerated powers even while "cherishing the hope that its beneficial objects may be attained by a resort for the necessary powers" to the procedures "providently marked out in the instrument itself [as] a safe and practicable mode of improving it as experience might suggest."[6] Madison thus had no objection in principle to federally financed internal improvements; he simply believed that Congress was without power to call them into being until what Bruce Ackerman would identify as "we the people" fabricated new powers for the national government and signified that fabrication through formal amendment.

To describe something as an (authentic) amendment is thus at the same time to proclaim its status as a legal invention and its illegitimacy as an interpretation of the preexisting legal materials. Concomitantly, to designate something as an interpretation, even if one is not persuaded by it, is to accord it a certain legal dignity that is not present if one disbelieves the very possibility that one could have offered it as a "good faith" exercise in interpretation. The latter will probably be described as an attempt to "amend" the Constitution surreptitiously, in violation of the approved procedures by which inventions are accepted into the constitutional fabric. This may be what Madison meant to suggest when he stated that "it was not possible to discover in [the Constitution] the power to incorporate a Bank,"[7] though perhaps he meant simply that it was indeed "possible"—Alexander Hamilton showed exactly how one could do it—but ultimately unpersuasive. (A pervasive problem in analyzing legal rhetoric, of course, is knowing when statements should be read as mere hyperbole—as in regular denunciations by one or another Supreme Court justice of a colleague's position as "without merit"—or as something else.)

Indeed, I think it can be a useful exercise for those of us interested in the theory of constitutional interpretation to ask what sorts of changes in our political system could be authorized through ordinary legislation and/or judicial interpretation and what sorts, on the other hand, would require the inventiveness of "amendment." Could, for example, Congress simply authorize by legislation, or the Court otherwise legitimize through judicial decision, the election to office of a foreign-born twenty-three-year old as president? Most analysts no doubt would believe this to be impossible, that this is a paradigm instance where "amendment" would be necessary and plausible "interpretation" unavailable. Even this may not be self-evident, as Professor Anthony D'Amato has recently argued,[8] though this doesn't overcome the fact that most persons within the contemporary interpretive community would regard D'Amato's argument, if presented within ordinary discourse, as "off the wall" and demonstrative of an inability to understand the working conventions of our constitutional system, one of which is the important distinction between interpretation and amendment and the entailed position that not *everything* can be inferred from preexisting legal materials.


## II


Having already introduced, through James Madison, the issue of the United States Bank, let me turn to John Marshall's opinion upholding the Bank in *McCulloch v. Maryland*,[9] justifiably regarded as perhaps the most majestic single opinion of the Supreme Court in our now two-century history. Technically, of course, it concerned only the constitutionality of the Second Bank of the United States, given that the first bank had expired in 1811. But I think it fair to say that *McCulloch* also serves as an advisory opinion that the First Bank was perfectly constitutional as well, thus joining the First Congress in rejecting Madison's advice that it was not. Just as important, of course, is the host of congressional legislation that could be now passed under the broad reading of national powers articulated by Marshall, who took the occasion to spell out an overarching theory of national power that can be read as assigning basically plenary authority to Congress. I will not rehearse all of what is surely familiar to most of you, including the functional elimination of the Tenth Amendment and the necessary and proper clause as meaningful limits on the federal government. I cannot resist, though, quoting one of the single most famous sentences of the opinion, where Marshall emphasizes that he is expounding a "constitution intended to endure for ages to come, and, consequently, to be adapted to the various crises of human affairs."[10] Interestingly enough, the word Marshall emphasizes is "crises." I prefer, in contrast, to put a bit more stress on the word "adapted."

The theory, even if not the particular result, of *McCulloch* concerned, indeed appalled, many eminent Americans of the time. For my purposes, among the most interesting reactions was that of Madison himself. Although Madison, sometimes denominated "the father of the Constitution," acquiesced in the constitutional legitimacy at least of the bill establishing the Second Bank of the United States, which he had signed as president, he had never formally repudiated his opposition, on constitutional grounds, to the First Bank, and he was clearly disturbed by the breadth of Marshall's opinion. Writing the great Virginia justice Spencer Roane following *McCulloch*, Madison wondered what might have happened some three decades earlier had the supporters of the new Constitution frankly articulated "a rule of construction . . . as broad and pliant as what has occurred." He could not "easily be persuaded that the avowal of such a rule [at the state ratifying conventions] would not have prevented its ratification."[11]

Consider in this context, then, a comment by Professor James Boyd White, who somewhat laconically writes that Marshall's opinion in *McCulloch* "seems to be less an interpretation of the Constitution than an amendment to it, the overruling of which is unimaginable."[12] What I find intriguing, especially coming from the pen of one so careful with his words as Professor White, is that he does not appear to be leveling a criticism against either the opinion or Marshall, even as he offers a kind of support to Madison's skepticism about the provenance of Marshall's opinion. White comes truly to praise Marshall rather than to criticize him. But if White captures our common understanding—that is, if we share *both* his perception of *McCulloch* as a *de facto* amendment *and* his willingness to commend Marshall's performance in *McCulloch*—then we need, I believe, to integrate that understanding into the contemporary debate about constitutional interpretation. This debate in substantial measure concerns the limits to the authority of constitutional interpreters, whether judges or others. It was Marshall, of course, who in *Marbury v. Madison* had defined the importance of a written constitution—the "greatest improvement on political institutions" put forth by the new American nation—as consisting in the specification of powers (and limits) of government. "The powers of the legislature are defined, and limited; and that those limits may not be mistaken, or forgotten, the constitution is written. To what purpose are powers limited, and to what purpose is that limitation committed to writing, if these limits may, at any time, be passed by those intended to be restrained?"[13] The problem, of course, is how we decide disputes about what the "writing" actually means. Is *McCulloch* an example of remembrance or forgetting?

And does Marshall exhibit a mastery of judicial craft or a much more ominous (to some) Nietzschean (or Humpty Dumptyish) mastery of text and language?[14]

In any case, we must decide on our own appellation for Marshall's exercise in constitutional interpretation in *McCulloch*. Marshall's own word to describe *McCulloch* is "adaptation"; White's is "amendment"; Jefferson, always more plain spoken, might well have used the word "usurpation," given his own response to the decision that described the judiciary as a "subtle core of sappers and miners constantly working under ground to undermine the foundations of our confederated fabric."[15]

The problem posed by Marshall and *McCulloch* is, of course, repeated in many other cases. Consider, as only one example, our treatment of the constitutional text stating: "No State shall . . . pass any . . . Law impairing the Obligation of Contracts." Most contemporary analysts "know" (and teach) that the "proper" reading of this patch of text is that states shall not pass laws *unreasonably* impairing the obligation of contracts. Recall the important opinion by Chief Justice Hughes in *Blaisdell*[16] that crucially interpreted the Contract Clause to mean less than the categorical prohibition the "naive" reader might have thought it required. Though Hughes's opinion is suffused with reference to the "emergency" facing the nation, he blandly insisted that "[e]mergency does not create power" but provides only the "conditions" for exercising otherwise legitimate power. That is, no "amendment" was necessary in order for the Minnesota legislature to meet the threat to economic stability posed by the Great Depression; ordinary interpretation sufficed to supply the power. But it is obvious that one could describe the result in *Blaisdell* (and its justification by Hughes) in terms White applied to Marshall's opinion in *McCulloch*.

There is nothing "special" about a case like *Blaisdell*, save for its particular dramatic import within the context of the New Deal. The identical problem, of course, is posed by any First Amendment case that ends up, in fact, allowing an infringement of speech. But it is well known that not even ardent members of the American Civil Liberties Union (ACLU) believe that false proxy statements or perjurious testimony should in fact be protected against federal sanctions, and few believe that "amendment" of the First Amendment is a prerequisite to regulation.

Can we hope to achieve a principled (and is this the same thing as saying "disinterested" or "nonpolitical"?) resolution of dispute about how we should describe cases like *Blaisdell* or its First Amendment equivalents? Are there formal criteria, teachable by constitutional adepts, that can be learned by students of the Constitution, that will allow us to agree, as presumed "factual" matter, on what constitute interpretations and amendments. (We could still disagree, of course, on the "value" attached to any particular proffered example.) If, as I believe, the answer is no, what might that tell us about our overarching topic—the constitutional theory of constitutional amendment?

## III

I thus arrive at an explanation of the title of my chapter. If White is correct and the doctrine enunciated—dare one say the constitutional reality brought into being?—by *McCulloch* is "in fact" an amendment to the Constitution, then it would seem to follow that the answer to my multiple choice question *cannot* be "(B) 26," however common that answer might be. That number refers simply—*merely*—to the number of explicit textual additions to the 1787 document, though even this way of putting it is not without its ambiguities given the multiple thrusts of several of the amendments. There is, for example, no reason whatsoever for the inclusion in the Fifth Amendment of the right to a grand jury before indictment together with the right to compensation for a taking nor would any sense of organic integrity be violated by joining what we call the Fourth and Sixth Amendments, together with the grand jury and self-incrimination portions of the Fifth, into a single amendment dealing with criminal procedure. Nor would it have been jarring for the Fourteenth Amendment to have been broken down into several separately numbered amendments.

What I want to argue (perhaps "assert" is the more accurate term) is that it is almost literally thoughtless to believe that the best answer to my conundrum is "26," at least if one means to be asking a theoretically interesting question. The only question to which one can be confident that that can be the best answer is "how many explicitly numbered textual additions to the Constitution have occurred since 1787?" Perhaps it is a part of what E. D. Hirsch might call "cultural literacy" to know that the answer to *that* is "26," but I will be so bold as to say that that answer, without more, demonstrates a theoretical illiteracy that is far more alarming than would be the failure to remember, say, that we have a Twenty-fifth Amendment to the Constitution. Knowing that there have been twenty-six explicit numbered textual additions to the Constitution demonstrates no more understanding of the American government than the knowledge of how many vice-presidents we have had (knowledge that I will freely confess I do not now possess). Central to understanding the American government—whether as lawyer or political scientist—is recognition, and concomitant assimilation, of the extent to which the Constitution has indeed been amended, been the subject of political inventiveness, by means other than the addition of explicit text. This is obviously the crux of Bruce Ackerman's magnificent work, and I do not want to steal too much of his thunder even as I suggest some problems with it.

Now you might think, on the basis of what I have just said, with its harsh criticism of "26" as the answer, that the answer at least cannot be "(A) 14." This would seem to follow from the proposition that there have been at least the twenty-six specifically numbered inventions plus *at least* one more (for example, Marshall's opinion in *McCulloch*). Of course, if there have been *hundreds* more, then the best answer is "(C) 420±100." Alas, I don't think we can so readily reject "14" as a candidate for the best answer.

Is the very existence of the numbered textual additions presumptive evidence that "amendment" was thought to be required and interpretation unavailing? Well, yes and no. Perhaps they are evidence that *someone* at the time of their adoption thought they were required, but an entirely separate question is whether *we* think they were required.

This issue of the "necessity" of amendment was present at the very beginning of the Constitution. After all, the principal impediment to ratification was the failure of the Convention to include a bill of rights. The supporters of the Constitution insisted that no such bill was necessary, for the national constitution, unlike its state counterparts, was adopted under a theory of "assigned powers." That is, the national government was not plenary, lacking only that power specifically excluded by the foundation document. Instead, it had only those powers specifically granted by the constitutional text. Alexander Hamilton made this the crux of his argument in the eighty-fourth *Federalist*: How could anyone seriously believe that Congress could have the power to regulate the press, given that it was nowhere assigned any such power? "[T]he Constitution ought not to be charged with the absurdity of providing against the abuse of an authority which was not given. . . ."[17] James Wilson had made a similar argument in an address to Pennsylvania ratifiers.

One problem with this analysis, of course, was the existence of Article I, Section 9, which specifically prevents the Congress from, among other things, passing bills of attainder or creating titles of nobility. Indeed, Hamilton specifically emphasizes the importance of Section 9 as providing basic protection; he does not, however, address the point that if Section 9 is in fact "necessary" in order to prevent such legislation, then the Hamilton-Wilson argument fails. Many opponents of the Constitution were not so restrained and gleefully pointed out the tension between Section 9 and the argument that the Constitution should be construed only as a grant of explicitly assigned powers.

Still, Hamilton's argument, if accepted, renders wholly "unnecessary" the First Amendment, for proper interpretation would preclude conscientious members of Congress from passing, the president from signing, or the judiciary from enforcing a bill abridging speech, establishing a national church, or whatever. It may be jarring to suggest that the First Amendment contributes nothing, strictly speaking, to the Constitution.[18] That effect may be evidence, however, only of the distance we have traveled from the original understanding of the Constitution as creating only a limited government of assigned powers. In any event, there is no reason to believe that even all of the representatives who voted for the First Amendment did so in the belief that it was "required" in order to preserve the liberties enunciated. They just as likely may have believed that it was required as a political gesture to anti-Federalists who might, if not appeased, use the very procedures of Article V to bring into being a new constitutional convention that would reconsider the Philadelphia handiwork ostensibly ratified by the state conventions.

It may be a nice thing to have a clear specification of the inability of Congress to regulate the press or establish a religion, but that is a stylistic more than a legal insight, for nothing would be lost, according to the Hamiltonian argument, by the absence of the amendment. From this perspective, as a matter of law the amendment is nothing more than a "guide to the dim-witted" who need the aid of textual specification, even though the rest of us would arrive at precisely the same destination through the use of acceptable techniques of constitutional interpretation. Thus, imagine asking supporters of a textual addition to indicate *precisely* why they thought it was required. It is far different to say, on the one hand, "because the Constitution cannot legitimately be interpreted to allow X, and the new text will authorize X" or, on the other, "because even though the Constitution, correctly interpreted, already contains X within it, there are purported interpreters who are either too stupid or politically malevolent to realize that, so we must add the explicit text as a guide to the dim-witted in order to achieve our purposes." I presume, for example, that many more supporters of the Equal Rights Amendment

(ERA) believed that it was "required" for this second reason than for the first. Among other things, incidentally, this model, if accurate, speaks to the priority that even sophisticates might give to "textualism" as what my colleague Philip Bobbitt calls a "modality" of interpretation. Other techniques seem too fancy but reference to a text seems to eliminate any problems.

One may look at other amendments, besides the first or the ERA, and equally doubt their legal necessity. Take, for example, the Thirteenth Amendment, abolishing slavery. Surely those who believed, with Frederick Douglass, that the Constitution never allowed slavery in the first place, could scarcely have believed that an amendment was necessary to abolish it.[19] Still, Douglass undoubtedly represented a minority position, and most partisans of the Thirteenth Amendment, including Abraham Lincoln, believed that it was legally necessary. But we in 1990 certainly need *not* believe, as a legal proposition, that the Thirteenth Amendment is "necessary" in order to abolish slavery. To hold such a view would require rejection of the propriety of practically every important commerce clause decision since 1937.

Can it conceivably be the case, for example, that a Congress authorized to tell the Darby Lumber Company that it must pay a minimum wage to its laborers is without the power to transform chattel slavery? If we accept the legitimacy of decisions like *Darby*, *NLRB v. Friedman-Harry Marks Clothing Co.* (the fascinating companion case to the more famous *Jones and Laughlin* decision), and *Wickard v. Filburn*, then we simply cannot believe that the Thirteenth Amendment is of much more than symbolic importance.[20] I do not berate symbolism—that was a good enough reason to support the Equal Rights Amendment, but there is an obvious difference between praising either the Thirteenth Amendment or the ERA as a symbolic artifact and asserting that it was "necessary" to transform legal possibility.

Similarly, I doubt that many contemporary analysts believe that the Fifteenth and Nineteenth Amendments are "necessary," given contemporary interpretations of the Fourteenth Amendment in regard to racial and gender classification concerning fundamental rights. And, if the Supreme Court was correct in *Harper v. Virginia Board of Elections*,[21] which found Virginia's poll tax for state elections to violate the Constitution, then surely the Twenty-fourth Amendment, which two years before barred a poll tax in federal elections, is wholly unnecessary. Only if one agrees with Justice Harlan's considerably less generous reading of the Fourteenth Amendment would it be the case that we would lose something legally significant were the Fifteenth, Nineteenth, and

Twenty-fourth Amendments suddenly to disappear from the text of the Constitution? Indeed, ironically (but fittingly) enough, there were some supporters of the Fourteenth Amendment who nonetheless argued that it was not at all necessary because it simply spelled out what a correct interpretation of the Constitution already required.[22]  Let me quickly concede that an accurate historical portrayal of the background of all of those amendments would take into account the perception of some of the best constitutional analysts of the day that they were indeed "necessary." But this evaluation only highlights one of the central mysteries of the doctrinal operation of what I call "constitutional faith": the process by which "best constitutional analysis" is subtly transformed by the passage of time so that a given legal doctrine, say the power of Congress under the Commerce Clause, becomes radically transformed without formal amendment ever being deemed necessary.

Someone who disagrees with Professor White's designation of *McCulloch* as an amendment—and disagrees as well with the description of any *other* decision as a *de facto* amendment—might well have an interpretive theory sufficiently generous to view at least a dozen of the explicit textual additions as unnecessary and spelling out what was already "in" the Constitution to be teased out through legitimate interpretation.  Once that move is taken, then "(A) 14" is clearly the best answer, certainly more sophisticated theoretically than "(B)."

## IV

I want to be clear about what I am arguing (and what I am *not* arguing).   I have proffered a distinction—an opposition—between interpretation and amendment even as I have indicated my belief that I cannot provide formal criteria by which to distinguish the two. Furthermore, I strongly suspect that clever analysts can repeatedly show that what are thought to be "interpretations" are "amendments" and, of course, just the opposite, that what were thought to be great constitutional inventions, such as women's suffrage—were "in fact" not necessary at all because already immanent in the existing constitutional regime.  Thus it may be that the opposition I am suggesting is what my colleague Jack Balkin has recently termed a "nested opposition,"[23] by which he refers to basic notions that structure our thought even as they are constantly subject to conceptual revision and "deconstructive" analysis. The philosophy from which such an approach is drawn is what has come to be called nonfoundational pragmatism: That is, regardless of our inability to provide an allegedly firm, and formalistic, conceptual grounding of our terms, we nonetheless find that we make our way through the world—or, more accurately, through the forms of life that compose *our* worlds—by recurrence to basic notions that we simply seem unable to leave behind. Balkin suggests that the public-private distinction is one such nested opposition. Even as the latest analyst proves once more that the distinction is, according to some abstract scheme, untenable, he or she will almost inevitably reinvent it, so even more untenable (and truly unthinkable) is a world that indeed collapses the two notions into one undifferentiated concept.

So, I suggest, is it the case with the distinction between interpretation and invention-amendment. As Stanley Fish would be the first to point out, each of us at every moment is quite able to construct—and even believe in—such a distinction so far as our own analyses are concerned. Certainly one cannot make the slightest sense of Bruce Ackerman's enterprise, which I personally believe to be the most important and imaginative work now being done in the area of constitutional theory, without accepting the distinction.[24] I do not know if Ackerman accepts White's description of *McCulloch* as an amendment (signifying a "constitutional moment," in Ackerman's language). But he must surely believe this to be the case of cases, like *West Coast Hotel v. Parrish* and the previously mentioned *Darby Lumber Co.*, even if he would correctly argue that the decisions must be placed within the context of a supple and complex process of amendment of which they were simply the final step. Ackerman rejects *in toto* the earlier New Deal historiography by which the decisions of 1937 were simply restorations of the initial (and presumptively legitimate) Marshallian vision as spelled out in *McCulloch* and *Gibbons v. Ogden*. Were they merely restorations, then there would be no need for him to construct his marvelously complex account of Publian politics and constitutional moments that provide an alternative rendering of the American political process. The most significant alternative, from the perspective of the traditional lawyer, concerns the relative displacement of Article V as the mechanism by which amendments occur. Not only have Americans been inventive in their use of Article V; more significant, their inventiveness has been manifested in the very process of invention itself. Just as the "scientific method" itself has been transformed in the process of conducting the operations of "science" itself, so has the method of constitutional governance been transformed in the process of actually governing ourselves over the past two centuries. It is our ignorance about the methods and procedures that we have actually used to provide the framework of constitutional governance that so disturbs Ackerman and drives his project. Our ignorance is not merely an academic affront; according to Ackerman, it leads to a fundamentally stunted view of political possibility and of our own capacities as potentially Publian citizens who can engage not only in constitutional "interpretation," but, more importantly, constitutional fabrication.

## V

I conclude with two comments. The first is that Ackerman has made not the slightest effort to delineate the method by which he recognizes something as an "amendment" rather than a legitimate "interpretation." He can hardly believe that we know it when we see it, given that his own historiography of the New Deal, as already suggested, contradicts the conventional restorationist understanding of the period. I obviously think that it would be unfair to expect Ackerman to present a fully worked out, formalizable theory that could be applied transhistorically and transculturally. But is it equally unfair to expect him to say more than he has? Does not a theory so dependent as his on the perceived difference between interpretation and amendment require an acknowledgment of the interpretive dilemmas just outlined in this particular paper? After all, unless one believes that the New Deal cases *do* signify amendments, there is literally no need for the complex apparatus of Ackerman's argument.

This first comment is directed at those interested in constitutional theory per se and, perhaps more particularly, at Bruce Ackerman himself. But my second comment is directed more at a broader audience, including, at the very least, political scientists and historians. One reason I am so fascinated by Ackerman's project is the sweep of his reconceptualization of American politics and the way it "really works." It is not irrelevant that Ackerman has a joint appointment in the Yale political science department, not heretofore known for its commitment to normative political theory per se. His central project is to establish the existence within the operative paradigms of American politics of an alternative to Article V as a process of amendment. This alternative process involves a complex mixture of behaviors and perceptions by the president, Congress, and the electorate. To examine adequately the plausibility of Ackerman's account requires immersion in the literatures, among others, of presidential leadership, public opinion, and the operation of the electoral process.

There may still be some political scientists who would respond that the purported distinction between interpretation and amendment is of no interest to them, that it can be freely ignored by those interested in the hard stuff of political behavior. Most of us, though, by now have been persuaded that this is an implausible account of the doing of political science, that one can scarcely ignore a culture's own self-understanding if one wishes to understand its behavior. Indeed, the very notion of behavior, we have been taught by Clifford Geertz and many others, can hardly be separated from the interpretive understandings attached to winks, raised hands, and other physical actions presumably the focus of our attentions. But one need not resolve this theoretical debate in order to believe that the distinction between amendment and interpretation is of import even to the most tough-minded political scientists. I would be astonished, for example, if the standard textbooks purporting to introduce "American government" to students did not, at some point, make implicit resource to the distinction by way of teaching the young how amendments are added to the Constitution. To the extent that such discussions focus exclusively on Article V, they are, to put it bluntly, wrong. But to expand the discussion beyond Article V demands *some* kind of structured analysis that rapidly leads into just the kinds of distinctions suggested in this chapter. Or at least this is my own central thesis.

I hope that I have demonstrated the genuine problems, well worth the investment of our intellectual energies, packed into the conundrum that provides the title for my chapter. Just as importantly, I hope to have demonstrated as well why I believe that there is no work going on within the legal academy that so demands a truly interdisciplinary meeting of departments across the entire university community.

## Notes

Earlier versions of this chapter were given at the American Political Science Association convention in September 1990 and at faculty colloquia at the University of Toronto and University of Texas law schools. I am grateful for the suggestions received on those occasions. I should also note helpful criticism, in some cases not yet sufficiently responded to, from Akhil Reed Amar, Scott Powe, Fred Schauer, and Jeffrey Tulis.

1. William H. Rehnquist, "The Notion of a Living Constitution," *Texas Law Review* 54 (May 1976): 693.

2. 252 U.S. 416, 433 (1920).

3. See Nomination of Robert H. Bork to Be Associate Justice of the Supreme Court of the United States, Hearings Before the Committee on the Judiciary, United States Senate, Part

I, Serial N. J-100-64, 284—286. For Meese, see Edwin Meese III, "Address Before the D.C. Chapter of the Federalist Society Lawyers Division," reprinted in *Interpreting Law and Literature: A Hermeneutic Reader*, ed. Sanford Levinson and Steven Mailloux (Evanston, Ill.: Northwestern University Press, 1988), 25—33.

4. See Philip Bobbitt, *Constitutional Fate* (Oxford: Oxford University Press, 1982) for an elucidation of six "modalities" of constitutional interpretation, all of which are joined *as* "interpretations."

5. Madison's speech to the House of Representatives is reprinted in Paul Brest and Sanford Levinson, *Processes of Constitutional Decisionmaking* (Denver, Colo.: Little, 1983), 11-13. Quoted passages can be found at 12, 13.

6. Richard B. Morris and Jeffrey B. Morris, eds., *Great Presidential Decisions* (Philadelphia: Lippincott, 1960), 81.

7. Madison in *Processes of Constitutional Decisionmaking*, 11.

8. See Anthony D'Amato, "Aspects of Deconstruction: The 'Easy Case' of the Under-Aged President," *Northwestern Law Review* 84 (Fall 1989): 250—257.

9. 17 U.S. (4 Wheat.) 316 (1819).

10. Ibid., 415.

11. Letter of September 2, 1819, in *Records of the Federal Convention of 1787*, ed. Max Farrand (New Haven: Yale University Press, 1937), 3:435.

12. James Boyd White, *When Words Lose Their Meaning* (Chicago: University of Chicago Press, 1984), 263.

13. 5 U.S. (1 Cranch) 127, 178 (1803).

14. Even Robert Bork is hesitant to condemn Marshall. He labels Marshall "an activist judge," but asserts that "his activism consisted mainly in distorting statutes in order to create occasions for constitutional ruling that preserved the structure of the United States. Although he may have deliberately misread the statutes, he did not misread the Constitution. His constitutional rulings, often argued brilliantly, are faithful to the document." See Robert Bork, *The Tempting of America: The Political Seduction of the Law* (New York: Free Press, 1990), 21. Bork would presumably vigorously disagree with White's analysis of *McCulloch*, not to mention Madison's criticisms as expressed to Spencer Roane. It is obvious, of course, that this raises significant problems for anyone who is, like Bork, committed to so-called "original intent" as the authoritative guide to constitutional meaning, for one can hardly resist asking why Marshall is a more authoritative guide to constitutional meaning than "Pops" Madison.

15. Quoted from *The Portable Jefferson*, ed. Merrill D. Peterson (London: Penguin, 1975).

16. *Home Building and Loan Association v. Blaisdell*, 290 U.S. 398 (1934)

17. *The Federalist*, ed. Benjamin Wright (Cambridge, Mass.: Harvard University Press, 1961), No. 84, 535.

18. Fred Schauer has suggested to me that perhaps the real importance of the First Amendment is its *incorporation* into the Fourteenth Amendment as a limitation on the states. If one predicate of eighteenth-century constitutional theory was the limitation of the national government only to its assigned powers, another was basically plenary powers of the states, which indeed made it crucial to establish bills of rights in state constitutions against the power of the otherwise unconstrained state. Without textual presence of the First Amendment, it would have been much harder to impose its norms on states. Perhaps, but surely one could have reached many of the same results either through interpretation of the "privileges of immunities" clause of the Fourteenth Amendment or the "republican form of government" clause in Article IV. It is undeniable that the existence of the First Amendment provided a powerful rhetorical resource, but this is quite different from arguing that it was "necessary" to attaining the ends sought.

19. For Frederick Douglass's argument (which was not original with him), see "The Constitution of the United States: Is It Pro-Slavery or Anti-Slavery?" in *Writings of Frederick Douglass*, ed. Philip Foner (New York: International Publishers, 1950), 2:467—480. Discussed in Sanford Levinson, *Constitutional Faith* (Princeton, N.J.: Princeton University Press, 1988), 31, 76—77.

20. Both Professor Schauer and Akhil Reed Amar have reminded me that I am overlooking one important legal consequence of the Thirteenth Amendment, at least given the argument in the text concerning the power of Congress to abolish slavery under the modern reading of the Commerce Clause of acquiescing to the use of slave labor in the states. Ordinary legislation, by definition, can be overridden by a subsequent legislature. Thus the Thirteenth Amendment is not a genuine parallel to the Equal Rights Amendment *unless* one adopts Douglass's view that the unamended Constitution, correctly read, was as hostile to slavery as the unamended Constitution, correctly read, is supportive of gender equality.

21. 383 U.S. 663 (1966).

22. See, for example, Michael Kent Curtis, *No State Shall Abridge: The Fourteenth Amendment and the Bill of Rights* (Durham, N.C.: Duke University Press, 1986), 90-91.

23. Jack M. Balkin, "Nested Opposition," *Yale Law Journal* 99 (May 1990): 1669—1707.

24. See Bruce Ackerman, "The Storrs Lectures: Discovering the Constitution," *Yale Law Journal* 93 (May 1984): 1013—1072; "Constitutional Politics/Constitutional Law," *Yale Law Journal* 99 (December 1989): 452—549. See also the first of a three-volume explication by Professor Ackerman of his reconceptualization of American constitutional history in *We the People* (Cambridge, Mass.: Harvard University Press, forthcoming).

# 16

## The Price of Metaphysics:
## Deadlock in Constitutional Theory

*Daniel R. Ortiz*

American constitutional theory faces an impasse. On the one side stand the so-called interpretivists or originalists, those people who hold that the Constitution must be interpreted according to the framers' or ratifiers' original intent. On the other side stand their antagonists, the noninterpretivists or nonoriginalists, those who believe that constitutional meaning hinges upon changing social value. Theorists on both sides have through the years strongly reinforced both camps' positions, but neither side has ever managed a rout or even a substantial advance on the other. As in the Trojan War, the particular heroes may change—Meese may battle Brennan, Bork may battle Tribe, or, most interestingly, the later Bickel may battle the earlier Bickel—but the debate remains stalemated. Battle's only reward is frustration, exhaustion, and despair.

Don't worry. I don't plan to champion one side or the other. I do have a side, but it's my thesis that arguing for it or for the other side, for that matter, would be futile right now. The very nature of the conflict demands that it have no current resolution. Instead of taking sides, I want to show why neither side has advanced on the other and suggest how conditions must change for us to carry the debate to a conclusion. My idea is that the divide in constitutional theory reflects an even deeper and more long-standing divide in philosophy and politics, a divide that has largely defined the history of our political culture and a divide that we now find it hard to narrow or cross.

Let me start by stating what my claim is not. I am not saying that constitutional theory is merely a form of personal philosophy employed by judges and academics to reach individually desired political results.

Some people do take this view. To them, the lesson of *Lochner v. New York*[1] and *Griswold v. Connecticut*[2] is that both conservatives and liberals invoke constitutional theories to reach particular substantive ends. They believe that in *Lochner* conservatives applied nonoriginalist methods to frustrate New York State's regulation of the employment market while liberals invoked originalism on the other side. In *Griswold*, by contrast, they believe the liberals used nonoriginalism to discover the constitutional right to privacy, a move that the conservatives blasted as a violation of original intent. Although these are somewhat dubious interpretations, they are widely shared and evidence the depth of belief that the Court employs theory in bad faith. Results, I am sure, do drive much of constitutional theory, but they are not all. The long-standing philosophical and political divide that I believe explains the failure of constitutional theory to move forward is greater than that separating the political agendas of conservatives and liberals.

To my mind, the conflict between originalism and nonoriginalism reflects the deeper tension between contractarian and certain communitarian political theories. Originalism allures us because it satisfies contractarian values that run very deep in our political culture. Nonoriginalism, on the other hand, appeals to us because it meets the opposite demands of communitarian theory, a theory that also runs very deep. The debate in constitutional theory largely arises out of this logically prior debate in political theory, and, because this other debate is unresolved, we should not be surprised to find a stalemate in constitutional theory. Indeed, we should be surprised to find anything else.

We cannot, moreover, resolve this other debate right now for very intriguing reasons. Just as constitutional theory reflects a divide in political theory, so too political theory reflects an even deeper and more troubling divide in metaphilosophy. I will argue that today's two popular brands of constitutional theory, together with a third brand now out of favor, ultimately spring from three widely opposed sets of metaphilosophical and ethical commitments. In short, natural law, a once prominent but now largely discredited means of constitutional interpretation, stands upon a foundation of Platonism in its broadest sense. Natural law grounds constitutional interpretation in what it sees as the actual reality of things and seeks to conform the law to truth itself. Originalism, on the other hand, follows from the opposite view that truth or, more accurately, its surrogate, authority, resides only in the individual. At bottom, originalism represents a radically subjectivist approach which denies that values have any intrinsic validity at all.

Finally, nonoriginalism springs from a still different conception, one that grants the community rather than objective truth or the self authority over our categories of thought and action. This third, pragmaticized view is the one I personally follow, but my aim here is not so much to persuade people to it. Instead of taking sides between the two views that predominate today, I want to argue why persuasion is so difficult. Although we each find we must throw ourselves into one camp or the other, the battle cannot be won—at least for now. At this stage of our development our political culture is too highly conflicted to permit either resolution. For now, the metaphilosophical and ethical stakes are simply too high.

Natural rights have a long history in the Supreme Court. As one of the leading intellectual traditions competing at the Founding, natural rights theory influenced constitutional interpretation from very early on. In *Calder v. Bull*, for example, decided in 1798, the Supreme Court's lead opinion argued that "[t]he genius, the nature, and the spirit, of our state governments, amount to a prohibition of [legislative overreaching]; and the general principles of law and reason forbid [it]"[3] even when the Constitution's express provisions are silent. Likewise, in *Fletcher v. Peck*, another early case, Chief Justice Marshall gave equal weight to natural law and constitutional text in determining the limitations on government. "The State," he said "was restrained, either by general principles which are common to our free institutions, or by the particular provisions of the constitution of the United States."[4] It did not matter which. Justice Johnson's opinion in this same case made clear exactly how far some thought the claims of natural law extended: "I do not hesitate to declare that a state does not possess the power [claimed here]. But I do it on a general principle, on the reason and nature of things: a principle which will impose laws even on the deity."[5]

At bottom, all such arguments appeal to a reality or truth independent of human existence and outside of history. Transcendent entities like Platonic forms, ideas in the mind of God, and objects of philosophical realism all define a truth greater than ourselves to which we should bend our efforts. In this view, the judiciary legitimately strikes down social arrangements whenever they deviate from the right. Judges, perhaps even more than the rest of us, have an obligation to bring social practice into ever more perfect alignment with objective truth. Political settlements should not deter them, for the political process enjoys at most presumptive validity.

In any event, we now discredit natural law. Except for a few dinosaurs among us, we have come to accept Jeremy Bentham's view that natural rights are nothing but "nonsense on stilts." Both American legal practice and changes in intellectual, social, and economic conditions have led to this result. First, natural law acquired a bad odor in constitutional theory as the Supreme Court increasingly used it to justify and protect particularly oppressive social arrangements. Most notoriously perhaps, the Supreme Court employed natural law to insulate some of the worst excesses of late nineteenth and early twentieth-century capitalism from legislative attack. By enshrining the right of free labor, "one of the most sacred and imprescriptible rights of man,"[6] in the due process clause of the Fourteenth Amendment, the Supreme Court barred nearly all state attempts to regulate and humanize economic markets. The Court similarly employed natural law to allow the state to prescribe oppressive social roles for women. In *Bradwell v. Illinois*, for example, those justices who most strongly believed in men's right of free labor held that Illinois could refuse to admit women to the bar because

> nature herself . . . has always recognized a wide difference in the respective spheres and destinies of man and woman. . . . The constitution of the family organization, which is founded in the divine ordinance as well as in the nature of things, indicates the domestic sphere as that which properly belongs to the domain and functions of womanhood. . . . The paramount destiny and mission of woman are to fulfill the noble and benign offices of wife and mother. This is the law of the Creator. And the rules of civil society must be adopted to the general constitution of things, and cannot be based upon exceptional cases.[7]

Second, beginning with the rise of Cartesianism and the new science, we began to doubt whether we had any reliable access to truth outside ourselves and then later whether such truth actually existed. As we began to doubt, we began increasingly to locate certainty and sometimes truth inside ourselves. The more optimistic or perhaps just conventional of us became idealists, like Kant; the more cynical became subjectivists, like Hobbes and Nietzsche, who located political and later general authority without any corresponding notion of truth within ourselves. As Hobbes put it: In the state of nature "nothing can be Unjust. The notions of Right and Wrong, Justice and Injustice have there no place."[8] It was our loss of faith in transcendence and our turn into ourselves that led to the rise of originalism among constitutional theories.

Because originalism has most often appeared as critique, people commonly misunderstand its argument. The standard originalist attack accuses nonoriginalists of imposing their own personal values on the people. This is obviously an illegitimate form of interpretation, if indeed it is interpretation at all. Given this standard charge, one might assume that the key to originalism lies in the way it prevents judges from imposing their own values on us. This cannot be its argument, however, for many other possible methods of judicial review—like coin-flipping or, even more arbitrarily, like consulting a particular law professor—could cabin judicial discretion at least as well. The key to originalism is not that it prevents judges from imposing their own values but rather that it forces them to apply the framers' values. The critical, but largely unspoken, part of its argument, is why applying the framers' values legitimates judicial review.

The theory goes something like this: Because we elect Congress and the president, their actions are ours. Law binds us, in this view, because we have bound ourselves. When the Court strikes down a properly enacted law, however, a problem emerges: the so-called countermajoritarian difficulty. Judges, who are unelected, cannot legitimately invalidate what the people have agreed to through their representatives. The task of constitutional theory is to describe the special conditions under which judicial nullification is legitimate. The originalist argues that a judge can legitimately strike down a law only when that law violates the terms of the framers' original social contract. That contract legitimately trumps our representatives' values because it reflects the privileged values of American society in 1789, which, the argument goes, match our own. In striking down a properly enacted law because it violates original intent, the judge is only imposing our own values against us. These are our highest values, moreover, because they are the ones we as a society have precommitted not to allow ourselves to change through ordinary legislation. In this view, judicial review possesses exactly the same legitimacy as ordinary contract enforcement. We may no longer want to observe a contract, but as we have agreed to be bound by its terms, a court acts legitimately in enforcing it against us. Originalism thus solves the countermajoritarian difficulty through contractarianism. The Constitution is, in this view, just a compact among individuals that specifies how they have agreed to be governed.

There are difficulties, of course, with this theory. Every link in the chain is at least a bit tenuous. The framers, for example, did not represent everyone in 1789. Women and blacks, just to mention two major groups, were excluded. Likewise, some groups today fall somewhat outside the prevailing social consensus. Most tenuous, however, is the link between 1789 and the present. Social values have changed greatly over the last two centuries and, to the extent they have changed, the original consensus no longer legitimates. Originalists tend to brush aside these difficulties by arguing that we today have consented to the original contract by choosing either not to amend it or not to move to a different country. Nonoriginalists, of course, claim that this argument will not do. To them, our failure to amend the Constitution or to leave the country proves at most acquiescence, a notion that, unlike consent, cannot satisfactorily ground judicial review.

The metaphilosophical underpinnings of this position are best, if unintentionally, revealed in Robert Bork's notorious 1971 *Indiana Law Journal* article, a good example of how not to write your way onto the Supreme Court. In that piece, Bork attacked *Griswold*, the case in which the Supreme Court had first found a right to sexual privacy. *Griswold*'s result, he said, was necessarily unprincipled:

> Every clash between a minority claiming freedom and a majority claiming power to regulate involves a choice between the gratifications of the two groups. When the Constitution has not spoken, the Court will be able to find no scale, other than its own value preferences, upon which to weigh the respective claims to pleasure. . . . Unless we can distinguish forms of gratification, the only course for a principled Court is to let the majority have its way. . . . There is no principled way to decide that one man's gratifications are more deserving of respect than another's or that one form of gratification is more worthy than another. Why is sexual gratification more worthy than moral gratification? Why is sexual gratification nobler than economic gratification? There is no way of deciding these matters other than by reference to some system of moral and ethical values that has no objective or intrinsic validity of its own and about which men can and do differ. Where the Constitution does not embody the moral and ethical choice, the judge has no basis other than his own values upon which to set aside the community judgment embodied in the statute. That, by definition, is an inadequate basis for judicial supremacy. . . . One of my colleagues refers to this conclusion, not without sarcasm, as the "Equal Gratification Clause." The phrase is apt, and I accept it, though not the sarcasm. Equality of human gratifications, where the document does not impose a hierarchy, is an essential part of constitutional doctrine because of the necessity that judges be principled.[9]

Bork's argument traces out the full political implications of the solipsistic turn. First, values have no objective or intrinsic validity. They are mere "gratifications," matters of taste, about which people can and do differ. Without any objective standard by which to judge them, all we can say is that particular individuals do or do not hold them. Bork, thus firmly rejects the God's-eye view upon which the natural-law model of interpretation depends. Second, because all we can say about values is that particular people hold them or do not, all values stand in some inherent relation of equality. Simply put, because only individuals can compare values, society itself must grant each value equal inherent respect. Thus, a judge who displaces one value by another because she thinks it better necessarily violates the foundational principle of equality of gratifications. In many ways, Bork's view represents a caricature of the metaphysical liberalism that Sandel found in Rawls's *A Theory of Justice*.[10]

The only question is why Bork allows the judge to displace values when the Constitution "itself . . . impose[s] a hierarchy"? After all, those values can possess no more intrinsic validity than others. Bork does not flesh out the affirmative side of his argument, but his discussion of legislation, I think, reveals it. Bork quite clearly states "that the principle [of gratification equality] is not applicable to legislatures. Legislation requires value choice and cannot be principled in the sense under discussion. Courts must accept any value choice the legislature makes unless it clearly runs contrary to a choice made in the framing of the Constitution."[11] What privileges the values of legislation cannot be intrinsic to the values themselves, so it must be intrinsic to the process of legislation. It is the legislative process itself that privileges values that themselves possess no substantive privilege. As Bork puts it, "in wide areas of life majorities are entitled to rule for no better reason [than] that they are majorities."[12] What counts is the number of people who hold a value, not what the value is. At bottom, then, the only authority values have comes from individuals' agreement to them. Majoritarianism legitimates because it represents the working consent of the governed. This same consent theory, moreover, underlies his limited account of judicial review: "Society *consents* to be ruled undemocratically within defined areas by certain enduring principles believed to be stated in, and placed beyond the reach of majorities by, the Constitution."[13]

Bork's outlook is strongly atomistic. It holds that we as a society cannot look into a value to judge it. Only individual people can do that, under whatever lights they have, and the Court's only job is to find and respect the majority of individuals' judgments. The Court cannot enforce a value because it is "good" but only because a majority of individuals has agreed to it. Social value is thus defined only as the aggregation of individuals' preferences.

At first glance, nonoriginalism appears to be nothing more than a short-cut method of originalist review. It too seeks the terms of our consent to be governed, but instead of tracing those terms through the social compact of 1789 down to the present, it appears to make a direct appeal to the values of individuals in contemporary society. In Justice Cardozo's time-worn *Palko* formulation, we might consult "the traditions and conscience of our peoples,"[14] only to cut out the middleman of 1789. In this view, nonoriginalism appears to be doing more directly exactly what originalism demands. Yet, if this is its aim, it too has problems. Most notably, one could ask why the Court can determine contemporary values better than the legislature. If only demographically, legislators are perhaps more representative than justices of the Supreme Court. It is at this point that nonoriginalism traditionally fails to persuade its opponents.

This description of nonoriginalism as a type of originalism but without the muss and fuss of appeals to 1789 mischaracterizes it, however. Nonoriginalism is searching for something different from contemporary majoritarian will. Whether we accept Cardozo's description of nonoriginalism as a search for "fundamental" values,[15] Alexander Bickel's description of it as a search for "principle,"[16] or Ronald Dworkin's more recent description of it as a search for "integrity,"[17] it is clear that nonoriginalism rests on assumptions quite different from contractarianism. Unlike originalism, nonoriginalism's inquiry into tradition and collective conscience aims not to determine the aggregate of individual preferences. Instead it looks to discover those values that are fundamental, not in the sense that they are encoded in hard natural law but in the sense that they define who we are as a political culture. As Cardozo again put it, they are those values that are "of the very essence of a scheme of ordered liberty."[18] This inquiry unabashedly judges values independently of individuals' agreement to them. A value is to be enforced not because a majority of individuals agrees to it but because it substantially helps define what the political community is—even when a majority of individuals within the community does not realize that or does not care. Put simply, nonoriginalism judges values according to their importance in maintaining the identity of our political community, not according to the extent of their popular acceptance. As you can guess from my description, the nonoriginalist position is strongly communitarian.

It is communitarian, however, in a very specific way. Unlike many versions of communitarianism, this type is less substantive than ontological. It employs community not as a value but as a ground for value. It commands not that politics enforce community but that any values politics does enforce enjoy community authority. Society, in other words, "grounds" values but these values do not themselves have to promote community. Thus, people like Rawls, Dworkin, and Rorty have lately grounded liberalism no deeper than in our cultural norms and practices.[19] In Rawls's words, theirs is a political not a metaphysical conception of liberalism, one that grants individuals rights not because the individual enjoys ontological primacy but because society, which does, believes some areas of life are better arranged autonomously. The community in this view enjoys priority over the individual, but the community grants the individual sovereignty in certain spheres. In other words, we respect the individual not because we believe the individual enjoys authority but because our political community, which does, commands it. In this view, the traditional contradiction between communitarianism and liberalism disappears. The community becomes the source of autonomy as a value.

This social ontology underlying nonoriginalism reflects a more recent metaphilosophical turn than does contractarianism. The earlier debate between natural law and contractarianism reflected a debate between Platonism and vulgar Cartesianism, a debate between external and internal certainty and, more particularly, a debate between truth and ultimately subjectivism. The move from truth to contract that occurred in constitutional theory represented the triumph of vulgar Cartesianism. As Heidegger noted in discussing Nietzsche, however, this triumph merely inverted things.[20] It replaced traditional metaphysics with its inverse, but it left a metaphysics nonetheless. Although this triumph privileged the opposite side of all the traditional dualisms, its effect was to reentrench even more deeply the traditional metaphysical picture. Our final vocabulary stood largely unchanged; only its valences were reversed.

The current debate between contract and community, however, reflects a different metaphilosophical debate. It is not a debate between two sides of the same old problem but rather a debate between the traditional view and a new one. The social ontology upon which nonoriginalism rests is largely a twentieth-century phenomenon. It reflects the decisive turn people like the later Heidegger, the later Wittgenstein, Donald Davidson, and Richard Rorty have made away from metaphysics and towards culture. Their ontology is defundamentalized, one that grounds all—if "ground" is not too strong a word—in social norms and practice. It rejects the old debate between natural law and originalism, between truth and contract, as merely flipping from one bad choice to another. Better to reject the problem that presents these choices than to waste time arguing between them. Our task should be to move beyond contract to community just as we moved before from truth to contract.

The interesting question is why this move has proven so difficult. My best hunch is that the ethical stakes are just too high. Both sides of the traditional metaphysical picture promise moral comforts. The Platonic choice of faith in truth outside us offers hope in a world more perfect than ourselves. We can put to rest worry about our past and present imperfections on the theory that the truth will eventually raise us. The Cartesian choice can offer us the same or different comforts. If we go idealistic and transcendental, like Kant, we can find a truth inside ourselves to guide us to a better world. This form of Cartesianism, after all, is just an inward form of Platonism. If we go in the opposite direction, on the other hand, we can have the comforts of Nietzsche and Hobbes. Following Nietzsche, we can look forward to recreating ourselves and to achieving a kind of power and freedom or, following Hobbes, we can at least escape responsibility for our condition. Without a privileged ideal to follow we may have no hope of finding something more perfect than ourselves, but then we can have no guilt for failing to attain perfection either. Hobbes presents a colder comfort, but a comfort nonetheless.

Neopragmatism offers something else entirely. Like contractualist theories, it sees nothing transcendent in which we can seek refuge from ourselves and our history. Unlike contractualist theories, however, it rejects the notion that nothing remains greater than the self. The choice is not between the absolute, on the one hand, and the selfish individual, on the other. Together we ourselves can create standards to judge ourselves by and so raise ourselves. Social ontology thus offers a kind of hope although one less bright than the traditional metaphysical kind. Social ontology, however, also offers responsibility. If we can create our own better world, if we have power to remake ourselves, only we can be guilty of our own condition. We can blame nothing else for our failure to rework our history for only we are responsible for what we are. In other words, neopragmatism, the metaphilosophical outlook upon which nonoriginalism rests, offers us a mixed blessing: hope with responsibility.

We should not be surprised, then, that constitutional theory now stands stalemated. If it took us hundreds of years to move from truth to contract and merely invert the traditional metaphysical picture, perhaps we should expect some difficulty in moving from contract to community and rejecting metaphysics entirely, particularly since the neopragmatic move entails the possibility of blame and failure. As a political culture, our current condition is odd. We seem both unhappy to remain in contract and fearful of moving to community. We are deadlocked right now. So, I offer no present comfort to constitutional theorists. As individuals, we must choose a constitutional theory and so enter the debate, but we must do so aware that we cannot win it. No matter which perspective we choose—originalism or nonoriginalism—our every move will be challenged from another deeply privileged vantage in our political culture. Not until we overcome our metaphilosophical indecision will we be able to begin to end the debate in constitutional theory.

## Notes

I thank Mary Anne Case, Patrick Crawford, Walter Benn Michaels, George Rutherglen, and William Weaver for commenting on earlier drafts of this chapter. Their criticisms helped me avoid many errors. Whatever errors remain are, of course, my own responsibility.

1. 198 U.S. 45 (1905).

2. 381 U.S. 479 (1965).

3. 3 U.S. (3 Dall.) 386, 388 (1789) (opinion of Justice Chase).

4. 10 U.S. (6 Cranch) 87, 139 (1810).

5. Ibid., 143 (Johnson, J., concurring).

6. Slaughter-House Cases, 16 Wall. 36, 110 (1873) (Field, J., dissenting).

7. 16 Wall. 130, 141—42 (1873) (Bradley, Jr., concurring).

8. Thomas Hobbes, *Leviathan*, ed. C. B. MacPherson (London: Penguin, 1968), 188.

9. Robert H. Bork, "Neutral Principles and Some First Amendment Problems," *Indiana Law Journal* 47 (Fall 1971): 9—10.

10. Michael Sandel, *Liberalism and the Limits of Justice* (Cambridge: Cambridge University Press, 1982).

11. Bork, "Neutral Principles," 10—11.

12. Ibid., 2.

13. Ibid., 3 (emphasis added).

14. *Palko v. Connecticut*, 302 U.S. 319, 325 (1937) (quoting *Synder v. Massachusetts*, 291 U.S. 97, 105 [1934])

15. Ibid., (quoting *Synder v. Massachusetts*, 291 U.S. 97, 105 [1934]).

16. Alexander Bickel, *The Least Dangerous Branch*, 2nd ed. (New Haven: Yale University Press, 1986).

17. Ronald Dworkin, *Law's Empire* (Cambridge, Mass.: Harvard University Press, 1986).

18. *Palko v. Connecticut*, 302 U.S. 319, 325 (1937).

19. John Rawls, "The Priority of Right and Ideas of the Good"; Rawls, "The Idea of an Overlapping Consensus"; Rawls, "Justice as Fairness: Political not Metaphysical"; Ronald Dworkin, "Liberal Community"; Richard Rorty, "The Priority of Democracy to Philosophy," cited in bibliography.

20. Martin Heidegger, *Nietzsche: Nihilism*, trans. Frank A. Cupuzzi (Cambridge, Mass.: Harper and Row, 1982): 4.164—165.

# 17

## Practice, Purpose, and Interpretive Controversy

*Steven Knapp*

In a series of writings since 1982, Walter Benn Michaels and I have laid out what we have been willing to call a "pragmatist" account of interpretive controversy. At the center of this account is the view that disagreement about the meaning of any text—when it really is disagreement about the text's meaning and not about something else—can never be anything other than disagreement about what the text's author or authors intended it to mean. And since there is no limit to what someone can intend something to mean—or, to put this another way, since anyone can use anything to mean anything—there is no point in trying to devise a general interpretive procedure, an interpretive *method*, that will help resolve interpretive controversies. The object of every interpretive controversy, when it really is an interpretive controversy, is always and only a particular historical fact, and there is no general way to determine what any particular historical fact might be. No general belief, or if one prefers, no *theory* about the nature of interpretation offers any help in deciding the meaning of any particular text.[1] Now this doesn't mean, absurdly, that no general beliefs play any role in interpretation. The belief that human authors in general cannot refer to persons born after the authors' deaths rules out, for interpreters who believe this, the possibility that when Thomas Aquinas mentioned "Aristotle" he referred to the second husband of a former First Lady of the United States. But even that interpretive consequence will only follow for interpreters who already happen to share the general belief in question, which is in any case a belief about certain limits on human nature and not about the nature of interpretation. Thus the anthropological belief that a human author can't refer to someone born after the author's death entails, once again, that Aquinas can't have referred to Aristotle Onassis. But neither an acceptance nor a rejection of the belief or the entailment in any way affects the fact that the object of interpretation is whatever Aquinas intended.

What makes this account of interpretation resonate with certain themes of American pragmatism is its assertion that, in any interpretive controversy, there is no higher court of appeal than the beliefs of the conflicting interpreters, and consequently no better way—indeed, no *other* way—to resolve the controversy than for the interpreters' beliefs to converge. In at least one important respect, however, it may seem rather strange to call the position I have been describing a pragmatist one. For it may seem to ignore the actual *practice* of contemporary interpretive controversies as these are played out in the pages of legal as well as literary journals. After all, it may seem that nothing is more obvious about such controversies than the frequency with which disputes about the meanings of particular texts turn into metainterpretive disputes among competing accounts of the value or purpose of literary or legal interpretation as such. In the apparent practice of contemporary interpretive controversy, a debate about the meaning of some portion of the Constitution, for example, can turn at any moment into a debate about the ethical or political purposes served by locating the Constitution's meaning in the history of previous decisions; or in the moral traditions of the Republic; or in the political praxis of current interpreters; or in the historical intentions of the Constitution's framers and/or ratifiers.[2] And yet the account I have been describing involves the surprising claim that such disagreements are irrelevant to genuine controversy about the meaning of any text, since there is only *one* kind of meaning that a genuine interpretive controversy can really be about, and that is the meaning actually intended by the text's author or authors. And, the account insists, the plurality of purposes for which we engage in interpretive controversy in no way affects the singularity of what every such controversy must be about.

Once again, I want to acknowledge how odd that assertion is likely to sound when uttered by a self-proclaimed pragmatist. For it may seem an unavoidable axiom for any pragmatist that, in any inquiry, our very concept of what we are trying to discover depends on the actual human purposes motivating, and embodied in, the socially constituted practice of the inquiry in question. After all, such purposes form a crucial aspect of our *practical* relation to what we are investigating, and a central point of pragmatism, at least on one understanding of it, is captured by the Peircian maxim that our concept of any object consists in what we take to be those effects of the object that, as Peirce puts it, "might conceivably have practical bearings."[3] Or, as Peirce later reformulated the maxim, "The entire intellectual purport of any symbol consists in the total of all general modes of rational conduct which, conditionally upon all the possible different circumstances and desires, would ensue upon the acceptance of the symbol."[4] Whatever one thinks of the details of Peirce's maxim, there would seem to be something suspiciously antipragmatist about the very notion of separating our concept of some object of inquiry from our sense of the purposes for which the inquiry is undertaken, since, on a pragmatist account, the modes of conduct that would ensue from our *adopting* a concept are inseparable from what we have in mind when we *conceive* the concept in the first place. Applied specifically to textual interpretation, this principle would seem to challenge the pragmatist credentials of any account that tried to separate our concept of what interpreters of texts are after—our concept, that is, of textual meaning—from what we take to be the *point* of interpreting texts. Shouldn't a pragmatist be the first to argue that the concept of textual meaning itself must vary with our interpretive purposes? And if theoretical debates over the purpose of interpretation can legitimately affect our concept of textual meaning, then doesn't it follow *a fortiori* that such debates can affect our interpretations of particular texts?

Of course, I think the answer to the first of these questions is "no," and consequently that the second question doesn't arise. To get at what's wrong with this line of thinking about interpretation, I will consider what happens if one tries to take seriously the notion that one can still make sense of interpretive controversy while supposing that the concept of textual meaning varies with the purposes of our interpretive practices. The most convenient way to address this issue is to consider the views of a legal philosopher who, though not a pragmatist himself, has tried to do exactly that. The philosopher I have in mind is Ronald Dworkin, and the views I will address are the ones he has presented in his book *Law's Empire*, and more recently in a lecture (unpublished as far as I know) titled "Interpreting Interpretation."[5] I should also say at the outset that my sense of Dworkin's views is indebted to discussion and correspondence with him following his delivery of the lecture at Berkeley in April, 1990.

Dworkin's account of interpretation, as I understand it, is essentially this. Interpretation involves the use of particular interpretive concepts; one such concept, for instance, is that of the meaning of a poem. But each interpretive concept is tied to a social practice, tradition, or enterprise. What all such practices have in common is that, despite their differences in other respects, each of them is understood *teleologically* by those engaged in it—that is, each practice is thought to have a point, a purpose, a telos. And the particular interpretive concepts tied to these practices are or ought to be, as Dworkin put it in his lecture, "sensitive" to the point of the practice in question. Thus, for instance, if one understands the point of common law to be to provide not simply formal guidance but "coherence of principle," one's concept of what a precedent is and therefore of what it can mean will reflect this broader understanding of the point of interpreting precedents in the first place.

Because it involves what he frankly terms the *imposition* of the interpreter's purposes on the object of interpretation, Dworkin, in *Law's Empire*, calls his theory of interpretation "*constructive*," opposing it to what he calls the "conversational" view, according to which interpretation "aims to decipher the authors' purposes or intentions in writing a novel or maintaining a particular social tradition, just as we aim in conversation to grasp a friend's intentions in speaking as he does." On Dworkin's account, "the purposes in play are not (fundamentally) those of some author but of the interpreter. Roughly, constructive interpretation is a matter of imposing purpose on an object or practice in order to make of it the best possible example of the form or genre to which it is taken to belong" (*LE*, 51-52).

As the mention of form and genre suggests, Dworkin's account of interpretation in *Law's Empire* begins with cases of what he calls "creative interpretation," such as the interpretation of works of art or social practices, since these bring out the role of interpretive purpose that he will claim is common to all interpretive practices. It soon turns out that even conversational interpretation is really constructive in the same sense; so is the interpretation of scientific data:

> Understanding another person's conversation requires using devices and presumptions, like the so-called principle of charity, that have the effect in normal circumstances of making of what he says the best performance of communication it can be. And the interpretation of data in science makes heavy use of standards of theory construction like simplicity and elegance and verifiability that reflect contestable and changing assumptions about paradigms of explanation, that is, about what features make one form of explanation superior to another. The constructive account of creative interpretation, therefore, could perhaps provide a more general account of interpretation in all its forms. We would then say that all interpretation strives to make an object the best it can be, as an instance of some assumed enterprise, and that interpretation takes

different forms in different contexts only because different enterprises engage different standards of value or success (*LE*, 53).

This passage from *Law's Empire* contains one explicit claim and one implication that I want to explore. The explicit claim is that "all interpretation strives to make an object the best it can be, as an instance of some assumed enterprise." The implication is that, since every object of interpretation in any practice always instantiates some broader enterprise—so that a given poem is interpreted as instantiating the broader enterprise of literature, and a given statute is interpreted as instantiating the broader enterprise of law—it follows that interpreters who disagree even about the general point of the enterprise in question are also disagreeing in some interesting sense about the meaning of particular objects. In other words, theoretical disagreements matter, and matter at the level of controversy over particular facts.

Let me begin, then, with the claim that interpretation strives to make an object "the best it can be." Consider a practice that is admittedly somewhat remote from what Dworkin mainly has in mind: the practice of interpreting utterances by people one meets on the street. Suppose someone approaches me and says, "Give me your money now, or I'll kill you." I interpret this utterance. According to Dworkin's account, my role in this situation is to give the utterance the meaning that will make it the best possible instance of a broader enterprise, presumably in this case the enterprise of accosting and addressing pedestrians. But what meaning would make the utterance in question the best it could be as an instance of street communication? Perhaps, preferring entertainment to assault, I should conclude that the speaker is promising to tell me a hilarious joke—in other words, he's saying, "This one will really *kill* you!"[6]

But no doubt that's the wrong way to understand what it means, on Dworkin's account, to make an utterance "the best it can be." In the passage I quoted a moment ago, Dworkin alluded to W.V.O. Quine's notion that our attempt to understand a speaker's utterance is guided by a certain "principle of charity." On this principle, I can only assign to a speaker an appropriate set of meanings, intentions, and motives if, as Dworkin has more recently put it (thinking especially of Davidson's account of the principle), "I try to eliminate inexplicable error" on the part of the speaker I am trying to interpret.[7] Thus, for instance, if someone uses words in a way that seems to make no sense, I will generally try to find other meanings for those words, or other causes of the speaker's action. Suppose the speaker says, "Give me your money now, or I'll *bill* you." Then I will indeed try to remove what seems to be an inexplicable error. I may conclude that when the speaker said "bill" he actually meant "kill." Or I may conclude that he is under a certain delusion, believing that he is a dentist and I am his patient: "Give me your money now—or I'll bill you." Notice that either of these choices would succeed in eliminating inexplicable error—precisely by *explaining* what the error was. But neither of them involves making the utterance the best it can be—at least on any principle other than relative explicability. In any case, in this situation, especially given my stake in the outcome, I don't want to know how good the utterance *might* be but exactly how good or bad it actually is.

My first example has been of an interpretive practice whose point is best served by making the object of interpretation not the best it can be but just as good or as bad as it is. But now consider another alternative to Dworkin's model. Why can't there be an interpretive practice whose point is best served by making its objects precisely the *worst* they can be? Why can't there be, for instance, an interpretive practice like what, in current literary criticism, is called "oppositional criticism," a practice whose point requires an interpreter to make the meaning of a particular literary work just as bad as possible? Suppose the point of an interpretive practice is to *undermine* or *overturn* a social structure that a given literary work (or a given legal statute) is seen to support. In that case, presumably, the point of the interpretive practice will best be served by concepts and procedures that make the object in question the worst instance of the broader enterprise that the interpreter's ingenuity can manage to make it. I suggest that only a forgivable remoteness from recent trends in literary criticism could have led Dworkin, in his account of "creative interpretation," to overlook this possibility.

So far I've been elaborating a single objection: Dworkin gives us no reason to think that a teleological account of interpretive practices—an account that makes interpretive concepts sensitive to our interpretive purposes—entails that interpreters should make their objects "the best they can be" as instances of some assumed enterprise. My second objection will take into account the possibility that Dworkin might grant what I've just said: that there might very well be interpretive practices, the point of which required us to make the *object* of interpretation no better than, or even worse than, it would otherwise be.

The second and more interesting question raised by Dworkin's account is whether interpreters who have different views of the general *point* of a practice can still have enough *in common* for their interpretive disagreements to be of any interest. According to Dworkin, as I understand him, people who disagree even about the fundamental point of a practice are still disagreeing with each other in an interesting way about the meaning of particular objects. Opposed to this is what he calls the crude view—my view, actually—that to think the point of interpretation is to make an object "the best it can be" is to give up the possibility of disagreeing in any interesting way with those who see the point differently—for instance, those who think the point of interpretation is to understand the acts of historical agents, no matter how good or bad those acts may have been.

Confining my attention for the moment to literary interpretation, I'll state my objection abstractly and then give an example. In the abstract, it seems to me obvious that people with fundamentally different conceptions of the very point of literary interpretation can perhaps disagree interestingly about that general issue, but they cannot disagree in any interesting way about the meaning of a particular text. They can't disagree in any interesting way because nothing that counts as an *argument* about the text for one of them counts as an argument for the other, and nothing that counts as *evidence* for one of them counts as evidence for the other. My example is *Paradise Lost*—I trust by now a familiar enough one in legal as well as literary theory, thanks to the work of a certain eminent contributor to both fields.

*Paradise Lost* is currently playing a prominent role in the debate about the canon of English literature. One symptom of this controversy is the fact that, only last year, my own department abandoned its long-standing requirement that all its doctoral candidates must have read substantially in Milton's works, including, at a minimum, *Paradise Lost*. Although there have been various debates about *Paradise Lost* in this century, the current one focuses mainly on the question of whether and to what extent the poem expresses a vision of patriarchal authoritarianism that should no longer be inflicted, at least without explicit warning, on innocent students.

Those readers who, unlike Berkeley doctoral candidates in English, *have* been required to read Milton, will remember that in one of the epic's stranger episodes, Satan is caught in Paradise disguised as a toad and squatting by the ear of Eve, in whose mind he is busily instilling an evil dream. At the touch of an angel's spear, he returns, explosively, to his original shape. Various challenges are exchanged between Satan and his captors; at one point, facing Gabriel and a phalanx of heavily armed angels, he makes a speech that concludes with the following proud and contemptuous remarks:

                    I alone first undertook
        To wing the desolate Abyss, and spy
        This new created World, whereof in Hell
        Fame is not silent, here in hope to find
        Better abode, and my afflicted Powers
        To settle here on Earth, or in mid Air;
        Though for possession put to try once more
        What thou and thy gay Legions dare against;
        Whose easier business were to serve their Lord
        High up in Heav'n, with songs to hymn his Throne,
        And practis'd distances to cringe, not fight.[8]

More than one student, reading these lines, and unschooled in the lexical history of the English language, has wondered whether Milton meant by the adjective "gay" in "gay Legions" what a current writer might mean by it. If such a student turns to the footnotes in an annotated edition, he or she will discover—provided, of course, that she accepts the authority of the edition in question—that the word "gay" did not, in Milton's period, and therefore probably but not certainly in Milton's own usage, mean homosexual, but simply bright, or at most, fancily dressed, like courtiers.[9] I say probably but not certainly because there is no reason in principle why Milton might not have been the first to use the word in its now current sense; in any case, the received understanding of what the word meant then is itself based only on fallible interpretations of how the word was used by particular authors.

But now suppose that an interpreter wants to follow Dworkin's proposal that the point of literary interpretation is to make the work the "best it can be" as an instance of the broader literary enterprise. Why not give the word "gay" its *present* meaning, in place of or in addition to its former meanings—in which case Satan becomes the inventor not just of gunpowder (which he invents in Book 6) but of homophobia? Does anyone want to deny that *Paradise Lost* would be *better* in some important sense if it condemned homophobia, in addition to, or even in place of, the more traditionally recognized evils Milton undoubtedly intended to criticize? Presumably very few people would want to deny this, now that, for instance, the Roman Catholic hierarchy officially counts homophobia as a sin. More generally, if one is impressed by the accusation that *Paradise Lost* is so reprehensibly and even dangerously authoritarian that it should be struck from the list of literary classics, why not change the meanings of its words wherever possible to bring them into line with whatever meaning will make the poem "the best it can be"?

In fact, I can see no reason why there might not be a practice of literary commentary that took exactly this form. I see no reason in principle why classes on *Paradise Lost* might not consist of collective efforts to change the meanings of as many of the poem's words as might be necessary to make it less offensive than an increasing number of its readers seem to find it. What I can't see, however, is how practitioners of this enterprise could enter into significant or interesting disagreements about the text's meaning with those for whom interpreting the poem still meant figuring out what Milton meant by it.[10] What argument, advanced by an interpreter committed to what Dworkin would call "historicism" (*LE*, 359-363), could possibly interest an interpreter committed to Dworkin's interpretive *optimism*?[11] Suppose the historicist appeals to the Oxford English Dictionary for evidence that a word "didn't mean that then." Of course, says the optimist; that's why we have to ignore what it meant then and opt instead for what we take to be its best meaning *now*.

I want to insist at this point that my aim is not to caricature Dworkin's theory. I am aware that, on his view, there are certain constraints that prevent a practitioner of any kind of interpretation from making a text mean whatever he or she would *prefer* that it mean; such constraints, internal to each interpretive practice, are what make it possible, he thinks, for two people to disagree fundamentally about the point of a practice and still engage in interesting disagreements about particular objects. In a passage I have already quoted, for instance, Dworkin mentions two constraints that are especially relevant to literary interpretation; he writes that "constructive interpretation is a matter of imposing purpose on an object in order to make it the best possible example of the *form* or *genre* to which it belongs" (*LE*, 52; emphasis added). Later in the same paragraph he adds a third constraint when he writes that "the *history* or shape of a practice or object constrains the available interpretations of it" (again, my emphasis; I take it that the mention of shape here merely underscores the earlier mention of genre and form). "History" here would seem to mean the record of previous interpretations because Dworkin later endorses Gadamer's view that interpreters "think within a tradition of interpretation from which they cannot wholly escape" (*LE*, 62). And in an earlier essay he compares interpreting a text to participating in a kind of historically continuous act of collective composition, like the writing of a chain novel.[12]

The trouble with this account—a trouble pointed out some time ago by Stanley Fish—is that it simply isn't true that considerations of form or genre impose any constraint whatsoever on what an interpreter can do

in order to make a work like *Paradise Lost* "the best it can be."[13]  Nor
does the record of previous interpretations.   For the genre and
interpretive history of any text are just as much subject to interpretation
as the meaning of the text's words.   Interpreters constantly debate
whether *Paradise Lost* is finally a tragedy, in which case we would have
been better off had Adam and Eve not eaten the fruit and remained in
Paradise, or a comedy, in which case the Fall is fortunate, and what God
wanted was precisely for Adam and Eve to rebel against the arbitrary
regime he pretended to impose.   And the history of interpretations of
*Paradise Lost* is nothing other than a history of controversies over,
among other things, the question of whether the poem is genuinely
authoritarian or secretly subversive.   Why not just pick the genre, or the
precedent in the poem's interpretive history, that best fits one's sense of
what it would take to make the poem "the best it can be" as an instance
of the broader literary enterprise?   Suppose, for instance, we stop
thinking of *Paradise Lost* as an epic *or* a tragedy, or as belonging to any
other genre that Milton might have known or cared about; suppose we
think of it instead as a kind of medieval, or perhaps Joycean,
dream-vision.   We can decide that the entire action of *Paradise Lost* is
only a feverish dream in the mind of Eve, whose awakening will signal
the return of matriarchy after the long nightmare of patriarchal
usurpation.   So much for the charge that *Paradise Lost* is complicit in
patriarchy.   By following similar procedures across the canon, what is
now known as the "problem of the canon" could be solved with extreme
economy—for instance, without even printing any new anthologies.

Perhaps, however, there are other considerations to which Dworkin
might appeal in order to show how an historicist and an optimist could
have enough in common to give one of them a reason to care about what
counts as evidence for the other.   At one point he suggests that there are
reasons, internal to optimism itself, that can motivate an optimist to pay
attention to evidence about an author's intention.   Thus he observes that
one prominent theory of art has located aesthetic value in the degree to
which a work "embodies individual creative genius" (*LE*, 60).   If we take
exhibiting an author's genius to be one of the points of the literary
enterprise, we can't make a poem better by *subtracting* something from
what the author's creative genius has produced.

But how would that principle work in the case I have imagined?
How would the value of Milton's creative genius be in any way impaired
by our expanding the range of evils his poem is taken to criticize?   We
could simply give Milton credit for putting into the poem what he put

into it, and then go about our business of adding things that would make it even better.

I'll mention one last constraint that Dworkin might invoke: aesthetic coherence. He might argue that to revise the poem in the free-wheeling way I have suggested would somehow damage its coherence, and being coherent is part of what it means for a poem to be the best it can be as an instance of the literary enterprise. But that won't work either: There is nothing incoherent about supposing that Satan's motivational set includes homophobia among its other evil dispositions. Indeed, it's worth noting in this connection that Satan, not God, is the inventor of heterosexual intercourse; before Satan's affair with his daughter Sin, *good* angelic sex, described in some detail by the archangel Raphael in Book 8, is emphatically *not* heterosexual. In general I see no reason to suppose that there is any limit at all to the number or the kind of meanings that one could give the words of *Paradise Lost* without producing a work that would be any less coherent than the work produced by Milton.

It seems to me, then, that Dworkin's account fails to constrain the optimist in a way that gives her any reason to argue with the historicist's findings instead of just ignoring them or taking them in stride. And the same failure of constraint would occur in the case of an interpreter who wanted to make a text mean the *worst* thing it could mean—thus engaging in a "pessimistic" mode of interpretation. This failure suggests the following general account of the relation between interpretive controversy and controversy over interpretive purposes. Of course, interpreters can disagree in interesting ways about the purpose of interpreting; they can disagree, for instance, about what to do with the *results* of interpretation once those are arrived at. Insofar as a disagreement remains at the level of what one does with the *result* of an interpretive inquiry—whether one enjoys it or deplores it or obeys it or ignores it—such disagreement may be interesting and important but is irrelevant to the question of what the interpretive inquiry itself is after.[14] But if a disagreement about the purpose of interpretation really did become a disagreement about what counted as an interpretation—if it really did reach all the way down to affect the concept of textual meaning and therefore the actual practice of assigning meanings to a particular text—then the disagreeing parties would be involved in activities so fundamentally different that what counted as a consideration for one of them would have no force at all for the other. In that case, only an equivocation on the term "interpretation" could make it seem that they were still engaged in a single controversy.

Let me recall, at this point, my reason for bringing up Dworkin's account in the first place. I wanted to explain why I doubted that we could make sense of interpretive controversy while supposing that the very concept of textual meaning varied with the purposes of our interpretive practices. But my criticisms of Dworkin's account, even if accepted, have not yet disposed of the apparent anomaly I began with: the apparent anomaly, that is, of a pragmatist's supposing that our concept of some object of inquiry can be independent of the purposes for which the inquiry is undertaken. For how, especially on pragmatist assumptions, could we ever arrive at such a concept? Am I asking us to imagine that a practice of inquiry could arise without any practical motivation? And am I then forced to posit some kind of impractical, disinterested desire for interpretive truth? In the remainder of these remarks, I wish, first, to show why an insistence on a single concept of textual meaning is compatible with an acknowledgement of the plurality of interpretive purposes, and compatible also with a denial that we are ever interested in the truth for its own sake (though I will also ask whether a pragmatist needs to deny that possibility). Second, and in conclusion, I will comment very briefly on the relevance of my present argument to the present state of literary and legal controversy.

The easiest way to show why a focus on intended meaning is compatible with acknowledging that we interpret for various reasons is to show that the practice of discovering intentions itself serves a variety of purposes. One reason to discover a speaker's intentions—the one most obviously relevant to the street encounter I imagined earlier—is that doing so provides one kind of basis for *predicting* the speaker's future behavior. Another reason is to acquire information to which we think the speaker has access. Indeed, it is only by treating a speaker as the sort of rational agent to whom we can accurately ascribe certain intentional states that can we be *informed* by what the speaker says. Suppose, for instance, someone says that a certain town in Greece was "visited by Aristotle." We can't be informed by this statement (at least not in the relevant way) unless we suppose, defeasibly, that the speaker has certain accurate beliefs about someone named Aristotle and intends the name "Aristotle" to refer to a particular person whom we believe we can identify. Until we resolve the second of these questions, we won't have any way to decide whether the speaker is telling us about the ancient philosopher or the modern tycoon.

Consider another reason for discovering a speaker's intended meaning (a reason that may already have occurred to those readers with a bent toward the law): We may want to determine whether an utterance was malicious and is thus deserving of punishment. (I specify malice because I am aware that it is possible in tort law for a party to be held accountable in some circumstances for the effects of a set of noises or marks for which she is responsible, regardless of what she might have intended those noises or marks to mean.[15]) I think it is fair to say that no interpreter of an utterance could count as being motivated by one of the purposes I've just described unless that interpreter was interested in, among other things, discovering the speaker's actual intended meaning. To suppose otherwise would be to endorse an extremely skeptical or paradoxical view: that the value of a prediction about someone's behavior has no relation to the accuracy of the data on which the prediction is based; or that there is no connection between what we can learn from a speaker's utterance and what the speaker intended to communicate; or that the speaker's actual intention is irrelevant to the question of whether her speech is malicious.

Each of the three purposes I've mentioned goes beyond an interest in discovering the speaker's intention; none of them amounts to an interest in intention for its own sake. Nevertheless, despite their diversity in other respects they converge on a single object of inquiry, the speaker's intended meaning. In other words, the notion of "the truth of the matter" that is involved in interpreting for the sake of prediction is the same as the notion of the truth of the matter that is involved in interpreting for the sake of being informed by what a speaker says or for deciding whether the utterance was malicious.

Now the convergence of these three purposes on a single object of interpretation, the speaker's or author's intended meaning, does not by itself show that the intended meaning is the only plausible object of interpretation. I won't go into the particular arguments for that claim that Walter Benn Michaels and I have presented elsewhere; in general, we argue that there is no plausible way to make sense of the notion that interpreters are disagreeing about the meaning of a particular text except to suppose that they are disagreeing about some particular intended meaning.[16] Most recently, we have tried to show why our position does not involve the sort of mentalistic confusion that plays so prominent a role, for instance, in popular debates about Constitutional "originalism"—I mean the confusion of supposing that the meaning intended by an author can be said to fix the extension of a general term she uses only if she already has in mind all the objects to which the term applies.[17] But my aim here, once again, has not been to repeat our previous arguments but only to show that an interest in discovering an author's intended meaning can be motivated by a variety of instrumental purposes. Hence the claim that a text means what its author intended does not require us to suppose that our practices of interpretation could arise, or survive, without any instrumental motivation. There may never be a case in which someone is interested in finding out what a text means, and therefore what its author intended, without having some instrumental reason for doing so.

On the other hand, I think it's worth asking whether pragmatism really does entail a denial that someone could be interested in discovering something "for its own sake." Even if we suppose, as I'm not sure we have to, that every practice of inquiry must have been motivated initially by some instrumental purpose, there is no obvious reason to deny that a practice that emerges for the sake of one kind of purpose might continue in the absence of that purpose. On the contrary, I don't see why a practice of inquiry can't take on a motivational force of its own. Thus if one of our purposes is to discover certain historical facts, it's no essential part of pragmatism to argue that *that* purpose has to be motivated by some *additional* purpose. In short, I don't see why pragmatism has to deny the possibility that *curiosity* exists and exists as a kind of practice in its own right. There is no reason to suppose that a practice has to be, as we say, "practical."[18]

A moment ago I raised the question of whether I was forced to imagine that there is "some kind of impractical, disinterested desire for interpretive truth." The answer turns out to be that nothing in the claim that a text means what its author intended it to mean forces one to say that there is, but nothing in pragmatism, rightly understood, requires one to say that there isn't. Whether or not we have a desire for truth that can exist apart from our various *additional* purposes in discovering it, our concept of what the truth involves in any given inquiry remains distinct from our sense of those various purposes.

But what, after all, is the practical bearing of this outcome? How should we apply it to the actual contemporary practice of legal or literary controversies, which are marked, as I have admitted, by a continual confusion of interpretive and metainterpretive concerns? Nothing in my account suggests that eliminating such confusion is possible, or even desirable, or that it should be equally possible or desirable in every institutional setting. In the case of literary interpretation, I have to say that the confusion does seem a little gratuitous. Because the outcome of interpretive controversy doesn't matter, and because it doesn't even matter whether an interpretive controversy is ever resolved, it's hard to see what moral or political or even professional interest is served by supposing or pretending that the question of what, if anything, a certain literary text is good for is the same as the question of what, if anything, the text means. Once two parties to a literary debate come to recognize that one of them is asking the first sort of question while the other is asking the second, it's hard to see why either of them would continue to find the controversy worth pursuing.

I am prepared to believe, however, that the case of legal controversy is different, if only for the obvious reason that certain decisions have to be rendered, no matter how deeply the contending parties disagree about the value and even the very *identity* of the object over which they are contending. For that reason, it may very well make sense for two lawyers to act *as if* they are debating, for instance, the meaning of the Constitution, even when they have radically different concepts of the very identity of the object over which they are arguing—one of them locating it in the meaning of the historical document, another in the meaning of some object or collection of objects that are metonymically linked to the historical document, such as a series of previous decisions or the nation's moral character. It is no part of my argument to claim that the Constitution lawyers and judges interpret *should* be identified as the historical document that bears that name, or that the meaning of any text is *ever* the actual object of legal controversy. Similarly, it is no part of my argument to deny that lawyers can have reason to stipulate that they are discussing the meaning of a particular text when what they are actually discussing is, for instance, the meaning of America.[19] Given our institutions, there may simply be no other way, in some cases, of pursuing what is really a disagreement about the *identity* of a text, or its *value*, or the grounds of its *authority*, than by pretending that the disagreement is about what the text means. In some cases, for all I know, this may amount to what Joseph Vining calls, in a related discussion, "a necessary and even desirable form of self-delusion."[20] I have no interest in correcting the practice of lawyers in this regard but only in insisting that there is no reason for a pragmatist account of interpretation to treat even an institutionally necessary fiction as anything more than that—to treat it, in other words, as competing in any epistemologically interesting way with what one takes to be the truth. For the pragmatist recognition that our only access to truth, in interpretation or anywhere else, is through a socially constituted practice of inquiry does not affect the distinction between truth and fiction, even when fiction suits our purposes better than truth.

## Afterword

Professor Dworkin's response, in a section of his chapter at the end of this volume, shows some annoyance at my having, as he sees it, "burlesqued" his account of interpretation. In fact, however, he has misunderstood my objections.

The main source of Dworkin's misunderstanding seems to be his assumption that an argument against *his* reasons must be an argument against *reason*. Thus he supposes that, because I deny that his optimistic theory can make sense of interpretation, I must think interpretation is nonsense. Because I deny that his theory allows for the sort of reasoned interpretive debate he thinks it does, I must be arguing that "there are no intrinsically good reasons for holding an interpretive position." But Dworkin's move from his reasons to reason as such is, as he likes to say, "too crude." Of course I think there are good interpretive reasons—even, if one likes, "intrinsically" good ones. But in my view, an interpretive reason's goodness is a function of our interest in figuring out what someone intends to say, and not of some other purpose.

Certainly I don't hold that the only good reasons are the ones that "produce consensus." For why suppose that the interpretation on which interpreters come to agree must be the *right* one? In my view, the right interpretation is just the one that correctly identifies the author's actual intended meaning: It by no means follows that interpreters inevitably arrive at the right interpretation, or even that they *ever* do. My only remark about consensus was the quite trivial observation that there is no other way "to resolve interpretive controversy than for the interpreters' beliefs to converge." But it doesn't follow that the way to get a correct interpretation is to resolve an interpretive controversy. Dworkin is assimilating my views to the wrong kind of pragmatism, the kind that confuses our inability to stand outside our beliefs with the notion that whatever we agree in believing is true.

The question, as I see it, is not whether *anything* constrains interpretation but whether anything *else* constrains it besides what we take to be the best evidence of what someone intends. One candidate for such a constraint, to which Dworkin remains unaccountably loyal, is genre. One would only deny the constraining power of genre, according to Dworkin, if one supposed, bizarrely, that "genuine interpretive constraints" had to work "in something approaching a physical way, like sentences fighting back to stop even the most determined interpreter for putting them in the wrong genre." This is an amusing response to Stanley Fish's metaphor, but it misses the point of the objection. The point is simply that what genre a work belongs to is no less subject to interpretation, and therefore to interpretive disagreement, than is any other feature of the work in question. Only *after* we decide what genre a work belongs to can genre play any role in constraining interpretation. But deciding what genre a work belongs to involves deciding what genre its author intended to adopt.[21] Once we decide *that*, then of course our notion of the work's genre enters into the "structured and complex mix of . . . beliefs and convictions, some of which . . . act as checks to others." My aim was not to deny the role of genre but to ask whether it could play its obviously important role *if* one accepted Dworkin's theory of interpretation. For on Dworkin's theory, we aren't supposed to care what genre an author intended to adopt. So either the genre enforces itself (in which case Dworkin *does* conceive it as something like a natural force) or we should simply pick the genre that makes the work "the best it can be" for the sake of our broader interpretive purposes (in which case the work's genre can hardly be said to constrain our interpretive choices).

Since I don't reject interpretive constraints but only the notion that they can operate apart from intention, I am puzzled by the use to which Dworkin puts my example from *Paradise Lost*. Dworkin writes that an interpreter who thinks the value of poetry lies "in the expressive imagination or genius of the poet" will be constrained from using the word "gay" to denote homosexuality—"*Unless*, of course, he also thinks that our contemporary use signals and depends on a kind of association between gaiety and homosexuality that Milton himself might in some way have sensed and anticipated." (Historically, I consider that possibility by no means a *reductio ad absurdum* but perfectly conceivable.) But we might be constrained to disagree with such an interpreter, Dworkin says, "if we found it too implausible that Milton might have anticipated a now-common association."

Dworkin asserts that I consider such constraints "illusory." The point of my example, however, was to suggest that they make perfect sense, provided one wants to know what Milton intended. And that point is simply confirmed by Dworkin's recasting of the example, for it isn't as though an interest in Milton's genius *by itself* constrains Dworkin's interpreter. It's only because an interest in Milton's genius involves an interest in figuring out what Milton intended that Dworkin's interpreter has any reason to care whether Milton anticipated a now-common association. In general, the constraints that interest Dworkin make sense in intentionalist terms not optimist ones.

So what's wrong, exactly, with intention? Dworkin's brief answer, in the present context, is "mentalism." Thus he writes that, according to my "mentalistic theory," "intentions are apparently independent of beliefs and meanings and have a fixed content that is independent of the purpose interpreters might have in trying to identify them." But this is a strange characterization of my account, which nowhere criticizes Davidson's holistic theory of intentional states and which starts from the Peircian denial that our concept of any object of inquiry can make sense apart from the role it plays in our inquiry itself. Dworkin's appeal to "purpose" simply skips over the purposes that are internal to a given inquiry and focuses instead on the various second-order purposes for which we can undertake such an inquiry. And he is right in saying that the content of people's intentions, in my view, is independent of second-order purposes for finding out what those intentions are—or, indeed, for disregarding them when we decide to do something else with a text besides interpreting it. But none of this has anything to do with "mentalism." Nor is it clear to me that Davidson anywhere holds that the logic of interpretation varies with the ulterior purpose for the sake of which we interpret.[22]

Dworkin's assumption that an interest in intention must involve some sort of "mentalistic" confusion is related to what is no doubt the primary source of his worries about intention, though he doesn't mention it here. In recent remarks on the subject published elsewhere, he summarizes and endorses the view of Charles Fried that, in the case of the Constitution, "The framer's opinions . . . are both unknowable and, *as they themselves thought*, irrelevant."[23] The claim as summarized is sufficiently remarkable, for if the framers' opinions are unknowable, how do we know they considered them irrelevant; and if their opinions are irrelevant, why should we care what they thought about their opinions? But this anomaly is symptomatic of a deeper confusion: Dworkin thinks that to suppose that the framers' text means what they intended it to mean is to be struck with their *opinions* as to how their intended meanings should be applied. But nothing in the claim that a text means what its author intended says anything about who has the best account of what to *do* with the author's intended meanings. To have the right account of interpretation is not to have, or even to imply, any account at all of what role interpretation ought to play in our legal and political practices.

# Notes

1. See entries in bibliography under Knapp and Michaels and under Mitchell.

2. For a recent account of the way debates about the Constitution's *meaning* turn into, or reveal themselves to have been all along, debates about the Constitution's *authority*, see Robert Post, "Theories of Constitutional Interpretation," *Representations* 30 (Spring 1990): 13—41.

3. Charles Sanders Peirce, *Collected Papers of Charles Sanders Peirce*, ed. Charles Hartshorne and Paul Weiss (Cambridge, Mass.: Harvard University Press, 1931—1935), V:402.

4. Ibid., V:438.

5. The lecture "Interpreting Interpretation" was delivered at the University of California, Berkeley, on April 3, 1990. Dworkin's book *Law's Empire* is cited in text below as *LE*. Full citation can be found in the bibliography.

6. I owe this particular twist on the example to Jeffrey Knapp.

7. From my notes on "Interpreting Interpretation."

8. *Paradise Lost*, Book 4, lines 935—945, in *John Milton: Complete Poems and Major Prose*, ed. Merritt Y. Hughes (Indianapolis: Odyssey, 1957), 300.

9. Hughes doesn't gloss the word at all, but many undergraduates will find the following gloss in *Paradise Lost*, ed. Scott Elledge (New York: Norton, 1975), 101: "in dress and behavior like courtiers."

10. Of course they could enter into *other* kinds of discussion, resulting in other kinds of agreement or disagreement; for instance, they might interestingly pursue their metainterpretive disagreement over the relation between meaning and intention. Conversely, there are other sorts of disagreement besides disagreement about the status of intention that might make further interpretive controversy pointless. Thus, as Stanley Fish pointed out in conversation, two interpreters who agreed that the object of interpretation was the author's intended meaning might radically diverge in their notions of what constituted evidence of authorial intention and for *that* reason have too little in common to engage in genuine interpretive controversy. But while disagreement about what counts as evidence *can* make genuine interpretive controversy impossible, disagreement about whether a text means what its author intends necessarily does so.

11. Dworkin's "optimism," both as an account of the logic of interpretation and as an attitude toward our legal institutions, is queried from a somewhat different perspective by David Hoy in "Dworkin's Constructive Optimism v. Deconstructive Legal Nihilism," *Law and Philosophy* 6 (1987): 321—356.

12. See Ronald Dworkin, *A Matter of Principle* (Cambridge, Mass.: Harvard University Press, 1985), 158—162. This argument originally appeared as a section of Dworkin's essay "Law as Interpretation," *Critical Inquiry* 9 (September 1982): 179—200.

13. In a critique of Dworkin's essay "Law as Interpretation," Stanley Fish calls attention to Dworkin's "assumption . . . that sentences, figures, and styles announce their own generic affiliation, and that a reader who would claim them for an inappropriate genre would be imposing his will on nature" ("Working on the Chain Gang: Interpretation in Law and in Literary Criticism," *Critical Inquiry* 9 [September 1982]: 209). Fish's response to Dworkin's essay is reprinted as Chapter 4 of his *Doing What Comes Naturally: Change, Rhetoric, and the Practice of Theory in Literary and Legal Studies* (Durham, N.C.: Duke University Press, 1989).

14. The point I am making here is a version of E. D. Hirsch's well-known distinction between "meaning" and "significance"; see E. D. Hirsch, Jr., *Validity in Interpretation* (New Haven: Yale University Press, 1967), 211. The difference between us is that I don't grant the distinction any *methodological* importance since I don't consider any inquiry into what Hirsch

calls "meaning" more "objective" than an inquiry into what he calls "significance." I don't think, in other words, that meaning as Hirsch construes it provides the "guiding idea" without which "self-critical or objective interpretation is hardly possible" (212).

15. Cf. Joseph Vining, "Generalization in Interpretive Theory," *Representations* 30 (Spring 1990): 4.

16. See especially Knapp and Michaels, "Against Theory 2" and "Intention, Identity, and the Constitution" (cited in bibliography).

17. Knapp and Michaels, "Intention, Identity, and the Constitution."

18. The distinction I am making here has affinities with the distinction between pragmatism and instrumentalism explored in relation to Holmes and Dewey by Thomas C. Grey in "Holmes and Legal Pragmatism," *Stanford Law Review* 47 (April 1989): 853—860.

19. My examples of these differing accounts of the Constitution's identity are taken, once again, from Robert Post, "Theories of Constitutional Interpretation."

20. Vining is referring to the practice of "reading" statutes: "The reading of statutes for 'their intent,' the paying of close attention to nuance and form in them, may be a necessary and even desirable form of self-delusion" ("Generalization," 5).

21. Provided, that is, that the author knew *how* to write in the genre he/she intended to write in. I am not denying that genres are conventional; and because they are conventional, no one can produce (or even *intend* to produce) a work in a given genre without following its conventions, just as no one can produce (or intend to produce) a meaningful utterance in English without following the rules of English.

22. What feature of Davidson's theory can Dworkin have in mind here? Davidson does deny that the concepts used by interpreters "have a legitimate place in explaining speech" apart from the extent to which "they can be shown to play a useful role in the construction of an adequate theory" (*Inquiries into Truth and Interpretation* [Oxford: Clarendon Press, 1984], 146—149). But the "theory" in question here is only what Davidson calls a "theory of interpretation" of a particular speaker's utterances. And according to Davidson, "We interpret a bit of linguistic behavior when we say what a speaker's words mean on an occasion of use" (141). Furthermore, to argue that the nature of this task varies without ulterior purposes in pursuing it would be to refute Davidson's claim that (necessarily) we can't ascribe intentions without at the same time ascribing beliefs and meanings. For if what we're after is whatever will make an utterance, say, therapeutically helpful, why should we necessarily care, as Davidson does, whether the resulting "interpretation" preserves the right interrelations among the speaker's various states?

23. "The Reagan Revolution and the Supreme Court," *The New York Review of Books* 38 (July 18, 1991), 23; emphasis added.

# 18

## Is Legal Originalism Compatible with Philosophical Pragmatism?

### David Hoy

In the law originalism is the doctrine that the meaning of the Constitution is what the framers originally intended it to mean. Originalism is thus a special case of the more general view in the theory of interpretation that the meaning of a text is the author's intention. This intentionalist thesis is held by some literary theorists who have been called "New Pragmatists."[1]  Stanley Fish is one who is sympathetic to both intentionalism and pragmatism, but two other theorists who have also worked out an original theory are Steven Knapp and Walter Benn Michaels.  Steven Knapp in particular has stated that he is an originalist (in a qualified way, of course) as well as a pragmatist.  Originalism and pragmatism are thus identified, or at least made closely compatible, in ways that I find difficult to reconcile with my own understanding of how pragmatism is understood in philosophy today.   In this chapter, therefore, I raise the explicit question "is originalism compatible with pragmatism?," and my answer will be, in brief, "no."

Before arguing for this answer, I must first explain how I understand pragmatism.  Any account of present-day pragmatism must reflect the writings of Richard Rorty, who has done the most to revive interest in the philosophical tradition of pragmatism.  Present-day pragmatism can, of course, be called "new" pragmatism, not because it conflicts with the classic pragmatism of Charles Sanders Peirce, William James, and John Dewey on points of doctrine but only because of the evolution of the position.  There will inevitably be intervening influences that have been absorbed by the new pragmatism and that could not have been reflected in classic pragmatism.  These influences come from later American philosophers like W.V.O. Quine and Donald Davidson as well as from

German hermeneutical philosophers like Martin Heidegger and Hans-Georg Gadamer.

Richard Rorty explicitly includes Davidson and Gadamer in his accounts of contemporary pragmatism. In the legal context the philosopher of law Ronald Dworkin is allied with Davidson, and thus I am inclined to count Dworkin as a pragmatist as well. But Steven Knapp in his contribution to this volume criticizes Dworkin and has also criticized Davidson in the past. One might therefore infer that there are two opposed camps of pragmatism today, one composed of Rorty, Davidson, and Dworkin, and another of Fish, Michaels, and Knapp. As the alleged allies might differ among themselves on crucial points, however, I will not pretend to argue for one camp against the other but will start with a more general characterization of pragmatism and then examine in more detail the different strategies for arguing the case about originalistic interpretation in constitutional law.

Since Dworkin's *Law's Empire* will feature centrally in what I have to say, I should make clear that I will not be using the term "pragmatism" as he does. In the more specific context of legal theory "pragmatism" is his label for a forward-looking approach to legal interpretation, one that disregards the connection of the law to the past and sees law as realists did, namely, as disguised predictions of what judges will say in the future or noncognitive expressions of desire.[2] Pragmatism in this special legal sense is a skeptical attitude toward the law and society (and I worry below that Steven Knapp shares this attitude). American philosophical pragmatism is not skeptical, however, and Dewey, for instance, was deeply optimistic about the possibilities for social reforms.

Two central features of contemporary philosophical pragmatism are (1) antifoundationalism, and (2) social optimism. There is no reason to think that (1) and (2) entail each other, and, indeed, what seems to separate Richard Rorty from Stanley Fish is that both accept antifoundationalism, but Fish rejects Rorty's social optimism. I will return to the question of pragmatism's social philosophy. Right now let me explain briefly three epistemological aspects of what is meant by antifoundationalism; each of these will feature in the attempt to reconcile originalism with pragmatism. These three aspects have to do with (a) truth, (b) realism, and (c) holism.

Although the connections between classic pragmatists' theory of truth and Donald Davidson's are complex, for present purposes I think that it will be enough to say that one central feature that they share is their rejection of the idea of a correspondence test for truth.[3] There is thus no way to get completely outside a set of beliefs to check them against reality. One must add quickly that pragmatists do not thereby reject reality, but have a different analysis of the concept of reality. Although there is controversy about Hilary Putnam's distinction between "metaphysical realism" and "internal realism,"[4] I invoke it now to suggest that in rejecting the idea of a reality that could be so independent of our beliefs that even at the ideal limit our best confirmed scientific theories could be wrong, the pragmatists need not reject the notion of reality altogether. Instead, reality will be conceived pragmatically as internal to our system of beliefs and our cognitive practices. Belief and meaning are thus related holistically, not atomistically, and confirmation involves testing beliefs against other beliefs, not against some metaphysically independent reality. This holism is worked into the pragmatist theory of interpretation of Dworkin when interpretation is said to aim at maximizing intelligibility by seeing the text in the best possible light, not at recapturing authorial intention.

This brief a sketch of philosophical pragmatism's antifoundationalism may be too abstract, so let me try to make the issues clearer by turning to Steven Knapp and Walter Benn Michaels, who have explicitly defended authorial intention and yet have also called themselves pragmatists. I will be challenging their theory of interpretation, in particular their claim that interpretation is necessarily of the author's intention. I will also examine Steven Knapp's critique of Ronald Dworkin's nonintentionalistic and nonoriginalist theory of legal interpretation, discussing Dworkin's adaptation of Donald Davidson's principle of charity.

The concept of truth is a good place to begin with any position calling itself "pragmatic." A well-known feature of early American pragmatism is that truth is not separated from usefulness, and that early pragmatists spoke of truth as cash value. Yet Knapp and Michaels let truth and usefulness come apart, even to the point of claiming that their intentionalist account is *true* but *useless*. In a response to my earlier critique of their position they conclude by claiming that their intentionalism has "no heuristic value." They insist that the advantage of their account over the hermeneutic view that I defend is "not that [intentionalism] is more useful but that it is true."[5]

This conclusion might give one the impression that their conception of truth is alien to the pragmatist conception of truth.[6] Yet in the paper published in this volume Knapp takes pains to say that he is not positing "some kind of impractical, disinterested desire for interpretive truth." So he wants to free his account from the impression that it presupposes an interest "in the truth for its own sake." But I am afraid that for me that impression still lingers. He seems to think that although the quest for truth is accompanied by certain purposes and interests at the beginning of inquiry, those purposes may eventually fall away and be replaced by others. He even seems to imagine that at some point an inquiry might be motivated by only one such "purpose," namely, mere curiosity, which seems to me like what Kant called "purposeless purposiveness." Such an endpoint begins to sound like "truth for its own sake" after all, especially when he sums up his view by saying that "there is no reason to suppose that a practice has to be, as we say, 'practical.'"

So even in Knapp's attempt to convince us that he is a pragmatist he sounds curiously unpragmatic. Either he continues to be attracted by the traditional epistemological desire for "interest-free knowledge" or he leaves the relation of truth and practice unexplained. This second possibility is suggested in Knapp's chapter, where he says, "For the pragmatist recognition that our only access to truth, in interpretation or anywhere else, is through a socially constituted practice of inquiry does not affect the distinction between truth and fiction, even when fiction suits our purposes better than truth." He might mean that even if inquiry is always socially constituted, it will still need an account of the difference between truth and falsity. But he tends to make a stronger claim of the independence of truth from socially constituted practices when he insists that "our concept of what the truth involves in any given inquiry remains distinct from our sense of those various [additional] purposes" that led to the inquiry in the first place. The intuition behind this claim about truth may be correct, but it does not seem like pragmatism's emphasis on "warranted assertability" and its tendency, in Knapp's own description, to show the connection between truth and socially constituted practice.

A difficulty with the intentionalists' account, then, is that it sees the truth of an interpretation as its correspondence to the object of interpretation, which is authorial intention. This object seems radically independent of the socially constituted practices of interpretation, and it even appears to be committed to what Putnam calls "metaphysical realism." Intention on this account risks becoming a metaphysical entity, the truth about which could always be different from what our best confirmed account might tell us. Pragmatism holds, in contrast, that the truth should not be construed as independent from the practices of inquiry, and thus is more akin to internal realism.

Aside from the epistemological stance of this intentionalism, the form of argument that Knapp and Michaels use to establish their account of intention also seems more antipragmatist than pragmatist. As Richard Rorty has made clear in much of his recent work, pragmatism must avoid giving transcendental arguments for the universal inescapability of its own conclusions and position. Yet Knapp and Michaels seem to be giving us a transcendental argument. In their view, it is an inescapable feature of all textual interpretation that interpretation be of the author's intention.

This claim appears axiomatic, and thus I have difficulty in understanding how it could be labeled pragmatic. Of course, I do not want to quibble about a label. They can label it "pragmatism" if they want, but then they should clarify the connection to practice, given the admitted "uselessness" of the idea. Steven Knapp wrestles with that problem in his chapter for this volume and raises the worry that Dworkin's position seems more pragmatist than Knapp's own, because Dworkin believes that interpretation can serve different purposes and that these different purposes might indeed result in different readings of the text. Knapp wants to say in contrast that these are not disagreements about the text (for instance, the Constitution) but about something else (for instance, "the meaning of America"). Knapp thinks that there can be disagreement over how to use the results of interpretation, but he thinks that these disagreements about the results cannot have affected the prior process of interpretation itself.

So Steven Knapp sees a distinction between interpreting the text's meaning and applying that interpretation to the present situation, a distinction rejected by Dworkin, along with hermeneutical philosophers like Gadamer. Knapp thus accepts Virginia English professor E. D. Hirsch's famous distinction between meaning and significance, except that, unlike Hirsch, he does not think that there is an objective answer to the question of what the actual meaning is. Instead, Knapp only thinks that if interpreters disagree, they must be disagreeing about the author's intention, whatever that was. Knapp, unlike Hirsch, does not think that there is any privileged evidence that will tell you what the intention really was. For Knapp *all* evidence would be evidence for the author's intention, so he has no way of preferring some kinds of evidence to others.

I am not disagreeing with this desire of his to avoid the sort of theory that would guide or constrain interpretation. I only want to point out that Knapp may not have identified other necessary conditions for disagreement. If we could not disagree about the text's meaning unless we disagreed about the author's intention, for us to disagree it might also be necessary that we accept similar kinds of evidence, similar kinds of inference, and comparable notions of the canon. If, for instance, two interpreters disagreed about what the author's intention was, and one thought that she knew by divine revelation what the author's intention was but the other did not accept divine revelation, they would still not be genuinely disagreeing about the text. So even if Knapp were right that a necessary condition of disagreement about the text was acceptance of the author's intention as an object of interpretation, it does not follow that there are not other things that are also necessary for disagreement.

One such thing might be what nonoriginalists call present meaning. That is, Knapp has not excluded the possibility of arguing that for disagreement about the text to be possible, there must also be disagreement about the present meaning of the text. Let's take the law as such a case. Two parties come before the court precisely because the legal statute or the Constitutional clause seems to them to apply differently. To make a long story short, the view that disagreement must be about the authors' intentions does not rule out the view that disagreement is about present application because both might be true. Knapp's claim that authorial intention is a necessary condition is a thin one and does not exclude other factors as well.

What I am suggesting is that Knapp does not have grounds for saying that in constitutional disagreements lawyers are only pretending to be disagreeing about the text when they are really disagreeing about larger social interests (which is what I take him to mean by his phrase "the meaning of America"). I do not see why in his own view the disagreement could not be about *both* the text *and* "the meaning of America" (which I see as inextricably intertwined). I admit to being puzzled by his concluding skeptical remarks about constitutional interpretation, and his acceptance of the view that arguments about getting the text of the Constitution right represent merely lip service, or "an institutionally necessary fiction." In trying to explain his skepticism to myself, I hazard the following guesses. First, I assume that he does not want his intentionalism identified with the originalism of Meese and possibly Bork. Second, he disagrees with nonoriginalism, which holds that authorial intention is irrelevant in settling legal disagreements. However, third, he seems to think that nonoriginalism is probably right about the way constitutional interpretation is really practiced, and that lip service to the intention of the Constitution is really only "an institutionally necessary fiction."

Even if these guesses are wrong, the more important worry is whether he is not shifting between thinner and thicker claims about intention. The minimal, thinner claim that I take him to be making is that authorial intention is a *necessary condition*. However, in this assessment of the originalism and nonoriginalism debate, he may be moving a thicker claim that authorial intention is the only object about which there can be genuine interpretive disagreement, and is thus a uniquely *sufficient* condition.  But this latter claim is arguably too strong to apply to legal discourse, especially because judges sometimes limit themselves.[7]

If Knapp were to demur from the stronger claim, I would then point out that not much follows from the thinner claim.  The claim that intention is a necessary condition would amount simply to insisting a judge who decided correctly that something was unconstitutional could do so because the original intent entailed that decision (even if one did not know what that intent was).[8]  But I say that not much follows because the judge could also decide not to rule that the action was unconstitutional, which is to say in effect that it was constitutional.  Conceptual analyses that identify necessary conditions are often overestimated in their substantive force.

Knapp's appeal to intention also has a less strong effect than lawyers who are familiar with the originalism debates might infer.  This comes out more clearly in an earlier piece by Knapp and Michaels, where they respond to my suggestion that they clarify how their intentionalism differs from originalism.  Their main objection to originalism is that it is "mentalistic."  By this I believe that they mean that for originalists authors are the best authorities for the meaning of their texts.  Indeed, I think that this characterization may apply only to some originalists.  Let me distinguish between these "mentalistic originalists" and "normative originalists."[9]  Whereas mentalistic originalists would reason from psychological generalizations on the historical facts about what the framers could have believed, a normative originalist like Judge Robert Bork would reason more generally from the *principles* and *values* the framers desired to protect.  So defined, there may not be as much of a gap between a normative originalist and a nonoriginalist like Dworkin, who also believes that the reasoning should be from principles and values.

From what Steven Knapp has said, his position still sounds like an originalist position, although more like normative originalism.  Let me quote a long passage from an earlier response to me:

> After all, if a text only means what its authors intend it to mean, aren't the authors of the Fourteenth Amendment the best authorities as to what the equal protection clause prohibits and permits?  Not necessarily.  For one thing, the authors might well be mistaken about their own intentions; or they might have forgotten them, or never have correctly understood them in the first place.  Or they might be lying or joking.  More interestingly, they might be perfectly correct about what their intentions were and perfectly sincere in reporting

those intentions, and still be mistaken as to what the equal protection
clause prohibits and permits.[10]

Knapp thinks, for instance, that the framers of the Fourteenth
Amendment wanted to guarantee equality but were simply mistaken in
their belief that segregated schools are intrinsically equal. Therefore, we
need not follow their belief about segregated schools, but only their
original intention, which was to guarantee equality.

So now we have some clarification of Knapp's special use of the
terms "meaning," "intention," and "belief." The law's meaning is the
original intention, but the intention is separate from the author's beliefs,
even to the extent that author's mistaken beliefs "in no way affect the
content of their intention itself."[11]     However, there are several
philosophical problems with this view. For one thing, the insistence on
principle and value may be so abstract as to become potentially divorced
from history, ignoring what Gadamer has called the *Wirkungsgeschichte*,
the concrete historical circumstances and their development. An overly
abstract account might lead to a blindness to the internal reasons for the
evolution of legal doctrine.[12] For another thing the account of intention
still seems "mentalistic," as opposed to "pragmatist." One could always
claim that one had a good, clear intention on this account, even if one's
actions or statements went awry because of the regrettable falseness of
one's beliefs. A pragmatist account, I would think, would want to tie
intentions and beliefs more closely together. In a pragmatist account it
would seem that what the intention was should be determined as beliefs
are, that is, holistically, looking at the general pattern formed by
statements and the world. In Donald Davidson's holism, for instance,
an interpreter does not simply attribute an isolated belief to a speaker,
but a pattern of interrelated beliefs. "Beliefs are identified and
described," says Davidson, "only within a dense pattern of belief."[13]
The principle of charity is roughly the additional requirement that this
pattern include mostly true beliefs, that is, beliefs that are true by the
lights of the interpreter. The interpreter does what is necessary to make
the "significant mass of belief" coherent.[14]

The upshot of the holistic account of interpretation is, then, that
beliefs and intentions are figured out as part of a circular process of
interpretation. Furthermore, the way to avoid "mentalistic" accounts is
to give up the idea of meaning in the sense of a purely mental object of
understanding, and think *extensionally* instead. That is, since the
interpreter does not have any access to what is inside the head, and may
even give up internalism about mental state (that is, the idea that there
is some special category of things "inside the head"), the interpreter

constructs an interpretation of the speaker's sentences, intentions, beliefs, and desires through what can be observed about the speaker's interactions in the world. The principle of charity does not mean that the interpreters impose most of their beliefs on the speaker, but only that they try to minimize unexplained error. So in the interpretation of intention and belief, although it may be necessary to interpret the interpreters as having some particular beliefs that seem to the interpreters to be mistaken, for the most part intention and belief must be intimately connected.

I go over all this to explain why in Knapp's account intention and belief threaten to become radically disjoint. Dworkin's position, in contrast, owes much to the Davidsonian account of interpretation, and particularly to its holism. The holism does not rule out considerations about the authors' intentions. But it does not make them the foundation of textual meaning in the way that Knapp implies. In particular, there is no reason to think that intention is the primary object that the interpreter is after. Davidson does not deny that sentences are uttered by intentional beings, but he thinks that intentions are complex. The problem with the intentionalists' appeal to intention, I would add, is that there are too many intentions, or at least, too many descriptions of intention to say that "*the* meaning" is "*the* intention." Just to take a simplified example, notice all the intentions that Davidson identifies in the following passage:

> Suppose Diogenes utters the words "I would have you stand from between me and the sun" (or their Greek equivalent) with the intention of uttering words that will be interpreted by Alexander as true if and only if Diogenes would have him stand from between Diogenes and the sun, and this with the intention of asking Alexander to move from between him and the sun, and this with the intention of leaving a good anecdote to posterity. Of course these are not the only intentions involved; there will also be the Grecian intentions to achieve certain of these ends through Alexander's recognition of some of the intentions involved. Diogenes' intention to be interpreted in a certain way requires such a self-referring intention, as does his intention to ask Alexander to move.[15]

The initial intention here may be the normal one with which to start the interpretation, but there are other intentions that the interpretation must take into account. The intentionalist account should say more about whether when the intentionalists' talk about *the* meaning and *the* intention, they mean a single one of all the intentions or a list of them all. I will note that this list would be a long one even for Diogenes' one-liner, and thus would be extremely long for even a short text like the Constitution.

So intention can come into the picture, but the story is complex, and which intentions are finally most relevant depends on which story one wants to tell. Davidsonian radical interpretation depends on constructing a truth theory, that is, a theory in which the sentences that are held true are recursively portrayed. Davidson has a complex story to tell about how speaker's meaning and utterance meaning are related, but he does not want to collapse this distinction, as Knapp and Michaels do. His holism entails that "radical interpretation cannot hope to take as evidence of the meaning of a sentence an account of the complex and delicately discriminated intentions with which the sentence is typically uttered," not because we should not ask about the intentions, but because "interpreting an agent's intentions, his beliefs and his words are parts of a single project, no part of which can be assumed to be complete before the rest is."[16]

The intentionalists are opposed to Davidson's account of interpretation, including his commitment to the distinction between speaker's meaning and utterance meaning. Therefore, they are also opposed to Dworkin, who acknowledges the Davidsonian elements in his account of legal interpretation. I would suggest that Dworkin be understood to be working within the general framework of Quine and Davidson, building on a conception of practical reasoning as "inference to the best explanation." However, for the record I should add that Dworkin is also claiming that Davidson's account of charity is merely a special case of a more general and inclusive account of interpretation that Dworkin is himself providing. Dworkin thinks that charity is a principle that applies mainly to conversational interpretation when two speakers confront each other. Davidson thinks that all interpretation must be modeled on this case, whereas Dworkin thinks that textual interpretation is different enough to require a more general account. Dworkin's view is thus that interpretation is the construction that makes the object of interpretation the best that it can be. Charity is the principle required for this constructive activity in speech encounters.

I will not spend time here discussing whether there are really grounds for debate between Dworkin and Davidson on this score. Let me assume that they are sufficiently allied, at least in contrast to Steven Knapp's position. Turning then to Knapp's counterexamples, let me play devil's advocate here and suggest that the counterexamples are not particularly telling.[17] To be provocative, let me argue that given Steven Knapp's claims about intention that I have just discussed, there may not be all that much difference between Knapp and Dworkin, especially on legal interpretation. If the intentionalists do not want to seem to share the conservative politics of originalism, but if they also object to the liberal politics of Dworkin's nonoriginalism, it seems reasonable to ask them where they do stand. Steven Knapp did imply that he was simply a literary critic and that literary interpretation does not make any difference in the real world. But now he is offering an account of legal interpretation as well, which he does think makes a difference. His claim, for instance, that legal reference to the laws' intentions is an institutionally necessary fiction seems to imply a deep skepticism about the rule of law in this country. Knapp, and perhaps Michaels and Fish, would thus share a skepticism about democratic society and the rule of law, in contrast to the social optimism of Dewey, Rorty, and Dworkin.

Focusing then on the details of Knapp's critique of Dworkin, let me suggest that Dworkin can resist the proffered counterexamples without too much difficulty. Knapp tries to undermine Dworkin's thesis that interpretation must always see its object "in the best light" by imagining a case where a mugger says to someone on the street, "Give me your money or I'll kill you." Knapp's reading of Dworkin suggests that in Dworkin's account the interpreter must make this into the most morally acceptable utterance imaginable, for instance, by inferring that the mugger really means to tell him a joke, one that will "kill him" metaphorically because of its humor. However, Dworkin's interpretation does not have to be high-minded and make this into a morally acceptable utterance. Dworkin's word, "best" can mean "best given the circumstances" or "best for practical purposes." So in this case the point of the practice is staying alive (as Dworkin himself remarked in response to Knapp), and the best interpretation is the one that will minimize unexplained error and maximize survival. So Dworkin's point about interpretation "in the best light" is perhaps a thin one, more like the Davidsonian model, which implies that the interpreter amends initial or standard understandings of sentences (what Davidson calls the "prior theory"), making up an intervening interpretation (what Davidson calls a "passing theory") that will minimize unexplained error and bring about the maximal coherence in the mass of belief shared by the two speakers. (Gadamer refers to this process as the "fusion of horizons.") Dworkin's position does not come down, then, to "knowing how good the utterance *might* be" in contrast to knowing "exactly how good or bad it actually is," as Knapp suggests. Dworkin's account rejects this distinction on Davidsonian grounds. Dworkin and Davidson are asking how real interpretations could succeed, and their answer is that they could succeed only if a significant mass of belief were shared.

Can there be "oppositional criticism" that makes the object the *worst* that it can be? Steven Knapp suggests that Dworkin simply overlooks that there are oppositional literary critics. But Dworkin, I would point out, certainly knows about oppositional legal critics, and a subtext in the book is clearly his worry about the Critical Legal Studies movement. But even though Dworkin is himself critical of this oppositional criticism, the question is whether his theory entails his preference for optimistic over pessimistic interpretation. Again, I believe that his main point is a thin one, in the Davidsonian manner, and should not be overestimated as a thicker, substantive doctrine. Dworkin's point is that deliberately trying to make something the *worst* it can be is either *incoherent* or *deceptive*. The activity would be *deceptive* if there were a better interpretation that one were deliberately suppressing. The activity would be *incoherent* if one were trying to show that the text did not make sense without making an effort to see what sense it could make. Now, of course, Dworkin realizes that interpreters can conclude that the text is seriously deficient and not good at all. But then they are still trying to make the object the best it can be, and saying that even given the effort to make it the best it can be, it is not good at all.

Dworkin's argument might thus seem reminiscent of the Platonic argument that one cannot really desire the bad, since if one wants what is bad, one must think that it is good, at least in more respects than it is bad. But the point is really more the Davidsonian one, which is that interpretation can succeed only if something makes sense, and something that really did not make any sense at all could not be interpreted. The evaluative term "best" should not confuse us into extending a semantic, cognitive point about how sense making is possible into some more value theoretic, substantive sense of what really is or is not "good."

The thinness of Dworkin's claim allows the oppositional critics in Critical Legal Studies to respond to him that in his own view Dworkin should recognize the coherence of their subversive readings of the law. They need not admit that they are trying to see the statutes in the worst light. They could claim that they are seeing the existing laws in the best light possible, since even in the best light the laws are disharmonious. This result would not be surprising, they could continue, because our society is a divided one. Their practice of showing that existing law lacks coherence could serve the purpose of showing that if we do not see this disharmony in the existing law, we will never achieve the "pure integrity" of abstract justice. These oppositional critics could contend that Dworkin's own attempt to show the "inclusive integrity" of existing law tends to blind him to the defects of existing law and thus to preserve rather than to overcome social division. The oppositional critics could use Dworkin's own theory of interpretation to defend themselves from his critique and to criticize his own optimistic readings.

Similar moves are possible in response to Steven Knapp's example of the conflicts about *Paradise Lost*. The example serves to make several points, but I would like to focus on only one. Oppositional criticism is defined by Knapp as "a practice whose point requires an interpreter to make the meaning of a particular literary work just as bad as possible . . . to undermine or overturn a social structure that a given literary work (or a given legal statute) is seen to support." So the critic shows that *Paradise Lost* is authoritarian, on the assumption that being authoritarian is bad. But here again Dworkin could respond that the critic is not really describable as making the work the worst that it can be but, instead, as showing that, at its best, the work is authoritarian and therefore bad. Because all interpreters share this obligation to see the work at its best, then this oppositional critic *can* disagree with other critics who say that the work is not really authoritarian, or more interestingly, that it is neither simply authoritarian nor simply subversive, but undecidable. Steven Knapp may be misreading Dworkin in thinking that the issue is how the work *might* be read. The issue is really how it *is* read, if it is read at all, where to read something means to make it intelligible. (Knapp seems to be dissatisfied with the possibility that "relative explicability" may be the only principle through which something is read in the best light, but this suggestion strikes me as being right because "explicability" may be simply another name for the principle of charity.)

So I think that Dworkin is right that there could be disagreement if intelligibility is the telos of interpretation and that there would be no need to posit intention as the ultimate object of interpretation. I also do not understand how Knapp's and Michaels's account applies to constitutional interpretation, where it is not really the author's intentions that count but the ratifiers' interpretations. In general, I think that the law is better accounted for not by an author-based account, as Knapp and Michaels offer, but by an interpreter-based account, as Davidson and Dworkin (and Gadamer) offer. Ratifiers are, after all, interpreters, not authors. But in the law even authors are interpreters in a more direct way than in literature because the body of law is a multiauthored amalgam. Statutes often have more than one author, and laws form a cumulative body such that the authoring of new law should be coherent with previous law. Factors like the authority of the ratifiers and the multiauthored character of law make for differences between law and literature, as does the authority that judges have and that literary critics lack in laying down their interpretations. Intentionalism seems to ignore these differences.

But finally I am not sure that in this particular debate between Knapp and Dworkin that there is much *practical* difference, when practice is what should be most important to self-described pragmatists like Knapp and Michaels. Knapp has allowed that intention is constructed by interpreters. No particular kind of evidence is any more likely to deliver the intention than any other kind, he adds, since all evidence is historical. So interpreters can reason equally well about present application as about original meaning; in either case they are supposedly talking about intention (or at least about intended principles as opposed to actual beliefs). Similarly, Dworkin posits in *Law's Empire* that if an ideal interpreter (his "Judge Hercules") could see the body of law as a whole, the interpreter would see the law as written by a single author, the "community personified" (225). The authorial intention would thus be a principle of integrity, the principle that the law be a "coherent conception of justice and fairness" (225).

I conclude therefore by noting at least this much convergence between Knapp and Dworkin. Both allow that intention is *constructed* by an *interpreter* in the process of interpretation. For both of them intention becomes an ideal endpoint of interpretation, even if one that is only approached asymptotically, like a Kantian regulative ideal. For both of them this construction is what makes genuine, rational interpretive disagreement possible. Is there any reason to think that Steven Knapp's account differs from Ronald Dworkin's in the end? Knapp might argue that he is talking about a real, historical individual author whereas Dworkin posits only a constructed author. However, even real individuals are constructs: They are constructed by interpreters and they construct themselves by interpreting themselves. If one's understanding of one's own intention is itself an interpretation, why not recognize that intention is never independent of interpretation, and not the only possible object or interest of interpretation?

My answer to the question of whether originalism is compatible with pragmatism is thus that there are epistemological commitments in intentionalistic originalism that are incompatible with the holism that I think is central to contemporary philosophical pragmatism. My arguments do not prove that originalism could not be amended to become more compatible with pragmatism, but they do suggest that Dworkin's antioriginalism is more consistent with pragmatism than either "mentalistic originalism" or "normative originalism." As a coda I would add that I myself find Dworkin's ideal optimism noble, but I worry that it posits an impractical endpoint to interpretation, one that could be reached only by ideal interpreters like Judge Hercules. Because I think that the conditions of finite interpreters are markedly different from those of ideal interpreters, I prefer a more limited and critical account of interpretation. But I will note that Dworkin's social optimism is consistent with the forward-looking cheerfulness of American pragmatism from John Dewey through to Richard Rorty. It is also reminiscent of the optimism of the American idealists like Royce and forgotten figures like William Hocking. However, if what I have said about Critical Legal Studies is correct, it too could be a variant of social optimism. A sufficiently complex account of interpretation should not pit such oppositional criticism *against* the optimists, as if optimism were invariably naive or reprehensible. Instead, the account of interpretation could aspire to showing how social optimism is still possible, despite social divisions. The "critical" account would add only that any optimism, however desirable, is to be tempered with a self-critical suspicion that there may be disharmonies, biases, and prejudices lurking at optimism's core.

## Notes

1. The anthology *Against Theory: Literary Studies and the New Pragmatism* (Chicago: University of Chicago Press, 1985) begins with an introductory essay, "Pragmatic Theory," in which the volume's editor, W.J.T. Mitchell, identifies Stanley Fish, Walter Benn Michaels, Steven Knapp, and Richard Rorty as principal "New Pragmatists" (1).

2. See Ronald Dworkin, *Law's Empire* (Cambridge, Mass.: Harvard University Press, 1986), Chapter 5. All references to Dworkin are from this work.

3. See Donald Davidson's rejection in his 1989 Dewey Lectures of his own earlier acceptance of the idea of correspondence: "The Structure and Content of Truth," *Journal of Philosophy* 87 (June 1990): 279—326, esp. 302—303.

4. See Hilary Putnam, *Reason, Truth, and History* (Cambridge: Cambridge University Press, 1981).

5. Steven Knapp and Walter Benn Michaels, "Intention, Identity, and the Constitution: A Response to David Hoy," cited in bibliography. In the same volume, also see my earlier discussion of their view, "Intentions and the Law: Defending Hermeneutics."

6. I do not mean to fully endorse the classic pragmatists' conception of truth. For a thoughtful critique of the pragmatistic slogan that truth is "what works" and a reformulation of classic pragmatism's theory of truth, see Robert Brandom, "Pragmatism, Phenomenalism, and Truth Talk," *Midwest Studies in Philosophy* 7 (1988): 75—93.

7. See Michael J. Perry, *Morality, Politics, and Law* (Oxford: Oxford University Press, 1988), Chapter 6.

8. See my discussion on page 484 of "A Hermeneutic Critique of the Originalism/Nonoriginalism Distinction," *Northern Kentucky Law Review* 15 (1988): 479—498.

9. Ibid., 481.

10. Steven Knapp and Walter Benn Michaels, "Intention, Identity, and the Constitution: A Response to David Hoy," manuscript pages 11—12.

11. Ibid., 14.

12. Steven Knapp would thus be susceptible to the same criticism made against Dworkin by legal historians. Mark Tushnet summarized such criticisms when he wrote: "[Dworkin] therefore can be required to produce evidence of an interpretivist sort that the framers knew that they were enacting provisions that embodied a moral content richer than their own moral conceptions. And, simply put, there is no evidence at all that they did. The distinction relies on modern theories of law that, I am certain, were quite foreign, indeed probably incomprehensible, to the framers of the Bill of Rights and the Fourteenth Amendment. Their theories of law were at the same time both more positivistic and more allied to theological versions of natural law than is the secularized vision of moral philosophy from which Dworkin draws his distinction." Mark V. Tushnet, "Following the Rules Laid Down: A Critique of Interpretivism and Neutral Principles," in *Critical Legal Studies*, ed. Allan C. Hutchinson (Totowa, N.J.: Rowman and Littlefield, 1989), 161.

13. Donald Davidson, "The Method of Truth in Metaphysics," in Donald Davidson, *Inquiries into Truth and Interpretation* (Oxford: Oxford University Press, 1984), 200.

14. Donald Davidson, "A Coherence Theory of Truth and Knowledge," in *Truth and Interpretation: Perspectives on the Philosophy of Donald Davidson*, ed. Ernest LePore (Oxford: Blackwell, 1986), 308.

15. Donald Davidson, "A Nice Derangement of Epitaphs," in *Truth and Interpretation*, 435.

16. Donald Davidson, "Radical Interpretation," *Inquiries into Truth and Interpretation*, 127. In "Communication and Convention," Davidson rejects what I take to be a central tenet of the intentionalism of Knapp and Michaels when he writes: "Of course the mere intention does not *give* the sentence the meaning. . . . Literal meaning and intended meaning must coincide if there is to be a literal meaning. But this fact, while true and important, is of no direct help in understanding the concept of literal meaning, since the crucial intention must be characterized by reference to the literal meaning." *Inquiries into Truth and Interpretation*, 271—272.

17. I have raised my own counterexamples and counterarguments to Dworkin in two essays: "Dworkin's Constructive Optimism v. Deconstructive Legal Nihilism," *Law and Philosophy* 6 (1987): 321—356; and "Interpreting the Law: Hermeneutical and Poststructuralist Perspectives," *Southern California Law Review* 58 (November 1985): 135—176.

# 19

## Pragmatism, Right Answers, and True Banality

### Ronald Dworkin

### I. Introduction

I have kindly been invited to discuss my work in relation to pragmatism. In this chapter, my interest is not in replying to the criticisms of my work found in this volume, but in two other goals. First, I shall try to explain, using the essays in this collection as evidence, why I believe that what Professor Rorty calls the "new" pragmatism has nothing to contribute to legal theory, except to provide yet another way for legal scholars to be busy while actually doing nothing. Second, I will try to explain why my view that there are right answers in hard cases is not, as it is often said to be, a daring but preposterous metaphysical claim that separates me from more sensible scholars, but an ordinary, commonsensical, extremely weak proposition of law that (as I have often said) it would be silly ever to announce if it had not been denied by so many legal philosophers.[1] These two projects are connected: The best account of why the new pragmatism has seemed exciting to some lawyers is also, I believe, the best explanation of why they have inflated the very ordinary right-answer thesis into a piece of incomprehensible nonsense.

I should like to link those immediate goals to a more general and important one: a plea for a more constructive jurisprudence. For more than a decade American legal theory has been too occupied in meta-theoretical debates about its own character or possibility. Creditable political aims inspired part (though only part) of this preoccupation. But, in the event, nothing came even of those political aims; those who discussed nihilism and deconstruction with social justice in mind could have done more for that cause by dealing with its problems more directly. We should now set aside, as a waste of important energy and resource, grand debates about whether law is all power or illusion or constraint, or whether texts interpret only other texts, or whether there are right or best or true or soundest answers or only useful or powerful or popular ones. We could then take up instead how the decisions that in any case will be made should be made, and which of the answers that will in any case be thought right or best or true or soundest really are.

## II. The New Pragmatism

Some lawyers who call themselves pragmatists mean only that they are practical people, more interested in the actual consequences of particular political and legal decisions than in abstract theory. But "pragmatism" is also the name of one kind of abstract philosophical theory. Professor Rorty, who says he is a philosophical pragmatist, includes within that tradition not just William James, Charles Sanders Peirce, and John Dewey, but also Ludwig Wittgenstein, W.V.O. Quine, and Donald Davidson, though the latter three philosophers have not so much supported as refuted Rorty's version of that tradition.

Rorty says that we must give up the idea that legal or moral or even scientific inquiry is an attempt to discover what is really so, what the law really is, what texts really mean, which institutions are really just, or what the universe is really like. We should give up the idea that one vocabulary of concepts, one collection of propositions, can be more faithful than another to some independently existing "reality." Instead, we should accept that the vocabulary we have is *just* the one we have, the one that seems to suit us, or to be useful to us. We should also accept that when that vocabulary of ideas and propositions no longer seems to be useful—no longer seems to suit us—we can and should change it, to see "how we get on" with a different one. Inquiry, so understood, is experimental. We try out new ideas to see how they work out, to see which ideas or vocabularies prove to be useful or interesting.

This sounds exciting, but it is philosophically a dog's dinner, as many philosophers have by now pointed out. I quote a succinct restatement of the point by Bernard Williams summarizing Hilary Putnam's devastating critique. "[Rorty's views] simply tear themselves apart. If, as Rorty is fond of putting it, the correct description of the world (for us) is a matter of what we find it convenient to say, and if, as Rorty admits, we find it convenient to say that science discovers a world that is already there, there is simply no perspective from which Rorty can say, as he also does, that science does not really discover a world that is already there, but (more or less) invents it."[2]

The point applies equally to law and morals. Ordinary lawyers practicing their profession think that some judicial opinions really get the law right or straight and that others do not. Ordinary citizens think that the war in the Persian Gulf really was just or unjust. They don't mean that it is amusing or interesting or helpful or useful to *say* it was, but that it really *was*, because expelling an invading army really *is* a just thing to do or because killing innocent civilians really *is* always unjust. It would be an understatement to say that this distinction—between what the law really is or what justice really requires and what it would be useful in some way to say or think—is important to us. It is crucial: We could not "get on" at all, let alone well, without it. If we thought the pragmatist was asking us to give up that distinction, we would reject his advice as pragmatically self-defeating: Taking that advice would make our "vocabulary" not more but much less useful to us.

So pragmatism self-destructs wherever it appears: It offers advice it tells us not to take. It must have surprised some readers, therefore, that in his contribution to this collection Rorty says that in law, at least, we have already *made* the changes his brand of pragmatism demands, that pragmatism and its allies have all but swept the field, that the long battle they fought is now largely won, and that in legal theory, at least, we are all pragmatists now. How can that be, because we still talk as if lawyers' statements of law are statements about what the law is, not what it would be useful to say it is, and because we still suppose that lawyers' statements can get the law right or wrong? The explanation lies in a diagnosis I have offered before, at some length, but will summarize now.[3]

Rorty and his followers apparently all distinguish, though without making this clear, between two levels at which people supposedly think and speak. The first is the internal level at which some practical enterprise like law or science or literary activities or moral engagement is carried on. That is the level at which people use the vocabulary that is useful to them: the level at which people rightly say, because that *is* useful, that science describes how the world really is and that the law is not just what it would be useful to think it is. The second is the external level at which philosophers and other theorists talk *about* these enterprises rather than participate in them. That is the level at which, according to Rorty and the others, some bad philosophers of science claim that science discovers how the world really is, and bad legal philosophers say that lawyers and judges try to discover, even in hard cases, what the law really is. This is the level Rorty means to occupy: He wants to say, himself now occupying that external level, that these external claims are metaphysical, foundational, and other bad things. Refuting these mistaken external descriptions, he thinks, will not change thought or speech at the internal level—the level of actual science and actual legal practices—except to free it from whatever confusion and obscurity has leaked into the practice from the bad external theories. So Rorty says that the triumph of pragmatism has only cleared the conceptual ground so that actual practice can continue liberated from that kind of confusion.

The difficulty with this defense, however, is that the external level that Rorty hopes to occupy does not exist. There is no external philosophical level at which the statement "science tries to describe the world as it is" can mean something different from what that statement means in the internal world of science, and no external jurisprudential level at which "the law, properly understood, allows affirmative action" can mean something different from what it means in court. Language can only take its sense from the social events, expectations, and forms in which it figures, a fact summarized in the rough but familiar slogan that the key to meaning is use. That is true not only of the ordinary, working part of our language, but of all of it, the philosophical as well as the mundane. Of course, we can use part of our language to discuss the rest. We can say, for example, what I just said: that meaning is connected to use. And, certainly, ordinary words can acquire technical meaning in the special practices of a particular profession: Lawyers use "consideration" in a very special way, for example. But we cannot escape from the whole enterprise of speech to a different and transcendent plane where words can have meanings wholly independent from the meaning any practice, ordinary or technical, has given them.[4]

So it is not enough for Rorty simply to appeal to a mysterious philosophical or external level. He needs to locate the bad philosophical statements in some context of use; he must show them to have some special technical or other sense, so that when a legal philosopher says that legal propositions are true or false in virtue of what the law really is, he is not merely saying, in a more general way, what an ordinary lawyer says when *he* says that a particular judicial opinion got the law wrong. Neither Rorty nor other pragmatists have actually tried to do that, however. It is difficult to see how they could succeed if they did try. They would have to paraphrase the philosophical statements in some way to bring out their supposedly special meaning, and in doing that they would have to fall back on other words and ideas that also have a perfectly ordinary and clear use, and they would then have to tell us how *those* words mean something different from what they do in that ordinary use.

Suppose the pragmatists tell us, for instance, that the bad philosophers' theories have a special meaning because these theories claim that the content of the real, external world is independent of human purposes, or independent of culture and history, or something of the sort. The difficulty is that these new phrases—about the independence of reality from purpose—also have ordinary meanings, and if we give the philosophers' claims that ordinary meaning, then what they turn out to be saying is ordinary, too. It is perfectly true, for example, that, using all these words in their ordinary way, the height of Mt. Everest is not relative to human purposes or history or culture, though the metric measures we use to describe its height, and the fact that we take any interest in its height at all, certainly does depend on purposes and cultures. So a pragmatist would then have to supply special meanings for such phrases as "independent of purpose," special meanings that once again try to explain why when the philosopher says that reality is independent of purpose he says something different from what ordinary people mean when they say it. And anything the pragmatist then said—any new paraphrase or translation he offered—would encounter the same difficulty, and so on and on. Would it help if the pragmatist said that though, for example, it is true that the height of a mountain is independent of our purposes, that is true only given how we go on, and that the bad philosopher denies or doesn't understand that? No, because once again given how we go on—that is, as a statement drawing its sense and force from the practices we have in fact developed—*this* claim is false. *Given* how we go on, the height of the mountain is not determined by how we go on but by masses of earth and stone.

I hope no one will think, incidentally, that I am now claiming that pragmatism is not skeptical enough, or that it is, in some paradoxical way, swallowed up in its own skeptical success. Let me repeat: Philosophical claims, *including* skeptical claims of different sorts, are like any other kind of proposition. They need to be understood before they can be embraced, and they can only be understood against the background of how the concepts they employ are used. So understood, the pragmatist claims we have been discussing are not triumphantly true but only, in a straightforward and pedestrian way, false. Given how we go on, it is not true but false that there is no reality for scientists to discover, for example, or that law is only a matter of power, or that there is no difference between interpretation and invention. These announcements sound fascinating, radical, and liberating. But only until we ask whether they actually mean, in the only language we have, what they seem to say.

I said, a moment ago, that Rorty's new pragmatists, their predecessors and allies, have made no genuine effort to answer the question I posed: What is the difference in sense between the philosophical or theoretical claims they reject and the parallel ordinary ones they accept? How can that be? How can they believe themselves to have refuted positions they have not described? Never underestimate the power of metaphor and other devices of self-deception.

The pragmatists use scare-quotes and italics like confetti: They say that the bad philosophers think not just that things really exist but that they "really" or *really* exist, as if the quotes or italics change the sense of what is said. Metaphor is their heavy artillery, however. They say that the bad philosophers think that reality or meaning or law is "out there"; or that the world, or texts, or facts "reach out" and "dictate" their own interpretation; or that law is "a brooding omnipresence in the sky." These metaphors are meant to suggest, as it were, that the bad philosophers are claiming a new, different, metaphysically special kind of reality, reality beyond the ordinary, a new, supernatural, philosophical level of discourse. But it is only the pragmatists who, in fact, ever talk that way. They have invented their enemy or, rather, tried to invent him. For if the pragmatist explained his heated metaphors, he would have to fall back on the mundane language of ordinary life, and then he would not, after all, have distinguished the bad philosophers from the ordinary lawyer or scientist or person of conviction. If saying that law is "out there" means that there is a difference between what the law is and what we would like it to be, for example, then most lawyers think that the law is out there, and the pragmatist has no perspective from which he can sensibly say that it is not.

## III. The Right Answer Farrago

My thesis about right answers in hard cases is, as I have said, a very weak and commonsensical legal claim. It is a claim made within legal practice rather than at some supposedly removed, external, philosophical level. I ask whether, in the ordinary sense in which lawyers might say this, it is ever sound or correct or accurate to say, about some hard case, that the law, properly interpreted, is for the plaintiff (or for the defendant). I answer that, yes, some statements of that kind are sound or correct or accurate about some hard cases.[5] (In fact, I say that some such statement is characteristically or generally sound in hard cases. But we can ignore that more ambitious statement in this discussion about the *kind* of claim I am making.)

The most natural way to support that legal claim is therefore to try to show what the right answer is in some particular hard case. I can only do that, of course, by making an ordinary legal argument. I have in fact made many such arguments about very hard cases: I recently argued, for example, that a correct understanding of the United States Constitution required the Supreme Court to reverse the Missouri Supreme Court in the *Cruzan* case.[6] Four members of the Court agreed with that conclusion. Five disagreed: They thought the best available arguments required the opposite answer—that they were required to affirm the Missouri court. I have now mentioned ten very different lawyers all of whom thought (or at least said) that there was a right answer in the *Cruzan* case, as a matter of ordinary legal judgment. And, of course, many thousands of other lawyers thought the same thing. Now it's your turn. Have you yourself found any ordinary legal argument on balance the soundest, in any kind of hard case? Then you, too, have rejected the no-right-answer thesis I take to be the target of my own claim.

Legal theorists have an apparently irresistible impulse, however, to insist that the one-right-answer thesis must mean something more than is captured in the ordinary opinion that one side had the better argument in *Cruzan*. They think I must be saying not just that there are right answers in some ordinary way, as an unselfconscious lawyer might say that, but that there are *really* right answers, or *really real* right answers, or right answers *out there*, or something else up the ladder of verbal inflation. Their mistake is just Rorty's mistake: Thinking that they can add to or change the sense of the position they want to attack by inserting these redundancies or metaphors in it. There is *no* perspective from which these inflated and decorated claims can have a sense different from their sense uninflated and undecorated, and that is the sense they have in ordinary legal life. So there is nothing in what I have said for them to deny except what most of them would think it perverse to deny.

If the skeptical no-right-answer thesis has any practical importance at all, therefore, it must be treated as itself, not a metaphysical but a legal claim. It claims that, contrary to ordinary lawyers' opinion, it is a legal mistake to think there are right answers in hard cases. So understood it stands or falls by legal argument. Philosophy and morality are certainly, and in many ways, pertinent to that legal argument. Legal positivists, for example, have argued that the one-right-answer thesis must be wrong, in law, as a matter of logic or semantics. (I tried to answer their arguments in an early article.[7]) Members of the Critical Legal Studies movement point to what they take to be pervasive internal contradictions in legal doctrine that, if they exist, would rule out right answers. (I have tried to show that this suggestion confuses contradiction with competition, however.[8]) Moral skeptics, including John Mackie, defend a kind of internal moral skepticism that, if sound, would also defeat the possibility of right answers.[9] No doubt other arguments with legal bite can and will be deployed in favor of the internally skeptical view. But these are legal arguments; if successful they call for reform, and if successful they can be made without the crutch of inexplicable metaphor. They are not like the pragmatist's objection, which cannot be made except by redescribing what I say in metaphorical terms, trying to hijack me to some mythical philosophical level where external skeptics hang out, vultures desperate for prey.

## IV. Rorty and Banality

I shall now comment individually on some of the chapters in this book, and I begin with Rorty's own. He says that pragmatism and legal realism have, in fact, now been accepted by almost everyone in legal theory, and he cites my own work at several points as evidence. Even I, he says, who might be thought not to be a pragmatist, actually am. He calls attention to a remark I made many years ago. I said that no concept of truth could escape "the fact that all our concepts, including our philosophical concepts, take the only meaning they have from the function they play in our reasoning, argument, and conviction."[10] He says this echoes Dewey and supports his pragmatism and also legal realism. But it is the same point that I have been making here, and I made it then, as I have here, in the course of showing that pragmatism, not its opponents, was trying to engineer that kind of escape. I made it, in fact, in the course of defending what Rorty concedes sounds like a most unpragmatic claim: the one-right-answer thesis I have just been discussing.

He has a good deal to say about that thesis, moreover, and it is all revealing. I said, in the article from which he quotes, that it would make no difference to my thesis if instead of saying that there was a single "true" answer in controversial cases I said that there was a single "most reasonable" answer. I was illustrating the point I have been pressing here: that some legal skeptics are drawn, as bulls to a red flag, by "true," which seems to them a second-level philosophical kind of word, even though they have no trouble with "reasonable," which seems an internal, ordinary word. But there is no pertinent difference between the two formulations of the one-right-answer view. The apparently less threatening talk about "most reasonable" answers assumes, after all, that there is a single true answer to the question of which decision is the most reasonable. Rorty confirms my general diagnosis when he says that my willingness to substitute "most reasonable answer" for "right answer" "takes away whatever antipragmatist and anti-realist force there might have been in the 'one right answer' slogan." If my "slogan" is antipragmatist when it claims only one right answer, however, it is equally antipragmatist when it claims only one most reasonable answer.

The example is typical. Rorty's claim that everyone is now a pragmatist turns out to mean only that very few people now say things that strike him as being said at the mythical philosophical level. He says, for example, that since my own views about adjudication are "not interestingly different from Cardozo's," it "is hard to see what the force of the phrase 'one right answer' is supposed to be." That is meant to suggest, I presume, that he would understand the force of the one-right-answer thesis if he could treat it as a crazy metaphysical claim about pulsing right answers "out there" in some "independent legal reality." The trouble is that I have long ago made plain that I don't have anything like that in mind: Indeed, that there is nothing like that *to* have in mind. So he is at loss. Why would any one want to say that there are right answers in hard cases unless he meant something crazy?

I just tried to answer that question. The only reason anyone has to say that there can be right answers in hard cases is that this has been denied, sometimes in an interesting, internally legal way, by many legal philosophers, and it is of great legal importance that their skeptical claim be understood to be false because practice would have radically to change if it were true. I said that there are right answers, that is, only because and after others said that there are not. Rorty does not find substantive jurisprudence of that kind "interesting." But he must take it up if he really does want to discover the "force" of my claim, which lies in legal theory not in his mythical metaphysics.

He has another, equally revealing, argument for the triumph of pragmatism, however, which I set out in full. "Since neither Dworkin nor Richard Posner nor Roberto Unger has any use for what Posner calls 'formalism'—namely 'the idea that legal questions can be answered by inquiry into the relation between concepts'—it seems plausible to say that the battles which the legal realists fought in alliance with Dewey have been pretty well won." Presumably what Posner and Rorty have in mind, as this kind of formalism, is a method of legal argument that tries to reach concrete legal conclusions by some method of logical or semantic entailment: a method that tries to decide what the due process clause covers, for example, by asking what follows from the conjunction of "due" and "process," as a matter of semantic entailment, with no attention to the point of the clause or the results it was supposed to or might achieve. Rorty is right to think that there are few legal formalists now; even the crude "original intention" school of constitutional interpretation, which he apparently thinks qualifies, plainly doesn't. I doubt, however, whether there ever *were* legal formalists of that sort, at least in Anglo-American legal history, and this is an opportune moment to repeat my request for names. William Blackstone, as I have pointed out in the past, will hardly do, nor will Joseph Beale or the others on the usual lists. I believe that the battle against formalism, so defined, was a famous victory over straw persons.

In *Law's Empire* I used the term "pragmatism" in a more substantial way, to describe a method of adjudication that some of the legal realists defended, and that is very far from either banal or universally accepted. A judicial pragmatist, in the sense I had in mind, believes that the triumph of justice or policy is all that matters and that consistency with the past, except so far as it advances that goal, is irrelevant. Rorty says that I misuse "pragmatism" because I equate it with "crass instrumentalism." Unless I misunderstand "crass," that is a serious misreading because I emphasized that a judicial pragmatist, in the sense I had in mind, might be dedicated to the triumph of any conception of justice or policy from utilitarianism to pure Kantian principles, which doesn't sound either crass or instrumental. I concede that my use of "pragmatism" is a special one. The name has no clear meaning, however, and my use has the advantage of capturing a genuine disagreement with important implications for actual legal practice.

But my use also has the great disadvantage, from Rorty's point of view, of picturing the disagreement between legal pragmatism and its antagonists as an argument within substantive jurisprudence about how judges ought to decide cases and why. He prefers to see it as a battle between confused platonists and pragmatists firing metaphors. For Rorty's purposes, the jurisprudential problems that actually occupy lawyers are indeed, as he so often says, boring. Once it becomes clear that I mean nothing metaphysically more ambitious than, for example, Cardozo did, Rorty finds that our opinions about adjudication, which are certainly different, are not "interestingly" so.

That same theme—that legal theory is interesting only when it recapitulates Rorty's imaginary battles—runs through his whole essay. "For myself," he says, "I find it hard to see any interesting *philosophical* differences between Unger, Dworkin, and Posner; their differences strike me as entirely political. . ." (emphasis in original). Those three people have philosophically in common, so far as I can see, only that none of them says the impossible-to-say things that mark an antipragmatist for Rorty, and it is yet another effect of his false distinction between ordinary and philosophical discourse that he thinks an argument cannot be philosophical if it is also political. So though Rorty is correct that pragmatism suddenly seems banal, he is wrong about how and why. Not because it has been accepted by everyone, but because it has become particularly clear, in the last several years, that there is nothing in it to accept.

## V. Grey and the Instrumental

Professor Grey suggests that the pragmatic tradition in American philosophy should be understood as the union of two ideas. First, pragmatism insists that our beliefs and convictions are "contextual," by which he means that they are the product of time, place, and culture rather than given by innate reason. Second, pragmatism is instrumental; the soundness and importance of some idea consists not in its abstract truth but in its usefulness to the community whose idea it is.

No sensible person would dispute contextualism, at least with respect to the greatest part of what we believe.[11]   Of course, I wouldn't have the opinions I do about science or religion or patriotism or abstract painting if I had been born into a very different time or place.  The most interesting beliefs I now have wouldn't even be available, as something that could be believed, in very different cultures.   But though contextualism provides a needed reminder to the complacent, it is essentially external to the argumentative and justificatory side of science, morality, and law.   It cannot count as an argument against someone's scientific or moral or legal opinions that he would not have had these in other times and circumstances.  If that were a sound skeptical argument, little would be left of our beliefs and convictions.

Grey thinks that the instrumental side of pragmatism, on the other hand, does have practical consequences for argument and justification.  But what are these?  Instrumentalism would not make much difference in the case of science, provided scientists were agreed that scientific theories are useful when they help us to predict and control events.  Usefulness in that sense is so strongly linked to truth as to make very little of practical importance turn on which we describe as the more fundamental.[12]   We might expect instrumentalism to make a far greater difference in morality and law, however, because there, as I said, we now draw an important difference between truth and usefulness.  But it would be a mistake to think that instrumentalism could provide any kind of independent standard of inquiry in these areas because the question of what counts as the right *kind* of usefulness is itself at the heart of any important dispute.  It would beg the question for a utilitarian to argue, for example, that his view would be the most useful because it would improve the general welfare.  His opponents deny that increasing general welfare is what moral reasoning or legal analysis is exclusively about, or even about at all.  The legal pragmatist I described in *Law's Empire*, who thinks that the only test of a good judicial decision is whether it advances some goal, does not think that the test of whether that goal is the right one can *itself* be instrumental.  So it would seem that pragmatic instrumentalism could play no decisive role in political or legal argument.  At some point a commitment is needed not just to usefulness, but to a particular conception of what true usefulness consists in.

Pragmatists obscure this important point by appealing darkly to "experience" or "seeing how we get on" or something of the sort.  That is meant to suggest that a particular proposal may prove itself, as time goes by, either by attracting a consensus or by producing unforeseen benefits that, once they are realized, seem plainly an improvement. In that way, the argument seems to run, moral and legal inquiry can be genuinely experimental. Of course, it is desirable to bring people together. But consensus alone is hardly an achievement; when important issues are in play it matters more which principles the consensus has settled on. No one who opposes abortion as immoral, for example, could accept, as a sensible moral experiment, a project of seeing how we get on if we assume that it is not, because he would find disaster, not confirmation, if a consensus did form around that view. The test of popularity, in any case, presupposes that people in the community will have some *other* standard for deciding whether the experiment has been a success; no principle becomes popular only because it is thought to be popular. So we cannot decide whether experience has vindicated some position unless we have some good idea what experience *would* vindicate it, and experience cannot, of course, itself supply that.

So the pragmatist's faith in the mysterious powers of experience does nothing to answer the objection that instrumentalism begs the question. There is, however, another, more subjective, interpretation of what instrumentalism might mean in law and morals. It might be said to mean that each of us should rely on his own sense of what, in the popular phrase, works for *him*—what he finds it comfortable and productive to believe. The suggestion fits well with other remarks that come easily to the new pragmatists. It fits the importance they attach to whether they themselves find some idea "interesting," for example, and to the experiment of "trying on" an idea to see how it feels. But it hardly delivers on the promise that usefulness can provide a significant test of political and legal claims, unless usefulness is now defined as nothing more than personal satisfaction or someone's success in getting others to feel as he does.

Do serious pragmatists really mean that personal satisfaction should be adopted as the final test of whether some practical or legal decision is justified? Grey's own extended example of instrumentalism at work might suggest that they do. But a closer look at his wise chapter shows something very different. He describes the history of his own reflections about the extremely difficult problem of how far a university or faculty should seek to protect its students from verbal racial or sexual harassment by other students. He began, he says, by recognizing two different "mentalities" that might be brought to bear—the "civil-liberties" approach, which he believes argues for freedom of speech on the campus, and the "civil-rights" approach, which he thinks argues for restraints on speech to protect minority groups from psychic harm. In the end he declined to choose between these mentalities, because after thought "both remain[ed] in the case" for him. Instead he constructed a solution for his own law school that, as he put it, borrowed elements from each mentality impressionistically, without benefit of any "overarching" principle dictating where and why each should yield to the other.

This autobiographical fragment is dominated by the assumption, so striking in much of Critical Legal Studies, that political attitudes naturally coagulate into "forms of consciousness" or "mentalities" or "conceptual schemes" and that these must, at least in principle, be embraced or rejected as packages. If we accept that idea, then we might well think that there is something strikingly radical, which exhibits a refreshing instrumentalism, in combining elements of these supposedly incompatible mentalities or visions. But if we reject the whole idea of "mentalities," as bad metaphysics of thought, we can state the problem Grey confronted in a more ordinary and I believe helpful way. Put roughly: In some circumstances two ideas most of us accept seem to conflict. The first is the principle that speech should only be restricted by institutional sanctions, in virtue of its content, in the gravest emergencies. The second is the proposition that racial and sexual invective, particularly in the form of sustained harassment, is peculiarly unfair and damaging to individual people, to groups, and to our entire social and political culture. These are not, as Grey himself rightly says, contradictory ideas, but ideas in competition, which is a very different matter.[13]

Some people who accept both ideas nevertheless insist that freedom of speech must be fully protected, even at a cost they agree is deplorable, because liberty means toleration even for the speech we hate. Others take a very different view: that universities and faculties should accept some compromise of free speech in these circumstances. How much compromise, and in what form? Those questions do not, of course, admit of precise answers. We might well be persuaded that a particular scheme of regulation, like the scheme Grey constructed for Stanford, is about right for the time and place for which it is proposed, and yet not be ready to accept any more abstract systematic theory about how liberty and equal respect should be accommodated from which that particular scheme could be derived. So we say, in effect: This scheme seems or feels right to us, for now, even though we are not prepared to defend any general and comprehensive theory of the matter. That is not to say, however, that the particular accommodation proposed for the present case is the best one *because* it seems or feels best to us.

This is a crucial distinction. We must be careful to distinguish between our belief that a particular accommodation is justified, though we cannot explain why by supplying a more comprehensive account into which it fits, and a very different belief we do *not* have, which is that our thinking or feeling it right makes it right or supplies any kind of justification for adopting it. The difference, as always, is reflected in the different social and practical expectations, including self-expectations, associated with these two very different ideas. Suppose Grey were asked to propose a scheme of regulation for some very different kind of association—for state-wide legislation, for example, or for a high school. If the accommodation he felt right was then a very different one, he would, I expect, feel some responsibility for explaining why the differences in the situation justified differences in the rules, even if he was still unable to supply a comprehensive, structured, and complete theory about when free speech should yield. He would not be satisfied to say only that he felt comfortable with a different accommodation in these different circumstances.

So Grey exaggerates the degree to which his own thinking about this problem followed either an unconventional or instrumental path. His response to a difficult problem is simply the familiar response of anyone whose political morality is complex enough to recognize different principles or goals that in some circumstances compete. We need no new pragmatism to explain that thoroughly principled approach. Why does Grey seem to think otherwise? The answer may lie in yet another metaphor popular in pragmatist circles: He says his thinking did not appeal to any "overarching" theoretical structure. This invokes, once again, an invented opponent who supposedly believes that we cannot justify any practical decision except on the basis of a structure of weighted and integrated principles so complete, precise, and dispositive as to settle all cases in advance.

There is considerable theoretical advantage in imagining such a structure as an ideal background for some kinds of decision, particularly adjudicative decisions, as I have myself argued. But no one in his right mind thinks that even adjudicative decisions, let alone legislative ones, are in practice unjustified because no mortal can construct that kind of structure. A decision is responsible when it is treated as *in principle* grounded in a structure of aims and principles. Its author accepts the responsibility, among others, to explain, particularly to those who are adversely affected, why different treatment of others in other circumstances is not capricious or arbitrary or discriminatory. I am confident, as I said, that Grey accepts that kind of responsibility.

## VI. Knapp and Interpretation

Professor Hoy, in the course of his instructive piece in this collection, answers much of Professor Knapp's criticism of me. I will not expand on Hoy's points, many of which I tried myself to make, though much less skillfully, in the conversations and correspondence to which Knapp refers. Hoy is right, for example, that Knapp's burlesque of my account of interpretation, through supposed counterexamples about mumbling muggers and oppositional critics, is much too crude. It is based on a misreading of what it means for the practice of conversation to achieve its assumed purpose during a hold-up and on too thin an understanding of what oppositional critics must want others to think they are claiming if they want to have any effect. Hoy is also right that Knapp's contrast, between making some object or practice as good as it can be and showing it as it really is, begs the central question in play.

It would be profitable, perhaps, to investigate Knapp's mentalistic theory about what intentions are, according to which intentions are apparently independent of beliefs and meanings and have a fixed content that is independent of the purpose interpreters might have in trying to identify them. Knapp never defends that view of intention, though prominent philosophers, including Donald Davidson, have raised very serious objections to it. If Knapp were on reflection to abandon that view, his opinions would presumably shift in two important ways. First, he would be less likely to insist that interpretation is necessarily and in all circumstances a matter of discovering the historical intentions of a particular person or group of people. Second, he might come to see why, even when interpretation *is* just a matter of that, its results are *nevertheless* sensitive to the interpreter's purposes in carrying out that project. We might well turn out to have different techniques for attributing intentions to gunmen in the street, for example, than biblical interpreters have for attributing intentions to Old Testament prophets, or psychiatrists for attributing unconscious motives to their patients, or lawyers for attributing purposes to legislators. If so, these differences would reflect the different assumptions we have about the points of these different enterprises.

I shall use Knapp's essay, however, not to explore these issues any further but to continue the general point I have been making. The new pragmatist argues in two steps. He first redescribes quite ordinary statements other people make, which have a familiar sense gained in ordinary life, in metaphors that seem to turn them into preposterous views no sane person could hold. He then announces some skeptical-sounding conclusion that seems to follow from the evident silliness of these redescribed views, as if one had to choose between the inflated metaphor and the skepticism of the pragmatic put-down. Knapp's piece contains several examples of this form of argument, of which I select two.

Consider, first, the basis on which he claims pragmatist allegiance:

> What makes [my] account of interpretation resonate with certain themes of American pragmatism is its assertion that, in any interpretive controversy, there is no higher court of appeal than the beliefs of the conflicting interpreters, and consequently no better way—indeed no *other* way—to resolve that controversy than for the interpreters' beliefs to converge.[14]

The metaphor is the key to the argument, which proceeds in these steps. People who think there can be good reasons for adopting one interpretation rather than another, other than the agreement of all interpreters, must think there is a "court of appeal" outside the convictions of the interpreters—phantom interpreter-judges in the sky—which has a privileged authority, as real courts of appeal do, to certify such reasons as good ones. But there is no such court of appeal. Hence there are no intrinsically good reasons for holding an interpretive position, only reasons that do or do not produce consensus. The fallacy lies, of course, in the first, metaphor-soaked proposition. No one with literary or moral opinions thinks there is anything even *like* a court of appeals where these opinions can be enforced. Knapp must find some other way to "resonate" with American pragmatism.

Now consider Knapp's extended criticism of my own views. He wants to show that on my "teleological" account of interpretation, there are no interpretive constraints. Anyone can say anything and get away with it. So (on my account) if we think *Paradise Lost* would have been a better poem if it condemned prejudice against homosexuals, we can capitalize on Milton's use of "gay" to say that Satan was a homophobe, even though "gay" only very recently acquired that sense. Knapp says, correctly, that I will reply that it is not true that an interpreter can say anything: If he is acting in good faith, he is constrained, among other things, by a responsibility to make coherent sense of the poem as a whole, by the formal requirements of the genre to which he assigns the poem, and by his overall sense of the point and value of poetry. I said, by way of example, that someone who takes the value of poetry to lie in the expressive imagination or genius of the poet is not free to interpret a poem to express ideas that he could not attribute to the poet, even as ideas the poet might have grasped (as we say) subconsciously.

Someone who took that view of poetry, for instance, would not think himself free to claim that Milton, in using "gay" in the way he did, was saying anything about homosexuality. *Unless*, of course, he also thinks that our own contemporary use signals and depends on a kind of association between gaiety and homosexuality that Milton himself might in some way have sensed and anticipated, so that Milton might have expressed, in Satan's description, a general slight that reflected among other things a latent homophobia. And unless he also thinks that reading the poem to include a Satanic slight of that kind reveals a set of other, related ideas that, once noticed, can be seen reflected in other passages. If a critic thought all *that*, then he would see Knapp's suggestion as a critical triumph not a *reductio ad absurdum*. But if we disagreed—if we found it too implausible that Milton might have anticipated a now-common association—then we would be constrained by our views about the point of poetry to reject the critic's interpretation as silly.

Knapp wants to show that constraints of this character are illusory, no constraints at all. He therefore offers metaphors to suggest what real constraints would be like. He borrows these from Professor Stanley Fish, a writer whose own work about interpretation is consistently undermined by the fallacy I am now describing. Knapp says that Fish "calls attention to Dworkin's 'assumption . . . that sentences, figures and styles announce their own generic affiliation, and that a reader who would claim for them an inappropriate genre would be imposing his will on nature.'" The point of these metaphors is clear: Genuine interpretive constraints, they suggest, must work in something approaching a physical way, like sentences fighting back to stop even the most determined interpreter from putting them in the wrong genre. Or in some other immovable way so that a person who challenges them is trying to violate a law of nature. But does anyone have that picture in mind when he says, for example, that some statesman is constrained by a sense of justice? Or that the House of Lords is constrained by precedent?

Constraints can be intellectual as well as physical or legal, and, of course, it is intellectual constraints I have in mind. What we think, about anything important, is a structured and complex mix of different kinds of beliefs and convictions, some of which, in virtue of their content, act as checks on others. No single one of these is absolutely foundational, in the sense of absolutely privileged, so that it can never be withdrawn in the face of others. But as a system these convictions nevertheless check and constrain one another in a variety of ways, as I just recognized in my description of how someone's various convictions, acting together, check what he can think of *Paradise Lost*. Of course intellectual constraints can be illusory, in their own way: They are illusory, as I have also pointed out, when the supposed constraints are only restatements of the views they are supposed to check. Someone who set out to show that all our interpretive convictions are like *that* would be aiming at an internal kind of skepticism; it would be extremely difficult to show, but well worth showing if it could be done. Knapp does not have hard work like that in mind: He wants to win his point by observing that if someone persists in an absurd interpretation, by our lights or even by his, he will not go to jail or run into a stone wall.[15]

## VII. Fish and the Subtlety of Practice

Professor Fish has been (as he might put it) on my case for almost a decade. He has written no less than three highly critical articles about my work,[16] which accuse me, among other vices, of "slipperiness" and "spectacular confusion"; he refused to allow a commissioned reply to one of these to be published; and he ends his enthusiastic review of Judge Posner's book, which is his own contribution to this collection, gratuitously reporting his "somewhat churlish" criticism of me in casual conversation.[17] I have no wish further to provoke so energetic an opponent. But his many articles about interpretation, including those critical of me, illustrate so starkly the features of pragmatism I have been discussing that it would be cowardly of me not to call your attention to them.

I said that pragmatists invent their opponents through bizarre metaphorical transformations of ordinary statements, and then defend that move by insisting that these supposed opponents are not talking in the ordinary way but are trying to occupy some special, external level of discourse that the pragmatist cannot actually describe but insists is there anyway. Fish's *oeuvre* confirms that diagnosis, but he adds a new and important twist: There must be a second, external level to interpretation, he says, because nothing of any interest can possibly be said from within an intellectual practice about it. A priori claims are always unbecoming to a self-announced antitheorist; but this one is a particularly serious mistake, because anyone who is blind to the critically argumentative and reflexive character of intellectual practices will understand almost nothing else about them.

That fear is realized in Fish's most recent account of what he thinks the cardinal enemy of pragmatism—foundationalism—really is. "By foundationalism I mean any attempt to ground inquiry and communication in something more firm and stable than mere belief or unexamined practice."[18] Notice the contrast: Mere unexamined practice—doing what comes naturally—on the one hand and "something more firm and stable" on the other. The contrast self-destructs in the way Rorty's parallel pronouncements do, because it is part—it is an indispensable part—of mere unexamined practice to think that some inquiry and some communication is indeed grounded in something more substantial than mere belief: facts, for example. Fish obscures the point by immediately producing the familiar list of bad ideas that someone who believes in "something more substantial" supposedly must take on. The usual suspects are all there: "ground . . . invariant across contexts and even cultures"; a "'brute fact' world"; a "set of eternal values"; "the free and independent self"; a method of inquiry that "will *produce*, all by itself, the correct result" (emphasis in original). But the fact that none of that nonsense is part of our ordinary practice doesn't mean that the distinction between mere belief and something more substantial isn't; it rather means that Fish doesn't grasp, or rather is trying to forget, what the distinction really does come to as a matter of "how we go on."

His first article on my work exploited the now-familiar metaphor strategy. He told his readers that in my view meanings are "just there" or "self-executing" or "already in place" or "just given" in the text, that literary works "announce their own affiliation" to form and genre, and that novels have an "uninterpreted core" that guides their own interpretation. He ended, however, by scrupulously reporting the curious fact that I myself had taken care to deny everything these metaphors might be thought to suggest; indeed that I might be thought to have anticipated everything he himself had said. But he said that my disclaimers, far from showing that his frightful metaphors were out of place, only revealed confusion. Someone who says that there is a difference between interpreting a text and inventing a new one, he said, *must* be assuming a "just there" or "uninterpreted core" picture of meaning, *whatever* he later says he is doing or assuming or thinks.

In his second article the two-level device became explicit. My slipperiness and spectacular confusion, he said, consisted in switching between two levels of discourse without warning my reader that I was doing so. The first is the internal level of a practice like interpreting or judging, the level at which ordinary scholars and judges just have beliefs and make decisions. The second is the external, more "general and abstract," level at which we might try to "characterize judicial activity in a decisive and illuminating way," or make "prescriptive or normative" claims about it. He applied this distinction to my claim that there is a difference between judges' following precedent and ignoring it, a distinction he had earlier flatly denied.

> Thus while there is, at the level of practice, a distinction between continuing the legal history and striking out in a new direction, it is a distinction between methods of justifying arguments and not between actions whose difference is perspicuous apart from any argument whatsoever. The difference, in short, is interpretive, and because it is interpretive, it can't be used to settle anything, for it is itself what is continually being settled. Dworkin is thus in a perfect bind: he can stick with the original . . . form of his distinction [which Fish, remember, took to mean texts fighting back, in spite of my protestations], in which case he fails to distinguish *meaningfully* (in a way that can be consulted or used) between judicial activity or anything else; or he can invoke it as a distinction within . . . practice, in which case it has no prescriptive or normative force because it is a distinction between contestable modes of self-description or accusation.[19]

We should look at this remarkable passage in some detail. The opening denial that the distinction between interpreting and inventing is not "perspicuous apart from any argument whatsoever" is the usual red herring, more "just there" stuff. No one ever thought the distinction was perspicuous apart from any argument, whatever that might mean. The related assertions—that the distinction between following and ignoring precedent itself involves an interpretive claim, that accusing some judge of having ignored precedent is a "contestable" accusation, that the distinction doesn't settle anything, and is always itself being settled—only mean, I suppose, that lawyers often disagree about whether a particular form of argument counts as interpreting or inventing, and that both lawyers' and legal philosophers' opinions about these matters are constantly shifting. No one has ever denied that either.[20] But so far nothing in the argument is pertinent to the question Fish is meant to be addressing: whether the distinction between interpreting and inventing can be used in an illuminating and critical way within interpretive practice, that is, giving the distinction only the sense Fish now agrees it has within that practice. Can it make sense to say, using the ordinary distinction, that some judge is not interpreting precedent but is striking out on his own? Can that count as a criticism of that judge?

Of course it can. If the ordinary distinction can't be used in that descriptive and critical way, then how can it be used? Of course we characterize judicial practice in an "illuminating" way when we say (if it is true) that judges accept a responsibility to interpret precedent rather than to ignore it. And, of course, it is an important normative claim to say that, whether or not they do accept that responsibility, they should. How can it lessen the force or cogency of these claims that they are themselves, as of course they are, interpretive claims? Or that they are inherently controversial and often unlikely to be "settled" in the sense of commanding a consensus? Why can't interpreting the practice be part of an interpretive practice?[21] Fish's two-level claim seems a casebook example of Wittgenstein's diagnosis of philosophical bewitchment: Theorists puzzling themselves out of common sense by some hidden a priori commitment. Fish's crucial assumption that an interpretive practice cannot be self-conscious and reflexive, an assumption presupposed in each of his countless charges about my moving in a confused way from one level to another, is undefended, counterintuitive, pervasive, and crippling.

The force of the assumption is consistently down-market: It makes interpretive practice seem unreflective and automatic.[22] It generates serious misunderstanding of both the activities it wrongly separates. It abandons interpretive theory to the external metalevel of invented enemies, and it leaves actual interpretive practice flat and passive, robbed of the reflective, introspective, argumentative tone that is, in fact, essential to its character. Both consequences are conspicuous in Fish's third article about my work. He repeated, first, that the battle between us must be understood, whatever I say, as taking place on an external logical plane wholly independent of interpretive practice. I try, he said, to occupy an Archimedean point outside all practice; my "law as integrity" is just a "stand-in for the general claim of philosophy to be a model of reflection that exists on a level superior to, and revelatory of, mere practice." His announced new argument for this description was that *Law's Empire* tries to give lawyers advice that they do not need, because they could not possibly act contrary to that advice anyway. The argument fails even in its own terms.[23] But it wouldn't work, for Fish's purposes, even if it did work in its own terms. Even if my claims about adjudication were all otiose and unnecessary, it wouldn't follow that they were in any way Archimedean or external; banality is all too internal and worldly. Fish has to show (as I said earlier any pragmatist must show) that he can assign the statements he finds offensive a sense sufficiently different from the sense they have within ordinary interpretive practice to justify his claim that they are deployed at a different, strange, and disengaged level of discourse. I am not aware that he has even tried.

Fish's second assumption, about the passive, unreflective character of interpretive practices, dominates his complaint that I am not content to report that judges think "within" a practice but insist that they should think "with" one:

> To think *within* a practice is to have one's very perception and sense of possible and appropriate action issue "naturally"—without further reflection—from within one's position as a deeply situated agent. . . . To think *with* a practice—by self-consciously wielding some extrapolated model of its working—is to be ever calculating just what one's obligations are, what procedures are "really" legitimate, what evidence is in fact evidence, and so on. It is to be a theoretician.[24]

But as any lawyer knows, there is no difference, in the case of law, between thinking in and with the practice: These are the same thing. A good judge will "naturally" and "without further reflection" see that it is part of his job to be self-aware and self-critical, to ask what his "obligations" really are, what "evidence is really evidence," and so forth. He will naturally see that he must be, in Fish's terms, a theoretician as well as, and in virtue of, occupying his role as a participant. That doesn't mean (I had better say) that lawyers or judges construct theories of their enterprise from scratch every time they speak. It rather means what I said in discussing Grey's views about "overarching" theory: that they recognize the argumentative character of even the views they hold unreflectively and that they understand that even these are, in principle, vulnerable to a theoretical challenge they have a responsibility to meet, if and when it arises, the best they reasonably can. Here as elsewhere,

Fish dramatically underestimates the complexity of the internal structure of practices that people can quite naturally fall into; he doesn't see that, in some jobs, theory itself is second-nature. Some things we do are more argumentative than throwing a forkball: Denny Martinez never filed an opinion. Even in baseball, moreover, theory has more to do with practice than Fish acknowledges. The last player who hit .400, fifty years ago, was the greatest hitter of modern times, and he built a theory before every pitch.[25]

## VIII. Conclusion

My comments on critics are meant, as I said at the beginning, not to continue quarrels I did not start, but to show that these are quarrels no one needs. Of course we should discuss what kinds of reasons, if any, count as supporting a decision at law, and whether, as I believe, legal argument is best understood and criticized as a form of interpretive argument, conducted over time like my chain novel example. But the particular critics I have been discussing do not, so far as I know, take any different substantive view of these matters from my own. I object only to the pointless metaphysical theater, the fierce campaigns against invented fools, the misleading, spuriously shocking dramas about interpretive truth being only interpretive power. Legal theory already has enough ways of wasting time.

## Notes

1. Some critics, including Brian Barry and Joseph Raz, suggest that I have changed my mind about the character and importance of the one-right-answer claim. For better or for worse, I have not. See Ronald Dworkin, *Taking Rights Seriously* (Cambridge, Mass.: Harvard University Press, 1977), Chapters 4 and, particularly, 13. See also my somewhat earlier article "Is There Really No Right Answer in Hard Cases?" which was reprinted as Chapter 5 in Ronald Dworkin, *A Matter of Principle* (Cambridge, Mass.: Harvard University Press, 1985); Chapter 7 of that collection; and Chapter 7 of Ronald Dworkin, *Law's Empire* (Cambridge, Mass.: Harvard University Press, 1986).

2. Bernard Williams, *London Review of Books* (January, 1991).

3. See note 1 above.

4. That is what makes it so difficult to state the issue, if any, that divides "realists" from "antirealists" in metaphysics, and, more generally, to formulate any philosophically very deep form of skepticism.

5. Notice that I do not claim that lawyers all agree about which side is favored by the best arguments. (I could hardly claim that because a hard case is one in which lawyers do disagree.) Nor do I claim that some algorithmic decision procedure is available that dictates what the right answer is. I have elsewhere described how I think lawyers should think about hard cases, and my description emphasizes how dense with individual judgment that process is.

6. Ronald Dworkin, "The Right to Death: The Great Abortion Case," *New York Review of Books* (January 31, 1991): 14—17.

7. See Dworkin, *A Matter of Principle*, Chapter 5.

8. Dworkin, *Law's Empire*, Chapter 7.

9. See Marshall Cohen, ed., *Ronald Dworkin and Contemporary Jurisprudence* (London: Duckworth, 1984), 271—275 and Chapter 7.

10. Ibid., 277.

11. It is a different question whether *all* our beliefs are contextual in that way—whether, for example, Immanuel Kant or Noam Chomsky were wrong in thinking that some fundamental faculties or ideas or categories belong to common human reason and are therefore not contextual. I do not know whether Grey means that a pragmatist must reject their hypothesis.

12. Crude forms of pragmatism may, I agree, get in the way of a subtle understanding of interesting questions about how scientific theories come to be accepted and then rejected and replaced by other theories, as the long discussion of Thomas Kuhn's views about paradigm shifts in the history of science has made plain. But if a scientist is told that the ultimate test of what he and other scientists have together done is the usefulness of their product in the long run, he will not in consequence change the kinds of evidence or other argument he takes to be relevant.

13. I discuss the difference in Chapter 7 of *Law's Empire*.

14. Steven Knapp, "Practice, Purpose, and Interpretive Controversy," 324 (Chapter 17 in this volume).

15. Concerning Professor Knapp's reply to me in this volume, I should say that I misunderstood his discussion about there being "no higher court of appeal" than agreement in matters of interpretation. I thought he was denying that there could be any inherently good reasons for accepting an interpretation except consensus, and I am happy to learn that he meant only that there could be no consensus without consensus. I am puzzled, however, why he would trouble to report the latter, quite unexceptionable, belief, or why he would think that embracing it allowed him to "resonate" with American pragmatism any more than with, say, Neoplatonic mysticism.

I had three purposes in mind in constructing my hypothetical argument about Milton, Satan, and homophobia. I wanted to show, first, that the constructive view of interpretation does not exclude attending to intention, but on the contrary provides a reason for doing so in some kinds of cases—those in which it is plausible that making the best of a creative project involves connecting it to the creative intelligence of its author. It is perfectly consistent to insist, for that reason, that interpretation must connect with authorial intention in literary criticism, but deny that it must do so in some other area, like legal interpretation, in which the constructive goal does not so plausibly require a connection with some author's intention. Second, I wanted to illustrate my claim that the content of intention (or, if you prefer, the conception of intention in play) itself depends on constructive purpose. For the kind of diffuse intention my suggested interpretation attributes to Milton, which involves an unconscious anticipation of a connection only later made explicit by others, would not count as an intention in other contexts—in a libel trial, for example, in which the question was raised whether Milton wrote with the intention of depicting Satan as a bigot. Finally, I wanted to illustrate the kind of constraint the methods of constructive interpretation impose on interpreters. I, of course, accept the claim carried in Knapp's familiar metaphors and in his burlesques: that there are no external, physical constraints on constructive interpretation. I emphasized instead the way one department of an interpreter's convictions checks the influence of others, if he is acting in good faith, and I used the Milton story as an example. Knapp replies that an interpreter's sense of genre, for example, cannot constrain his interpretation, because genre is itself the product of interpretation. That was, however, my point: An overall interpretation is a complex structure of sub-interpretations, no one of which, as I said, is absolutely privileged, but which acting together, in the familiar way of complex theories, control and vouch for the whole.

The question of mentalism I raised in passing is too complex to be pursued in great detail here. But it is worth noticing the flaw in Knapp's explanation of why his account of intention is "holistic" rather than mentalistic. The difficulty in attributing intentions to people that Davidson pointed out lies in the fact that intentions, beliefs, and motives are interdependent in the sense that our view of the content of any one of these presupposes assumptions about all three. But how are we then to prefer one holistic description, which deploys one overall and consistent view of intentions, beliefs and motives, to others that deploy very different but also consistent holistic accounts? We must find our standard in the purposes we have in seeking explanations of people's mental lives. But what are our purposes? Knapp, as I understand him, argues that we must distinguish between our first-order purposes in seeking to discover someone's intention and the different second-order purposes we might have in using the information once we have discovered it. That sounds like a distinction, because we presumably seek explanations of behavior for purposes at least closely connected to the purposes to which we hope to put them. But when Knapp explains how he makes the difficult distinction, he says, so far as I can tell, only that this distinction lies in this: that our first-order purpose in discovering an intention is just to discover that intention, so that *any* other concern we might have is just a second-order concern about how to put what we discover to best use. But that is a hopeless reply given the initial assumptions I described. If our view of what someone's intentions are depends on our overall account, and the overall account we select depends on some purpose we assume we have in seeking an overall account, that purpose cannot be just the purpose of discovering what his intentions really are. That circle has much too small a radius to be of any use at all. So I concluded, out of what I thought was fairness to Knapp, that he rejected any Davidsonian account of intention in favor of a more mentalistic-fact-of-the-matter view of intentions.

Many philosophers now answer the question of interpretive purpose in roughly this way: Our purpose in seeking an overall account of someone's intentions, beliefs, and desires is to facilitate interacting with him in the various ways people do interact, and, to that end, to increase our power either to predict his behavior in different circumstances or to our power wither to explain his behavior attributing to him the minimum of inexplicable error. This rough formulation plainly includes much of what Knapp would call second-order purpose, and so resists the firm distinction he has in mind. But it leaves room for a new, much less sharp, distinction between the general aim of interpretation—to put the interpreter in the best general position for interacting—and the more specific purposes of some particular circumstance or context. Once the distinction is made that way, however, there seems little point in insisting on a single, canonical sense of intention constant across interpretive contexts and practices and insensitive to the differences in purpose amongst these. In some contexts even the most general purposes of interpretation are so different from those of normal conversation that a somewhat different standard for selecting the best overall account, and so a different standard for assigning intentions, comes into play. So a critic's reconstruction of Milton's intentions is sensitive to different information and argument, as I said, from that of a libel lawyer, and a constitutional lawyer's account of a particular statesman's intentions in legislation is different from an historian's.

In some circumstances or practices our interpretive purposes are disconnected from interaction or prediction altogether, and then we find it natural to speak of the meaning of, for example, a statute or a string of precedent decisions without intending any description of the mental life of any particular individual at all. Knapp thinks this is a mistake because he thinks that meaning *must* involve human intention. He therefore urges lawyers to say, not that the Constitution, properly understood, declares racial school segregation unlawful, but that properly understood it does not, because the authors of the Fourteenth Amendment plainly did not intend it to, but that the Supreme Court should declare school segregation unlawful anyway, because what the Constitution means is not decisive of what judges should do in their role as its guardians. That bewildering jurisprudential thesis supposes that we must choose between two ideas: that Supreme Court justices must exercise their constitutional power to strike down majoritarian legislation only in accordance with the concrete intentions of statesmen from another age, who anyway didn't intend their concrete intentions to count in that way, or that the justices are free to exercise that great power with no responsibility to show how their decisions flow from a compelling interpretation of the Constitution's text and history. That is a false dilemma, and we should be suspicious of any theory of meaning that thrusts it on us.

16. These are now collected in Stanley Fish, *Doing What Comes Naturally* (Durham, N.C.: Duke University Press, 1990). See "Working on the Chain Gang: Interpretation in Law and Literature," Chapter 1; "Wrong Again," Chapter 2; and "Still Wrong After All These Years," Chapter 16. See also pages 384—392.

17. Judge Posner's book is characteristic of that phenomenally prolific author's virtues and defects. It is clear, erudite, punchy, knock-about, witty, and relentlessly superficial. He sets out, as his main theoretical aim, to attack what he describes as the right-answer thesis. He has in mind the thesis I described and tried to clarify earlier. He says he means, in claiming that there is no "objective" answer in hard cases, that the experts do not agree in such cases. As it is exactly that feature—disagreement—that makes such cases hard, he wins a quite total victory, for it is undeniable that the experts do not agree in cases in which they disagree. But, of course, that is not what the "right-answer" argument is about. As I said earlier, it is about a legal question of jurisprudential size and philosophical dimension. I described, earlier, some of the facets of that question that other writers have taken up. Posner fastidiously avoids them all, sticking to his trivial claim about disagreement. There is a good deal of interest and fun in his book, and he does range over a wide variety of issues, discussing, for example, statutory and constitutional interpretation.

18. Fish, *Doing What Comes Naturally*, 342.

19. Fish, "Still Wrong," in *Doing What Comes Naturally*, 111—112.

20. It might seem that Fish is appealing here to what I have elsewhere called the demonstrability thesis: that nothing can count as a good argument for any view unless it is demonstrably persuasive, that is, unless no one who is rational can or will resist it. So nothing can count, within practice, as showing that a particular argument is an example of inventing unless everyone agrees that it is. If that is Fish's point, this is just another example of importing standards of good argument that are foreign to a practice into it from some external level of skepticism. Fish has said, however, that he agrees with me that this kind of external skepticism is pointless. See "Still Wrong," in *Doing What Comes Naturally*, 370—371.

21. See *Law's Empire*, Chapter 2.

22. Fish recently offered a more dynamic account of the epistemic structure of interpretation; indeed, one that seems congenial to the account I offered earlier, in reply to Knapp, about how interpreters are constrained. Fish says, for example, "Even though the

mind is informed by assumptions that limit what it can even notice, among these is the assumption that one's assumptions are subject to challenge and possible revision under certain circumstances and according to certain procedures. . . ." That seems to recognize that interpretation can be internally critical, at the level of practice, which Fish denied in the passage quoted earlier. But he does not suggest that he has changed his mind, perhaps because he presents this dynamic account not as an explanation of the reflective character of interpretive practice but more passively as an explanation of how interpretive styles can come to change. See Fish, *Doing What Comes Naturally*, 146.

23. Fish says that it would be impossible for judges to be pragmatists in the sense I described earlier because judges cannot help but be influenced by their legal training. That is a non sequitur; the fact that judges are still recognizably acting as judges when they ignore precedent doesn't mean that is not what they are doing. He says that because interpretation is necessary in reading any statute, the style of adjudication I called conventionalism is impossible. But I defined conventionalism as holding that law is a matter of uncontroversial interpretation, not no interpretation. He says that because even a judge who rejects any responsibility of continuity with the past nevertheless will make a principled decision in *some* sense, it follows that *some* sort of integrity is inevitable. But not, of course, the demanding kind of integrity I described as essential to law as integrity.

24. See Fish, *Doing What Comes Naturally*, 386—387.

25. Part of Professor Fish's response to my essay (Section V, Chapter 3 in this book) is welcome: He not only recognizes that theory is very much part of some practices, but he also acknowledges a key component of the best explanation of how theory works within interpretive practices like law. He says that in such practices "competent practitioners operate within a strong understanding of what the practice they are engaged in is *for*, . . ." He might have added that this fact accounts for the argumentative and dynamic character of such practices. Lawyers often puzzle and disagree about what the law, properly understood, really requires in some situation because, though they share a sense that law is for *something*—that the various rules and practices that form law's history have a point—they have different, rival and controversial, accounts of what that point is, either in general or with respect to particular departments or doctrines or rules of law. So legal reasoning is best understood as interpretive in the following way: Lawyers reason about what the law in new or controversial cases is by constructing what they take to be the best justification for past rules and practices, and then trying to extrapolate that justification forward into those new cases. In that way they interpret and re-interpret their institution's past, formulating, re-formulating, testing and probing rival justifications. They disagree with one another when and because they adopt somewhat different justifications for the same history, or extrapolate much the same justification differently. This process is not self-conscious or explicit in every case: "Easy" cases are those in which any plausible interpretation of the past would dictate the same decision now, and the new decision therefore seems unreflective and near automatic. But every appellate judge, at least, faces hard cases, in which the process of justification and extrapolation becomes more self-conscious and explicit, closer to the fully reflective and explicit form it takes in, say, classroom argument, which is only another, differently structured and motivated, forum in which the same practices unfolds. (In *Law's Empire*, I try to defend the views about adjudication summarized in this paragraph.)

If Fish had continued his account in that way, he would have given an intelligible and accurate account of how legal theory "folds into" legal practice, and also of how academic lawyers and legal philosophers can try to help that enterprise. He is not yet ready, however, to give theory so prominent a place in interpretive practices. So he continued in a very different way more congenial to his former antitheoretical stance. He says that though lawyers understand that law serves a point, their understanding is "not theoretical in any interestingly ymeaningful way" because it "generates without the addition of further reflection a sense of what is and is not appropriate, useful, or effective in particular situations." He still wants, in other words, to picture lawyers and judges as like natural, unreflective athletes: instinctive craftsmen who react unthinkingly to legal problems, deciding as they have been trained to do, as no one trained in that way can *help* but do, obeying the ancient practices of their profession because it would be unthinkable to do otherwise, supplying justifications for these rules only if asked, and then just by repeating empty phrases they memorized in law school, idle justifications that have nothing to do with their actual practice, except to impress like hydraulics textbooks on a plumber's shelf.

That is an exceptionally poor description of actual legal practice. Fish's account leaves no room for puzzle or progress or controversy or revolution: It cannot explain how lawyers can worry or disagree or change their minds about what the law is. As I said, his account of interpretive practices leaves them flat and passive. He insists, for example, that judges are simply incapable of challenging settled procedures of adjudication: He thinks it would be as "unthinkable" for them to reconsider conventional principles of court hierarchy and precedent as it would be for them to decide cases by randomized Shakespearian citation. But legal history is choked with examples of judges who called procedural orthodoxy into question. Some challenges ended in failure—those federal court judges who claimed the right not to follow past Supreme Court decisions when they thought the Court was about to change its mind, for example, have so far persuaded no one else and have been overruled. In other cases the challenge was dramatic and successful; a few decades ago, for example, the House of Lords, Britain's highest court, suddenly announced that contrary to settled practice it would no longer be bound by its own past decisions, and though the new practice was thought shocking by some British lawyers, few of them question it now. These are only random examples: Legal history or legal process could provide hundreds of others. In almost all such cases the challenge to orthodoxy and convention was wrapped in an argument of the same underlying structure: that the purposes of adjudication, precedent, hierarchy and the rest—at least as seen by those proposing the change—would be better served by some more or less radical departure from what had seemed beyond question.

Fish makes parallel claims about substantive legal principles. He says that lawyers would be dumbfounded if asked for a justification of the "tools" they use in considering contract cases, like the doctrines of offer and acceptance, mistake, impossibility, frustration, breach, and so forth; he says lawyers no more rely on theories or justifications in using these doctrines than carpenters rely on theories to use nails. But any standard history of how contract law developed in the centuries after *Slade's Case* shows how bad an analogy that is, how thoroughly it misstates the role theoretical argument and disagreement played in that process. Each of the doctrines Fish mentions changed in content from period to period, and they still differ from jurisdiction to jurisdiction in the common law world; the changes and differences reflect, among other things, different emphases on the relative importance of freedom of contract, efficiency in commerce, imposing fairness on commercial practice, and protecting people with inadequate bargaining power, just to name four of a large number of theoretical claims lawyers have made or rejected about the point and justification of contract law. Any contemporary contracts case book, moreover, shows how vivid these controversies remain. For the doctrines Fish calls second-nature tools are intensely controversial. It is controversial not only what should count as an offer or an acceptance or a mistake, for example, but also how central these ideas should be to the law's enforcement of consensual transactions, as the development of doctrines of quasi-contract and contracts of adhesion, and the limited replacement of contract by status, among other trends, seems plainly to show. Once again, the heart of these controversies is the kind of theoretical argument—urging and challenging different justifications—that Fish wants to treat as merely decorative. As I said earlier in this article, legal skeptics challenge one ordinary assumption of legal argument—the assumption that legal questions have right answers. But these skeptics insist, as much as anyone, that legal argument is nevertheless theoretical in just the way Fish denies, because they describe it as an attempt by each side self-consciously to advance its own vision of private law.

I therefore believe that though Fish's views are now less radical and shocking than once they seemed, he still seriously misunderstands the role of theoretical argument in interpretive practices like law and literary criticism. But I must point out one passage, near the end of his response, that might suggest a different conclusion. If I am right, he says, that a lawyer or judge must engage in theoretical reflection just to carry out his role competently, then "there seems little reason to call it theory," since it is simply the quality of being skilled at one's job. But if, on the other hand, "theory is used in a more exalted sense . . . we are back in the realm of meta-commentary and high abstraction." The first of these claims must have surprised every reader. It is surely part of a philosopher's or a cosmologist's or a welfare economist's being "skilled" at his job that he be able to engage in very complex theoretical argument, and we have, in that fact, not "little" but compelling reason to call what *they* do theory. Does Fish really mean that theory plays no "meaningful" role in the work of any profession? Or does he mean only that he, for his part, will not use the word "theory" to describe any form of thinking, no matter how self-conscious, that goes with skill at a job, but will reserve that word to describe mental processes that somehow float free of practice in the never-never land of "meta-commentary and high abstraction?" If so, we would finally have nothing left to disagree about, except that since I don't believe in the never-never world I use "theory" in the normal way.

# Selected Bibliography

Addams, Jane. *Democracy and Social Ethics*. Cambridge, Mass.: Harvard University Press, 1964.
_____. *The Long Road of Woman's Memory*. New York: Macmillan, 1916.
_____. *Peace and Bread in Time of War*. Boston: G. K. Hall, 1960.
_____. *Forty Years at Hull House*. New York: Macmillan, 1935.
Apel, Karl-Otto. *Diskurs und Verantwortung: Das Problem des Ubergangs zur Postkonventionellen Moral*. Frankfurt: Suhrkamp Verlag, 1985.
Bell, Derrick. "The Supreme Court, 1984 Term—Foreword: The Civil Rights Chronicles." *Harvard Law Review* 99 (November 1985): 4—84.
Bork, Robert H. "Neutral Principles and Some First Amendment Problems." *Indiana Law Journal* 47 (Fall 1971): 1—35.
Cardozo, Benjamin. *The Nature of the Judicial Process*. New Haven: Yale University Press, 1921.
_____. *Selected Writings of Benjamin Nathan Cardozo: The Choice of Tycho Brahe*. Edited by M. Hall. New York: Bender, 1947.
Cohen, Marshall, ed. *Ronald Dworkin and Contemporary Jurisprudence*. London: Duckworth, 1983.
Cover, Robert M. "The Supreme Court, 1982 Term—Foreword: Nomos and Narrative." *Harvard Law Review* 97 (November 1983): 4—68.
Delgado, Richard. "When a Story Is Just a Story: Does Voice Really Matter?" *Virginia Law Review* 76 (February 1990): 95—115.
Dewey, John. *Art as Experience*. London: George Allen and Unwin, 1934.
_____. *Experience and Nature*, 2nd ed. New York: Dover 1929.
_____. *John Dewey: The Later Works*. Edited by Jo Ann Boydston. 47 vols. Carbondale, Ill.: Southern Illinois University Press, 1986.
_____. *Logic*. (New York: Holt, 1938).
_____. "Logical Method and Law." *Cornell Law Quarterly* 17 (December 1924): 17—27.
_____. *The Moral Writings of John Dewey*. Edited by James Gouinlock. New York: Hafner, 1976.
_____. *The Quest for Certainty: A Study in the Relation of Knowledge and Action*. New York: Minton, Balch, 1929.
Dewey, John, and J. H. Tufts. *Ethics*, rev. ed. New York: Holt, 1936.
Dworkin, Ronald. *Law's Empire*. Cambridge, Mass.: Harvard University Press, 1986.
_____. "Liberal Community." *California Law Review* 77 (May 1989): 474—504.

_____. *A Matter of Principle*. Cambridge, Mass.: Harvard University Press, 1985.

_____. *Taking Rights Seriously*. Cambridge, Mass.: Harvard University Press, 1977.

Elshtain, Jean Bethke. "Antigone's Daughters." *democracy* (April 1982): 46—59.

_____. *Meditations on Modern Political Thought*. New York: Praeger, 1986.

_____. *Public Man, Private Woman*. Princeton, N.J.: Princeton University Press, 1981.

Farber, Daniel. "Legal Pragmatism and the Constitution." *Minnesota Law Review* 72 (June 1988): 1331—1378.

Feyerabend, Paul. *Against Method*. London: New Left Books, 1975.

Fish, Stanley. *Doing What Comes Naturally*. Durham, N.C.: Duke University Press, 1990.

Gilligan, Carol. *In a Different Voice: Psychological Theory and Women's Development*. Cambridge, Mass.: Harvard University Press, 1982.

Grey, Thomas. "Hear the Other Side: Wallace Stevens and Pragmatist Legal Theory." *Southern California Law Review* 63 (September 1990): 1569—1595.

_____. "Holmes and Legal Pragmatism." *Stanford Law Review* 41 (April 1989): 787—870.

_____. "Langdell's Orthodoxy." *University of Pittsburgh Law Review* 45 (Fall 1983): 1—55.

Habermas, Jürgen. *The Theory of Communicative Action*. Translated by Thomas McCarthy. Cambridge: Polity, 1984.

_____. *Wirklichkeit und Reflexion*. Edited by Helmut Fahrenbach. Pfullingen, FRG: G. Neske, 1973.

Hirsch, E. D., Jr. "Counterfactuals in Interpretation." In *Interpreting Law and Literature*, edited by Sanford Levinson and Steven Mailloux, pp. 55—68. Evanston, Ill.: Northwestern University Press, 1988.

_____. *Validity in Interpretation*. New Haven: Yale University Press, 1967.

Hollinger, David. *In the American Province: Studies in the History and Historiography of Ideas*. Bloomington: Indiana University Press, 1985.

James, William. *The Meaning of Truth*. Edited by Fredson Bowers. Cambridge, Mass.: Harvard University Press, 1975.

_____. *Pragmatism*. Edited by Fredson Bowers. Cambridge, Mass.: Harvard University Press, 1975.

_____. *Talks to Teachers on Psychology and to Students on Some of Life's Ideals*. Edited by Fredson Bowers. Cambridge, Mass.: Harvard University Press, 1983.

_____. *Varieties of Religious Experience*. Edited by Fredson Bowers. Cambridge, Mass.: Harvard University Press, 1985.

_____. *The Will to Believe and Other Essays in Popular Philosophy*. Edited by Fredson Bowers. Cambridge, Mass.: Harvard University Press, 1979.

Kennedy, Duncan. "Freedom and Constraint in Adjudication: A Critical Phenomenology." *Journal of Legal Education* 36 (December 1986): 518—562.

Kloppenberg, James T. *Uncertain Victory: Social Democracy and Progressivism in European and American Thought 1870—1920.* New York: Oxford University Press, 1986.

Knapp, Steven, and Walter Benn Michaels. "Against Theory." *Critical Inquiry* 8 (Summer 1982): 723—742.

_____. "Against Theory 2: Hermeneutics and Deconstruction." *Critical Inquiry* 14 (Autumn 1987): 49—68.

_____. "Intention, Identity, and the Constitution: A Response to David Hoy." In *Legal Hermeneutics: History, Theory, and Practice,* edited by Gregory Leyh. Berkeley and Los Angeles: University of California Press, forthcoming.

_____. "A Reply to Our Critics." *Critical Inquiry* 9 (June 1983): 790—800.

_____. "A Reply to Richard Rorty: What Is Pragmatism?" *Critical Inquiry* 11 (March 1985): 466—474.

Kuhn, Thomas S. *The Structure of Scientific Revolutions.* 2nd ed. Chicago: University of Chicago Press, 1970.

Levi, Isaac. "Escape From Boredom—Education According to Rorty." *Canadian Journal of Philosophy* 11 (December 1981): 589—601.

MacIntyre, Alasdair. *After Virtue,* 2nd ed. Notre Dame, Ind.: University of Notre Dame Press, 1984.

_____. *Whose Justice? Which Rationality?* Notre Dame, Ind.: University of Notre Dame Press, 1988.

MacKinnon, Catharine A. "Feminism, Marxism, Method, and the State: An Agenda for Theory." *Signs: Journal of Women Culture and Society* 7 (Spring 1982): 515—544.

_____. *Feminism Unmodified.* Cambridge, Mass.: Harvard University Press, 1987.

_____. *Sexual Harassment of Working Women.* New Haven: Yale University Press, 1979.

_____. *Toward A Feminist Theory of the State.* Cambridge, Mass.: Harvard University Press, 1989.

Margolis, Joseph. *Pragmatism Without Foundations: Reconciling Realism and Relativism.* Oxford: Blackwell, 1986.

Matsuda, Mari J. "Looking to the Bottom: Critical Legal Studies and Reparations." *Harvard Civil Rights—Civil Liberties Law Review* 22 (Spring 1987): 323—399.

_____. "Public Response to Racist Speech: Considering the Victim's Story." *Michigan Law Review* (August 1989): 2320—2381.

Michelman, Frank. "Law's Republic." *Yale Law Journal* 97 (July 1988): 1532—1537.

_____. "The Supreme Court, 1985 Term—Foreword: Traces of Self-Government." *Harvard Law Review* 100 (November 1986): 4—78.

Minow, Martha. "The Supreme Court 1986, Term—Foreword: Justice Engendered." *Harvard Law Review* 101 (November 1987): 10—95.

Mitchell, W. J. T. *Against Theory: Literary Studies and the New Pragmatism.* Chicago: University of Chicago Press, 1985.

Mulvaney, Robert J., and Philip M. Zeltner. eds. *Pragmatism: Its Sources and Prospects.* Columbia: University of South Carolina Press, 1981.

Nagel, Thomas. *The View From Nowhere.* Oxford: Oxford University Press, 1986.

Peirce, Charles Sanders. *The Collected Papers of Charles Sanders Peirce.* Edited by Charles Hartshorne and Paul Weiss. 8 vols. Cambridge, Mass.: Harvard University Press, 1934.

_____. *Writings of Charles S. Peirce.* Edited by Christian J. Kloescl. 5 vols. Bloomington: Indiana University Press, 1986.

Posner, Richard A. *Cardozo: A Study in Reputation.* Chicago: University of Chicago Press, forthcoming.

_____. *Law and Literature: A Misunderstood Relation.* Cambridge, Mass.: Harvard University Press, 1985.

_____. *The Problems of Jurisprudence.* Cambridge, Mass.: Harvard University Press, 1990.

_____. "The Regulation of the Market in Adoptions." *Boston University Law Review* 67 (January 1987): 59—73.

Posner, Richard A., and William Landes. *The Economic Structure of Tort Law.* Cambridge, Mass.: Harvard University Press, 1987.

Putnam, Hilary. *The Many Faces of Realism.* La Salle, Ill.: Open Court, 1988.

Putnam, Hilary, and Ruth Anna Putnam. "William James's Ideas." *Raritan* 8 (Winter 1989): 27—44.

Quine, W.V.O. *From a Logical Point of View,* 2nd ed. Cambridge, Mass.: Harvard University Press, 1980.

Radin, Margaret. "Justice and the Market Domain." In *Markets and Justice (Nomos 31),* edited by John W. Chapman and J. Roland Pennock, 165—198. New York: New York University Press, 1989.

_____. "Market-Inalienability." *Harvard Law Review* 100 (June 1987): 1915—1936.

_____. "Reconsidering the Rule of Law." *Boston University Law Review* 69 (July 1989): 781—823.

Rawls, John. "The Idea of an Overlapping Consensus." *Oxford Journal of Legal Studies* 7 (1987): 1—25.

_____. "Justice as Fairness: Political not Metaphysical." *Philosophy and Public Affairs* 14 (Summer 1985): 223—251.

_____. "The Priority of Right and Ideas of the Good." *Philosophy and Public Affairs* 17 (Fall 1988): 251—277.

_____. *A Theory of Justice.* Cambridge, Mass.: Harvard University Press, 1971.

Rorty, Richard. *Consequences of Pragmatism*. Minneapolis: University of Minnesota Press, 1982.

_____. *Contingency, Irony, and Solidarity*. Cambridge: Cambridge University Press, 1989.

_____. *Philosophy and the Mirror of Nature*. Princeton: Princeton University Press, 1979.

_____. "Pragmatism Without Method." In *Sidney Hook: Philosopher of Democracy and Humanism*, edited by Paul Kurtz, 295—275. Buffalo, N.Y.: Prometheus, 1983.

_____. "The Priority of Democracy to Philosophy." In *The Virginia Statute for Religious Freedom: Its Evolution and Consequences*, edited by Merrill D. Peterson and Robert C. Vaughan, 257—282. Cambridge: Cambridge University Press, 1988.

Sandel, Michael. *Liberalism and the Limits of Justice*. Cambridge: Cambridge University Press, 1982.

Simpson, Evan, ed. *Anti-Foundationalism and Practical Reasoning: Conversations Between Hermeneutics and Analysis*. South Edmonton, Canada: Academic Printing and Publishing, 1987.

Sleeper, R. W. *The Necessity of Pragmatism: John Dewey's Conception of Philosophy*. New Haven: Yale University Press, 1986.

Smith, John E. *Purpose and Thought: The Meaning of Pragmatism*. Chicago: University of Chicago Press, 1978.

Stephen, James Fitzjames. *Liberty, Equality, and Fraternity*, 2nd ed. London: Smith, Elder, 1874.

Thayer, H. Standish. *Meaning and Action: A Critical History of Pragmatism*. Indianapolis, Ind.: Hackett, 1965.

Unger, Roberto. *The Critical Legal Studies Movement*. Cambridge, Mass.: Harvard University Press, 1986.

Wells, Catharine. "Tort Law as Corrective Justice: A Pragmatic Justification for Jury Adjudication." *Michigan Law Review* 88 (August 1990): 2348—2414.

West, Cornel. *The American Evasion of Philosophy: A Genealogy of Pragmatism*. Madison: Wisconsin University Press, 1989.

White, Morton. *Social Thought in America: The Revolt Against Formalism*. New York: Viking, 1949.

Williams, Bernard. *Ethics and the Limits of Philosophy*. London: Fontana, 1985.

Williams, Joan. "Critical Legal Studies: The Death of Transcendence and the Rise of the New Langdells." *New York University Law Review* 62 (June 1987): 429—497.

_____. "Deconstructing Gender." *Michigan Law Review* 87 (February 1989): 797—845.

Wittgenstein, Ludwig. *Philosophical Investigations*. Translated by G.E.M. Anscombe. New York: Macmillan, 1953.

# About the Book and Editors

Social thinkers in the Deweyan pragmatist tradition have always been optimistic about the prospect of social progress. But the recent pragmatist revival has tended to emphasize the destructive side of pragmatism: Truth is not absolute, and there are no foundations or even a privileged standpoint from which to theorize.

But when truth becomes what is good in the way of belief, when law becomes what judges say it is, and when no discourse has a unique claim to "getting the world right," the question becomes, "What constructive role can pragmatism play either in structuring public debate or in dealing with life"? What, if anything, in the way of a positive social program does pragmatism have to offer?

In *Pragmatism in Law and Society,* leading scholars from law, literature, philosophy, and political science offer contrasting and stimulating responses to these questions.

**Michael Brint** is assistant professor of government and foreign affairs at the University of Virginia. He is also the author of *Tragedy and Denial: The Politics of Difference in Western Political Thought* (Westview, 1991) and *A Genealogy of Political Culture* (Westview, 1991). **William Weaver** is working toward his J.D. and Ph.D. in political theory at the University of Virginia.

# About the Contributors

**Lynn A. Baker** is assistant professor of law at the University of Virginia School of Law. Her works on family law and state and local issues have appeared in a number of law journals.

**Ronald Dworkin** holds joint appointments as professor of jurisprudence, Oxford University and professor of law, New York University School of Law. He is author of *Law's Empire*; *A Matter of Principle*; and *Taking Rights Seriously*.

**Jean Bethke Elshtain** is Centennial Professor of Political Science at Vanderbilt University. Her works include *Meditations on Modern Political Thought*; *Public Man, Private Woman*; and *Women and War*.

**Stanley Fish** is Arts and Sciences Professor of English, professor of law, and chair of the Department of English, Duke University. He is author of *Doing What Comes Naturally*; *Is There a Text in This Class?*; *The Living Temple*; and *Surprised by Sin*,

**Milton Fisk** is professor of philosophy at Indiana University, Bloomington. Professor Fisk's works include *Ethics and Society: A Marxist Interpretation of Value*; *Nature and Necessity: An Essay in Physical Ontology*; and *The State and Justice: An Essay in Political Theory*.

**Thomas C. Grey** is Nelson Bowman Sweitzer and Marie B. Sweitzer Professor of Law at Stanford University. His publications include "Hear the Other Side: Wallace Stevens and Pragmatist Legal Theory"; "The Hermeneutics File"; "Holmes and Legal Pragmatism"; "Langdell's Orthodoxy"; "The Uses of an Unwritten Constitution"; and "Serpents and Doves: a Note on Kantian Legal Theory."

**E. D. Hirsch, Jr.** is author of *The Aims of Interpretation*; *Cultural Literacy*; and *Validity in Interpretation*. He is Kenan Professor of English at the University of Virginia.

**David Hoy** is currently chair of the Department of Philosophy at the University of California, Santa Cruz. Widely published in hermeneutics and contemporary continental philosophy, he is author of *The Critical Circle: Literature, History, and Philosophical Hermeneutics*.

**Steven Knapp**, professor of English at the University of California, Berkeley, co-authored the essay "Against Theory" with Professor Walter Michaels. In addition to many articles, he is also author of *Personification and the Sublime*.

**Sanford Levinson** is Angus G. Wynne, Sr. Professor of Civil Jurisprudence at the University of Texas at Austin and author of *Constitutional Faith*. He has also edited *Interpreting Law and Literature* (with Steven Mailloux) and *Processes of Constitutional Decisionmaking* (with Paul Brest).

**Martha Minow** is professor of law at Harvard University and author of "Justice Engendered" and "When Difference Has Its Home." With Elizabeth V. Spelman, she has coauthored "Passion for Justice."

**Daniel R. Ortiz** is professor of law at the University of Virginia. His recent publications include "Affirmative Action Under the Constitution" and "Federalism, Reapportionment, and Incumbency."

**Richard A. Posner** is a judge on the United States Court of Appeals for the Seventh Circuit and senior lecturer at the University of Chicago Law school. He is author of *Cardozo: A Study in Reputation*; *Law and Literature: A Misunderstood Relation*; and *The Problems of Jurisprudence*.

**Hilary Putnam** is Walter Beverly Pearson Professor of Mathematical Logic at Harvard University. His works include *The Many Faces of Realism*; *Reason, Truth, and History*; and *Representation and Reality*.

**Margaret Jane Radin** is professor of law at Stanford University. Her works include "Justice and the Market Domain" and "Reconsidering the Rule of Law."

**Richard Rorty,** University Professor of Humanities at the University of Virginia, is author of *Philosophy and the Mirror of Nature*, *The Consequences of Pragmatism*, and *Contingency, Irony and Solidarity*.

**Elizabeth V. Spelman,** professor of philosophy at Smith College, is author of *Inessential Woman: Problems of Exclusion in Feminist Thought*.

**Catharine Wells** is associate professor of law at the University of Southern California Law Center, and author of "Tort Law as Corrective Justice: A Pragmatic Justification for Jury Adjudication."

**Cornel West** is Director of Afro-American studies, Princeton University and author of *The American Evasion of Philosophy: A Genealogy of Pragmatism*.

**Joan C. Williams** is professor of law at the American University, Washington College of Law. Her publications include "Deconstructing Gender" and "Critical Legal Studies: the Death of Transcendence and the Rise of the New Langdells."

# Index